Making African
Christianity

Making African Christianity

Africans Re-imagining Their Faith in Colonial Southern Africa

Robert J. Houle

LEHIGH UNIVERSITY PRESS
Bethlehem

Published by Lehigh University Press
Co-published with The Rowman & Littlefield Publishing Group, Inc.
4501 Forbes Boulevard, Suite 200, Lanham, Maryland 20706
www.rowmanlittlefield.com

Estover Road, Plymouth PL6 7PY, United Kingdom

British Library Cataloguing in Publication Information Available

Library of Congress Cataloging-in-Publication Data
Making African Christianity : Africans reimagining their faith in colonial southern Africa / edited by Robert J. Houle.
     p. cm.
   Includes bibliographical references.
   ISBN 978-1-61146-081-0 (cloth : alk. paper) — ISBN 978-1-61146-082-7 (electronic)
   1. Christianity and culture—Africa, Southern. 2. Christianity—Africa, Southern.
3. Africa, Southern—Church history. 4. Missions—Africa, Southern—Influence.
5. Zulu (African people)—Religion. I. Houle, Robert J., 1969-
   BR1450.M335 2010
   276.8—dc23   2011024219

∞™ The paper used in this publication meets the minimum requirements of American National Standard for Information Sciences—Permanence of Paper for Printed Library Materials, ANSI/NISO Z39.48-1992.

Printed in the United States of America

Contents

Photographs   vii

Map   xiii

Prelude   xv

Acknowledgments   xix

Introduction   xxi

1   In the Beginning . . .   1

2   Being Zulu and Christian   43

3   Conflicting Identities   89

4   Revival   145

5   Naturalizing the Faith   189

6   A Zulu Church   227

Conclusion   279

Bibliography   287

Index   303

About the Author   311

Photographs

Umtwalume Chapel, undated. Courtesy Pietermaritzburg Archives Repository, c5521.

Zulu Pastors and Evangelists with Drs. William and Sydney Strong, 1903. Courtesy Pietermaritzburg Archives Repository, c5555.
Standing, left to right: Gardiner Mvuyana, Mbiya Kuzwayo, Garnet Mthembu
Sitting, left to right: Charles Ransom, Joel Bhulose, J.D. Taylor

Revs. Ransom and Taylor with Theological Class, undated. Courtesy Pietermaritzburg Archives Repository, c5553.
Standing, left to right: Rev. W. J. Makanya, Rev. Mabuda Cele, M. Shabane, unknown, Madikane Cele, Rev. Joseph Gobhozi, Chief James (David) Mbhale, Rev. Jeremiah Langeni, John Mdima
Middle row, left to right: Henry Mbesa, Rev. Bryant Cele, Sivetye, Dr. William Strong, Dr. Sydney Strong, Rev. C.K. Goba, Rev Daniel Zama, Rev. P. J. Gumede
Bottom row, left to right: N. Mseleka, J. Msabala, Jack Cele, Willie Shabane, Rev. J. Bhulose, William Mthimkulu, Rev. Gardiner Mvuyana

Inanda Seminary, 1897. Courtesy Pietermaritzburg Archives Repository, c5578.

Beatrice Street Chapel, undated. Courtesy Pietermaritzburg Archives Repository, c5582.

Map

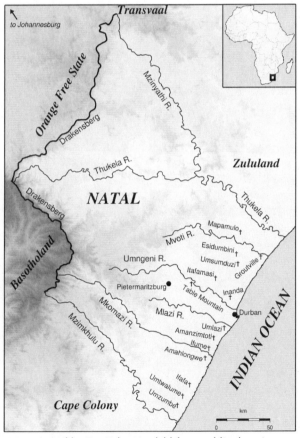

Map created by Dr. Kelsey Jordahl from public domain sources.

Prelude

On a gorgeous Sunday in June of 2001, I attended Sabbath services at Groutville, one of the oldest and most important of the stations of the American Zulu Mission (AZM), the southern African branch of the American Board of Congregationalist Foreign Missions (ABM). The church stood on the same spot as it had for a century and a half and the graves of generations of *amakholwa* ("believers" in Zulu) littered the slopes of the hill that sprawled up from the back of the building. The church, a simple building whitewashed and gleaming in the sun, opened up through great wooden doors into a large hall whose walls were only lightly adorned in proper Congregational fashion. Well-worn wooden floors held well-worn wooden pews, a slightly raised altar held a cross and a candle, the walls behind adorned with a tapestry and a few hand-drawn signs, including one wishing all those in attendance a happy Father's Day. Almost two hours before services were scheduled to begin several deacons arrived to assist in preparing communion. An hour later the faithful started to trickle in and within fifteen minutes the pews filled. Spontaneous singing soon erupted, as one strong voice after another introduced hymns and others joined in, praising Jesus. A Zulu hymnal that dated some of its works back to the very earliest translations by the AZM lay unused by those with whom I shared a pew, its contents already long since memorized.

By the time the service commenced, the hall was full. Some three hundred parishioners squeezed in tightly together; older members were given prominent seats up front while the young and late arrivals were left to stand along the walls or sit around the altar. Unlike the revivals (which form the fulcrum of this book) at the turn of the century, when George

Weavers, a revivalist from Iowa, and Mbiya Kuzwayo, his Zulu interpreter, had led both day and night sessions here, this was the only service for the day and those in attendance made the most of it. Lasting nearly two hours, the service was far removed from the staid Congregationalism of the United States. Closer in spirit and tone to an African American Baptist service, participants clapped and danced when they sang, raised their hands in prayer, and exuberantly vocalized their appreciation for particularly moving moments. Among the most prominent in this regard were the dozens of men and women dressed in the uniforms of their revival groups—organizations who devoted time during the week to visit the homes of those who had not recently attended church, or those few who never had. The women belonged to *isililo* (literally "wailing," but a society of Christian women) and dressed in blue and white skirts and blouses, while the men, dressed in khakis and simple blue shirts, belonged to Soldiers for Christ (SFC).[1] The two groups, now split along gendered lines, were directly descended from *amavoluntiya*—the body perhaps most responsible for spreading the revival message—and it was clear that the spirit of that early group continued to live in the men and women whose actions animated the worship service I now attended.

In the middle of the service, during a particularly impassioned moment of impromptu praise and singing, the pastor of Groutville took an elaborately carved walking stick and passed it to one of the SFC. The congregation cheered and the man raised the staff in triumph, singing a Zulu hymn with particular gusto. Later the walking stick was passed on to another participant with a similar momentary rekindling of spirit. It was clearly an important, if highly ritualized, moment and it caught my attention as it did everyone's. Other aspects of the service could have occurred anywhere and I never doubted that I was attending a Christian service and that this was part of what might be called the universal church, the community of Christians spanning time, distance, ethnicities, and even denominations. After the better part of two hours, the service slowly wound down and the community greeted each other as we made our way outside.

Later, while waiting for the pastor to finish with the children's Sunday school that followed, I chatted with several church members about the history of the mission, about the revivals a century earlier, and about the nature of their Christianity. Universally they laid claim to membership in what they considered mainstream Christianity and rejected any suggestion that the nature of their faith was somehow syncretic, an amalgamation of African and Christian beliefs. By then my research was winding down, and I was both sympathetic to their annoyance with such a question, and convinced that they were right in regarding such a hypothesis as faulty. Their church and their Christianity were not syncretic, but they, and more particularly those who had come before them, had managed to build a faith that was both fully local and firmly orthodox. In this they followed what Christians around the world have done for millennia.

This, it strikes me, was fundamentally what the revivals had accomplished. Before them, as we will see, African Christians struggled to fill gaps in their systems of belief by retaining traditions connected with the ancestral spirits. That was syncretism. Revivals armed *amakholwa* with theologies that allowed believers to claim Christian orthodoxy while also making it relatively easy for others to follow. What occurred now, before me, was a fully realized African Christianity that the congregation lived deeply as its own.

After the service several deacons walked me through the graveyard and pointed out tombstones of the very first *amakholwa*—their ancestors and the very people I had been researching. As we talked about the just concluded service I eventually asked about the walking stick. This, I was told, was the symbol of authority within the SFC. When evangelists went out to pray and preach in surrounding homesteads, leaders carried these walking sticks as a marker of spiritual status.[2] Within the church it acted as a sort of transfer of authority, the pastor handing over a bit of sacred legitimacy with it giving the person holding it the right to lead the congregation in praise. Here, of course, was another key to the lasting importance of revival—for congregations today continue to claim empowerment of the Holy Spirit, a critical step in fully realizing Christianity on the continent. In the Congregational church it was even more, a transcending experience that essentially recaptured the moments of religious revivals from a century earlier.

Then, much to my amazement for I had not yet begun asking these men about those revivals, I was told that the artfully crafted staves were much like that which Elder Weavers himself had used to traverse the hills of Natal. But of course, I shouldn't have been surprised. As I will argue, the Holiness message preached by Weavers offered a Spirit-filled religious experience that struck those who participated in the awakenings as familiar, empowering, and life-altering. It was particularly important moment for *amakholwa* because it occurred at a time when the identity they had originally constructed had begun to collapse. Weavers' message offered them the promise of both sacred and secular legitimacy, a powerful combination that kept many within the orbit of the Congregational Church while allowing for important local alterations of the Christianity practiced. All of this occurred within the realm of a colonial settler government particularly hostile to any signs of African independence. The men and women at Groutville were evidence of the power of their ancestors to affect and maintain the transformations necessary for Christianity to survive on the continent.

NOTES

1. Deborah Gaitskell has tracked *isililo* back to 1912, when a group of Congregational women formed the group in response from criticism directed at them by men that they were not doing enough to prevent loose sexuality among their children. Deborah Gaitskell, "Devout Domesticity? A Century of African Women's Christianity in South Africa," in *Women and Gender in South Africa*, in Cheryl Walker (ed.), *Women and Gender in Southern Africa to 1945*, (Cape Town: David Phillips, 1990), 259–263.

2. Captain Mgobhozi and Mr. Brightman Mbambo, interview, Groutville, June 24, 2001.

Acknowledgments

For the family, friends, colleagues, mentors, archivists, editors, and assistants who made this possible, you are too many to name and I am indebted and grateful.

Introduction

This is the story of how Christianity became an African religion. That it is so now seems indisputable, but how this occurred is still not fully understood, for scholars have tended to examine this as a single distinct moment—the individual decision to convert accompanied by all its social and political implications. But the making of African Christianity should not be thought of as the story of conversion alone, for the really important changes occurred long after that initial moment as slowly, across generations, African believers molded their faith to local realities during the colonial era and beyond. Some did so deliberately, expressing dissatisfaction with aspects of the missionary message, coming to their own understanding of biblical passages and theology, and perhaps even voting with their feet and attending the services of preferred denominations. Most did so less intentionally; in the enthusiasm they expressed for some Christian rituals over others, the continuation of certain traditional practices in the face of missionary hostility, the clothing they wore, books they bought, religious symbols they erected, or the many other small ways African Christians signified their belief to those around them. In time, however, these two strands of action wove together to transform the faith into a religion that Africans now call their own.

I tell this history by closely examining the ways in which a particular group of converts, nineteenth and early twentieth century Zulu from what would become South Africa, gradually developed a Christianity that felt familiar; that served their cultural, political, *and* spiritual needs. They transformed Christianity over several generations both in response to the unique demands of different eras, but also because it took time for believers to digest the multifaceted workings of their adopted faith, give voice to that which attracted them, reject what did not, and lay claim to the spiritual and political legitimacy that both converts and missionaries believed necessary to ultimately effect change. Part of this process lay outside of South Africa, for just as the conditions of individual believers changed over the years, so too did global Christianity. The message believers consumed was not static and Zulu Christians (known as *amakholwa*, or believers) transformed their faith by treating the theological foundations of the religion as an open buffet, picking and choosing what appealed to them from any number of theological traditions and ecstatic movements that flowed through the Port of Natal. In other words, Zulu both shared and participated in the great transformation of the faith then underway across the globe—a project that would eventually produce the two most important religious movements of the last several centuries: Pentecostalism and Evangelism.

What resulted provides a lens into understanding the phenomenal popularity of Christianity today, for once armed with a locally coherent message, Zulu evangelists began aggressively spreading the Word at the end of the nineteenth century, a duty several generations of believers had previously avoided. The Zulu churches quickly grew as the population responded to the carefully crafted appeals of *amakholwa* that combined access to a world religion while being imbedded into the soil around them. It is this model, the translation of the faith into local idioms over several generations, which other Christians replicated in their own ways across sub-Saharan Africa as they appropriated the faith and turned Christianity into an African religion.

This book will also highlight the ways early African believers wrestled with what it meant to be both African and Christian during the colonial era. While the project of transforming Christianity into an African religion was still underway it proved a difficult task for many to find the right balance between two occasionally discordant identities. Writing of Jomo Kenyatta's well known anecdote—"When the white man came to our country he had the Bible and we had the land. The white man said to us, 'Let us pray.' After the prayer, the white man had the land and we had the Bible"—Takatso Mofokeng has argued that this demonstrates the "incomprehensible paradox of being colonized by a Christian people and yet being converted to their religion and accepting the Bible, their ideological instrument of colonization, oppression, and exploitation."[1] Other scholars, picking up on this tension, have emphasized this dissonance by offering alternative explanations to the classic missionary conversion narrative (hagiographies which generally highlighted the heroic sacrifice of missionaries struggling to free heathens from barbaric practices and the miraculous nature of the successes they experienced) for why so many Africans chose the colonizer's religion. Norman Etherington, in his seminal work on Zulu Christianity, almost totally excluded the pull of religious faith from his analysis of early conversion; many believers, he instead argued, entered the faith for functional reasons such as the easier access to land, trade, or government positions that education in mission schools provided.[2] So masterfully did Etherington paint this image that for the better part of two decades few scholars bothered following his lead in studying what was one of the most important social and cultural shifts on the continent. One reason for this, of course, is that he was right, functional reasons played a particularly important role in the early conversion narratives of Africans across the continent. However, as I discuss in this work, not only does sincere religious interest need to be accounted for among the early converts, but a purely functional explanation for the popularity of Christianity also fails to explain either the dramatic growth of congregations in later years or the sustained belief of subsequent generations of Christians during the later colonial period when any tangible benefits to adopting the faith became much more difficult to discern.

In Natal, the southern African British colony that would eventually become part of South Africa, the advantages enjoyed by the first Christians had largely faded by the 1880s in the face of a white settler economy designed to marginalize all Africans. At Groutville, one of the first mission stations established in Natal, members of the American Zulu Mission (AZM), a Congregational organization that lies at the heart of this work (in part because they were the largest mission body in the area for nearly a century) became relatively wealthy growing sugar in the early 1870s. Less than two decades later the sugar mill they established went bankrupt as larger white owned plantations squeezed them out of the market; a reality facing many *amakholwa* businesses at this time. Yet despite their spiral into poverty, the Groutville congregation continued to grow as did all other AZM churches in subsequent years. Did many continue to see membership as a pathway to success in a rapidly changing world? Undoubtedly. Literacy, if nothing else, must have remained a powerful draw. But why remain? However they arrived, Christianity clearly offered more to converts than a few additional coins in the pocket and believers responded to this by appropriating the faith with great zeal.

Similar to functional arguments for conversion, scholars are inarguably correct in seeing mission churches as important sites of colonization, particularly through cultural transformation.[3] What I do not accept is the assumption of some that the success of Christianity in Africa is solely attributable to colonialism. The thinking being that the imposition of the later led hand in glove to the former. It is undeniable that missionaries often shared a symbiotic relationship with colonial officials (albeit a frequently uncomfortable and at times even antagonistic one for both parties) but such a position makes the false assumption that missionaries were the central actors in the spread of Christianity. This simply wasn't the case.

Jean and John Comaroff have perhaps best articulated the connection between Christianity and colonialism in their studies of London Mission Society evangelization among the Tswana of southern Africa. Noting the power of the early exchanges of goods (and the ideas embedded in those goods) between Tswana and missionaries they argue that the gifts given by the Christians "anticipated the more complex transactions that would incorporate the Tswana into the culture of empire."[4] Certainly such dialectics can be found at work between the AZM and their congregations as well. The mission, for example, ran "family schools" during its early years in which children were indentured to missionaries by local families. As I discuss in chapter 2, these children learned to read and write, received religious instruction, but also worked to earn their way—a case ripe for interpretation employing what the Comaroffs call the "colonization of consciousness," a model for the ways mission Christianity prepared Africans for absorption into the British Empire. Yet a deeper examination of these day schools suggests that they weren't nearly as hegemonic as the "colonization of consciousness" argument might lead us to believe. Some children were baptized, some took on the cultural trappings of their employers (such as Western clothing or a sense of a formal working day) but most returned home unconverted, gave the money they had earned to their fathers, and went back to herding cattle with their brothers and friends.

More importantly, those Africans who converted did not simply receive Christianity (and with it the European cultural trappings long since adhered to the faith) as if it were poured into them. The Comaroffs claim to be highlighting the "Long Conversation" between missionaries and congregations, but ultimately Africans play a passive role in their narrative of Christianization; they are significantly transformed by the Western and imperial political and economic accoutrements of Christianity without actively articulating the meanings of their adopted faith. I am not the first to note this troubling lack of African agency. Among the most effective critiques, Elizabeth Elbourne, Paul Landau, and J. D. Y. Peel have all argued that the Comaroffs' focus on the intertwining of Christianity and colonialism has overestimated the importance of missionaries while ignoring the critical role of African evangelists in reimagining and spreading the faith.[5] This may be because the Comaroffs essentially treat Christianity as a foreign and hostile cultural force, any African embrace of which gives off the whiff of collaboration in their own conquest. Or as Landau writes; "The Comaroffs read Africans' embrace of Christianity as a temporary surrender."[6] The irony here is, as a number of scholars have demonstrated, that embracing Christianity seems to have ultimately produced any number of nationalist movements. Jonathan Draper has noted how Magema Fuze, one of the earliest *amakholwa* public intellectuals, worked to produce a "prophetic nationalism infused by Christian symbolism" designed to protect Zulu identity and the remnants of the Zulu state against further erosion by colonial forces.[7]

Yet Africans effected just as they were affected and many of the very same shirt- and trouser-wearing youth employed by missionaries also assisted in translating the gospels—an act that ensured Christianity assumed a local character from the earliest moments of its birth.[8] Naturalization (that is the process by which Christianity was stripped of many of its foreign trappings and became increasingly local) was not, however, a smooth evolutionary development.[9] On several occasions *amakholwa* radically reimagined the nature of their community and their faith as it became clear that their previously constructed identity did not meet current needs.[10] These shifts often proved traumatic for congregations, but after each the link between local realities and lived Christianity grew stronger—further distancing the faith from its mission origins.

The first generation of African Christians appears to have viewed their faith as fundamentally a new clan affiliation, with loyalties transferred to the *amakholwa* community and their missionary "headmen." Missionaries encouraged this thinking, not the least by doling out cattle and land much as did Zulu chiefs looking to grow their base of dependents. Perhaps not surprisingly, many early Zulu Christians demonstrated little enthusiasm for active evangelization among traditionalists. Some seem to have seen conversion as a sort of zero-sum game in which additional *amakholwa* were likely to simply dilute the worldly benefits that accrued to this new tribe. But this functional argument cannot fully explain the lack of interest among converts for this activity and it also must be understood within the context of early Christians having only just begun the project of transforming the faith—it seems likely that converts so keenly felt the holes in their new spiritual lives that they did not have confidence in the message missionaries asked them to disseminate. Only when they created a Christianity they could truly call their own did evangelization efforts begin in earnest—and met with success among traditionalist Zulu (known as *amabhinca*, a term I will use interchangeably with "traditionalists" throughout this book.) The nature of this success was replicated across Africa as Africans first came to terms with their adopted faith only when they had adapted it to local needs and only then did aggressive evangelization begin in interest. It was from that moment that the faith truly took root on the continent, for African evangelization proved critical to the spread of the faith.[11]

Today there are some 360 million Christians on the continent, a number that is expected to nearly double by the middle of this century.[12] These figures are all the more staggering when compared to Europe, the historical home of Christianity which counts some 500 million baptized, but where the faith slowly withers and the great medieval cathedrals now house only the remnants of aging congregations. Indeed observers have argued that the coming century will almost certainly be one in which Africa (along with Asia and Latin America) assumes leadership of almost every one of the major Christian denominations.[13] That this will be so says much about who the typical Christian is today; no longer is it a European, or even an American, but much more likely someone in the global south. As Philip Jenkins has recently noted, "By 2050 only about one-fifth of the world's three billion Christians will be non-Hispanic whites. Soon, the phrase 'a white Christian' may sound like a curious oxymoron, as mildly surprising as 'a Swedish Buddhist.'"[14] As Christianity has waned in the West, Africans have embraced this new faith in numbers and with an enthusiasm that almost staggers the imagination.

Nor should it be assumed that these figures are somehow illusory, Africans as Christians in name only as someone reading Barbara Kingsolver's bestselling *The Poisonwood Bible* might be led to believe.[15] As is true in much of the rest of the continent, Christianity is one of the most important social forces in today's South Africa—resonating at nearly every level of society. Churches, from the grandest cathedrals to those that are little more than a few roughly hewn pews in shacks, litter the countryside and every conceivable form of the faith is represented, from Roman Catholicism, to all the mainstream Protestant denominations, to every shade of Pentecostalism, and to those, such as the amaNazaretha, that have stretched the fundamental tenets of the faith to the breaking point. More importantly, unlike Europe and increasingly America, South Africans fill those churches. Nearly 80 percent of the country claims membership in a Christian church and on Sabbath mornings the streets are packed with parishioners making their way to services that often last the better part of the day.[16] In KwaZulu-Natal (KZN), the most populous of the country's provinces, women and men dress in the uniforms of their particular prayer groups (organizations within the church designed to encourage and support the faith of individuals) and take mini-bus taxis in which bobble-head Jesuses watch over passengers from the dashboard. For foreign researchers riding along, it is not uncommon to be asked with great concern the state of one's own salvation, a question hinting at the dramatic reversal in the relevance of Christianity between the North and the South that has occurred since the religion was first introduced to the area some 150 years ago.

Indeed given the striking success of the faith in South Africa it is difficult to imagine that a century ago very few Africans called themselves Christian here or anywhere on the continent outside of Ethiopia (where it has a longer history than it does in most of Europe). Mbulasi Makanya, the first Zulu convert, was baptized in 1846 and her son followed eleven months later to help form a congregation of less than a half dozen.[17] By 1848, after a decade of proselytizing, the American Zulu Mission could count only eleven converts. To the American missionaries who arrived in the area confident in their ability to quickly build a self-sustaining church, the results of their early labor were deeply disappointing. A generation later little had changed and as late as 1895 the African Christian community of Natal remained insignificant; numerically, politically, and even within their own churches.

By the end of the next decade, this had all changed. Congregations grew beyond the capacity of the founding churches to hold sufficient services for everyone interested in attending. Missionary organizations, including the AZM, quickly ordained a host of African pastors to meet demand, and new churches blossomed across southern Africa. It would take another generation before Christianity became the dominant faith of the land (and not until independence before the religion dominated certain parts of the continent such as East and Central Africa) but the gains it made at the turn of the century proved enduring. Today the majority of Zulu call themselves Christian and the faith is as deeply rooted in South African society as any other place on the planet.[18]

Why did this happen? What occurred in the first quarter of the twentieth century that came to so dramatically alter worldwide Christianity? Most scholars now agree that Christianity has thrived because it was first appropriated by Africans and then spread by armies of unpaid evangelists who deserve more attention than the white missionaries who preceded them.[19] Unfortunately the study of African Christianity has moved little beyond this abstract conclusion and very few accounts exist highlighting either the actions of individual Africans involved in the process of naturalization, or the relatively lengthy time this took. We now know that their collective efforts shifted the religious landscape of a continent, yet their stories remain largely untold outside of the churches they helped make viable and self-sustaining institutions.

This work seeks to fill this lacuna by presenting the narratives of *amakholwa* like Ntaba, one of the earliest Zulu converts who approached the missionary at Mvoti in 1846 with a cow for sale because he was "ashamed to go unclad any longer," and Nguzana (Rufus Anderson), who converted in the 1860s after spending time as an assistant to an itinerant merchant who bought and sold goods to *amakholwa*, and Mabuda Cele, who struggled to understand why his Christianity should preclude drinking *utshwala*, the Zulu beer missionaries came to hate, or Grace Jwili who as a woman became one of the first *amakholwa* of any gender to take up missionary work outside of Natal in the early 1870s; and finally Mbiya Kuzwayo, whose story begins in this book with a Holiness revival in 1896 and dominates the final chapters because it was he who guided Christianity through its most important transformation in Natal—changes that soon after led to a Zulu-dominated Congregational pastorate and an enthusiastic lay preaching force. During this half century *amakholwa* re-imagined what it meant to be Christian on several occasions—first moving their religious identity from a separate ethnicity that distinguished them from traditionalist neighbors to a muscular faith closely connected to career choice and material possessions, before finally absorbing theologies outside Congregational orthodoxy, particularly spiritualist ones found in Holiness, and coming to terms with some of the more difficult theological aspects of Christianity. Only then could they call the faith their own and fully tackle their evangelical obligations. The final step in the evolution occurred around the turn of the century and it was only from this moment that congregations across the mission quickly grew and leadership of the churches finally passed out of white missionary hands.

Oddly, however, those individuals mentioned above have largely been forgotten outside of the church. Instead it is *amakholwa* like John Dube, the founding president of what would become the African National Congress (ANC), and Pixley ka Seme, who would become one of the organization's early presidents, whose political activities have dominated the imagination of historians.[20] However, Dube's mission, in particular, was a modernizing not a religious one, and while he saw the two as connected, he seems to have drawn very few into the faith. He believed, as I discuss in chapter 5, that Zulu Christians needed training in the industrial arts before any other education, religious or otherwise—a belief that eventually led him to pursue political organization. So while the activities of Dube were undoubtedly important to the eventual political fortunes of not only his fellow Christians but all Africans, he had very little to do with the popularization of the faith.

While the Celes, Jwilis, and Kuzwayos of colonial Natal were also interested in events outside of the church, their greatest contributions are not as well regarded because, in part, they are much more subtle and, frankly, so much more difficult to tease out of the primary sources.[21] Men and women like these were engaged in appropriating Christian theology to assemble a Christian message that was eventually enthusiastically received because it met needs at the local level while retaining its universal principals. Critical to this naturalization of the faith was the theological experimentation *amakholwa* (like Christians everywhere) engaged in; for the Christian message brought by missionaries contained ideas that held wide-spread appeal such as salvation and life after death, but was also burdened by Western cultural trappings woven into missionary sermons. As long as it seemed Zulu needed to transform themselves into Americans in order to be Christian, the faith would have had very little success. But once African evangelists naturalized the faith, their Christianity became significantly more palatable.

Nor am I suggesting that this process was necessarily one of syncretism (although that was certainly one possible outcome), rather Africans spent generations deconstructing and reconstructing, over and over again, what it meant to be Christian within the context of local beliefs but fully enmeshed in the long Christian conversation. Adapting sermons, selectively reading biblical texts, re-imagining the nature of prayer, and picking from an abundance of new and often radical religious ideas emanating from post-Civil War America, in doing all this Africans actively wrestled with what the faith might mean in their lives. Much to missionary consternation, Zulu Christians proved more than willing to cross the theological boundaries of whatever denomination they happened to belong. Witnessing someone "struck down by the Spirit" is certainly not what one might expect to find in a Congregational church in New England, but from the late 1800s forward this became a regular part of the experience for Africans in the churches of the AZM. Missionaries warned their congregations against "excessive emotionalism" but this experience became so ingrained that it is a regular feature of both regular and revival services in these churches to this day.

What is extraordinary in this experimentation is that it did not lead to the collapse of the mainline churches (that is those "traditional" Western institutions such as the Congregational, Methodist, Anglican, and Catholic churches that first sent missions to southern Africa). That is not to say there weren't defections; some, such as the Methodists whose central structure was inherently weak, experienced relatively high rates of schism.[22] But few lost more than half of their congregations and many, such as the AZM, held on to the majority. This was rarely a result of an enlightened missionary attitude. Indeed it is remarkable how frequently missionaries defied both the desire of African congregations to assume responsibility for their churches and the urgings of their central leadership back home to speed up the transfer of authority. The AZM, for example, was a branch of the American Board of Commissioners for Foreign Missions (ABM), the leading missionary organization in the United States for most of the nineteenth century. The ABM expanded rapidly throughout the world in the early 1800s, committing considerable resources to India, China, Turkey, and southern Africa. By the middle of the century however, this devotion to a truly worldwide mission had taken a financial toll and the home office urged its missions to hand over the churches to a less expensive native pastorate so it could recall, or simply not replace, the majority of its American overseas workers. Missionaries of the AZM, like those elsewhere, resisted this request and it took nearly half a century for Africans to assume control of the pulpits.

If missionaries were resistant to the transfer of leadership to Africans why did so many *amakholwa* remain in mission-led churches? While this study points to several possible answers, two are particularly persuasive. The first is that by the end of the nineteenth century an internal, theological revolution that effectively separated missionaries from direct control over individual churches by moving Christianity out of their hands was already underway. I examine this in greater detail in chapter 6, but even the inherent ethnocentrism of missionaries couldn't withstand the tradition embedded in the gospels that when a congregation demonstrated command of the faith they were given responsibility for their own church. A millennium of Christian history pointed to local practices of the faith holding primacy, something even the Roman Catholic Church at the height of its hegemony couldn't prevent.[23]

The second is that many of the faithful had simply invested too much into their membership in the traditional churches to leave. Members of the AZM, like Christians everywhere, gathered communities together from scratch, built churches with their own hands, paid for the hymnals, pews, and altars that filled those buildings, and were baptized, received communion, wedded, and buried their ancestors in the same. They were, quite simply, too deeply committed to their lives in the churches to leave (although this also speaks to the enormity of the decision for many who left). Given what they were required to surrender, to many it must have seemed far better to engage in the spiritual and political battles necessary to make the churches their own while also engaging in the difficult process of reimagining what forms their Christianity would ultimately take.

For the same reason that John L. Dube has attracted attention, academics have also long been fascinated by those who ultimately did break away and formed their own congregations. These African Independent Churches (AIC), as they have become known, have received considerable attention from historians, anthropologists, and political scientists as formative sites of anti-colonialism.[24] Because of this (and also, in fairness, because so many African Christians are now members of an AIC or Pentecostal congregation) most scholarship on Christianity in southern Africa has focused on the history, reach, and power of these institutions.[25] This work, however, seeks to shed light on the other half, those who remained in the traditional churches and wrought change from within. Theirs is a particularly important story not only because it has gone largely ignored, but also because in retaining their membership in the traditional churches they lent authority to the alterations of the faith they made along the way. Quite literally, I would argue, the legitimacy they gained from maintaining "respectability" allowed for radical experimentation without the sort of schismatic rupture that so frequently pulled breakaway congregations of the day (whether they be in the United States or Africa) outside the orbit of ecclesiastical law to the point that few, if any, other denominations accepted them as Christian.[26] In thinking about respectability I borrow from the work of Robert Ross and Elizabeth Elbourne who have both argued that the concept captures the aspirations of African Christians during the colonial era, in particular their desire to force their way up the hierarchy of colonial society by adopting many of the cultural trappings of the western world.[27]

While respectability speaks to the political and economic aspirations of *amakholwa* vis-à-vis the colonial setting, it also explains much about inter-African relations at this time. This study concludes just as the *amakholwa* elite had begun to successfully translate their standing into positions of power among the Zulu nobility. And here I use "the *amakholwa* elite" deliberately, for it has become commonplace to assume that all African Christians slid into the category of "educated elite" both by dint of their faith, and the truth that the majority of those who led independence movements across the continent in the middle of the twentieth century, attended mission schools in their adolescence. But the vast majority of Christians should not be thought of in this way as they were often as marginalized as their traditionalist neighbors. Both economic and political poverty have been the common experience for all Africans.

Frustratingly for many Christians, some of their marginalization came early at the hands of fellow believers. As I argue in chapter 3, Zulu Christians also actively engaged in sorting out what "respectability" (or the lack of it) meant among themselves from the very early moments of the church in Natal.[28] For example, membership in one of the founding AZM churches (like Groutville and Inanda) was clearly more prestigious than being affiliated with one of the numerous smaller "outstations" that branched off from the original congregations. This was in part because of the perceived spiritual power imbued in the bricks and mortar of those original buildings, but also because missionaries (who until the end of the nineteenth century still presided over most of the central churches) were regarded as important political allies, fonts of doctrinal truth, and offered the easiest access into the worldwide Church. Indeed one of the important consequences of the revival I discuss in this work was to disconnect spiritual from secular respectability by giving all believers the ability to claim religious authority regardless of place of birth or color of skin. By the beginning of the twentieth century one could be a noteworthy Christian without embodying the other trappings of success generally connected with respectability and the "educated elite."

What *amakholwa* did share, regardless of their class, was a belief that their Christian identity signified a connection to the wider world. While it can be argued that in adopting Christianity believers hoped to force entrance into the British colonial economy, it becomes increasingly clear when reading the sources that African Christians quickly understood that theirs was a faith shared across time and space. Early African believers sought, again and again by a myriad of means, to connect with the wider Christian world. Christians of the American Zulu Mission, for example, wrote letters to the secretary of the ABM, to missionaries away on sabbatical, to other Christian organizations, and to Christians in other ABM missions in Africa and elsewhere. They participated in worldwide days of prayer. They became members of transnational Christian organizations like the YMCA, and a few of the very gifted and very determined made their way overseas to pursue advanced degrees, often supported by funds from Westerners committed to evangelization. A few went out on mission. Maintaining respectability meant all this was possible and one could participate in Christianity as a universal religion—leaving the churches to join an AIC made all this significantly more difficult. Africans understood that leaving the mission churches hurt in a number of ways, not the least of which is that it crippled their own claims of Christian legitimacy.

It is this aspect of respectability I am particularly interested in, for it is here that *amakholwa* secular aspirations intersected with Christian religious identity and reinforced a commitment to a certain, historically based, ecclesiastical authority. What this meant was that, frankly, the relationship between missionary and convert often mattered less for understanding how Africans perceived their Christianity than did how they related to each other. It also seems possible to make an even bolder claim—had a core body of *amakholwa* not remained within the church it seems entirely possible that Christianity would have disintegrated or been absorbed into traditional belief systems before the faith had become entrenched into Africa as part of a world-wide system of like-minded faithful.[29] For this reason alone the study of those who remained in the churches is at least as important to understanding the success of Christianity in Africa as any examination of those who did not.

As scholars such as Lamin Sanneh have noted, the single most important act performed by early Christians was "translating" the gospels.[30] Sanneh is particularly interested in the most literal meaning of this term, the act of rendering the Bible into local languages, but I would argue that it is in Sanneh's secondary understanding of this idea that the key to the success of Christianity across the continent is truly found. Christianity needed to be culturally translated as well, transposed into local milieus and here the religious overlap could be occasionally found. As I argue in chapters 4 and 5, for Zulu Christians disconnected from the daily presence of the *amadhlozi* ancestral spirits, an alternative needed to be found and the Holy Spirit eventually served as substitute. That isn't to say that this Christianity was syncretic, but rather that Zulu cosmology, whether Christian or traditional, was incomplete without this type of active, ever-present, religious figure. Elsewhere in Africa other needs demanded to be filled and in doing so first African evangelists, and then the wider African Christian community, retained their ethnic identities even while assuming the faith. Yoruba Christians were Christian, but still Yoruba, just as Zulu Christians remained Zulu.[31] J. D. Y. Peel makes this point nicely when noting that any focus on change when discussing conversion "has to be grounded in an appreciation of the continuities through change."[32]

For those who remained in the churches revival was perhaps the most important tool in re-imagining their faith. Often connected to the events told of in the Acts of the Apostles, revival is actually a difficult concept to define because it has meant so many different things to so many different groups over the last several hundred years. Scholars have been particularly interested in the frequent intersection between disruptive social changes and revival; indeed perhaps the most important work on revival in Africa, Karen Fields' *Revival and Rebellion in Colonial Central Africa* argues that a millenarian revival in early twentieth century Zambia was a rational response to the societal upheavals of colonialism.[33] I don't dispute Fields' conclusions but would argue that the political ramifications of revivalism on the continent are only one aspect of a much larger phenomenon. As I describe throughout chapter 3, this work is also interested in disruptive social changes (colonial and otherwise) but is so within the context of understanding the process by which African believers altered their faith in response to these challenges.

Most Christians seem to agree that at their core revival movements seek to reignite the spiritual fervor of both listless congregations and straying believers.[34] That is to say that generally revivalism invigorates churches by inciting those within them to a more impassioned faith—the former a desired and expected outcome of the latter. Because this is most often the goal, revival movements are often not evangelistic in nature. Conversion certainly occurs, indeed "come to Jesus" narratives are the bread and butter of revival sermons, but generally the target audiences are those already in the churches and the core message is one of a return to spiritual purity.[35]

Indeed, when a wide-ranging revival occurred among *amakholwa* of the AZM at the end of the nineteenth century, the focus was foremost upon altering the faith lives of those within the churches. As discussed in chapter 5, very few if any non-Christians participated in the first year of the movement and when members from the earliest revived churches organized groups they called *amavoluntiya* (the Volunteers) to spread the message; these groups initially travelled to other Christian churches, not among their traditionalist neighbors. It was clear to those who participated that this was a religious experience directed at and for those who already believed. In no small part this is because the message was drawn from Holiness, a theology just then emerging from the American heartland that argued that Christians could attain a state of absolute purity through the Holy Spirit which would allow them to lead lives free of sin.[36] While Holiness advocates were certainly interested in reaching "heathens" their message was of primary interest to those who already considered themselves Christians but wanted to achieve a "higher state of perfection" in their spiritual lives. This revival wasn't, then, about converting Africans, it was about altering the structure of their lived faith.

This leads me to an additional observation: revival is most often a deeply contradictory event, both reinforcing and challenging the leadership of clergy. For many, the experience represents a time when lax members are drawn back into full participation with their congregations, reaffirming the authority of the churches and crystallizing power in the hands of whomever speaks from the pulpit. Indeed revivals have frequently occurred in places of great social discord such as frontier lands, newly urbanized areas, or blighted cities (think here of the revivals that gripped Appalachia in the early nineteenth century and Los Angeles a century later.)[37] In these places individuals often gravitated toward revival as a means of maintaining their identity in the face of apparent social chaos.

But revivals also open up revolutionary space for individuals within congregations to create new identities or even, as I argue here, to re-imagine the nature of their community and their faith. This is accomplished in no small part because of the fluidity of leadership and legitimacy during these events. In normal times, the hierarchy of churches is generally clear and pastors carefully control the message while following liturgical and doctrinal structure established by centuries of practice. While revivals possess their own organization, they are also seeded with moments that are explicitly designed to collapse the bonds of normal behavior in the expectation that this will free participants to become open vessels for the Holy Spirit. Free prayer, extended singing, dancing in the aisles, moaning, wailing, collapsing comatose—all of these and more signal participation in revival while also transgressing what the historical churches viewed as acceptable behavior.

The problem for church authorities is that this is a difficult genie to re-bottle, for revival participants almost always long to maintain (or recapture when it is lost) the power of the experience, and rightly recognize that it is in the original breaking of normal bonds that they were empowered. So revival echoes not only spiritually, but also temporally as congregations lay claim to at least some authority from church authorities who are forced to readjust normal church practice to meet these demands. Particularly important in this regard is that revival also encourages prophetic expressions by participants whose utterances are directed not only at individuals, but also toward shaping the future of local churches, the denominations they are part of, and even worldwide Christianity. While nearly everyone experiences some prophetic moment during revival, it is generally recognized that the utterances of a few particularly "blessed" members carry greater weight. Strikingly, these individuals often emerged from amongst the masses and rarely were armed with previous liturgical training. Perhaps not surprisingly their utterances have not always aligned with accepted doctrine—sometimes this resulted in schism, but most church authorities sought to soften and adsorb the potentially heretical whenever possible. Indeed it is just this approach that animated missionaries of the AZM even when they believed revival had stretched acceptable boundaries—a process discussed in more detail in chapter 6.

For missionaries of the AZM this reality was further exacerbated by the theology of Holiness that animated the revival in their churches. Holiness, as practiced by the revivalist that introduced it to South Africa, called on participants to be "sanctified," an event they believed made them free of sin and in so doing allowed for the Holy Spirit to take up permanent residence in their souls. Once so filled, the sanctified believed they had achieved a state of "perfection" that made them vessels of Christian might and power. It was in this state that for the first time *amakholwa* could claim spiritual equality with their missionaries, if not even more than equality—for AZM missionaries almost universally refused to engage in the activities necessary to achieve sanctification (the public confession of sins that marked most services was deemed too unbecoming) and in this failure the missionaries opened space for congregations to claim the moral high ground, to reasonably believe that they were now closer to God and better understood His will than the missionaries themselves. The American missionaries, who initially welcomed the revivals, soon came to understand this turn and openly fretted over the "overly emotional" nature of the movement. In response they sought to tamp down revival, to soften its power in their congregations.

But it was too late. Armed with this newfound spiritual legitimacy, *amakholwa* transformed Congregational services, making them more open and dynamic. Focus shifted from the autocratic workings of the pulpit to a significantly more democratic and participatory spirituality emanating from the pews, and missionaries frequently found services spinning out of their control as congregations asserted their own religious needs over normal practice. Within a decade of the first revivals the American missionaries acknowledged that their time leading individual churches had passed, and that going forward congregations and services would be led by African pastors and deacons. During this often tumultuous transition very few *amak-holwa* chose to break away from the AZM. They did not need to, for they were well underway with an internal revolution, a spiritual coup, if you will, that kept Africans in the churches not so much because of their successful assertion of political control (although this certainly played a role in the maintenance of unity) but rather because Africans demanded that their Christianity reflect their own needs and reality. Missionaries may not have liked this, but it was the only way their ultimate goal, the establishment of the Christian church in KwaZulu-Natal, could have succeeded.

Unfortunately, even though this is a story of the re-imagining of Christianity that focuses first and foremost on how converts dealt with the internal workings of their adopted faith, the colonial government ultimately forced its way into even this deeply personal process. As I make clear in chapter 6, the state became increasingly uneasy about the degree of freedom the *amakholwa* community came to enjoy following revival. After a number of Ethiopian movements sprang up, several of which were connected to the AZM, the white settler state of Natal moved aggressively to corral the ecclesiastical freedoms enjoyed by Zulu Christians as a result of their appropriation of the faith. Missionaries and Zulu Christians alike both recognized the effect that this was bound to have as from the end of the first decade of the twentieth century forward converts increasingly turned to churches outside of state influence. So, far from encouraging Christianity as a tool of suppression, the colonial state early on discouraged it for fear of its liberating aspects and in so doing likely fueled the growth of the AICs. While this might be regarded as having the opposite effect of what the state desired, it likely also ensured that future international criticism of South Africa's racist policies would be muted as many in the AICs were cut off from the power of the larger church. This is not to say naturalization was somehow crushed by the colonial state, whose Secretary for Native Affairs (SNA) slowly imposed the draconian measures that would become the basis of apartheid, but rather that the process also did not result in a church fully sheared from its mission roots—surprisingly something that remains true to this day.[38]

Across the continent the growth of Christianity proceeded in a similar fashion to what had occurred in South Africa. Almost universally, local forms of African Christianity underwent a number of revisions as African Christians explored what it meant to be Christian, and transformed themselves and their faith as need and experience demanded. Part of this was through reading, or often publicly performing, particular passages from the Bible. As Gerald West has argued, "Ordinary African interpreters of the Bible are less constrained than their scholarly compatriots in the strategies they use to appropriate the Bible" and this has resulted in a willingness to play with biblical texts until local coherence is achieved.[39] Another site of transformation has been the large public gatherings of Christian celebration that are common throughout the continent, but was particularly remarkable during the massive revivals that occurred in Central and Eastern Africa shortly before independence during the middle of the twentieth century. These animated an intense reimagining of Christianity which ultimately led to an explosion in church membership and the formation of the *Balokole* (the saved ones), a revivalist group dedicated to reimagining traditional churches while maintaining an orthodox Christianity.[40] Empowered by revival to claim both Christianity and the traditional churches as their own and then able to mold them to their own needs, Africans ensured that the faith not only survived, but flourished across the continent.

What follows in this work tells how this happened in one small part of Africa, but in so doing serves as a model for understanding the larger process of Christianization that has occurred across the continent over the last two centuries.

NOTES

1. Takatso Mofokeng, "Black Christians, the Bible and Liberation," *Journal of Black Theology* 2 (1988), 34. Mofokeng's comments must be understood within the particular context of apartheid, the system of repression and exploitation formally established by the white, largely Afrikaner, National Party in 1948. This web of laws and practices kept the minority white population in economic and political power until the first free elections in 1994 swept most, if not all, of the trappings of white establishment away with the election of Nelson Mandela and the African National Congress (ANC). Christianity among Africans survived the insistence of the National Party that their institutionalized racism was ordained by God, although many, like Mofokeng above, came to question the relationship between the religion and the system of repression.

2. Norman Etherington, *Preachers, Peasants and Politics in South-east Africa, 1835–1880* (London: Royal Historical Society, 1978); and Etherington,"Recent Trends in the Historiography of Christianity in Southern Africa," *Journal of Southern African Studies,* 22 (1996); David Sandgren, *Christianity and the Kikuyu: Religious Divisions and Social Conflict* (New York: Peter Lang Publications, 1989).

3. Comaroff, Jean and John, *Of Revelation and Revolution: Christianity, Colonialism, and Consciousness in South Africa, Volume 1 & 2* (Chicago: University of Chicago Press, 1991 & 1997); David Chidester, *Savage Systems: Colonialism and Comparative Religion in Southern Africa* (Charlottesville: University of Virginia Press, 1996); Leon de Kock, *Civilizing Barbarians: Missionary Narrative and African Textual Response in Nineteenth-Century South Africa* (Johannesburg: Witwatersrand University Press, 1996); V. Y. Mudimbe, *The Invention of Africa* (Bloomington: Indiana University Press, 1988). For the view of missionaries as agents of imperialism in its most

strident form see, Nosipho Majeke, *The Role of Missionaries in Conquest* (Alexandra: Cumberwood Press, 1952.)

4. Comaroffs, *Of Revelation and Revolution*, 183.

5. Elizabeth Elbourne, *Blood Ground: Colonialism, Missions, and the Contest for Christianity in the Cape Colony and Britain, 1799–1853* (Montreal: McGill-Queens University Press, 2002); and Elbourne, "Word Made Flesh: Christianity, Modernity and Cultural Colonialism in the Work of John and Jean Comaroff," *American Historical Review* 108 (2003): 435–459; Paul Landau, "Hegemony and History in Jean and John L. Comaroff's *Of Revelation and Revolution*," *Africa* 70 (2000): 501–519; J. D. Y. Peel, "Colonization of Consciousness," *Journal of African History* 33 (1992): 328–329.

6. Landau, "Hegemony and History," 512.

7. Jonathan Draper, "The Bishop and the Bricoleur: Bishop John William Colenso's *Commentary on Romans* and Magema Kamagwaza Fuze's *The Black People and Whence they Came*," in Gerald West and Musa Dube (eds.), *The Bible in Africa: Transactions, Trajections, and Trends* (Boston: Brill Press, 2000), 447–448.

8. For an excellent discussion of this process among Tswana of southern Africa see; Stephen Volz, "Written on our Hearts: Tswana Christians and the 'Word of God' in the Mid-Nineteenth Century," *Journal of Religion in Africa* 38 (2008).

9. Although scholars have recently turned to "naturalization" to explain the process by which Christianity was absorbed, adopted, and adapted by local peoples, it is not a new idea. In the early 1900s Edward Caldwell Moore made the argument that Christianity could only be successfully transmitted to new lands if missionaries understood the cultural transformation it must undergo in doing so. Pointing to the past and noting that it became a Greek faith to the Greeks and an African one to the Carthaginians he argued, "It was not merely clothed with the garments of new times and places but fed with the food, vitalized with the rich blood, of the new races, domesticated, naturalized, nationalized, transmitted from father to son, as all part and parcel of the mystery of the transmission of life." Edward Caldwell Moore, "The Naturalization of the Christianity in the Far East," *Harvard Theological Review* 3 (1908): 254. For a recent use that mirrors Moore see, Kenneth Mills, "The Naturalization of Andean Christianities" in R. Po-Chia Hsia, ed., *Cambridge History of Christianity: Volume 6, Reform and Expansion 1500–1660* (Cambridge: Cambridge University Press), 2007.

10. Here I am indebted to Benedict Anderson's, *Imagined Communities: Reflections on the Origins and Spread of Nationalism*, (London: Verso, 1991), whose discussion on the socially constructed nature of the nation state I deliberately echo. Unlike Anderson, I am speaking of a religious community, but similar to his argument that a modern nation is by necessity "imagined" because the members of even the smallest state cannot know each other and therefore think vertically about the nature of their national identity, so also was it the case with Zulu Christians, who formed a new community and had to work to fix even elastic borders across this non-organic identity.

11. Adrian Hastings, *The Church in Africa, 1450–1950* (New York: Oxford University Press, 1996), 437-41.

12. David Barrett, George Kurian, and Todd Johnson, *World Christian Encyclopedia*, 2nd ed. (New York: Oxford University Press 2001), 13–15.

13. When Pope John Paul II passed away in 2005 one of the names frequently mentioned as a possible successor was Cardinal Francis Arinze, a prelate from Nigeria. Arinze's ascension mirrors the rapid growth of Catholicism across the continent which now annually produces more candidates for priesthood than Europe from amongst a population of practicing faithful that will soon pass the number of active European Catholics. In the same way, the number of active Anglicans on the continent dwarf the number in England, leading to very real troubles for the Church of England which finds itself split between African bishops calling for conservative positions on social issues such as gay marriage and consecration of women and the far more liberal views of its English and North American leadership. Mark Rice-Oxely, "Jerusalem Conference May Widen Anglican Rift," *Christian Science Monitor,* June 20, 2008. Mandy Morgan "An African Priest: Shortage of American Priests leads to More Diversity in the Nation's Catholic Churches," *National Catholic Reporter,* October 17, 2003.

14. Philip Jenkins, *The Next Christendom: The Coming of Global Christianity* (New York: Oxford University Press, 2007), p. 3.

15. Barbara Kingsolver, *The Poisonwood Bible* (New York: Harper Torch, 1998). Kingsolver's work, while masterfully painting the internal family dynamics of an American missionary family living and working in post-WWII Congo, portrays African converts as either insincere or particularly shallow in their beliefs. This caricature is fine for a novel that needs a static idea of African tradition to serve as a foil for the antihero missionary at the center of the book, but it does not serve to explain the subsequent success of Christianity in the Congo and elsewhere.

16. Statistics South Africa, *Census 2001: Primary Tables* (Pretoria: Statistics South Africa, 2004) and can be found online at http://www.statssa.gov.za/. At 69 percent of the total population, Christianity is not quite as dominant in KwaZulu-Natal as it is elsewhere in the country.

17. This work draws extensively from a number of archives, the most important of which are those connected to the workings of the ABM in the United States and the AZM in South Africa.

18. For an overview of the contemporary strength of Christianity in South Africa see, Richard Elphick and Rodney Davenport, *Christianity in South Africa: A Political, Social, and Cultural History* (Berkeley: University of California Press, 1997).

19. Richard Gray, *Black Christians and White Missionaries* (New Haven: Yale University Press, 1991).

20. Shula Marks, *The Ambiguities of Dependence in South Africa: Class, Nationalism, and the State in Twentieth Century Natal* (New York: John Hopkins University Press, 1986); Heather Hughes, "Doubly Elite: Exploring the Life of John Langalibalele Dube," *Journal of South African Studies* 27 (2001): 446. Hughes notes that in the past, Dube received more attention for his work beyond the political realm, but that today "he is remembered primarily as a political figure."

21. Here my work deliberately echoes several works written about historically marginal southern Africans. I am particularly indebted to Paul la Hause's *Restless Identities*, a work that rescues the stories of two *amakholwa* preachers (neither from the AZM) whose life histories tell us much about the social and political realities of early twentieth century Natal. La Hausse's work provided a clear path

for understanding the potential significance of even those individuals who were lightly regarded in their own times. Jeff Peires' *The Dead Will Arise*, on the other hand, tells the story of Nongqawuse, a young woman living on the margins of Xhosa society who experienced a transformative vision that called on Xhosa to sacrifice all their cattle and grain in the expectation that great riches would befall them. The end result of this apocalyptic moment was Xhosa mass starvation and the loss of independence to imperial England. The theoretical engine of Peires' work is built around the idea that even such a seemingly irrational event contains within it an "internal logic"—an idea in this case built around religious belief. It strikes me that *amakholwa* who remained with the mission churches even when the functional reasons for doing so no longer existed could be accused of their own irrationality, but they had their reasons for remaining and these, like the Xhosa before them, were embedded in their faith. Where my work differs is that I have chosen to emphasize the religious life of African converts over their political one. I do this knowing that Christians often stood at the forefront of popular political movements throughout the colonial period (and into the era of apartheid) but if we are to understand how Christianity was successfully absorbed and transformed then the emphasis must be on the critical spiritual moments in this process. Thankfully others have already examined the more secular lives of these early believers. Paul la Hausse, *Restless Identities: Signatures of Nationalism, Zulu Ethnicity and History in the Lives of Petros Lamula and Lymon Maling* (Pietermaritzburg: University of Natal Press, 2000); J. B. Peires, *The Dead Will Arise: Nongqawuse and the Great Xhosa Cattle Killing Movement of 1856–57* (Bloomington: Indiana University Press, 1989).

22. For a fuller discussion of this phenomenon see, James Campbell, *Songs of Zion: The African Methodist Episcopal Church in the United States and South Africa* (New York: Oxford University Press, 1995).

23. Stephen Neill, *A History of Christian Missions* (New York: Penguin, 1986), 151–154.

24. Scholars are currently split over what the "I" in AIC should stand for. A growing minority now use "Initiated" instead of "Independent." I have cleaved to convention here.

25. As just a sample see, Bengt Sundkler, *Zulu Zion and Some Swazi Zionists* (London: Oxford University Press, 1978); Jean Comaroff, *Body of Power, Spirit of Resistance: The Culture and History of a South African People* (Chicago: University of Chicago Press, 1985); J. Mutero Chirenje, *Ethiopianism and Afro-Americans in Southern Africa, 1883–1916* (Baton Rouge: Louisiana State University Press, 1987); David Maxwell, "Historicizing Christian Independency: The Southern African Independence Movement, 1908–1960," *Journal of African History* 40 (1999); and Maxwell, *African Gifts of the Spirit: Pentecostalism and the Rise of Zimbabwean Transnational Religious Movement* (Athens: Ohio University Press, 2007); Birgit Meyer, "From African Independent to Pentecostal Charismatic Churches," *Annual Review of Anthropology* 33 (2004).

26. Examples on both continents are legion, but two obvious cases are the Church of Jesus Christ of Latter-day Saints (commonly known as the Mormon Church) in the United States, and Isaiah Shembe's amaNazarite church that may

claim as many as a million adherents (mostly Zulu) in South Africa. Both consider themselves Christian institutions, but are regarded as so doctrinally in error by other Christians as to lie unredeemably outside the Christian world.

27. Elbourne, *Blood Ground*; Robert Ross, "Missions, Respectability and Civil Rights: the Cape Colony, 1828–1854," *Journal of Southern African Studies* 25 (1999).

28. For the role of Zulu Christians in laying the groundwork for modern Zulu nationalism in the 1920s see; Nicholas Cope, *To Bind the Nation: Solomon kaDinuzulu and Zulu Nationalism 1913–1933* (Pietermartizbug: University of Natal Press, 1993); Shula Marks, *The Ambiguities of Dependence in South Africa: Class, Nationalism, and the State in Twentieth-Century Natal* (New York: John Hopkins University Press, 1986).

29. This is not only speculation on my part. For an example of exactly this coming to pass, see John Thornton, *The Kongolese Saint Anthony: Donna Beatriz Kimpa Vita and the Antonian Movement, 1684–1706* (New York: Cambridge University Press, 1998) in which the collapse of denomination authority leads to the gradual dissipation of what had been a thriving Catholicism.

30. Lamin Sanneh, *Translating the Message: The Missionary Impact on Culture* (Maryknoll: Orbis, 1989).

31. For a particularly horrifying reminder of this see the 1994 genocide in Rwanda, where Hutu Catholics often butchered Tutsi Catholics with little regard for shared faith (although, as evidenced by the charnel houses that several churches became, many Tutsi hoped and prayed that their shared faith might matter.) Philip Gourevitch, *We Wish to Inform You That Tomorrow We Will be Killed with Our Families: Stories from Rwanda* (New York: Picador, 1998).

32. J. D. Y. Peel, *Religious Encounter and the Making of the Yoruba* (Bloomington: Indiana University Press, 2000), 255.

33. Karen Fields, *Revival and Rebellion in Colonial Central Africa* (Princeton: Princeton University Press, 1985).

34. Works discussing how to start and maintain revivals are a cornerstone of Christian presses. For some examples see, Hank Hanegraaff, *Counterfeit Revival: Looking for God in all the Wrong Places* (Nashville: World Publishing, 1997); Ian H. Murray, *Pentecost Today?: The Biblical Basis for Understanding Revival* (Cape Coral, FL: Founders Press, 1998); Roberts Liardon, *God's Generals: The Revivalists*, (New Kensington, PA: Whitaker Press, 2008).

35. Once "revival" has occurred, however, the expectation generally is that churches will support and encourage their members to vigorously proselytize.

36. Vinson Synan, *The Holiness-Pentecostal Tradition: Charismatic Movements in the Twentieth Century* (Grand Rapids: Wm. B. Eerdmans, 1971); Melvin Dieter, *The Holiness Revival in the Nineteenth Century* (Metuchen, NJ: Scarecrow Press, 1980); Shuanna Scott, "'They Don't Have to Live by the Old Traditions': Saintly Men, Sinner Women, and an Appalachian Pentecostal Revival," *American Ethnologist* 21 (1994).

37. Ellen Eslinger, *Citizens of Zion: The Social Origins of Camp Meeting Revivalism* (Knoxville: University of Tennessee Press, 1999) Cecil Robeck, *The Azusa Street Mission and Revival: The Birth of the Global Pentecostal Movement* (Nashville: Thomas Nelson, 2006).

38. This may not be an entirely fair comment, as several of the former churches of the AZM, such as Inanda and Groutville, share a relationship with the United Church of Christ which still sends American missionaries to serve in these places at their request.

39. Gerald West, "Mapping African Biblical Interpretation: A Tentative Sketch," in Gerald West and Musa Dube (eds.), *The Bible in Africa: Transactions, Trajectories, and Trends* (Boston: Brill Publishing, 2000), 39–40.

40. Thomas Spear, "Toward the History of African Christianity," in Thomas Spear and Isaria Kimambo (eds.), *East African Expressions of Christianity* (Athens: Ohio University Press, 1999), 8–13; Heike Behrend, *Alice Lakwena and the Holy Spirits: War in Northern Uganda, 1985–1997* (Athens: Ohio University Press, 1999).

1

In the Beginning . . .

In the opening of *Cry, the Beloved Country*, Alan Paton writes of the land he called home: "There is a lovely road that runs from Ixopo into the hills. These hills are grass-covered and rolling, and they are lovely beyond any singing of it."[1] This may be one of the most fitting descriptions ever penned, for no other feature so marks Natal, the South African province where most of this history takes place, as its hills.[2] All along the coast the land rises up almost from the point where the Indian Ocean touches sand. For the first twenty miles or so the hills are gentle, easily tilled and harvested. In a fortunate congruence, it is also here that much of the rain falls on the province and today, as it did shortly after its introduction a century and a half ago, sugarcane blankets the area in a great waving sea of green. After this short stretch, however, the earth rises sharply and the next thirty miles, encompassing much of the land set aside for African residence by early British authorities, is dominated by steep ridges and deep valleys. While beautiful, this dramatic land is difficult to plow and agriculture is further hampered by unreliable rains. It is just as difficult now as it was during colonial days for a Zulu homestead, or *umuzi*, to support itself by living off the relatively small plots of land available here.[3]

The city of Pietermaritzburg marks the middle of the province and here again the hills change, becoming smoother and progressively larger as they march toward the towering Drakensberg escarpment that lines the western border of Natal. Early white colonialists found this area, with its broad, mist covered valleys, particularly conducive to farming and gradually, through force and legislation, removed Africans from what is now known as the Midlands. Some of those removed were settled in several reserves established near the Drakensbergs, where the great massifs make farming difficult. To the north and south Natal demarcated its borders with rivers. The Thukela River tumbles out of the Drakensbergs as a mere stream but quickly gains size as it weaves, sometimes drunkenly, at other times with a terrifying ferocity, along Natal's northern border.[4] The hills here are sharp, rocky, and dry, and much of the land is suited for nothing better than raising the goats ubiquitous to the area. To the south, the Umzimkhulu River marked the southern border of the province and serves today, much as it did during the colonial period, as a demarcation between Zulu and Xhosa—two people culturally and linguistically similar but with distinct political histories.

Most of the American Zulu Mission stations fell within either of the first two geographical regions found moving inland from the coast, and the economic fortunes of early *amakholwa* were often determined by the locations of their home churches. For members of Groutville, near the coast and ideally situated for growing sugar, the land could provide bountiful harvests as it also frequently did for members of the Umlazi, Amanzimtoti, and Inanda stations. For those stations located on more rugged land, such as that found at Mapumulo, Esidumbini, Umsunduzi, Itafamasi, and Amahlongwa, financial success was significantly more difficult to secure and even during colonial Natal's boom years the African Christians here struggled to free themselves from poverty.

HEAVEN'S PEOPLE

Just what forces lay behind the creation of the Zulu state in the early 1800s remains a contentious issue.[5] What has become clear, however, is that the society that emerged from the kingdom's consolidation of power under the leadership of Shaka, its founding regent, remained, at best, an amalgamation of local chiefdoms. These chiefdoms were themselves composed of various *imizi* (plural of *umuzi*) and were bound to the central state by sending their young men to participate in the regimental *amabutho* system. These regiments not only provided a ready means of projecting royal power, but also an effective labor pool which the state could deploy to increase its wealth, police its subjects, and maintain a proper degree of separation between themselves and the unassimilated peoples, known as *amalala*, on the geographic margins of the kingdom.[6] Most of what became Natal, and those living there, fell into this category and many (although certainly not all) chose to abandon the area during the worst of the Zulu state's excesses in the late 1820s as it sought to maintain the *amabutho* system by keeping the regiments busy either on campaign or raiding for cattle.

For nearly a century to be Zulu (which can be translated as "People of Heaven") was to be a member of the Zulu royal house, an identity John Wright has noted was jealously guarded by the inner-core of the state and to which conquered people rarely aspired.[7] It was not until the early twentieth century that "Zuluness" became a desired marker for a broad swath of African peoples across KwaZulu-Natal. Those perhaps most responsible for this movement were, interestingly, those who saw themselves as bound for heaven: missionaries and *amakholwa*. In their desire to produce a translation of the New Testament, missionaries flattened local linguistic differences while their converts eventually turned to the Zulu royal house for both affirmation of their relative success and out of frustration as paths of economic, social, and political advancement were increasingly shut down to them by the colonial state. For its part, the state of Natal found this coalescing identity both frightening, for the specter of Zulu martial skill, and necessary as it allowed for the African population to be more easily, and cheaply, administered under one system discussed below.

MARGINAL EUROPEANS AND THE ZULU STATE

In April 1824, the first whites settled permanently in the area under the leadership of Francis Farewell and Henry Francis Fynn, both Englishmen. Landing at one of the few natural harbors in the region (which they called Port Natal and would become the city of Durban), they came seeking their fortunes in the lucrative ivory trade, hoping to undercut the Portuguese operating out of Delagoa Bay to the north.[8] In recognition of the power of the Zulu state, one of the party's first acts was to visit the kingdom's capital at kwaBulawayo, returning with several head of Shaka's royal cattle in what amounted to his tacit permission to settle and their acceptance of a status as homestead heads under his authority.[9] The handful of white fortune seekers grew steadily until by 1838 some forty or so had settled in the area, most with ties to various Cape Colony trading firms.[10]

As the number of whites grew so too did the number of Africans returning to the area to resettle. Within six months of their initial arrival, Fynn reported the presence of black refugees seeking the protection of the small band of whites.[11] Most of the traders proved happy to play the role of "white chief" and collected families under their protection in exchange for labor, food and, occasionally, female companionship.[12] Still, this initial trickle of refugees remained just that until 1828 when Shaka was assassinated by a group of conspirators led by his half brother Dingane who, following a brief struggle for succession, claimed the throne for himself. In the tumult that followed, several chiefdoms, such as the Qwabe and the Cele, took advantage of the power vacuum and fled south into Natal, seeking independence. It was from among people such as these that missionaries would later claim their first converts.

As Natal became a refuge for the disaffected of Zulu society, relations between the Zulu state and merchants at Port Natal steadily deteriorated. On several occasions Dingane found it necessary to impose cattle fines on the whites and more than once the traders, fearing for their safety, abandoned their settlement to flee into the surrounding bush with their African dependents. This tenuous relationship reached a breaking point in 1835 when, tired of the steady stream of defections of individuals, households and whole chiefdoms, Dingane demanded that the traders return all future refugees to his charge. Intimidated, the traders initially conceded, but within three months felt secure enough to break the agreement. Dingane retaliated by cutting off the whites from trading across the Thukela and an uneasy truce lasted until 1837, when Afrikaner Voortrekkers descended into Natal from the Drakensbergs after fighting their way across much of the highveld.[13]

Led by Piet Retief, the Trekkers arrived at Mgungundlovu, the Zulu capital, seeking a grant of land south of the Thukela in which they hoped to establish an independent nation. Dingane, hearing of the Afrikaners' successes against his longtime foe, Mzilikazi's Ndebele, recognized the danger they posed to the Zulu kingdom and laid an ambush for Retief and his party. After initial success Dingane failed to press his assault, and the surprised Trekkers rallied their remaining strength, defeated a large Zulu force at Ncome River (later renamed Blood River by Afrikaners in memory of their victory) and proceeded to split the nation in two by supporting Dingane's half-brother Mpande's claim to the throne.

Following Dingane's death, Mpande assumed the mantle of Zulu king and "awarded" his Afrikaner supporters the land south of the Thukela River (including Durban and its white settlers.) The Trekkers called it the Republic of Natalia, but it was country doomed to a short life. British authorities in the Cape Colony, alarmed by the unrest created by Afrikaner actions, finally acted on a long-standing request by the Durban merchants to annex Natal, and in 1842 a British force occupied the town. Initial Trekker resistance was quickly overcome and the following year Natal became part of the British Empire.[14] Many Afrikaners who had left the Cape Colony to escape English control now moved west, back across the Drakensberg Mountains and out of reach, temporarily, of British oversight.

For Mpande, even more than Dingane, one of the primary challenges of rule proved to be maintaining the cohesiveness of the Zulu kingdom. With first Afrikaner and then English overlords, Natal offered a tempting sanctuary for the more marginalized peoples that made up the Zulu polity and during the 1840s many moved south of the Thukela. So serious did the problem become, that Mpande removed the population located along the river and replaced them with military posts in the hopes of blocking such flight.[15] It was not, however, only Zulu moving into Natal at this time. From the south and west *amalala* began to return to their homelands and English settlers, arriving in increasing numbers throughout the mid-1800s, found a land they had presumed empty filling at a rapid pace.

HER MAJESTY'S DOMINION

Before British annexation, Afrikaner farmers had stated their intention to forcibly expel all returning Africans who they declared "had no right or claim to any part of this country" and acted on this assertion by conducting raids on returning refugees who they accused of squatting on their land.[16] British settlers proved equally jealous of the land, and the assumption that Natal had been "empty" when whites arrived colored the first Locations Commission, set up in early 1846 to delineate land for African settlement. Under the Commission's recommendations Theophilus Shepstone, the first Diplomatic Agent to the Native Tribes and later the first Secretary for Native Affairs (SNA), relocated some 80,000 Africans under fifty-six *amakhusi* (chiefs) onto reserves.[17] Not wanting to anger an already volatile Afrikaner population, the new Natal administration abandoned the commission's recommendations for establishing locations in areas deemed most desirable by white farmers and instead established the reserves (called locations) on land rejected by whites.[18]

By the beginning of the 1850s, most Africans in Natal lived on locations under what has become known as the "Shepstone System," a patchwork of "native customary law" which allowed the Natal government to rule a numerically superior people on the cheap by supporting the "traditional" rights of chiefs over their people and allowed for the continued practice of social and political traditions not deemed within the purview of the colonial state.[19] For those matters deemed important to the state, Shepstone became almost the sole arbiter of policy and as David Welsh has demonstrated, chiefs found some of their key powers, such as calling up young men into *amabutho* regiments, severely restricted—while at the same time they were given additional authority by Shepstone to collect taxes and muster press gangs for the colonial state.[20] It has recently been argued that this taking with one hand while giving with the other might have been part of Enlightenment-era thinking designed to propel Zulu through the lower stages of development, it is difficult to imagine Shepstone mulling the notions of David Hume while laying the groundwork for what would eventually evolve, as Welsh argued, into apartheid.[21]

Legally, the SNA ruled the African population in conjunction with the colony's lieutenant governor, but in practice Shepstone ruled over his department and the people it served as his own personal fiefdom until he retired from the post in 1875. The fact that Shepstone almost alone established policies should not, however, be confused with an ability to consistently impose those policies at the local level. A web of nineteen salaried resident magistrates covered Natal and were charged with insuring that the Secretary for Native Affairs' orders were carried out, this they did with varying degrees of effectiveness as often the best they could hope for was a negotiated agreement with the chiefs through whom "traditional" law flowed. It was meant to be a self-supporting administration and in 1848 Colonial Natal imposed a "hut tax" on every homestead to pay the costs of maintaining the reserves without calling on funds from the colonial treasury.[22] But outside of moving part of the African population onto reserves and collecting taxes, the colonial state maintained a minimal presence in the daily lives of the average *umuzi* and ultimately had very little impact on the ways in which *amakholwa* transformed Christianity. Indeed, for most of the nineteenth century the colony of Natal looked to missionaries to effect social change among its African population.[23]

THE WORD COMES TO NATAL

Considering their willingness to engage in polygamy, it is unsurprising that the merchants who established Port Natal showed little interest in spreading the Christian message. Only when Captain Allen F. Gardiner arrived in the colony in 1835 did proselytizing began in earnest. A member of the Church of England, although not formally affiliated with them as a missionary, Gardiner resigned his commission with the Royal Navy following his wife's death and committed himself to spreading Christianity.[24] In February, shortly after his arrival, Gardiner obtained an audience with Dingane and, despite his assurance to the king that "any intention to interfere with either their laws or customs was the farthest removed from my thoughts: as, next to the fear of God, honour and respect to kings and all in authority, was a prominent feature in the religion which was taught in 'the book' and which I was so anxious to make known to them," he failed to received the king's permission to establish a mission within kwaZulu.[25]

Rebuffed, Gardiner returned to Port Natal and played a conspicuous role in the town's development over the next several years. He solicited funds from the traders for the establishment of the settlement's first church, and later a school for the growing African population, and in May of 1835, he finalized the treaty between the merchants and Dingane that promised to return to the king any fugitives who might seek asylum among the whites. In accord with the treaty, Gardiner personally returned four such refugees, for which Dingane reversed his earlier decision and agreed to allow the missionary to work within the kingdom.

Before doing so, however, Gardiner returned to England the following year and appealed to the Church Missionary Society (CMS) for financial support and additional manpower. The society responded by sending Rev. Francis Owen, a recent graduate of Cambridge, with Gardiner on his return to Natal in May 1837. Owen arrived in Natal with a mandate from the CMS that resembled the working plan of most of the missionaries arriving in the area over the next half century, he was to preach the Gospel, translate the scriptures, and establish a Christian school for Zulu children.[26] After difficult negotiations, Dingane allowed Owen to establish a station near the royal residence. He made little headway, however, for in February of the following year he witnessed the assassination of Piet Retief and his party.[27] Appropriately alarmed he abandoned the station and fled to Durban, quitting the area entirely by 1839. Gardiner, embroiled in a dispute with the merchants of Durban, followed Owen shortly thereafter.[28]

Gardiner's absence did not leave the area without missionaries, however, for in 1835, responding to a call from the London Missionary Society, the American Board of Commissioners for Foreign Missions (ABM) sent six of its members to South Africa to minister to both the Zulu and Ndebele peoples. Like Owen, the Americans abandoned their stations during the crises of 1837, but several of the brethren returned over the following years and by the 1840s they had established themselves as the largest and most influential mission body in Natal, a position they held (and exploited) through the rest of the century.

Other mission bodies followed shortly after the Americans. The Wesleyans expressed interest in sending a mission to the Zulu as early as 1825, but did not do so until 1842, when Rev. James Archbell arrived with the British troops sent to take Durban from the Afrikaners.[29] Archbell, like the two Methodist ministers that followed him in 1846, worked almost exclusively with the growing English populations of Durban and Pietermaritzburg. Only in 1847, when W.C. Holden arrived under appointment to establish a church in Durban for the African population, did they finally reach out to Africans.[30] That same year James Allison, another Methodist, arrived from Swaziland, complete with several hundred members of the church he had founded there in 1844. Driven out by war, he and his followers landed in Natal and formed a new church near Durban on land granted by the colonial government. Allison later quarreled with the local Wesleyan leadership and once again led his congregation away from trouble, this time assisting them in purchasing a six-thousand-acre farm near Pietermaritzburg they named Edendale.[31] Others from Germany, Norway, France, and elsewhere eventually followed and by 1860 seventy-five missionaries from across the Western world occupied thirty-five stations in Natal, making it, at the time, one of the most densely proselytized regions in the world.[32]

THE AMERICAN BOARD AND THE ORIGINS OF MISSIONS

Founded in 1810, The ABM emerged out of the missionary spirit that first gripped American churches in the earlynineteenth century as part of the Second Great Awakening that swept America from the 1790s through the middle of the following century. During this period of heightened religiosity, revivals swept across the campuses of eastern universities, while on the western frontier Methodists competed with Presbyterians and Baptists to win souls in great camp meetings, exhorting their audiences to claim their place in heaven prior to imminent arrival of the millennium.[33] In New England, Congregational theologians dismantled the Calvinist theory of predestination, replacing it with a theory of free will in which individuals needed to take personal responsibility for their own salvation. This was a necessary precursor to foreign missions, for if God had already determined those to be saved Christians need feel little responsibility to spread the Gospel. These two theological strands, of the coming millennium and a belief in individual salvation for all, merged in the American church to produce a deep sense of urgency for those who had yet to hear the Word of God, an urgency that translated into personal obligation to save the "heathen."[34] Reflecting their shared roots, mission societies organized by the committed were modeled along the same lines as the abolitionist bodies just beginning to make their mark on America and to which many missionaries also belonged.[35] The first of these societies to reach out from the new world was the American Board.

The ABM began life as a students' organization, begun in 1806 by five undergraduates from William's College in western Massachusetts who claimed to have hatched the plan while seeking shelter in a haystack from a passing thunderstorm.[36] Their goal, "to effect, in the person of its members, a mission to the heathen" was deemed so controversial at the time that the original members vowed to keep their existence a secret lest they be thought "rashly impudent and so injure the cause they wished to promote." But this secrecy did not last long and soon the organization spread to other campuses and four years later students from Andover Theological Seminary approached the General Association of the Congregation to propose that Congregationalists take up the cause; a plan the denomination eventually approved.[37] Once founded, the Board, consisting of a "prudential" or executive committee of nine members and one secretary charged with the daily workings of the organization, received a steady supply of applications from young men eager to serve. Most were graduates of the seminaries of New England, a few came from as far away as Ohio, and by 1840 some 170 of them had travelled to China, India, the Middle East, and Africa.[38]

While women enthusiastically supported the mission project it was generally only men who received the early appointments to overseas service. That is not to say women did not go; they did, but generally only as wives of missionaries. It appears to have been an unwritten rule that only married men could serve overseas. Many of the early missionaries to South Africa received their appointments while still single and then spent several frantic months finding and wooing wives. The February 1849 wedding of Josiah Tyler and Susan Clark is representative. After learning of his acceptance to become a Board missionary and the imminent departure of the *Concordia*, a ship bound for Cape Town, Tyler rushed to Northampton, New Hampshire the home of Ms. Clark, a woman he had only recently met.[39] They married hurriedly at a funeral-like service in which the vows could not be heard over the "sobs and sighs" of her family. Unable to openly resist Tyler's "Godly duty," the family seems to have mustered the family physician to their cause in an effort to dissuade the young man from taking their daughter to Africa. The doctor met with Tyler, warned that Ms. Clark was delicate and thrust a box into his hands while saying, "Here is a box of medicines I present to you. Keep her alive as long as you can, but before the year is out I expect to hear of her death." Despite this warning the newlywed couple hurried off the day after the wedding to Tyler's ordination and from there boarded the *Concordia*. By the middle of the century, however, unmarried women were allowed to join the Board, but only as teachers and principals, never as fully vested missionaries.

The first two missionaries sent out by the Board arrived in India two years after the Board's founding. Much to their surprise, they were not well received and had difficulty establishing a station. The East India Company viewed the Americans as meddlesome and dangerous and the War of 1812 prompted British threats to expel them. Surviving these initial setbacks, the Board encouraged future missionaries to avoid political matters and, in particular, to steer clear of angering their English hosts,[40] a concern that would, as we will see, continue to color the Board's actions a century later.

Difficulties for these pioneers did not come from the British alone. To their surprise, converts were few and far between. Missionaries responded by taking local children into their homes to raise as Christians. In exchange for small sums of money or food nearby families indentured children to missionaries, likely understanding that they might lose some of them to

conversion. These children worked, but missionaries were primarily interested in the schooling, hymns, and prayers that also made up the typical
day for the youth. The "family school" approach, as it came to be called,
proved enduringly successful and as ABM missionaries established themselves across the globe, children of a multitude of nationalities began learning hymns and Bible stories while holding a broom.

THE AMERICAN ZULU MISSION

By 1833 the Board had placed missionaries on every inhabited continent
but Africa. Recognizing this oversight (and urged to do so by John Philip,
the renowned leader of the London Missionary Society in the Cape Colony)
they organized two separate parties bound for the southern Africa.[41] The
first group, consisting of three graduates of Union Theological Seminary,
the preeminent institution for the Presbyterian church in America (which
had joined the ABM two years earlier), landed at Cape Town in February
of 1835, and proceed into the interior with their wives to administer to
the needs of those they called the "Interior Zoolahs"—the Ndebele under
Mzilikazi.[42] The second party, consisting of two graduates of Andover Theological Seminary, their wives and Dr. Newton Adams and his wife, landed
at Port Natal later that year and proceeded into the lands held by Dingane
to work among the "Maritime Zoolahs."[43] Both groups hoped to befriend
their respective kings, convert them, and then reap the benefits of a sort of
"trickle-down" Christianity in which royal pressure led to mass conversion.
This approach was understandable given the dramatic success of Board missionaries in Hawaii in 1822 where the conversion of the aristocracy had led
to baptisms by the thousands.[44]

Within a year of their arrival, however, the mission to Mzilikazi withdrew
after staggering from one disaster to the next. Mzilikazi proved willing to
use missionaries for trade and diplomacy, but opposed their efforts to
preach to his people and showed no interest in converting himself. Even
without his opposition the mission stumbled badly, for the Americans
arrived ill-prepared for the cold winters on the southern African highveld
and by September the entire band had fallen gravely ill with rheumatic
fever. Before they could recover, Mzilikazi's capital came under attack by
Afrikaner forces, routing the Ndebele and leaving the Inland mission with
little choice but to join their brethren in Natal.[45]

Matters proved little easier along the coast. Dingane only grudgingly allowed the Americans to build in an area well removed from the royal capital at Umgungundhlovu. The station they opened, near the Umlovi River
in contemporary kwaZulu, experienced initial success, and the Americans

wrote home pleased with their progress. However Dingane also took notice, and when word spread of his displeasure the congregation dropped to
a stalwart few.[46] Before they could respond to this challenge, however, the
Americans were swept up in history as Piet Retief's Trekboers came stream-
ing over the Drakensbergs. His death and the subsequent war sent the
Americans fleeing Natal back to the Cape Colony in June 1838.

The Americans only returned to Natal hesitantly and in piecemeal.
Daniel Lindley worked as a pastor among Afrikaners for seven years
before again taking up mission work to Zulus. Dr. Adams also stayed in
southern Africa, returning to Natal shortly after fleeing and setting up the
American's first permanent mission in South Africa. The others all sailed
for America and among them only Aldin Grout returned to continue his
work. The Prudential Committee looked aghast on the series of disasters
its two "Zoolah" missions suffered and voted in 1843 to discontinue the
work in southern Africa. By then, however, the Zulu mission had already
been given a fresh life, for the British, moving to stabilize the northern
Cape frontier, took Natal in 1842 and, as part of this effort, asked the
Americans to stay on. The missionaries stayed, six more joined them soon
after and in 1849 the Board responded to a warning from Grout that "our
society will move so slowly, that others will step in before to reap the
harvest of souls" by sending three additional mission families to join the
work in Natal.[47]

By 1849 the AZM had grown to twelve American missionaries with their
families. It was a fortuitous moment to become the largest mission body
in southern Africa, for the British administration had just established a
Locations Commission to map out where it wanted to settle the African
population of the province. For both practical and moral reasons the land
question deeply interested the Americans. As early as 1845 Lindley wrote
home expressing concern over native land rights, presciently noting:

> I began to be afraid that the rights of the Crown may interfere with the rights
> of the natives. Reserve so little land that they will not be able to subsist on it,
> and the thing will be accomplished; for they will then have to ask permission
> to live on the lands of others, which will be granted on condition that they
> labor for their landlords. Here in their own country they will be made servants
> and beggars . . . [48]

A few years later Dr. W. Stanger, the surveyor-general for the newly formed
province, confirmed the fears of the missionaries when he uttered what
would become an oft-repeated opinion among Natal's European population: "This country is too good for natives, it should be in the hands of
civilized men who would turn it to good account."[49] Knowing that many
settlers jealously eyed some of the choicer land they used for their mission

stations, the Americans happily accepted appointments for two of their own, Lindley and Adams, on the Locations Commission.

The Commission began meeting in 1846 and over the next year mapped out ten different reserves that would have covered nearly half of the colony.[50] The intention of the commissioners, influenced by a "village plan" already launched by the AZM on several of their stations (discussed in more detail in the following chapter) was to provide nearly twenty acres per family in the hopes of creating an African peasantry; small farms centered around small towns similar to those found throughout rural America.[51] With these allotments, the original plan also called for the building of roads, schools and other infrastructure, all with the intention of dragging local African society into the "civilized" world. The Colonial Office in London declined to pay for the plan, however, and the government of Natal, always sensitive to the demands of its white settlers, scaled back the size of the reserves and located the majority of them in marginal land undesired by white settlers. Only those fertile areas already occupied by American missionaries, such as Inanda, Umlazi, and Umvoti, remained open to black settlement.

The hunger by white settlers for land, as well as cheap African labor to work it, led the lieutenant-governor of Natal, Benjamin Pine, to comment in an 1852 interview with members of the AZM that it was his intention to break up the reserves, including the mission stations, all together, dispersing their Zulu residents across the white owned farms to act as tenant labor.[52] Alarmed, the missionaries sought reassurances, and following a protracted struggle, the Governor of the Cape Colony, Sir George Grey, intervened on behalf of the "civilizing potential" of the missions and agreed, in 1855, to grant land in title to the American Board and several other mission bodies. The grants were of what they called a "glebe," a core 500 acres considered the mission's property to do with as they wished, and from 6,000 to 8,000 acres surrounding the glebe held in trust by the mission for Africans upon which they could settle and farm.[53] Twenty such "mission reserves" were established at this time, twelve of which went to the AZM. Management of the mission reserves was through a board of trustees consisting of officials from Natal and missionaries, although in practice the missionaries ran their reserves as their own personal fiefdoms for much of the rest of the nineteenth century.[54]

Prior to 1855, the Americans had chosen stations for practical reasons. When A. T. Bryant established himself at Ifumi in 1847, he did so because it was ideally situated in the middle of many Zulu, was not overly far from other AZM missionaries, was easily accessible by wagon, and was well supplied with wood, water, and other building materials.[55] The first homes and churches were often models of Yankee ingenuity, and the finer craftsmen among the missionaries threw up large three to four room structures in a matter of weeks.[56] Missionaries often hired nearby Africans to assist in these efforts and parties of Zulu descended on the new missions for afternoons of clearing away brush, gathering thatch, cutting timber and making un-burned bricks.[57] Later this work devolved to the members of the churches who assisted in constructing the churches, schools, and often the pastor's house.

As the missionaries built their churches, Zulu residing near the stations did their best to come to terms with how these odd men fit into their society. Local residents tested the power of these men who claimed a con-nection with Nkulunkulu (the Zulu high god) by asking them to pray for rain—and several did just that, bragging of their successes (which they attributed to a higher power, of course.) For some they were sources of em-ployment or even refuge, but others often thought of missionaries as a new type of *inyanga* (healer). One woman came to Bryant seeking a release from her husband's ghost, which, she claimed, had come to her in the middle of the night, cut a hole in her side, and begun to consume her vital organs. Bryant gave her medicine along with a message that it was not so much the medicine as the power of God over ghosts that would heal her; she returned later for more medicine, if not the deity that accompanied it.[58]

As colonial Natal extended its reach in the countryside, the people sur-rounding the mission stations turned, for a time, to missionaries to act as mediators between themselves and the state. Africans, particularly chiefs, quickly realized that missionaries were much better positioned than them-selves to promote their interests with the government and they acted ac-cordingly. At Mapumulo, Umkhonto, the local chief, occupied the sensitive land along the Thukela River that divided Natal from the Zulu. Recogniz-ing his tenuous position he encouraged the American missionary Andrew Abraham to settle on his land. When Abraham did so, Umkhonto sent his people to assist in gathering building materials and even constructing huts. At the first Sabbath service Umkhonto sat in front, glaring and throwing rocks at those who laughed or slept and sending a runner after a party that attempted to slip out early.[59] Diplomatic services, it seems, could be ex-changed for religious observation and in this function, missionaries wrote letters, made appeals and attempted to mitigate conflicts.[60]

SOWING THE SEEDS, 1845–1865

In the early months of 1846 Umbalasi, an old widow once married to a distinguished chief, became the first Zulu to make a public profession of faith and be baptized into the American Zulu Mission church. In August of that year, two young men at Umlazi joined her, the vanguard of a very slowly rising tide to come. It is not a simple matter, of course, to determine the reasons why the first generation of converts chose to join the Christian church. What can be said, certainly, is that they did not make the decision lightly, for it meant turning their backs on old beliefs and customs and accepting new ones that demanded they interact with the world around them in unfamiliar and often deeply unpopular ways. It is also important to note that for most entering the early church, conversion was often just a final step in a long, slow process that led them there. Despite the wishes of many missionaries, the first Zulus attending Sunday services did not convert en masse, regardless of how persuasive the sermon.

Nor, as is often thought, were the majority of the early converts refugees, witches, or other undesirable characters. This stereotype is burned into the historical record as a result of Norman Etherington's particularly pithy description of early Zulu Christians that reworks a passage from the gospel of Matthew to suggest a hopeless condition for those who initially came to the churches: "They were the poor in spirit, kingdomless men who were glad enough to find a place in the kingdom of heaven. They were the meek, landless men who longed to inherit the earth."[61] He is certainly correct that the majority of Zulu had no interest in converting when missionaries first arrived, but his characterization of those who did doesn't capture the experience of most of the early church members for whom the reality of conversion was much more mundane, significantly more complex, and followed a well-trodden path that rarely began with them as "outsiders." Before conversion most of these early African Christians found employment with missionaries, became students, and often only much later did they enter into communion with the church. To explode this canard, however, requires carefully unpacking the often tortuous route many converts did take into the church, something made easier by a number of narratives that can be constructed from the early records of the AZM and that begins with the American missionaries but frequently has very little to do with them. Only in doing so can understand who the bulk of the first converts were and why they joined the church.

Understanding conversion as a lengthy process also helps explain why, by all accounts, mission efforts in Natal were dismal failures in their early years.[62] After nearly two decades, the AZM could barely count two hundred Zulu as members of their churches. For missionaries who believed that they would enter into Natal, raise up a self-sustaining church, and move on to the next "heathen" area within one generation, this dreary rate of success became frustrating. Missionaries may not have had the success they yearned for in those early years, but they were creating a pool of *potential* converts, men and women who attended a service or two, heard the Word but did not immediately act upon any interest it stirred in them. The narratives of converts, as we shall see, suggest that this frequently occurred and interest might only flower into active faith in the far future.[63]

Like missionaries of every age, Americans of the early AZM believed that they lived their lives as the Gospel told, each moment thickly imbued with spiritual signification in which the goodness of their own lives might serve as an inducement to conversion. Thus, early in the AZM's time in Natal, Aldin Grout happily reported that he had not set out across Natal on his own. Like most whites traveling in southern Africa he did so only by employing skilled African teamsters. For Grout to make the many days journey to northern Natal he needed to hire not just a wagon driver, but also a native to lead the oxen and another to handle other smaller choirs. Three employees, three potential converts exposed to daily prayers before meals, scripture verses read from the Bible in the evening, and a life led without cursing, drinking, or other "unChristian like acts."[64] While none of those thus employed may have converted, they certainly returned home having heard, and likely grasped, the basic meaning of the message.

Once settled missionaries found a host of additional reasons to employ Zulu and the size of their working households increased dramatically. A cook was required, "not a professional one" but simply one to be taught the basics, "with much patience and some vexation."[65] Someone to assist the cook, by fetching firewood and preparing the stove needed to be hired. Another servant was required to haul water, often from streams from as far as two hundred yards away. No fences bordered the mission property so several herding boys were necessary to keep cattle from trampling the mission gardens and running amok in the fields of Zulu neighbors. A stable hand needed to watch over the horses and several attendants were necessary to accompany the missionary when he went on itinerant preaching trips through the rough countryside of Natal, boys who carried food, water, and bedrolls. Mission work, it soon became clear, was a labor-intensive business that provided its own captive congregation.

Most of those employed in the missionary's household were young men and women, often just children but frequently teenagers. At least initially, parents of those so employed contracted out the services of their children, often for periods of service of two years or more.[66] In return the parents received money, livestock, or the promise of both when the contract was complete. Frequently, these children lived with the missionaries, slept under same roofs, ate with them, were clothed by them, prayed with them and, most importantly, were taught by them. Although it varied, the children who worked for the Americans, in addition to their normal duties, were also required to spend several hours a day, usually in a morning and an evening block, learning to read and write, studying arithmetic and history, and receiving religious instruction.[67] Lewis Grout referred to the practice as the "Manual Labor School System," perhaps a more apt description than the "Family School" label it acquired over the course of a half-decade of use by the AZM.[68]

Almost all of the early converts of the American Zulu Mission came out of the family schools. In 1848 Aldin Grout reported that outside of one couple and one old man, all of his church members, seventeen in all, were young men, aged sixteen to twenty-one, whom he had employed over the previous two years. He was also particularly pleased to report that, entirely independent of any action on his part, a group of young men in his employ had maintained a prayer service over the course of the year.[69] James Bryant acknowledged that the system, which allowed him to employ anywhere from ten to twenty children at any given time, did not reach the same number of potential converts as itinerant preaching, but argued that "what is lost in magnitude—is gained in efficiency from greater concentration of effort."[70] For Bryant, as for all other missionaries, the family schools served as a sort of religious apprenticeship, and those who showed the promise of accepting the Word of God were encouraged to take up residence on the stations following their terms of service. For this purpose, early catechists received land and, as we shall see below, frequently the assistance of the missionary in establishing a homestead.

Of course most Zulu children did not succumb to these Christianizing efforts. Lewis Grout, who admitted to taking in any and all presented by parents as long as he had worthy employment to offer, reported that of the twenty children he had engaged during his first year in Natal four had run away, two were dismissed, six others learned to read the gospels and three of those expressed a desire to "forsake their sins and live according to the Word of God."[71] The remaining eight, apparently, rather quietly served their terms, acquired the requisite capital for their fathers' *umuzi*, and slipped back into a traditional way of life. Still, for most of the early converts, the path into the church was often first through the family schools and their identity as Christians was a circuitous one at best as work led to education, residence on or near the stations, and eventually, conversion.

Of course the "family school" model did not apply universally to early *amakholwa*. Other conversion narratives were more dramatic, particularly those of the early female Christians. For many women, the mission stations offered a welcomed opportunity in a society that appropriated their productive and reproductive powers, restricted their political voice and limited their ability to determine their own fate.[72] In 1858 Hyman Wilder noted that the majority of girls in his employment had fled their homes in order to escape forced marriages.[73] Over time the "girl fleeing the old polygamist" became a dominant trope in mission correspondence. Audiences back home obviously enjoyed hearing of these dramatic tales, but their increase also suggests a shift in mission ideology; with the rising power of colonial Natal, missionaries proved increasingly willing to confront what they considered to be the excesses of Zulu patriarchy. And while the phenomenon of "runaway girls" also needs to be considered outside of the religious question, reflecting as it did, both a response to changes in the nature of the Zulu homestead and an awareness by Zulu youth that the stations could be utilized as leverage in improving their situations back home, it remains clear that many of the young women who eventually joined the AZM in its first twenty years, did so after first using it to advance their own cause.

Refugees from *ubuthakathi* (witchcraft) accusations gave missionaries (and, it seems, historians) the most dramatic, if far rarer, conversion narrative. Like many Africans, Zulu engaged in a number of supernatural practices most of which, as performed by *izangoma* and *izanuse* (diviners) and *izinyanga*, were considered therapeutic for society but which could also occasionally be twisted to serve evil purposes by those with malice in their hearts.[74] In colonial Natal *ubuthakathi* was obsessed over by nearly everyone. As Karen Flint and Julie Parle have noted, "African communities who suffered its consequences sought to discover and expose those who practiced witchcraft, while whites aimed to protect the accused and persecute accusers. Each saw their intervention as necessary, just, and preventing imminent death."[75]

The rare moments when missionaries became enmeshed in this drama were ones they excitedly retold as often as possible. Aldin Grout frequently related the story of one woman whose husband had been killed for witchcraft and who had fled her homestead fearing for the lives of herself and her family if the taint of *ubuthakathi* spread to her. Like the Israelites, she wandered in the wilderness for a time before realizing that the missionaries offered her the only hope of avoiding starvation. Showing up at Grout's door with her small son at her side and her four-year old daughter hidden safely in the bush, she begged for shelter. Given a place to stay she proclaimed: "Teacher you have saved me. I shall never leave you. I will die with you, and my children, let them be taught and educated as you think best, and in the meantime serve you as best as they can."[76] Not surprisingly she proved true to her word, becoming one of Grout's first converts, followed by her children. For the son, Umkalo, who showed up at his mother's side, the experience proved lasting. Grout, many years later, proclaimed him "one of our best and most consistent Christians."[77]

Local trouble also sent Umehlwana, a grizzled veteran of Shaka's army, onto the mission station. Lewis Grout learned, long after Umhelwana had taken up residence, that he had originally settled at the station as a way to "vex his chief who had decided against him in the case of some cattle."[78] Perhaps unsurprisingly Umhelwana, like many who joined the church under questionable pretexts, could not bear the expectation to lead a "pure" life that accompanied mission station residence and he eventually left his new home.

Considering that the majority of those who became church members during the first decades of the AZM did so along the "family school" path and were, therefore, of local origin, it seems unlikely that local Zulu viewed stations simply as shoals upon which troublemakers washed up. Still, the missionary habit of welcoming disturbed souls and questionable characters must have bothered many neighbors. At Umlazi, for example, an old widow well known as an *umthakathi* (witch), lost her powers and failed after much effort to restore them. She became deranged by the experience and in 1849 wandered the countryside for a time before taking up residence in the decrepit remains of the abandoned Umlazi chapel. After much persuasion by her family she returned to the homestead of her son, who had recently moved closer to the mission station. Her next step along the margins of Zulu society was to begin attending Sunday services at the mission as well as an all-female prayer group in which she showed much promise, a hearty interest in the message, and a desire to convert. For her family these interests no doubt proved her continued madness, while for the missionary they instead evidenced a full recovery into sanity and an escape from demonic possession.[79]

It must be stressed again, however, that while dramatic conversion narratives proved popular reading for American audiences, and no doubt offered plenty of gossip for Zulu women in the fields and men at council, they were far from the norm. Much more common was the case of another woman at Umlazi who had heard the Christian message many years earlier, found that it left a lasting impression, and returned to the church many years later, after the death of her husband.[80] As a widow she had little to lose and perhaps more to gain than most from joining the Christian church, yet she did so against her family's wishes, choosing to respond to the message of redemption instead of remaining within the comfortable confines of kraal life. For many this combination of necessity and interest proved to be the exact formula for drawing them into the fold, accepting the missionaries' message and lasting through the rigorous demands of dramatically altering their lives.

THE MESSAGE

Zulu attending Sunday service heard diverse and at times contradictory messages about the nature of the new faith. God, as described by the missionaries, was both a loving father and an all-knowing judge perfectly prepared to pass the most horrible of sentences for moral failings. Like the reasons for conversion, it is difficult to come to a precise understanding of how those who first heard the missionaries' messages came to interpret them. Still, what emerges from the letters of the missionaries is a people struggling to fit new ideas into older forms, of people occasionally accepting or rejecting this new message whole, but more often taking that which they preferred and weaving it into their own cosmology as they best saw fit. For early converts, however, this option, by far the easiest in coming to terms with the Christian message, often proved untenable in the face of persistent missionary efforts to insure their true acceptance of the faith, and over the years an accepted orthodoxy dictated to them by an increasingly dogmatic mission steadily replaced divergent beliefs.

The message presented by the early missionaries took, essentially, two forms.[81] The first, the "Good News" presented the message of salvation within the body of the risen Christ. This message—that Christ had died for the sins of mankind and in his rising had promised that all who accepted him into their lives, followed his commands, and placed themselves within the church, would be assured a place in heaven—would be enough, many of the missionaries hoped, to inspire the masses to convert. When this proved a vain hope, however, most of the missionaries resorted to unsheathing the God of the Old Testament, who, they warned, would willingly cast listeners into the fiery pits of hell for their unbelief and for failing to turn away from their sins. Part of this reaction, as Benedict Carton has noted, stemmed from an inability to effectively communicate the gospel in Zulu, a linguistic shortcoming a number of American missionaries suffered from, and which led some of their number to engage in racial stereotyping.[82]

But missionaries who resorted to fire and brimstone often found that it most often simply ended conversations, far from the desired effect. A dying man proved eager for A. C. Bryant's company in 1847, happy to chat about his cattle, goats and chickens, but when the missionary turned to the man's condition as sinner and the risk he ran of dying without salvation, the man sat in silence although he "felt compelled to give respectful attention to an unwelcome message." J. L. Döhne, who was well known for his fully developed righteous fury, often stomped from kraal to kraal railing against the people for failing to attend Sabbath, for the sinfulness of their customs and habits, warning them of the "evil consequences resulting from their practices."[83] Zulu, already burdened with a strong sense of the active nature of evil in the present life, were unlikely to respond to a message that threatened more of the same in the later.

But, at least occasionally, forceful sermons stuck home. Years after he had heard one such homily, a young man near Ifume approached Döhne and related a message that had stuck: "God could use force, if he liked, and take a stick in order to bring us to believing in Jesus Christ but does not as he wants them to decide for themselves . . . "[84] The sermon, mixing the Zulu approach to disciplining children with the biblical allusion to a benevolent father, effectively captured the imagination of at least one listener and likely rattled around in the conscious of many more. The second generation of missionaries, while stepping up the pressure on *amakholwa* to abandon traditional customs they held onto, frequently employed sermons that connected Christianity with "civilization." Christians were repeatedly warned that their continued connection with the customs of their fathers threatened to pull them back into the "degraded" condition missionaries had found them in. This message, as we see in the following chapter, quickly became a central tenant of *amakholwa* identity.

As in churches everywhere, congregations sat in the pews on Sunday and listened to sermons designed to steer them towards salvation by calling on familiar themes. Not surprisingly, considering the pervasiveness of cattle in popular Zulu idioms and culture, Christ became not a shepherd but a herder and the riches of the word of God were represented not as gold and brightly colored jewels but as a "large fold of cattle in which every man may enrich himself."[85] For the congregation at Umvoti, which, in 1878, became known as Groutville, composed largely of those who had fled the wrath of the Zulu kings, Aldin Grout's sermon that non-believers would, "probably sleep till the Almighty Spirit awakens some to flee the city of destruction and Satan, raging, awakens the rest to pursue in hot haste to capture the refugees" must have struck particularly close to home.[86] For those already converted, the message seemed clear; their decision allowed them to avoid the horrors they had experienced, placing them within the safe confines of the mission station. The unconverted were left to mull over their fate had they not chosen to flee before Shaka, or his successors Dingane, and Mpande. By 1864, at least, American missionaries understood that they needed to adjust their message to incorporate local themes and idioms. Daniel Lindley wrote that year that he believed his fellow missionary Seth Stone was "not a wise preacher" as he had failed to adjust his message to local conditions, preaching a series of sermons on "systematic theology" instead.

When, during a Christian wedding at Umsumduzi (sometimes spelled Umsumduze by missionaries) in 1851, Lewis Grout urged traditionalists attending the event to return for the following Sabbath, he noted that "they were called not so much by us as by their maker, their heavenly King, to attend worship not only on that but on every other Lord's day." Those in the audience may have puzzled over his authority in laying claim to their time; but they understood the meaning of this claim, for it simply played upon the familiar trope of the ability of Zulu royalty to demand their presence at ceremonial occasions.[87] While couching attendance at services in such familiar terms made the missionaries' desires understandable, the difficulty inherent in translating such theological principles as passing "from death into life" or being "born again" limited the ability of the early congregations to understand the complexity of the message, frustrating both missionaries and themselves.[88]

Equally confusing for those Zulu who interacted frequently with the early missionaries must have been their response to traditional Zulu belief systems. For the early missionaries may have thought Zulu spirits evil, but they frequently seemed to acknowledge the active role they might play in everyday life. When Bryant provided medicine to the woman who claimed to be infested with her husband's ghost he reminded her that: "God was more powerful than all the ghosts in creation . . ." hardly a refutation of the woman's fears.[89] Ghosts, demonic possessions and unseen malevolent spirits resonated with the missionaries' concept of evil much as they did for Zulu, and at least initially those who brought these fears to missionaries were presented with an ambivalent message that did not so much deny their existence as suggest God's mastery over them.

Less nuanced was the missionary reaction to snakes. For Zulu snakes could be dangerous, but they also might be the tangible form taken by *amadlhozi*, the Zulu ancestral spirits. Bryant used the occasion of a young boy being bitten by a snake, a bite bad enough to put his life into temporary danger, to prove a point.[90] The youth, and his fellow compatriots employed in Bryant's family school, were reminded "of the dangers to which they are constantly exposed, and the necessity of being always prepared for death." Bryant also chided the children for failing to kill the snake after the attack, dismissed their concerns that doing so would have destroyed an ancestral spirit, and marched them out in search of the offending creature. Once found he led the boys in clubbing the reptile to death.

No such interaction is recorded, but it seems likely that congregations, on hearing the creation story and the role of Satan as embodied within the serpent, puzzled over missionary refusal to accept that the creatures might be a vehicle for the spirits. Indeed some missionaries further fueled such skepticism by attempting to appropriate Zulu religious symbolism as evidence that God worked in their favor. One local kraal-head, disturbed by the effects of Lewis Grout's sermons on his people, threatened to remove his household to a far distant place if the missionary did not cease coming around and preaching. Grout responded by recalling another *umnumzane* (male head of the family) who had reacted similarly, commenting: "Yes such a one went away last year for fear of the Gospel and for fear that his children would repent and become Christians. But where is he now? And what did his leaving us profit him? Was he not soon bitten by a snake in his new abode, and did he not die almost immediately?"[91] For Zulu such retribution was frequently the province of the ancestors, a belief not far removed from the divine anger many missionaries argued for.

As time passed, however, and a second generation of American missionaries replaced the first, the younger missionaries, armed not only with the Bible but also a belief in the hard scientific "truths" then emerging hand-in-hand with the rapid expansion of the Industrial Revolution, sought to close the loopholes of sacred possibility created by earlier missionaries.[92] One young man, returning from sacrificing a cow to quell angry *amadlhozi* spirits, found himself accosted by Josiah Tyler over his beliefs in this custom:

"Do the spirits come and drink the beer?"
"Yes."
"What form do they assume?"
"That of snakes."
"Do you see them?"
"No."
"What reason do you have to believe there are any?"
"The *Izanusi* says so, and our forefathers have taught us."
"Does the beer or meat devoted to the spirits disappear?"
"I don't know, I suppose so."
"Then you believe this because you have been thus taught?"
"Yes."

Taylor then asked the man to listen while he instructed him "away from the traditions of the elders to the great truths of the Bible."[93] If Tyler found any hint of the ironic in the above exchange he did not evidence it, nor did he record if the young Zulu man found the nerve to point out the ephemeral nature of the "truths" proclaimed by Taylor.[94]

For those in attendance at Sunday services, confusion over the nature of the missionaries' message was not to be the only difficulty they had in coming to grips with the new religion. The forms and functions of the new faith, its basic rules, could prove equally exasperating to grasp. At Mapumulo, the local chief arrived at one of the station's first Sabbath services with his ten wives in tow, each of them carrying a large basket of corn the chief planned to sell. The missionary, despite interest in the grain, informed the chief that, according to the strictures of his faith, he was forbidden to make any purchase on Sunday. The following Sabbath the chief returned, without grain, but approached the missionary after the service to enquire if he could return with items for sale the following day. The missionary, now annoyed, replied that he could not even discuss matters of business on the Sabbath.[95] Even for members of the family schools, no doubt thoroughly instructed in the sanctity of the Sabbath, the rules governing this day proved difficult to keep. On a warm late spring Saturday in 1850, Lewis Grout sent several of his pupils out to fetch thatch for his roof. Instructed to return with a wagon-full of the material that evening, the boys tarried on the road and were forced to camp away from the station for the night. Grout, concerned by their intentions for the following day, sent a runner out to inform the youths that they should remain on the road until after Sunday, "lest we should have an example of the violation of the Sabbath upon the station."[96] Elsewhere, the congregation at Umvoti demonstrated, "plainly enough," that the Gospel message had "not yet got hold of their hearts" by laughing before and after the services,[97] although Aldin Grout at least felt it a small victory that congregations remained attentive during his sermon.

Still, a picture slowly emerges from the mission correspondence of a people grappling with the message offered. Chief Usingela, who expressed an early interest in Christianity and invited Adams to preach at his *umuzi* in 1849, listened intently while Adams lectured on the meanings of the seventh commandment. Afterwards the chief, looking for an example of what might constitute a break of that commandment, asked that his people's sins be pointed out and later approached the missionary to inform him that he understood the seventh commandment but believed his people did not fully appreciate it and wanted it explained to them.[98] In response to such questions, Adams founded the first formal Bible study in Natal that same year, weekly sessions in which the scriptures were read and explanations given for their meaning.

A few years later, Grout, located at Umvoti, expressed surprise at the level of sophisticated interaction with the Christian message his congregation evidenced in the questions they asked of him:

If David was a good man why did he have so many enemies?
How can goodness be reconciled with prayer to destroy his enemies?
How is it that David boasts of his righteousness?
Will infants dying in infancy be saved?
Can one take the life of another in self-defense?
If God is perfectly good why does he allow evil or man to be lead into sin?
It is said of Abraham that he was both a good man and a rich man. Why is it
    so hard for a rich man to enter heaven?
Why was the young rich man required to sell everything he had?
Is war ever justified?[99]

Converts clearly did not accept the entire message uncritically; they engaged with it, finding discussions about it morally and intellectually stimulating and, at some level, deeply satisfying. One of Aldin Grout's first converts informed him: "The sermon you preached on repentance two months ago made such an impression on my mind that though I have struggled hard against it, [s]till I resolved decidedly to repent of all my sins."[100]

EARLY TROUBLES

Not surprisingly, the growing Christian community often experienced a profound alienation from surrounding *amabhinca*. Converts saw themselves as the "People of God" and while their seclusion from those around them was neither complete nor desired, they made sustained efforts to promote the unique identity they claimed for themselves through conversion.[101] And it seems clear that it was the act of conversion that ultimately determined the boundary between those within *amakholwa* society and those without. Merely attending church, which many Zulu did early on, rarely either alienated one from surrounding friends and family, or ensured ones' place within the Christian community. Indeed the missionaries, and later the congregations themselves, required converts to make a public profession of their new faith, an act which ensured recognition by all of their new status as "believers." Accompanying this profession, of course, was baptism. In the eyes of the church, participants in baptism quite literally had their past lives, their old beings, washed clean. In the white garments they wore on such an occasion, Zulu converts declared themselves freed from their former lives and desirous of living a Christ-centered life.

Often, of course, this initial profession of faith was accompanied by other acts that further separated converts from traditionalists. Clothes were worn, homes built, and changes in economic activities pursued. For older men, of which there were relatively few in the early years of the AZM, it became common to cut off their *isicoco*, the headring made from woven hair and beeswax, worn by older men as the most visible symbol of their masculinity, status, and power in Zulu society.[102] Much more difficult for older men considering conversion, was the question of what to do with multiple wives, signs of both wealth and prestige in the polygamous Zulu society, but also serious responsibilities not as easily removed as an *isicoco*. One older man with three wives made the difficult decision to "put away" the most recent wives, remaining with his first, the mother of his children. Another man had the decision made for him when his first wife, opposed his becoming Christian, refused to remain with him once he did so. Female converts in polygamous households, unable to "put away" their husbands, found themselves in a significantly more ambiguous position and during the latter half of the nineteenth century both missionaries and *amakholwa* congregations engaged in a never-ending discussion over their status. At least initially, however, they were welcomed into communion with other believers, not yet required to separate themselves from their husbands' *umuzi*.

For the majority of early *amakholwa*, physical relocation accompanied their spiritual one. Indeed for most, moving onto the mission stations occurred well in advance of conversion.[103] In a stinging indictment of the twenty years of itinerant preaching that preceded his arrival, William Mellen wrote in 1867 that he had yet to "learn of the first instance where a native has become a believer before he has lived at a station, been instructed, and clad."[104] Mellen later extended this belief, arguing that not only was station residence a necessary precursor of conversion, but also critical in maintaining the Christian character of the believing community. Speaking of a young *amakholwa* off of the station, he noted: "He may possibly content himself to remain in ignorance in his native dress, and in the midst of snuff and beer and filth and sit and sing himself away to everlasting life. But I imagine he will have as his to do in heaven as on earth. That he will not belong to that class of angels spoken of who are sent forth to minister to the saints of earth."[105]

Missionaries were not alone in seeking this sort of radical separation. As the size of *amakholwa* community began to grow, *amabhinca* actively distanced themselves from nearby missions. For believers this meant making a choice, oftentimes, between their family and their newfound faith. Lewis Grout wrote of one young man's despair, when his family moved to the far reaches of the reserve in order to escape the Word's reach: "Few in Christian lands know to what test of Christian character some are put when they propose to renounce the world and embrace the gospel." In what Grout called "a heart-touching sacrifice," the young man refused to follow his family, despite his mother's pleas, and "seemed willing to give up father, mother, brothers, and sisters for Christ."[106] Other families, alerted to the dangers of losing members to the church, moved before such a tragedy struck.

Building a family could also be difficult for young converts. Particularly early on in the history of the stations, when many of the adherents were young men freshly emerged from the family schools, converts found it difficult to find partners interested in marrying them or families willing to allow this to happen. Traditionalists broke off old engagements, returned *lobola* cattle, and forbade their daughters to have anything to do with these young men who had abandoned the old ways. At Ifumi a young convert asked his would-be future father-in-law to allow his daughter to receive an education on the mission station before their marriage. The father refused and returned the four head of cattle delivered by the groom as part of the engagement payments. The young man, not wanting to accept them and thus provide evidence that he was agreeing to this change in plans, asked his brother to hold them for a time. His brother, however, refused to allow the cattle of a *amakholwa* to be mixed with his own, forcing the young Christian to place them with his missionary. The father later relented and allowed his daughter to go to the station in return for the four head of cattle.

Once on the station, however, the bride informed the young man that she would refuse to marry him if he insisted on abandoning the customs of their people. The young man sadly bade her goodbye and once again recovered his cattle.[107]

What becomes clear, while reading these early accounts, is that the mission stations became an early site for the forms of generational conflict that were to become pervasive throughout colonial southern Africa in later years. For youth, the stations offered an ideal escape from the hierarchical realities of the Zulu homestead, where an *umnumzane*, backed by the authority of tradition, held impressive power over the affairs of his family. Young men, eager to demonstrate their abilities and begin their own families, needed to look beyond their fathers' kraal gates. In colonial Natal this often meant faction fights and cattle raiding, but as the power of the state grew this avenue toward manhood became increasingly risky and instead of independence it could lead to the arduous labor of the *isibhalo* gangs.[108] Colonial authorities in Natal had, by the mid-1800s, begun to check the cattle raiding practices of Zulu youth and with this long-standing rite of passage blocked, young men turned elsewhere for the means by which they could declare their adulthood. For Zulu youth looking for alternatives, mission stations offered a viable path toward autonomy. Girls shook off familial obligations by fleeing to the stations and young men struck out on their own in much the same way. The Bible became a basis for youthful rebellion.

The relationship between the early missionaries, the youth they employed in their family schools, and the families of the youths was, as we have already seen, fraught with conflict and contradiction. Many parents viewed such employment as a unique opportunity to increase the wealth of their *umuzi*, just as many were disturbed by the results. In reaction to Christianizing influences, parents simply removed their children and forbade them to have anything more to do with the church or its schools. Children who wore clothing at the mission stations removed them before they returned home or risked having them tossed on homestead fires alongside the books many received as farewell presents from missionaries.

Some children proved intransigent, however, and efforts to reintegrate them into traditional society provided painful reminders to all of the distance that separated the church from the kraal. In an inversion of the biblical tale of the prodigal son, Unomutya, a young girl at Umsumduzi, returned home in 1849 after serving for a time at a family school.[109] Her father, joyous at her homecoming, slaughtered a cow and welcomed his neighbors for a feast. Joy turned to anger, however, when Unomutya refused to participate in the celebration, rejected the traditional beaded outfit made for her, and declined to dance with those who had come to welcome her back. Her father, outraged, tore the Western clothes from her back. Later, when opportunity arose, Unomtya slipped back to the mission, received baptism, and fended off attempts to entice her to return to the family's fold.

Powerlessness in the face of the breakup of their families led many patriarchs to angry responses. Missionaries, confident in the protection afforded them by God, if not always the British authorities, rarely felt swayed by angry outbursts. It was, they generally insisted, up to the child to decide where he or she chose to reside.[110] After Umlawu, a young man at Umvoti, joined the church in April of 1848, his father became so enraged that he drove the boy's mother away, blaming her for failing to prevent his son's conversion.[111] The collapse of his family continued unchecked, however, as soon another son expressed interest in joining the church and his daughter declared that she would not marry a heathen. It must have been with grim determination that this father returned to the station and led his daughter away after her three years of service expired (for which he received a cow). Once home the man made her remove her Western dress, put on traditional skins, forbade her to read her books, and required her to drink medicine designed to cleanse her of the "sickness" of Christianity.[112]

At Inanda in 1860, William Mellen refused numerous requests by the father, mother, and brothers of one young woman to return her home after she fled to the station to avoid an unwanted marriage.[113] After repeated pleading the father arrived one day armed with two spears. Approaching the missionary in great excitement, the *umnumzane* handed one of the weapons to the missionary and exclaimed: "Take this spear of mine and cut off my head and let me die at your feet. You have taken my child, she is dead to me, let me die at your feet." When the missionary declined to either cut the man's head off or return his daughter, the father took his other spear, placed it onto his stomach and began turning it, drawing the skin into folds of flesh around the point. Mellen, unmoved by the man's threat to disembowel himself, once again refused to allowed him to take his daughter home and the father, defeated, returned to his *umuzi*, gut and head intact but without his daughter.

After they had chosen their new life in the church, many converts found themselves cut off from their old family and friends. As we have seen, many *amabhinca* simply moved away, putting distance between themselves and the sites that had swallowed up loved ones. But for most within the early *amakholwa* community, the separation they endured for their new faith was more metaphysical than spatial. Some suffered little more than a cold shoulder at a relative's wedding; others had their sanity called into question. Many of the early converts were seen as choosing a lesser way of life and families responded to their perceived irresponsibility by cutting such wayward children off from their inheritance. This was a particularly serious blow for young men, who relied on their fathers' cattle herds to round out *lobola* payments, an option many were denied should they become Christian.

Yet, even early on the disconnect between the *amakholwa* community and their traditionalist friends, families, and neighbors, should not be exaggerated. Missionaries may have preferred to think of the borders of their stations as towering castle walls protecting the souls of the converts from the horrors of heathenism, but this was never reality. Instead, even through occasional difficulties, converts and traditionalists maintained relationships based on familial ties, friendships, business, and mutual need. Converts did attend weddings of their relatives (although the mission maintained that these were dangerous occasions of immorality) just as traditionalists packed the churches when converts celebrated any one of many church ceremonies. Daily life meant constant small interactions, whether in collecting water and washing clothes at nearby streams, herding cattle, or gathering firewood; both groups had little choice but to interact and, within a short time, the initial open hostility emanating from each side began to wane. When Utambusa, the oldest member of Lewis Grout's "family school" converted in the late 1840s, his father reacted by refusing to see his son, moving away and threatening to disown the young man. Despite these threats, Utambusa remained at Umsumduzi and slowly, through persistent effort, melted his father's hostility to this new life. Remarkably, the father returned, and Utambusa helped his father build a new homestead near the mission in a demonstration of their renewed ties.[114] The previous year, Grout witnessed another example of the resiliency of *amakholwa*-traditionalist relationships when a rumor of war with the Zulu nation gripped Natal. Far from staying to defend the church, the young men of the station bade apologetic goodbyes and returned to their families' homesteads to help ward off possible attacks from across the Thukela.[115] Far from delineating a sharp division between Christian and traditionalist, the borders of the mission station proved to be extremely permeable and relationships of every nature flowed both ways.

RUFUS ANDERSON

In 1870 the American Zulu Mission ordained its first Zulu minister, Rufus Anderson (whose Zulu name was Nguzane).[116] As part of his candidacy, and because the American missionaries understood that its supporters back home would appreciate hearing about this groundbreaking individual, the soon-to-be-ordained pastor gave a full and descriptive account of the process which led him into Christianity. It is a remarkable document in many ways, not least because Anderson's narrative highlights so many of the so-cial forces I have sketched out in the preceding sections of this chapter. [117]

Anderson did not come easily to his new faith. In fits and starts he drew near the mission and then pulled away, each episode marked by a tangle of explanations and events for his flirtation. Far from being a classic "I was a sinner and then I saw the light" tale, Anderson's history suggests the more nuanced journey I have argued for and through which the majority of con-verts passed on their way into the Christian church. Numerous individuals influenced him toward his ultimate decision, white traders and farmers, missionaries and *amakholwa*, and while the quest for a comfortable living drew him back, on several occasions, to the mission, it was ultimately the acts of those who proclaimed themselves Christian that opened his heart to their message. This is his story.[118]

Like many of those who came to live in Natal in its first years as colony, Anderson was born in Zululand but crossed over the Thukela when only a small child. He returned, however, after only a few years and lived with his uncle, caring for his cattle. It was in Zululand that he first heard the Chris-tian message, told to him by a passing *amakholwa*. Shortly after returning across the Thukela, and into his father's homestead, Ncapair, a *amakholwa* related to Ntaba at the Umvoti mission, offered him employment. This his father vigorously opposed, but the seed had been planted in Anderson's mind and one day, fearing that his father might beat him after the cattle under his care had gotten out and eaten up another man's garden, Ander-son left to join Ncapair. His stay at the mission did not last long as several days later his brother came and brought him back to his father's *umuzi*. His father applied his lesson with a whip exclaiming "You rascal, why do you live with the native Christians? It will be all right if you go and work for some white man, but the Christian natives have no money to pay you." When drought stuck shortly after the incident, Anderson took his father's words to heart and sought employment from Europeans.

After an Afrikaner had refused to hire him, Anderson turned to Josiah Tyler, the nearest missionary. Unfortunately for Anderson he arrived on the Sabbath and before he could ask the American, he was rebuked by a group of *amakholwa* who proclaimed: "It is not proper for you to do so on this day." Admonished, he traveled further, finally landing a job as a herder for an Afrikaner who promised him a cow in exchange for a year's labor. Before the year was up, however, Anderson had run away, afraid of receiving a whipping for failing to control a team of oxen on a trip to Durban. In the city, Anderson lived with his brother and cousin, eventually finding work in the same kitchen as his brother. After being dismissed from this job, An-derson stayed in Durban another two months before departing for home.

A series of short employments with various white farmers followed until Anderson began working for Mr. Smith, a trader who took goods from Durban into Zululand. Anderson enjoyed working for Smith, considered him a good man and was impressed by his commitment to Christianity, a depth of faith that he shared with his workers, taking them into his house for daily prayers. The youthful Anderson stayed with Smith "a long time," but eventually he returned to his father's *umuzi* with his wages. This was to be a familiar pattern throughout the history of the area, young men, and occasionally woman, working off the reserves in cities, farms, plantations and mines for short periods, returning home with their earnings for a season or two before seeking employment once again. This held true for Anderson as well, for after a few months at home, he found employment with a farmer, Mr. Duff at Umdhloti, who also treated him well, "served God," and from whose manifest "Christian character" Anderson came to believe that there must be a God. For unexplained reasons, Anderson's mother came and took him away from Duff after only four months.

Instead of settling in at his family's homestead, Anderson chose to work again for the trader, Mr. Smith. By this time, however, Smith's fortunes had changed, for he had lost a shipment of goods in a shipwreck and could not pay any of his workers who, one by one, left him. Anderson, displaying remarkable loyalty, stayed on, noticing the trader's "steadfulness in serving God even though he was poor." Anderson's friends ridiculed him for remaining, calling him a fool and remarking "Why do you work for a poor white man who has no money?" After many months without receiving a wage Anderson finally allowed his brother to talk him into leaving.

Once again Anderson took up employment with a farmer in the Umdhloti area, this time a Mr. Baugh, who put the young man to work driving plow oxen for four shillings a month. One night, though, an incident occurred that troubled the young man greatly. The farmer's hen house, built on the edge of a steep cliff, had become an inviting target for snakes, and Baugh insisted that Anderson accompany him in dispatching a troublesome serpent. With the young man's assistance, the farmer chopped off the head of the snake with an axe, and while Anderson doesn't illuminate this point in his narrative, it clearly stuck with him as a moment of omen, a point of preparation for the passage he was about to embark upon. For shortly after this event Anderson traveled with Baugh to buy a wagonload of corn from *amakholwa* living around Lewis Grout's station at Umvoti. It was a bitterly cold winter's Saturday, and as Baugh drove the wagon back, Anderson attempted stay warm by huddling amongst the sacks of grain. As rain came down, however, Baugh lost control of his team on a steep downhill, upsetting the wagon and sending its contents, Anderson included, spilling down the track.

Baugh returned with Anderson to Umvoti, injured, but too cold to determine how badly. Once there, a *amakholwa* took him in, bound his wounds and worked hard through the night to revive him. Within a few days Baugh, impatient at the delay, trundled the battered young man back into his wagon for the return trip. But for Anderson his experience with the *amakholwa* had proved profoundly moving and he recalled: "My heart saw the kindness of the Christian natives, and I loved them."

Following this experience, Anderson completed his contract with Baugh, took his money home, and returned once again to work for the English trader Smith, whose fortunes had improved. During this stay, the trader's sons taught the young man his ABC's and he begin attending church services in Durban, some four miles away from Smith's residence. Mrs. Smith, who also spoke to Anderson about God, made the young man a shirt, and he purchased a pair of trousers and a coat; proudly, he wore the outfit to services, an outward sign of the direction he was attempting to steer his life. He was well prepared than when one day, as he practiced his letters in the dirt outside of Smith's store, Thomas Hawes, a local *amakholwa* who Smith had hired to thatch his house, noticed Anderson and asked him if he wished to learn to read. Anderson responded enthusiastically, and Hawes suggested he move to Inanda.[119] After a short time, during which the young man scrutinized the station and its people during a corn-buying trip, he approached Smith and asked for permission to leave his contract early and go live at the mission. Smith consented and provided Anderson with a letter of recommendation to Lindley, the resident missionary.

Upon his arrival Lindley asked him if he wished to live with the Christian natives or reside in the mission house to work and be taught. Anderson chose the latter and worked for the missionary for two months before joining several other young men at Amanzimtoti Seminary, the first formal school of the mission. He soon moved past the alphabet and realized his goal of learning to read. Here also the faith he had nibbled at finally began to take form. The young men were led in daily prayer by their instructors, the missionaries Rood and Wilder, held prayer meetings on their own every Saturday and met together to discuss Bible lessons. The latter particularly moved him and as he read the gospels, Anderson found that "the words of God were sweet and piercing to me" and in time his companions began to ask him to lead their prayers: "and as I prayed, I felt my heart rejoice. It was now plain to me that there was a God."

Anderson finished his work at Amanzimtoti and moved back to Inanda and although he struggled with "evil thoughts" entering his heart, he battled whatever demons these may have been (at this age he likely had been betrothed back home) through prayer. His righteousness was soon recognized by Thomas Hawes, who invited him to join the church. Anderson did not take this matter lightly, believing that taking this step meant giving himself fully to the Lord, and he mulled the matter over before approaching the missionary and asking for permission to enter into a covenant with the other Christians. The missionary asked him if he loved Jesus and when Anderson replied in the affirmative the matter was placed into the hands of the congregation, who voted in favor of his joining. At his baptism Anderson celebrated his entry into this new life by selecting the name Rufus Anderson. His life as a *amakholwa* had only officially begun with the baptismal waters flowing over his forehead, although the path he walked to arrive inside the church doors was long and winding.

NOTES

1. Alan Paton, *Cry, the Beloved Country* (New York: Scribner, 2003), 31.

2. KwaZulu-Natal did not become one united province until the elections of 1994. The historical separation of Natal from KwaZulu was largely theoretical following the Anglo-Zulu war of 1879 when the Zulu heartland came under British administration. The Natal government held dominion and English settlement schemes divided up the land. For the purposes of this work, however, it serves as a practical geographical limit as the American Zulu Mission did not officially operate in Zululand for most of its existence and the Zulu kings still reigned unhampered at the beginning of this history.

3. John Lambert, *Betrayed Trust: Africans and the State in Colonial Natal* (Pietermaritzburg, University of Natal Press, 1995), 11; Charles Ballard, "The Repercussions of Rinderpest: Cattle Plague and Peasant Decline in Colonial Natal," *International Journal of African Historical Studies* 19 (1986). Among Zulu the homestead generally consisted of an *umnumzane*, (the male head of the household) his wife or wives, their children, and any dependents he may have acquired. Adam Kuper, "The 'House' and Zulu Political Structure in the Nineteenth Century," *Journal of African History* 34 (1993): 473–76.

4. A Zulu word, it is also common to find *uThukela* spelled in its Anglicized version, Tugela. The river marked the border between Natal and Zululand until 1897. Still, the two remained distinct in many ways and most of those who lived in the area continued to view the Thukela as a significant social and cultural boundary even if it no longer represented a political one.

5. The stick that stirred this debate is Julian Cobbing, who has suggested that the Zulu state emerged in reaction to European slave trading on both their southwestern and northern frontiers. As others have noted his evidence for this claim is shaky, but the thesis is intriguing and a legion of papers, articles, and books have flowed out of this debate. See, Julian Cobbing, "The Mfecane as Alibi: Thoughts on Dithakong and Mbolompo," *Journal of African History* 29 (1988); Elizabeth Eldredge, "Sources of Conflict in Southern Africa, C.1800–30: The "Mfecane" Reconsidered," *Journal of African History* 33 (1992); Carolyn Hamilton (ed.), *The Mfecane Aftermath: Reconstructive Debates in Southern African History* (Bloomington: Indiana University Press,

1996); and Norman Etherington, *The Great Treks: The Transformation of Southern Africa, 1815–1854* (New York: Longman, 2001).

6. For a masterful look at the careful husbandry of this inequality see, Carolyn Hamilton and John Wright, "The Making of the AmaLala: Ethinicity, Ideology and Relations of Subordination in a Precolonial Context," *South African Historical Journal* 22 (1990). The authors detail how peoples on the periphery of the state were ruled as "outsiders," ethnically inferior to those of the central state and used by the kingdom as a source for menial labor and easy cattle collections, but also as a foil upon which they could maintain internal loyalty by insuring that those within the Zulu state, those known *amantungwa*, sought to avoid becoming *amalala*, or despised people.

7. John Wright, "Reflections on the Politics of Being 'Zulu,'" in Benedict Carton, John Laband, and Jabulani Sithole (eds.), *Zulu Identities: Being Zulu, Past and Present* (New York: Columbia University Press, 2008), 35–43.

8. Nathanial Isaacs, *Travels and Adventures in Eastern Africa: Description of the Zoolus, Their Manners, Customs, etc.* L. Herman and P. R. Kinkby (eds.), (Cape Town: Struik, 1979), 31.

9. John Bird, *The Annals of Natal: 1495–1845* (Pietermaritzburg: 1888), 79. This was, essentially, a *ukusiasa* relationship—that is cattle loaned out by a patron. The client, in exchange for minding *siasa* cattle, kept milk products from the loaned herd and received a certain number of the offspring produced under his watch. The patron ensured that his cattle would be cared for, protected them from catastrophic loss by spreading them out, and, in a land where the number of humans under one's control was the most direct representation of power, bound additional households to himself.

10. Charles Ballard, "Natal 1824–44: the Frontier Interregnum," *Journal of Natal and Zulu History* 5 (1982): 58–60.

11. Fynn, H. F., J. Stuart and D. McK Malcom (eds.), *The Diary of Henry Francis Fynn* (Pietermaritzburg: University of Natal Press, 1950), 22–24. Although Cobbing has argued that this may simply have been back-writing history, justifying both the presence of the white traders in Natal and their later calls for Britain to annex the area. See Cobbing, "The Mfecane as Alibi."

12. Charles Ballard, "Traders, Trekkers and Colonists," in Andrew Duminy and Bill Guest, (eds.), *Natal and Zululand From Earliest Times to 1910: A New History* (Pietermaritzburg: University of Natal Press, 1989), 118. While Fynn records that the first Africans to reside among them were refugees from one of Shaka's campaigns to the north, it is just as likely that these were the remnants of local chiefdoms shattered as a result of the Zulu kingdom's policy of keeping its southern border free from potential threats.

13. The Voortrekkers were white pastoralists of Dutch descent who, feeling aggrieved by British rule at the Cape, began a near biblical search for a "promised land" in the mid-1830s by slipping across the frontier zone onto the highveld of the southern African interior. Always only loosely confederated, by 1838 they had split into three distinct bodies, each going its own way and causing chaos among the various African societies they frequently and violently interacted with. For a particularly astute analysis of the Trekker movement and its outcomes see Etherington, *The Great Treks*.

14. When the British Home Office finally agreed to the annexation on August 25, 1845, Natal became an anonymous district of the Cape Colony. Not until 1856 did the Colonial Office separate Natal from the Cape and grant them an independent administration. Edgar Brooks and Colin Webb, *A History of Natal* (Pietermaritzburg: University of Natal Press, 1965), 75.

15. Peter Colebrander, "The Zulu Kingdom, 1828–79," in Duminy and Guest, *Natal and Zululand From Earliest Times*, 99.

16. John Bird (ed.), *The Annals of Natal: 1495–1845, Volume I,* (Pietermaritzburg: Natal Society Publishing, 1888), 644. As part of these raids Trekkers carried off both cattle and child "apprentices," a practice common along the Cape frontier and one they continued in subsequent years. This custom, along with the decision by the Natalia government to remove all Africans not originally in Natal at the time of the Trekkers' arrival into the northern lands of the Eastern Cape, finally convinced a reluctant colonial secretary, Lord Stanley, to annex Natal for Britain.

17. David Welsh, *The Roots of Segregation: Native Policy in Colonial Natal, 1845–1910* (London: Oxford University Press, 1971), 15; John Lambert, "Chiefship in Early Colonial Natal, 1843–1879," *Journal of Southern African Studies* 21 (1995): 272.

18. With responsible government the Natal legislature, dominated by the sugar-barons along the coast and the Midland farmers, turned its attention to its first priority, insuring an abundant and cheap African labor supply. It was hampered in this effort, however, by the staggering demands for labor exerted by the Witwatersrand goldfields and the higher wages the mines provided. Farmers did not respond to this challenge by increasing their own wages, but rather by attempting to close off other options for Africans, particularly the popular and profitable tenant farming practiced by so many. For more see, Henry Slater, "Land, Labour and Capital in Natal: The Natal Land and Colonisation Company 1860–1948," *Journal of African History* 16 (1975): 272; and Patrick Harries, "Plantations, Passes and Proletarians: Labour and the Colonial State in Nineteenth Century Natal," *Journal of Southern African Studies* 13 (1987).

19. Norman Etherington, "The 'Shepstone System' in the Colony of Natal and Beyond the Borders," in Duminy and Guest, *Natal and Zululand*, 170–192.

20. Welsh, *Roots of Segregation*, 83–84, 150–155.

21. Jeremy Martens, "Enlightenment Theories of Civilization and Savagery in British Natal," in Benedict Carton, John Laband, and Jabulani Sithole (eds.), *Zulu Identities: Being Zulu, Past and Present* (New York: Columbia University Press, 2008), 122–132.

22. This forced Africans into the labor market to search for the cash necessary to pay taxes. In addition to this tax, Shepstone also occasionally demanded *isibhalo*, the traditional labor given by subjects to their chief to, say, harvest the chief's crops, for work on roads or as border guards at a reduced wage.

23. Outside of the resident magistrates the colonial government's presence remained remarkably thin until the mid-1890s. No reserve police force existed until the 1870s and even then its 200 members seemed hopelessly inadequate for the task. Instead punishment was meted out after the fact and crimes were rarely reported.

24. Gardiner is remarkable in that his missionary impulse did not run particularly deep within Western society where, until the late eighteenth century Wesleyan revival, little interest was manifested for traveling great distances and experiencing greater hardships for the sake of bringing the Gospel to the "heathen." Early Methodists, inspired by John Wesley's motto, "The world is my parish" (although he himself failed in his brief attempt to bring the Gospel to American Indians) became the first Protestants to take evangelization seriously.

25. Allen F. Gardiner, *Narrative of a Journey to the Zoolu Country in South Africa* (Cape Town: Struik, 1966), 296.

26. J. Du Plessis, *A History of Christian Missions in South Africa* (Cape Town: Struik, 1965), 441.

27. Francis Owen, Sir George E. Cory (ed.), *The Diary of the Reverend Francis Owen* (Cape Town: Van Riebeeck Society, 1926).

28. Unlike Owen, however, Gardiner did not give up on mission work, instead moving on to Bolivia where several years later, he died from starvation after being trapped by winter storms in the Andes. Jesse Page, *Captain Allen Gardiner of Patagonia* (London: Pickering and Inglis, 1830).

29. B. J. T. Leverton, ed., *Records of Natal, Volume One, 1823–August 1828* (Pretoria: 1894), p xxix.

30. William C. Holden, *A Brief History of Methodism and of the Methodist Missions in South Africa* (London: Wesleyan Conference, 1877), 406.

31. Edendale became the most prosperous Christian community in Natal and is widely viewed as representative of the *amakholwa* community at this time. This is probably unfortunate, as in many ways they were an anomaly, outsiders both ethnically and economically, property ownership was a central feature of Edendale identity although it remained relatively unusual for most *amakholwa*. See Sheila Meintjes, "Edendale, 1850–1906: a Case Study of Rural Transformation and Class Formation in an African Mission in Natal," PhD thesis (University of London: 1988).

32. Lewis Grout, *Zululand: Or Life Among the Kaffirs of Natal and Zululand* (Philadelphia: Presbyterian Publishing Society, 1864), 253.

33. Those asserting the impending end of the world confidently pointed toward the French Revolution as a sign; Napoleon, it was assumed, must assuredly be the Antichrist. William McLoughlin, *Modern Revivalism* (New York: 1959), 12–14.

34. The 1832 *Missionary Herald* declared that church members, "were redeemed by his precious blood, and renovated by the Spirit, and are preserved in faith and hope, and blessed in providence—not, chiefly, that they may have the comforts of this life, and the consolations of piety, and be fitted for and ultimately received to heaven—but that they may be 'the salt of the earth' and 'the light of the world'—the means of diffusing, as extensively and rapidly as possible, the knowledge and blessings of true religion," *Missionary Herald* "Twenty-Fourth Report of the Prudential Committee," 1832, 22–23.

35. The president of the Union Theological Seminary, a significant contributor of missionaries to the Board, declared at the turn of the century: "I am most fully convinced that slavery is the greatest evil in our country, except whiskey." Edwin Smith, *The Life and Times of Daniel Lindley* (New York: Library Publishers, 1952), 41.

36. AZM D/1/90, report of the 89th annual meeting of the American Board, Brooklyn New York, October 15–18, 1895.

37. Clifton Jackson Phillips, *Protestant America and the Pagan World: The First Half Century of the American Board of Commissioners for Foreign Missions, 1810–1860* (Cambridge: Harvard University Press, 1969), 21–23.

38. Phillips, *Protestant America and the Pagan World*, 37–38; David Kling, "The New Divinity and the Origins of the American Board of Commissioners for Foreign Missions" In Wilbert Shenk (ed.), *North American Foreign Missions, 1810–1914* (Grand Rapids: Eerdmans, 2004), 11–38.

39. The following is taken from: Josiah Tyler, *Forty Years Among the Zulus*, (Boston: Congregational Publishing Society, 1891), 19–21.

40. The Prudential Committee's instructions to its Indian missionaries were explicit on this point: "Wherever your lot may be cast, you will withhold yourselves most scrupulously from all interference with the powers that be; and from all intermeddling with political concerns. You will sacredly remember who has said, 'Render unto Caeser the things that are Caeser's, and unto God the things that are God's. ABM, *First Ten Annual Reports of the American Board of Commissioners for Foreign Missions* (Boston: Crocker and Brewster, 1834), 39. This policy remained a potent deterrent to overt criticism of a host nation's actions throughout the decades to follow. In one example, American missionaries who believed British policy had dealt unjustly with Afrikaners were asked to hold their opinions during the South African War.

41. The correspondence with Philips, initiated by a seminary student and passed into the hands of the Board, "laid open to our view a promising and accessible field." *Missionary Herald*, "Mission to Africa," (Boston: 1833), 89–90. The Board had considered the possibility of placing missionaries in Africa as early as 1812 but the fear of "the fever" held them back. ABM, *First Ten Reports of the American Board of Commissioners*, 49.

42. The Presbyterian Church, anxious to involve itself in foreign missions, agreed to unite with Congregationalists, under the auspices of the ABM, in 1833. This arrangement broke down under the strains of southern Presbyterian support for slavery a decade later.

43. The Board did not drop its reference to "Maritime" and "Interior" Zoolah until after the collapse of the mission to Mzilikazi's people.

44. Phillips, *Protestant America and the Pagan World*, 94. Two analogous examples in Africa include the Kongo empire and the kingdom of Buganda. The Kongo prince Alfonso I converted to Catholicism, overthrew his pagan brother, and established a Christian state in 1509. In Buganda, the ruling king maintained a delicate balance between Muslim traders, Catholic priests, and Protestant missionaries for a short time before the Christian faction successfully staged a coup and rid the capital of both traditionalists and Muslims. See, John Thornton, *The Kongolese Saint Anthony: Dona Beatriz Kimpa Vita and the Antonian Movement, 1684–1706* (Cambridge: Harvard University Press, 1998), 31–34; Jean Brierley and Thomas Spear, "Mutesa, the Missionaries, and Christian Conversion in Buganda," *The International Journal of African Historical Studies*, 21 (1988): 602.

45. Edwin Smith, *Life and Times of Daniel Lindley*, 106–110.

46. Alan Booth, *Journal of Rev. George Champion* (Cape Town: Struik, 1967), xii.

47. AZM 175/45, Grout to Anderson, June 19, 1845. Grout was particularly concerned by the Wesleyan plan to create a mission site at Pietermaritzburg. The Americans reached an agreement with the Wesleyans later that year that forty to fifty miles inland from the coast would be AZM territory while the rest of the colony was reserved for the Methodists. A few exceptions were eventually made, but only after a general geographic distribution had been settled upon. AZM 175/406, Group Letter to Anderson, September 1849.

48. AZM 175/87, Lindley to Anderson, December 12, 1845.

49. AZM 175/857, A. Grout to Anderson, March 1, 1847.

50. Smith, *Lindley,* 254.

51. Ibid, 259. Also see, John Lambert, *Betrayed Trust,* 10–11. The commissioners may have also looked to the south, where missionaries to the Mfengu had introduced a similar plan in the 1820s with favorable results. Colin Bundy, *The Rise and Fall of the South African Peasantry* (London: James Currey, 1988), 33–40.

52. AM 175/463, Annual report of the AZM, September 15, 1852.

53. David Welsh, *The Roots of Segregation,* 47.

54. The system made few of its participants happy. As we will see, missionaries complained of their relative powerlessness to remove "troublemakers," Africans frequently requested, but rarely were allowed, to buy the land outright, and the Natal government made several attempts to take control of the land.

55. ABM 175/695, Bryant to Anderson, April 30, 1847.

56. Josiah Tyler, one of the few early missionaries without industrial training, lived out of his wagon for several weeks before graduating to a Zulu hut. Here he lived for nearly two months before his house at Esidumbini was finished. Despite his pleas, the owner of this hut refused to allow him to cut out a door and Tyler was forced to enter and exit his temporary residence as would any Zulu, on his hands and knees. ABM 176/717, Tyler to Anderson, June 29, 1850.

57. Alan Booth, *Journal of George Champion,* 58; and ABM 175/67, Grout to Anderson, June 22, 1846.

58. ABM 175/731, Bryant to Anderson, March 31, 1849.

59. ABM 175/598, Abraham to Anderson, March 20, 1850.

60. As the community of believers grew on the stations, missionaries proved increasingly unwilling to fulfill the more active duties of this role for traditionalists and later missionaries were often dumbfounded by the brazen nature of such requests. But as late as 1867, Andrew Abraham reported: "A man came here a few weeks ago, complaining that one of his neighbors had taken three of his cattle and eaten them. He requested me to write and inform the Magistrate, saying that if I would do so, he and all his people, of whom he said he had a great many, would come to meeting every Sabbath." ABM 175/610, Abraham to Anderson, July 24, 1867.

61. Norman Etherington, *Preachers, Peasants, and Politics in Southeast Africa, 1835–1880* (London: Royal Historical Society, 1978), 115.

62. David Welsh, *The Roots of Segregation,* 44–48.

63. See also Belinda Bozzoli, *Women of Phokeng: Consciousness, Life Strategy, and Migrancy in South Africa, 1900–1983,* (Portsmouth: Heinemann, 1991), 36, for a particularly stark example of this process among Tswana of the western

highveld. After an early missionary's message was rejected he departed for Durban. But "the missionary left our tribe like a man who planted a seed in a dry soil, knowing well that one day rain would come to water the soil and the seed would grow and bear results." And so it did, for within three years a group amongst whom the "germ" had sprouted traveled to Natal to learn more about the Christian message, eventually only returning after securing the services of another missionary.

64. ABM 176/17, Grout to Anderson, April 16, 1847.

65. ABM 177/11, Joint Letter to ABM, March 7, 1864.

66. In a joint letter of the mission to the Board directors in Boston, the AZM missionaries attempted to win an increase in their salaries by noting that much of their income went towards paying parents 10 shillings per month for the services of their children in the family schools. ABM 177/111–12, Joint Letter, March 7, 1864.

67. ABM 175/387, Bryant to Anderson, September 12, 1849. It is likely that the children apprenticed to the missionaries came from poorer families, willing to exchange the valuable labor of their children for future wealth. A wealthier Zulu household, marked, as it was by the number of cattle it possessed, would have needed its boys to attend the herds.

68. ABM 175/186–187, L. Grout to Anderson, September 1851. Although the system died slowly, it had fallen out of favor by the late 1860s by which time, as we will see, the normal day schools operated at such a level that missionaries no longer found the time to devote the individual attention necessary to make this system of Christianization work.

69. ABM 175/873, A. Grout to Anderson, April 24, 1848. Young men made up the bulk of the early family school members, but in time mission wives began employing young Zulu women as domestics. Lucy Lindley recalled her angst at the decision to give up Thomas Hawes, her personal assistant, and bring in young Zulu girls to train in the proper use of soap, dishes, and tablecloths. The girls often slept on the floor of the kitchen and their first duty upon rising was to light the stove. Smith, *The Life and Times of Daniel Lindley*, 281

70. ABM 175/387, Bryant to Anderson, September 12, 1849. Twenty children appear to be the maximum number any missionary felt capable of taking on, and this only when pressed.

71. ABM 175/186–187, L. Grout to Anderson, September 1851. Grout, in a possible criticism of his fellow missionaries (something he was to become notorious for) noted that he used no compulsion to retain those he employed, and abided no violence in any being taken away from him, but rather lived by the motto "freedom to go or stay as they may choose" even if the child's time of engagement had not expired.

72. Jeff Guy, "Gender Oppression in Southern Africa's Precapitalist Societies," in Cherryl Walker (ed.), *Women and Gender in Southern Africa to 1945* (London: David Phillips 1990), 43–44. Sean Hanretta has argued persuasively, however, that women in pre-colonial Zulu society, particularly those connected to the royal house, wielded a surprising degree of power through their role as *izangoma*, or diviners. He argues that this provided a discursive model for women throughout the area and was accessed in part through a possession known as *indiki*. Hanretta, "Women,

Marginality, and the Zulu State: Women' Institutions and Power in the Early Nine-teenth Century," *Journal of African History* 39 (1998): 398–99. Julie Parle does not fully disagree with Hanretta's argument, but cautions against thinking of *indiki* in solely political terms, instead she makes the persuasive argument that spirit posses-sion could just as likely be mental illness and that there is worth in studying this phenomenon even if it wasn't a gendered form of protest. Julie Parle, *States of Mind: Searching for Mental Health in Natal and Zululand, 1868–1918* (Pietermartizburg: University of KwaZulu-Natal Press, 2007), 150–151. Perhaps even more powerfully, Sifiso Ndlovu has argued that academics would be better served if they didn't at-tempt to shoehorn Zulu gendered relations into western modes of feminist analyses that have produced, what she calls, a "gender oppression school" that has ignored that "pre-colonial Zulu women were neither automatically subordinate to Zulu men, nor barred by tyrannical patriarchs from the inner circles of Zulu power and monarchy." Sifiso Ndlovu, "A Reassessment of Women's Power in the Zulu King-dom" in Benedict Carton, John Laband, and Jabulani Sithole (eds.), *Zulu Identities: Being Zulu, Past and Present* (New York: Columbia University Press, 2008), 111, 119.

73. ABM 176/1029–1030, Wilder, Station report for Umtwalume, May 28, 1858.

74. Karen Flint, *Healing Traditions: African Medicine, Cultural Exchange, & Competi-tion in South Africa, 1820–1948* (Athens: Ohio University Press, 2008).

75. Karen Flint and Julie Parle, "Healing and Harming: Medicine, Madness, Witchcraft and Tradition," in Benedict Carton, John Laband, and Jabulani Sithole (eds.), *Zulu Identities: Being Zulu, Past and Present* (New York: Columbia University Press, 2008), 313.

76. ABM 175/881, A. Grout to Anderson, September 12, 1848 and ABM 178/164, A. Grout to Anderson, October 24, 1864. In this story, as it is to a lesser degree in the family school system, the missionary replicates, probably knowingly, the very type of patron-client relationships that marked pre-colonial and pre-mfecane chieftain-ships in Natal. Prior to their reification under the Shepstonian system, membership in a particular chieftaincy was not immutable. Clients could, and often did, shift their allegiances to patrons who could offer them greater protection, better eco-nomic terms or even present bribes of *isasa* cattle.

77. ABM 178/164, A. Grout to Anderson, October 24, 1864. This was, appar-ently, one of Grout's favorite stories, for he repeated it on numerous occasions throughout his thirty-year career. In its original telling it was Umkalo who was left in the bush and his sister who accompanied his mother to Grout's door after they went hungry in the wilderness for two days. Subsequent renditions switched the gender of the two children.

78. ABM 176/319, L. Grout to Anderson, September 2, 1852.

79. ABM 175/661, Adams to Anderson, September 20, 1849.

80. Ibid. While, as we shall see, family frequently played a role in pulling poten-tial converts away from the church, it also worked the other way, for in the this case the old woman encouraged her daughter to attend church. The daughter later left her polygamous husband and joined the congregation, much to the consternation of her husband and the rest of the woman's traditional family.

81. Although the family schools began producing a literate church almost imme-diately, the earliest congregations had limited access to the Word of God in its written

form. The AZM published a small selection of Zulu readings in Genesis in 1846, followed by a hymnal with twelve songs in 1847. The entire gospel of Matthew was published in 1848 followed by a catechism in 1849 and Psalms in 1850. This limited availability to the Word left the early *amakholwa* community reliant on missionaries to translate the meanings inherent in the text. This is not to say that Zulu catechists did not debate these meanings, they did with great vigor, simply that missionaries, backed by the authority of the *entire* Bible, acted as the final arbiter of its meaning. This position of authority eroded slightly with each new work published and collapsed almost entirely once the finished Bible was finally published in October of 1883. That said, there is no evidence to suggest that the AZM deliberately withheld the Gospel from its congregations, if anything the mission considered the completion of a Zulu language Bible to be of the highest importance and in 1879 Stephen Pixley took John Nembula (later Dr. Nembula), a third generation *amakholwa*, with him to America where they worked on translation for over three years. ABM 180/29, annual report, 1867–69; D. Roy Briggs and Joseph Wing, *The Harvest and the Hope: The Story of Congregationalism in Southern Africa* (Johannesburg: United Congregational Church of South Africa, 1970), 131. For an insightful examination of the role of translation in the creation of vernacular Christian communities see Lamin Sanneh, *Translating the Message: The Missionary Impact on Culture* (Maryknoll: Orbis, 1990).

82. Benedict Carton, "Awaken *Nkulunkulu*, Zulu God of the Old Testament," in Benedict Carton, John Laband, and Jabulani Sithole (eds.), *Zulu Identities: Being Zulu, Past and Present* (New York: Columbia University Press, 2008), 133–152.

83. ABM 175/834, journal of Döhne, October 3, 1853. Döhne came to the AZM from the Berlin Missionary Society. It is difficult to say if this approach alone accounted for his relative lack of success. It seems likely, however, that his abrasive personality, which many of the other missionaries found difficult, at best, to deal with, hurt any chance he had of developing a loyal congregation and it fell to an *amakholwa* preacher years later to develop a sustainable congregation at Table Mountain.

84. Ibid.

85. Jackson, Jr. to the Secretaries, February 7, 1860, archives of the Wesleyan Methodist Mission, as quoted in Etherington, *Preachers, Peasants and Politics in Southeast Africa, 1835–1880*, 146.

86. ABM 175/461, Annual report of Umvoti, September 15, 1852.

87. Although Grout proved disappointed with the results of this appeal, nearly a quarter of those who attended the wedding came to services the following Sunday, proving some success of the idiom he chose to employ. ABM 176/186, L. Grout to Anderson, September 1851.

88. ABM 177/60, unknown author, May 29, 1861; ABM 177/74, annual letter, 1862–63.

89. ABM, 175/737, personal journal of A.C. Bryant, April 2, 1847.

90. Ibid, April 9, 1847.

91. ABM, 176/313, Lewis Grout to Anderson, September 2, 1852.

92. It should be noted here that Benedict, following the lead of Jeff Guy, has argued persuasively that the American missionaries were consistently less open to engaging with and understanding Zulu cosmology than were men like the Revs. Allen

Gardiner, Henry Callaway, and Bishop John Colenso—all whom contributed enormously to our understanding of Zulu religious systems by their willingness to put preaching aside and listen. See, Benedict Carton "Awaken *Nkulunkulu,*" and "Faithful Anthropologists: Christianity, Ethnography, and the Making of 'Zulu Religion' in Early Colonial Natal', in Benedict Carton, John Laband, and Jabulani Sithole (eds.), *Zulu Identities: Being Zulu, Past and Present* (New York: Columbia University Press, 2008), 153–167; and Jeff Guy, *The Heretic: A Study of the Life of John William Colenso, 1814–1883* (Pietermaritzburg: University of Natal Press, 1983).

93. ABM, 180/85, Tyler to Anderson, March 29, 1863.

94. Such truth claims, backed up by the visual evidence of the relative success of Western ways of life, became increasingly plausible to Zulu audiences as the colonial presence increased throughout the area.

95. ABM, 175/597, Abraham to Anderson, March 20, 1850. Later, in 1866, Abraham was to recount the incident as a humorous anecdote for how far the people of the area had come under his guidance.

96. ABM, 176/90, L. Grout to Anderson, November 1848.

97. ABM, 175/857, A. Grout to Anderson, March 1, 1847.

98. ABM 175/660, Adams to Anderson, September 20, 1849. The seventh commandment is: "You shall not commit adultery."

99. ABM, 176, A Grout to Anderson, June 20, 1855.

100. ABM 175/871, A. Grout to Anderson April 24, 1848. The man, probably Ntaba Luthuli of whom we will hear more of in the next chapter, explained that he had decided to abandon his plan of acquiring a second wife, for whom he had already paid three cows.

101. ABM 175/1089, Ifume station report, 1853–54.

102. ABM 175/661, Adams to Anderson, September 20, 1849; ABM 177/490–91, Abraham to Anderson, November 28, 1865. While the missionaries seem to have approved of this step, at least as a symbolic act, it was not required, making it both an extraordinary act of fealty to their newly chosen faith and a very loud statement of their decision to separate themselves from their past lives.

103. Although well into the early 1900s, the majority of those living on the mission reserves remained unbelievers.

104. ABM 177/266, Umsumduzi Station Report, June 1867. His claim, outside of women in polygamous households, is nearly impossible to prove, although certainly numerous examples can be given of individuals drawn to the new faith prior to living on the stations, but of these perhaps all lived near the churches prior to their actual baptisms. Mellen, an early proponent of "Americanizing" the Zulu congregations (see chapters 2 & 3) firmly believed that civilization and Christianity went hand in hand.

105. ABM 181/159, Mellen to Clark, May 31, 1874.

106. ABM 176/126, L. Grout to Anderson, March 19, 1849. The odd syntax is Mellen's.

107. ABM 175/731–32, Bryant to Anderson, July 12, 1849. Although unlucky in love, this young man was fortunate to have his cattle returned. Many Christian men needed to undergo long and difficult struggles to regain even a portion of the *lobola* they had already paid when engagements were broken off.

108. From 1848 on, the colonial government made extensive use of *isibhalo*, a labor tax originally imposed by Zulu kings on young unmarried men and women. For six months the government expected these conscripts to work on the roads and public projects of the colony for wages substantially less than workers received elsewhere. It was, not surprisingly, a thoroughly despised system that most made every effort to avoid. Keletso Atkins, *The Moon is Dead! Give Us Our Money!: The Cultural Origins of an African Work Ethic, Natal, South Africa, 1843–1900* (Portsmouth: Heinemann, 1993), 53, 129–135.

109. ABM 176/130, L. Grout to Anderson, July 12, 1849.

110. Surprisingly early on Zulu in Natal seemed to have felt the presence of British authority. Bryant wrote, in 1849, that while converts had been harassed by *amabhinca* they did not fear physical attack as "all the people know that they live under British law and they would not dare, even were they so disposed, to proceed to open violence against those who embrace the gospel." ABM 175/386, Bryant to Anderson, September 12, 1849.

111. ABM 175/873, A. Grout to Anderson, April 24, 1848.

112. ABM 175/881, A. Grout to Anderson, September 12, 1848. While there is no record of young men receiving such medicine, it was frequently used for girls to "make them right." In combination with the medicine, they could also have their heads shaved. ABM 176/127, L. Grout to Anderson, March 19, 1849.

113. ABM 171, Inanda station report, 1859–60.

114. ABM 176/126, L. Grout to Anderson, March 19, 1849.

115. ABM 176/95, L. Grout to Anderson, September 1848.

116. Unlike most of the converts of the AZM Anderson chose to change his name upon baptism, selecting for himself the name of the former secretary of the ABM. Unfortunately Anderson provides no dates or ages for the events that happen to him, but clearly the events occurred across his youth and young adulthood.

117. It is also a remarkable document for the insight it gives into the often-complex process by which Zulu were drawn into the growing capitalist economy of Natal and how most skated along its margins; entering into and leaving working relationships as best suited them.

118. The following is taken from ABM 179/552–59, Robbins to Clark, June 2, 1870.

119. Thomas Hawes was the son of Joel Hawes, one of the more noteworthy figures in the early church. Thomas became one of the first Zulu pastors of the AZM. His brother, Benjamin, also assumed a leadership role in the church.

2

Being Zulu and Christian

In 1846 Ntaba Luthuli, one of the first residents of Umvoti mission station, led an ox to Aldin Grout, the resident American missionary. Untaba acknowledged that he had thought of using the beast to acquire a second wife but, after a particularly persuasive sermon by Grout, abandoned the plan, determined to lead a Christian life. For Untaba the first steps in walking the new path were now clear. "He was," he declared, "ashamed to go unclad any longer" and he urged Grout to take the animal, sell it, and use the money to purchase clothes such as the missionary wore. He did not want blankets, as most Zulu who covered their bodies in the presence of whites then dressed themselves, but pants, shirts and a jacket.[1] The money left over from these purchases he committed to the work of the mission.

Over the next several years Luthuli diligently pursued the visible symbols of his newly assumed identity. Instead of the typical Zulu wattle and daub round beehive hut, Ntaba and his wife remarried under Christian rites and moved into a square house, complete with a thatched roof built by Ntaba with the assistance of Grout.[2] After a brief education, he began working as a teacher and used his earnings to begin acquiring a variety of Western goods.[3] Like many male converts, he purchased a plow but, to his missionary's dismay, also carefully squirreled away shillings for a wagon and the large team of oxen needed to pull it. On trips to Durban he bought European spades, wooden pails, sickles and other contemporary implements of Western agriculture that marked him as distinct from his traditionalist friends and family. With these he planted two acres of cotton, hoping to supplement his teaching income. In the midst of all this activity he did not neglect his faith and he and his wife dutifully attended Sunday services, daily prayer meetings, and Bible studies. As the number of believers grew, building their own homes on the station, Luthali celebrated the special passages of life in communion with them. Some of these, such as births, marriages, and funerals were not new rites, and these Christians celebrated in communion with traditionalists. Others, however, such as Easter and Christmas were occasions of special importance for the community of believers alone and they celebrated their passing in prayer, public worship, hymns, and feasts.

Church, school, work, home: Luthali, like so many *amakholwa* to follow, actively pursued a full experience of what it meant to be Christian. He and other early converts pieced together an identity centered on their Christianity, but which frequently had less to do with what was found within the church walls than with the many opportunities the station offered to embrace "civilization." However, just as with their faith, Zulu Christians did not accept or welcome Western civilization whole cloth. They freely pursued recognition of their newly acquired status, for they longed to belong, but did so on their own terms, accepting aspects of Western civilization that appealed to them, rejecting those that did not.

Understanding the series of revivals that occurred on the stations of the American Board from 1896–1901 requires understanding that by the end of their first fifty years in existence, *amakholwa* came to perceive themselves as a unique community, occupiers of a fine-edged middle ground between western and traditional worlds. This chapter examines this *amakholwa* sense of identity by examining the bits and pieces of the Zulu Christian experience that they gradually pieced together. For certainly, by the middle of the nineteenth century, when *amakholwa* entered the church on Sunday (itself a key component of their identity) they felt part of something larger, a sense of belonging that extended to neighbors who dressed, worked and lived like them, but also who believed in a theology that connected them across local and national borders, across oceans of water, race, and time. Yet their community was also intensely local, and only those who shared in the act of taking communion with Zulu hands could understand this experience.

Some scholars have argued that the world built by African Christians was not truly a world of their own making, that despite its possibilities, the missionaries' faith was essentially a trap, another site of oppression.[4] While this may have held true elsewhere, it appears an insupportable thesis in the case of *amakholwa*. For these Christians, as Gerald West has argued, the Bible (and, I would add, the church itself) became a place "with their own hermeneutics of resistance and survival with which they 're-member' the Bible and constructed 'lived' and 'working' theologies."[5] Certainly, as we will see, Zulu Christians built their identity from a set of practices generally approved by the mission, and which linked them to the colonial state. But, as already discussed, *amakholwa* actively maintained connections to *amab-hinca*, neither wanting nor pursuing full separation from their past—instead they aggressively built a profitable middle ground which depended on carefully balancing their newly acquired Western identity with their older, Zulu-based one. African Christians constructed their community from a series of small, largely every day, decisions and actions, such as wearing clothes, hitching their cattle to plows, and attending prayer services. But surprisingly few of these were imposed by missionaries, instead *amakholwa*, many of whom, such as Rufus Anderson, worked in the homes of whites, sought out particular signifiers of identity that appealed to them. Zulu Christians bought plows not because they felt obligated, but because they understood that doing so provided them with significant advantages over their traditional friends and family. And once converts committed the transgressive act of hitching oxen to plows, it became easier for them to move onto transport riding, a career choice most of the American missionaries strongly disproved of, but which nevertheless became an important component of what it meant to be *amakholwa*. So too did early Zulu Christians alter other acts, such as wearing clothes and attending church, to meet their own expectations and needs. The initial *amakholwa* identity than cannot be understood as imposed, but rather as part of a larger process in which Zulu Christians wove the tapestry of their own community by slowly building a sense of what it meant to live and work on the stations of the AZM and what it meant to believe, to be people of faith.

ACCUMULATING IDENTITY

The early missionaries frequently made a simple assumption linking Western clothing to Christianity. They followed a narrow equation in which the *umutsha*, a loin cloth made of animal pelts worn by men or the *ukaka*, a short leather skirt worn by unmarried girls (who traditionally did not cover their breasts until marriage,) represented "savagery" and thus "heathenism" and the suits and dresses they wore represented "civilization" and thus Christianity.[6] Zulu quickly picked up on this and many of the first conversion narratives follow a distinctive pattern in which clothing is necessary not only as a Christian, but as a critical first step towards Christianity. It was believed that each piece acquired brought catechists closer to a full covenant with the church.[7] But Zulu did so within their own framework. Thus, although it frequently either amused or horrified the Americans, a catechist felt perfectly suited to attend Sunday services, attend classes, and even make social visits around the station, dressed in nothing but a long sleeved shirt, the tails of which served as adequate cover for the lower half of the body.

Much to the missionaries' relief, pants were often the next article of clothing acquired, followed, frequently, by a suit coat and even top hats. Initially, at least, women's wear was simpler; girls often received plain cotton dresses from missionaries, who then taught them to sew similar garments.[8]

This clothing, often stitched together by mission wives from rough material such as drapes, was often removed and carefully hung in the schools and churches when children went home.[9] When they returned to the mission an easily assumed identity hung ready for children to take down from the hooks and assume—both literally and figuratively. In the end this was a lesson in the mutability of identity many readily learned. Ironically, traditionalists employed the missionaries' obsession with clothing against them, excusing themselves from Sunday services by noting that they were "ashamed to appear in church unclothed where the great mass are clad."[10] Interestingly, *amakholwa* frequently acquired shoes, often if ever, well after conversion. The relative expense of shoes played a role in this, but *amakholwa* also successfully resisted the very idea of shoes and, late into the nineteenth century, even Zulu preachers went unshod outside of church.

Converts soon found ways to adapt the new convention of cloth in unexpected ways connected both to the past and their present.[11] Women, taught from the earliest to sew, quickly moved beyond the simple dresses of their early Christianity and hunted out brightly colored and fancifully styled fabric to which they attached the beads and leather used in traditional dress. For men the uniforms of the British military proved enduringly popular. Following the British seizure of Natal, the pews of the churches could well have been mistaken for regimental services, as men happily put on the garments castoff by the triumphant British army, and following the Anglo-Zulu war of 1879, young *amakholwa* men wore pants with white patches on their knees and shirts with red or blue sashes draped over their shoulders, emulating the British officer corps.[12] By the middle of the century, *amakholwa* attire became so elaborate that missionaries found it necessary to speak out against the "grand dress parades" they feared church services had become. One missionary thought it best to inform catechists coming to his door seeking pants that what they really needed were the "garments of salvation," the white robes "which the king of heaven is ready to give all who ask."[13] There is no record of how his listeners responded to this suggestion, but by the middle of the nineteenth century, they likely would have found a creative use for such a fantastic cloth.

In addition to resisting shoes, Christian men also tenaciously held onto the Zulu habit of carrying several different wooden "walking" sticks some of which were knobbed and could be used as weapons.[14] Zulu boys began using these staves from the moment they took up their fathers' cattle. In addition to serving as a means to prod along stubborn beasts they also kept snakes at bay and, most famously, were used in stick-fighting by boys, a highly evolved, and valued, martial skill in Zulu society and one carried through into adulthood. Indeed after initiation young men began engaging in *umgangela*, a frequently bloody and potentially deadly combat that pitted young men from competing tribes.[15] At least initially the kit carried by *amakholwa* included two or three long, often beautifully carved, staves of varying sizes and purpose. In time missionaries recognized their martial history and Christians were obliged to leave their sticks resting outside of church doors, but for some time, few would be found traveling any distance without them.

The problem for *amakholwa* was that clothing as a marker of identity became something of an arms race. As more and more Zulu adopted Western modes of dress toward the end of the century, the wide-reaching eclecticism evidenced by early Christians faded.[16] Young men enrolled at the Boys Training School at Adams wore a sober uniform replete with starched, stand-up collars and well polished boots. *Amakholwa* preachers wore three-piece suits with hats and dress shoes, and their wives rarely ventured beyond simple, carefully pressed dresses with flats or sandals. Clothing, in some form or another, had become so common among Africans that *amakholwa* needed to more carefully emulate Europeans if they desired to be accepted as "civilized"/Christian. This was, of course, a costly proposition, and as economic problems of the late nineteenth century left more and more *amakholwa* unable to dress the part, they searched for alternative symbols to mark their faith.

THE *AMAKHOLWA* HOME

Outside of clothing, no other aspect of early *amakholwa* life so marked their outward identity as living in a European style house. Building on the mission stations placed an individual "under" the missionary, both politically and religiously and also provided dramatic physical evidence to all those around of one's new identity. Not only were upright homes different in appearance from the beehive shaped wattle and daub structures of *amabhinca*, they were also free of the sites most closely linked with the worship of the *amadlhozi* (ancestors.) Most Zulu homesteads consisted of several *indlu*, the beehive-shaped huts which surrounded a central cattle enclosure, or *isibaya*. Public ceremonial events occurred within the *isibaya*, for the ancestors resided alongside the cattle. Private rituals were conducted inside, around the fire pit located at the center of the *indhlu*. Christian homes had no central *isibaya*, nor, constructed with rooms, did they provide an obvious center, as did the fire-pit. Ironically, the Western home, while itself symbolic of

belief, provided no obvious space for worship.[17] Yet Zulu Christians did not
entirely throw off the old ways, for there is also a sense of the familiar in
their near universal approach to building a home only after marriage. Like
their traditionalist friends and family, Christian men connected the act of
raising the walls of a structure with raising a family and young unmarried
amakholwa rarely lived on their own.

Slowly, as Christian men met and married Christian women, or brought
traditional wives onto the stations to become Christian, homes, often
nothing more than "neat cottages," began dotting the mission reserves.[18]
Missionaries encouraged this construction by providing technical knowledge, materials, tools, and even their own muscle. The Americans carefully
recorded each new house built, viewing this construction as evidence of
the success of their larger undertaking. By 1868 this fixation on development evolved further, with missionaries subdividing their count between
wooden houses and those built with brick, a material that allowed for
grander structures and gave a deeper sense of permanence to the entire
undertaking. The number of brick homes in 1868 was still relatively small,
with Umvoti, generally the wealthiest of the stations, lagging slightly behind Amanzimtoti six to four.[19] Following the cash infusion into the *amakholwa* community (as indeed throughout Natal) brought by the Anglo-Zulu
war, the number of upright homes on the stations rose dramatically, to
the point where missionaries rarely felt inclined to comment on them and
gradually discontinued keeping statistics on their number.

Almost universally, the first generation of Christians built their new
homes on the mission glebe, the small 500-acre plot of land set aside on
the mission reserve by the Natal government for missionaries to do with as
they pleased. The reasons for this are three-fold: First, early converts sought
the protection, spiritual if not physical, of surrounding themselves with
other like-minded individuals. There were also financial benefits in doing
so, not only did missionaries frequently provide assistance in building, they
also often provided land. Finally in traditional society, a newcomer moved
onto land assigned to him by his *inkosi* (headman or chief) after paying
his respects and asking his permission in the practice known as *khonza*.[20]
It is likely that the first generation of *amakholwa* interpreted the suggestion
by missionaries that they build near the church as carrying an equivalent
authority; after all, missionaries encouraged comparisons of themselves to
headmen. Missionaries, for their part, gradually developed a belief that the
ideal spiritual state for all of God's children, regardless of ethnicity, was the
small agrarian community similar to those found in rural Middle America.
The "village plan" as it came to be called, was promoted throughout the
nineteenth and well into the twentieth century. The plan consisted of small
plots of land in town surrounded by plowable fields radiating outward

from the center on which *amakholwa* could raise crops, allow their herds to graze on communal grounds, and keep in daily contact with each other and the church while doing so.

As it did in almost every material category, the station that came closest to achieving this ideal was Umvoti. Founded in 1844, the second oldest of the stations after Inanda, the residents of Umvoti enthusiastically embraced the village plan. The reserve, relatively small at 9,000 acres but strategically located only 45 miles from Durban on what would become prime sugar-cane growing country, was not, unlike most of the other mission reserves, connected with a nearby native location, making it much easier to set aside divisible land. A village was laid out and residents built houses on half-acre lots which they then owned outright. Surrounding the village were 160 lots of fifteen acres each, which were distributed among the people to do with as they wished.[21] Later, particularly during the troubles that followed the Anglo-Zulu war, the Americans expressed regret at having allowed owner-ship of the lots, but even then they did not abandon the basic premise of the plan, preferring instead to create idyllic rural villages in which the lots were leased, not sold.

On the other stations, where land ownership by Africans was never permit-ted, the ideal represented by Umvoti never had a chance of being fully real-ized. Umtwalume (initially spelled Umtwalumi by missionaries) stands as a typical example of what happened at the other stations of the AZM. There, by 1867, the eighty residents, who had demonstrated a "great desire" to be-come owners of land, had surveyed, at their own expense, lots of twenty-five acres each. The mission, initially willing to permit ownership, hesitated at the last moment and asked residents to demonstrate prior to ownership that they could effectively occupy the land, make improvements, and successfully cultivate it while leased from the mission. The issue dragged on through fol-lowing decades, and, as we will examine in the following chapter, became a contentious issue between the mission and their congregations.[22]

This plan also lent itself more readily to the larger fields Christians put under the plow and the carefully delineated plots surrounding the station contrasted sharply with the small patches traditionalists generally farmed alongside streams or close to other water supplies.[23] Most of the stations were surrounded by hills dotted with traditional homesteads. But this image, of a tight knot of Christians laagered in against a sea of unbeliev-ers, while seductive was, as I argued earlier, deeply misleading from the earliest, for the border between the two was always permeable. But there was a boundary to be crossed, a symbolic line that separated out those who lived in this new style of home from those who didn't. Inevitably, the sheer neighborliness that emerged from these living arrangements rein-forced a common identity. As will be examined in the following chapter, this blueprint began to break down in the decade prior to the revival of 1896–97, as outstations branched out from the central stations and new converts stayed put, remaining in the rural hinterlands and not bothering, or being unable to afford to build in the Western style as had the older generation of believers.

Unlike the wide creativity evidenced by Zulu Christians in clothing themselves, the exterior façade of homes seemed to not be strong sites of self-expression and *amakholwa* followed the forms laid down by missionaries, varying only in size. But while there were certain conventions Zulu obeyed in interior design, their tastes were not necessarily of the mission's making. At Umsumduzi, Lewis Grout believed that after purchasing a set of clothes and building a home, Christians required relatively little; patches, needles, and thread to repair their clothes, soap to wash them and, importantly, dishes to eat on.[24] These he believed were the essential items that made up the civilized life of new Zulu Christians. Yet, as evidenced by Ntaba Luthuli, most *amakholwa* sought a range of other goods, eager to acquire symbols of their new community. Western furniture, in particular, became an essential ingredient in the developing Christian identity and men bought axes, saws, augers, chisels, planes, and hammers that they employed in great sprees of building. Tables, chests, shelves, bed frames, wooden washtubs and, above all else, "American" style chairs were produced with varying degrees of craftsmanship.[25]

Once built, *amakholwa* begun slowly filling up their cabinets and shelves. Books became increasingly popular, and for many years the American printing press could not meet the demands of their increasingly literate, and apparently voracious, Zulu readership. *Amakholwa* bought ink, fountain pens and paper, keeping up an active correspondence with friends on other stations, Christians in other parts of the world, and even "their" missionaries away from the stations.[26] Women, many who had worked in the kitchens of missionaries as girls, carefully equipped their homes with items they now believed were found in a "proper" Christian household, buying iron pots, cutlery, china and cloth—great reams of cloth to make everything from napkins and tablecloths to bedspreads, drapes and, of course, clothing. These purchases added up to an interior space identifiably "Christian," one that informed visitors of the owners' belief and, perhaps more importantly, which constantly reminded the owners of the choice they had made. When Nqumba, a preacher/teacher at an outstation of Adams hosted a visiting missionary touring outstations in August of 1881, his main room appears typical of the material aspirations of the *amakholwa* community.[27] Central to the room was a homemade table around which sat several chairs, although in this case backless, more like milking stools than the high backed "American" chairs favored by so many other Zulu Christians. On one wall hung a series of roughhewn shelves, topped with a few pieces of crockery, a Zulu Bible, several works on the scriptures, hymnals, and Nqumba's book of notes taken while attending Adams Theological School (known for most of its history as Amanzimtoti Seminary). On the other walls hung decorative pictures cut from various English and American tabloids. Taken together they represented a sparse, yet fairly effective, statement of identity, a faith that encompassed a wide range of European material culture and differentiated its owner from the interior items of a traditional *umuzi*.[28]

The degree to which the emerging *amakholwa* community could afford the rapid acquisition of a "civilized" life remained a persistent concern for both converts and missionaries. The desire to demonstrate one's "Christianity" through material goods produced a persistent low-level anxiety throughout the AZM, and one that hung heavier on those from the poorer stations. At Umtwalume the wages of Christians there were so small that it took "all they can earn by diligent industry to clothe and feed themselves in the plainest style." So impoverished did the act of buying "decent garments" leave the church members there, that "their food is often of the plainest kind and of the scantiest quantity."[29] At Umsumduzi converts found themselves in similar straits, buying clothing impoverished them and left them unable to afford cattle, the marker of traditional wealth that Christians refused to part with. So too could building a home leave one with precarious finances; a Christian at Umtwalume built a comfortable house for himself and his family, lost it in a fire and rebuilt, but doing so left his family dependent on charity for food. At Amahlongwa the desire to live like the English had caused the *amakholwa* there to wear more and better clothing, to secure household furniture, wagons and plows; but all at the price of station residents falling into large debts, a process the American there feared had "hindered the spiritual progress of this and other stations."[30] Progress came at a cost, but one the early *amakholwa* community seemed willing to pay.

Working

During one particularly cold winter in the early 1880s, a chief from the location surrounding Amahlongwa spoke wistfully with the missionary of the nearby church. The chief, a relatively young man, had frequently expressed the desire that his people pursue the benefits of European civilization.[31] That his people had failed to do so was a source of frustration for the young chief and in his conversation with the missionary he explained their hesitancy; to seek such wealth, people feared, was to risk calling down upon themselves injurious witchcraft by jealous neighbors. Ultimately this fear "prevented many of the people from striking ahead of their neighbors and acquiring new forms of wealth." Although there is no record of such a response, missionaries rarely missed these opportunities to boast of the freedom *amakholwa* felt from such restrictions. From the earliest, members of the community pursued economic opportunity with the great zeal of those freed from traditional limitations. Teacher, preacher, trader, farmer, laborer, and craftsman, all of these proved enduringly popular for *amakholwa* who frequently practiced multiple trades at once in their pursuit of wealth. In these ways the early Zulu Christian community built a sense of communal identity that revolved as much around their ability to pursue new economic opportunities as it did shared religiosity.

Of course, as we have already seen, it was the willingness of homestead heads to exchange the labor of children for a cow or two that provided missionaries with most of the first generation of converts who then, not surprisingly, proved more than willing to break free of traditional economic models in pursuit of wealth. When children refused to return home, one can reasonably speculate that many Zulu must have regarded their neighbors, who for payment in cattle had sent their children to work in the homes of missionaries, as having called down the wrath of ancestors. Later, after deserting their families' kraal, many of these children received their first wages from missionaries. Luthuli worked as a teacher for Aldin Grout at Umvoti as early as 1846, joining at least one other Zulu teacher there. At Umlazi, Adams employed Umembula from 1847 on, providing the Zulu believer with sufficient income to move from his family, settle on the station, and later build an upright house.[37] As part of the belief that they would raise up a self-sufficient church within a generation of their arrival, Americans employed early catechists as teachers and preachers with the hope that such men could spread the Word far more rapidly than could foreign missionaries. But *amakholwa* soon began chasing more lucrative opportunities. In 1848 Grout reported the peculiarity of one of his station residents buying a cart and a span of oxen "which have full occupation taking goods to market."[33]

This initial experiment at Umvoti clearly succeeded, for others, first at Umvoti and then on elsewhere, soon followed. Less than a decade later, by 1856, Zulu Christians on four different stations owned a total of seven large wagons, twelve carts, twenty-nine plows and 250 trained oxen to pull the entire lot.[34] Early Christians had a decided advantage over their traditionalist friends and family when pursuing this new career. They earned salaries, hard cash from missionaries that *amabhinca* only began demanding after the imposition of the hut tax in 1849 and even then not exclusively until much later.[35] Cut off from traditionalist family, young *amakholwa* could accumulate capital unburdened by familial responsibilities.[36] They could also yoke their oxen and cattle to wagons, mishandling them, in the eyes of *amabhinca* for whom the beasts represented not only food and wealth, but also an important site of spiritual belief.[37] The striking statement by Christians in the construction of a house instead of a homestead was further reinforced by the willingness of the men of these households to travel long distances away from them. Where a homestead head did not hesitate to send his children off to distant pastures, to the mines, or to Durban, he himself stayed put, managing his *umuzi*. In contrast, *amakholwa* men rode long distances as transport-riders and traders, seeking out profits over the hills of Natal.

Unfortunately there is no official "log" of the *amakholwa* trading trips. But certainly, in carefully gleaning the records, one senses an enormously active people. John Dunn and other white traders who lived in Zululand deeply disliked missionaries. Not, I suspect, so much because they resented the condemnation rained down upon them by preachers for engaging in polygamous relationships with Zulu women, but rather because they viewed the mission stations as home to their primary competition; *amakholwa* who undercut their primary business of trading between Africans and Europeans.[38] It was in this middle ground that *amakholwa* made their profits by activating their liminal identity and trundling over the hills of Natal to buy loads of maize and other produce that they took to colonial markets.[39] It was work perfectly suited to a people who lived in both worlds and while many *amakholwa* traders lived on the margins of profitability, industrious individuals moving wagonloads of produce about could accrue handsome earnings.

For those willing, trading further abroad offered both greater risks and greater rewards. As early as 1860, if not much sooner, *amakholwa* filled their wagons with goods and ventured across the Thukela River into Zululand, over the Drakensbergs onto the Highveld, and at least as far as southern Mozambique.[40] Most of this early trade, before the gold mines opened and transport riders began making regular trips to Johannesburg, occurred in Zululand, as Christians sought to extract from that country the one currency that also translated well in the new economy, cattle. Christian merchants carried a wide assortment of goods, everything from feathers, fur, silk, and satin, to sugar, coffee, snuff, tobacco, and jewelry.[41] These were the luxury goods of the Western economy most sought by Zulu society and some of the few items for which they were willing to part with cattle. *Amakholwa* used newly acquired herds to secure other trade items, sold them for cash, or, significantly, used them to reconnect with traditional society.[42]

The transport trade also encouraged a number of agriculture ventures. Adoption of the plow allowed them to out-produce their traditionalist friends and family and the excess went for sale to the cities of Natal, frequently, especially early on, for handsome profits. In the early years of the mission this meant maize, but Christians quickly expanded their interests, branching out into various citrus and passion fruits, sweet potatoes and other vegetables. When cash crop opportunities arose, *amakholwa* did not hesitate to adopt these as well. The residents of Umvoti, well situated in what became prime sugar growing country, quickly took to the crop and for a short time it proved profitable. The Natal government, in one of the few instances of the colony promoting African agricultural interests, established a sugar mill at Umvoti in 1863. The first crushing from the mill yielded seventy tons of sugar, which, at $128 per ton, represented a significant cash influx into the small community of believers.[43]

While the bulk of the transport trade remained in the hands of those nearest Durban, Christians on other mission reserves also sought their fortunes in the occupation. To make a go of it men from the poorer stations along the fringes of Natal frequently formed business cooperatives. At Ifumi, in 1854, several residents formed a joint company, bought a wagon and pieced together a team of oxen before hitting the road. While buying grain they took advantage of the local natural resources and began transporting timber, a venture that soon proved profitable and occupied most of their buisness.[44] At Umtwalume, after decades of poverty, residents there finally scraped together enough money to afford a wagon in the early months of 1870, an important if belated step. Those unable to secure the necessary credit for goods often acted as independent operators, hiring their wagons out to other *amakholwa*, white merchants, big farmers or the military.[45]

Those that could afford it took to the profession with zeal. Despite losing nearly all their oxen in the lungsickness outbreak that swept north from Hintsa's land in the latter half of 1856, the residents of Umvoti recovered sufficiently by 1861 to claim fifteen wagons, two of those owned by one man, two hundred inoculated and trained oxen and thirty plows.[46] By the end of the 1860s the 433 church members of the mission owned nearly fifty wagons, many more carts and the hundreds if not thousands of oxen needed to pull all of them.[47] They were well positioned to profit from the Anglo-Zulu war a decade later that, particularly after the British defeat at Islandwana, meant hauling great quantities of war supplies across the Thukela River.

The war itself was meant to be a quick victory by an imperial power wrestling with itself over whether to fight at all against an opponent keen to avoid a conflict with a neighbor it had long wooed as an ally against the Afrikaner republic to its west. But the Zulu king Cetewayo could not overcome British desire to ease administration of southern Africa by confederating its various independent states. Sir Bartle Frere, the British High Commissioner for Southern Africa, believed defeating the Zulu would demonstrate English commitment and might, and despite Colonial Office resistance he pushed through a war that eventually cost the British not only their worst defeat at the hands of Africans, but also eventually confederation.[48] The British army, desperate to wash away their embarrassment with the complete dismantling of the Zulu state, hired out nearly every wagon in the colony at extraordinarily high prices and *amakholwa* of the AZM earned "hundreds, if not thousands of pounds" in two to three months of work before the last battle at the Zulu capital of Ulundi shattered the remaining Zulu regiments and effectively ended the kingdom's independence.[49]

It proved a time of unprecedented prosperity for the community and those who did not already own the necessary equipment rushed to do so, mortgaging what they could to buy wagons at inflated prices. Those fortunate enough to own teams prior to the war bought additional ones, built impressive homes, and purchased fine clothing and other "luxury" items generally reserved for the wealthiest of Natal's white society. This process did not go uncommented on, however. Even in the decades prior to the war, *amakholwa* had heard what they could only interpret as an increasingly contradictory message from missionaries on the subject of the transport trade. Missionaries praised the industriousness of their people, favorably compared them to the best New Englanders, and happily noted that when *amabhinca* regarded their *amakholwa* neighbors they needed to admit that: "Even in temporal matters it is clearly seen that Godliness is profitable."[50] Yet missionaries regarded the profession as harmful to the tightly woven Christian agricultural community envisioned in the village-plan.

William Ireland seemed pleased in 1854 that most *amakholwa* were "getting on" in their local businesses "probably as fast as is for their good" while managing to not "allow their worldly engagements to interfere with their attendance upon the weekly prayer meetings and the daily school."[51] By 1863, however, the AZM called in their annual letter for the development of enterprises on the stations as a necessary step to keep Christians from engaging in nomadic trading habits "which always and everywhere are so baneful to a true and steady growth of character either as respects a manly industry or a manly Christian life."[52] Much to the despair of *amakholwa*, their mission's desire for a more sedentary congregation was realized in the decade following the end of the Anglo-Zulu war, as an economic depression blanketed the land and enterprising Christians could not find work for the wagon teams they had bought at staggering rates in the 1879 boom.[53] For those able to struggle through the next decade, however, the discovery of gold on the Witwatersrand Main Reef in 1886 opened new opportunities and *amakholwa* again took up the challenge of moving goods into the interior. By 1894 the church at Mapumulo, the originating site two years later of the revival discussed in following chapters, had so many people off "either with wagons or seeking work" that the Zulu preacher in charge could not gather together sufficient members to hold a service.[54]

In addition to affecting the attendance at Sunday services, transport riding delayed the development of a Zulu church leadership. This was first felt at Umvoti, where, for a lack of teachers, Aldin Grout temporarily closed the school in 1853.[55] The salaries Grout could provide simply failed to attract *amakholwa*, who, he noted, could earn significantly more in transport riding. Even at Umsumduzi, one of the poorer stations, Lewis Grout found it difficult to raise up a Zulu leadership, noting that converts found it so profitable to trade, or work with wagon and plow, that most did not stay in school long enough to become teachers and pastors. He was particularly vexed by the habit of teachers and preachers starting well, but falling short in their obligations when they attempted to balance churchly duties with profitable businesses. When confronted over poor performance, he also noted, most were likely to pursue the path of mammon rather than that of the Lord's.[56] For most *amakholwa*, faced with an 1866 salary range of 10 shillings to £3 per month teaching, as opposed to the possibility of earning several hundred pounds a year trading, the choice must have seemed clear.[57] Throughout the mission, one promising teacher after another left after short stints to take up the transport trade, leaving positions vacant.

Those few *amakholwa* who stayed on, such as John Hlonono, often did so only by successfully balancing both their economic and spiritual obligations. Hlonono a teacher and preacher who established a new outstation just off of the Mapumulo reserve at Imushane, preached every Sabbath, taught three days a week, and went to great pains in between to cut a workable wagon path over the rough hewn hills of the area; his faith neatly tempered by a keen sense for a new business opportunity.

Still, there were a few cases of *amakholwa* "wholly called" to serve their faith; those willing to live ascetic lives by ignoring material gains in favor of spiritual ones. Mbiyana Ngidi, one of the first Zulu given his own congregation, declared in 1867: "Such is my walk in the work of the Lord. It is pleasant to me. There is no work so great, or so delightful; no there is not, I deny that there is."[58] It does not take a deep reading to see sharpness in this proclamation born of frequent exchanges with Christians less interested than he in pursuing "the work of the Lord." Still, even before the wealth that the Anglo-Zulu War generated, the unwillingness of young men to pursue the teaching degrees offered at Amanzimtoti Seminary caused the principal there to note: "The subject is at present assuming so serious a character as to demand the prayerful and thoughtful consideration of the mission."[59] The economic downturn following 1879 slowly reversed this process, (although, ironically, financially strapped Zulu Christians found themselves often unable to afford the rising school fees charged by the mission) and many *amakholwa*, unable to find work for their wagons, turned to the financial security of working for the mission.[60]

By the end of the 1880s the mission employed a significant number of *amakholwa* teachers and preachers.[61] For the most part these were relatively well-educated individuals, certainly more so than their fathers a generation earlier. The family schools gave way to regular day schools by the 1860s and, significantly, Amanzimtoti Seminary offered Christians a secondary education. As well-financed individual Europeans, larger firms, and later the railroads, squeezed *amakholwa* out of transport-riding, Christians turned to the schools to provide their children with a future off of the roads. For many this education led directly to careers with the missions. In 1868 the government began offering small grants to the mission bodies that had, and would continue to until the apartheid government took control much later, assumed full responsibility for the education of natives in Natal. This grant, combined with small contributions from the congregations, allowed the mission to offer livable wages to its employees.

Many of the new teachers took up positions in the expanding ring of outstations, building one-room schoolhouses that doubled as homes and often churches. Inanda was typical in this regard, with five such schools surrounding the central church by 1881. Nomtimba taught three miles from Inanda in a hut built for that purpose, as did Sara who taught four miles in the opposite direction. Jwili, a graduate of Amanzimtoti Theological Seminary, taught courses under the shade of a large yellowwood tree, four miles from Inanda along a path that ran west from the station. Lewis, five miles from Inanda, used a £100 grant from the government to establish the most permanent structure, an iron shed that served as schoolhouse and doubled as a church on Sundays. He also managed to build an upright house from which his wife taught sewing to the local girls.[62]

By 1883 the mission felt compelled to bring some structure to their increasing work force and started what became an annual event, the Teachers' Institute. Rotating between Inanda and Amanzimtoti the weeklong event offered classes for teachers to hone their own education, provided help with curriculum, brought some degree of standardization, and gave the Americans an opportunity to judge the comparative qualifications of the teachers. It was a professional event that marked the foundations of an "educated elite." But as *amakholwa* graduated with higher degrees, many also came to the realization that the racist settler state actively sought to block opportunities they hoped their education had earned them.[63]

Education

As the first generation of *amakholwa* came of age and had children of their own, they came to regard it "of the very first importance" that their children be educated.[64] This deeply held belief, promoted by missionaries who revered learning, drove a rapid growth in the educational opportunities offered by the AZM. The family school system, a staple of early missionaries, could not meet the demands placed upon it, and slowly a network of "day schools" began to dot the landscape in and around the mission glebes. Often little more than one room huts (or initially even a shady spot under a tree) these allowed for greater numbers of pupils, more hours taught, and higher degrees attained. While the family schools focused on the educational value of hard work and often included only a few hours of instruction in the fundamentals, the day schools slowly expanded their offerings from the basics of reading, writing, and the gospels. Courses in mathematics, geography, American and English history, music, and science, became common subjects in the day schools. Even with these new subjects, however, the classrooms could become tedious places for the brightest students. Outside of biblical tracts, few books were available in Zulu, and missionaries worried that the "same few books are read over and over again."[65] To compensate, the AZM increasingly relied on Zulu teachers (when, of course, they could be had), both to fill the positions and to translate the more difficult lessons.

Despite their deficiencies, the day schools grew steadily. In 1848, 155 children attended mission schools, by 1861 this increased to 264 and then nearly doubled to 475 by 1864 and nearly doubled again to 762 by 1868 before leveling off to numbers consistently in the 800s throughout the 1870s.[66] The number of schools doubled during this time as well, from ten in 1848 to twenty-one in 1874 (although the lack of *amakholwa* willing to take on teaching wages forced the mission to cut these back to seventeen in 1877.) Among Christian parents, the popularity of the school indicates an early recognition of the importance of education. Children quickly grasped it as well. It is not surprising that up to fifty children a day packed the school at Umvoti in 1859, filling the yard in eager expectation an hour before the first bell was rung.[67] Nor is it surprising that given the limited space, children who attended made the most of their experience. By the late 1850s, missionaries drew favorable comparisons between their Zulu pupils and their American counterparts, particularly in their ability to master the three Rs of reading, writing, and arithmetic.[68]

From the earliest, missionaries introduced English into the curriculum.[69] By the late 1850s, as increasing numbers of *amakholwa* interacted with and hoped to prosper from the growing western economy, Zulu Christians actively demanded English instruction. Most missionaries had always offered some instruction in English, but slowly this became formalized, both in the day schools and at night classes in Durban, where young Zulu men learned the language of their employers. Unfortunately for converts, instruction was often haphazard at best, a casualness that only changed in 1865 when the colonial government tied new educational grants to the sole stipulation that English become a regular feature of the school day.[70] While the Natal government avoided direct responsibility for African education, they slowly increased their control over mission schools by offering larger grants in return for several concessions.[71] While some of the wealthier stations could have managed without this money, for Christians from poorer stations these grants were a necessity and many steadily increased the number of hours devoted to English instruction as a consequence.[72]

As the number of literate *amakholwa* expanded so too did their desire for reading materials. Within its first few years, the mission published the gospel of Matthew, a catechism, the book of Psalms, a hymnal with sixty-seven songs and two small pamphlets containing selections from the gospels and Genesis, all in Zulu.[73] Without its own printing press, however, publication slowed down after the first decade. At Ifumi, Christians regularly prodded the missionary there for new titles, prompting him to note: "At most of our stations there are persons who have read and reread all the books printed in the Zulu language, tell they can almost repeat them . . . "[74] When a press finally arrived from America in 1859 it soon churned out new texts; within the first six months it had put out a series of half sheet lessons for the schools, a translation of Acts, and a text on Zulu grammar.[75] In many ways the press acted as a unifying force, bringing together those who could read with a shared set of experiences; each new publication was eagerly awaited, devoured and discussed. In 1865 it began printing a Zulu language newspaper, put out 1,000 copies of a Zulu hymnal enlarged to 181 songs and, with the assistance of several of the mission's brightest *amakholwa*, the first full New Testament published in Zulu.[76] As Christians went about their business in Natal and the growing cities of Durban and Johannesburg, they did so armed with pamphlets, testaments, and hymnals.

From the earliest days the American missionaries hoped to establish a high school with a seminary attached. It was from such an institution that missionaries envisioned great masses of Zulu teachers, preachers and pastors emerging to lead the churches. In 1851, Lewis Grout, frustrated by the slowness in translating the Bible, noted that the process would drag on interminably until he had well educated Zulu assistants. To this end he called for the establishment of a seminary so that the "most promising sons" could be trained in "something more than agricultural pursuits and mechanic acts" of which, he noted, "the Zulu is probably better equipped than the English anyway."[77] Four years later the mission opened a temporary high school at Umvoti. Taught by two missionaries, its first class featured twenty-five Zulu students ranging in age from late adulthood to under twelve, their primary qualification being that all could read the Psalms in Zulu. The project proposed to raise up a Zulu "preaching force for their own people" but was hampered by a lack of texts and financial shortfall; within a few years it had closed.[78]

In 1864, faced with the acute shortage of teachers discussed above, the mission made another attempt at establishing secondary education. This time, at Amanzimtoti, the project took, opening in 1865 with sixteen youthful students.[79] As a boarding school, Amanzimtoti took in pupils from throughout the mission (and from several other missions) and the classes provided young men with an opportunity to mingle, often for the first time, with *amakholwa* from the far corners of Natal.[80] The education they received was surprisingly complete and those that graduated left not only well prepared to teach, but also to fill the scattering of mid-level managerial and bureaucratic positions open to them in Natal and Johannesburg. Evidence for the quality of students produced at Amanzimtoti even came from an unlikely source when, in 1867, the Natal Superintendent of Education visited the high school, tested the students, and afterwards declared that few whites had "higher attainment" than some of those from Amanzimtoti. The number of students steadily increased (with fifty attending in 1874) but took until the mid-1880s to reach the figures the mission initially expected.[81] Nevertheless the mission remained committed to the effort and in 1871 built an impressive brick building at Amanzimtoti that included a general schoolroom, three smaller recitation rooms, and a library.

By 1877 three missionaries and Christian teacher, Jeremiah Mali, staffed the school.[82] Boys took courses in English grammar, English history, general and biblical history, arithmetic, geography, algebra, English composition, dictation, and the structure of sentences. English became the required medium and was not only obligatory in the classrooms, where all instruction was carried on in English, but also in the dining room. Interestingly, Sunday services remained in Zulu, the missionaries perhaps feeling that this was the one time in the week when the students needed to fully understand what was being said. Jeremiah Mali not only taught the students, but also conducted popular military exercises for the youth, marching them in formation up and down the yard. Of the 154 students who attended Amanzimtoti by 1877, sixty-five stayed for all four years and forty-one spent at least short periods as teachers. Amanzimtoti (with the Anglican-run Lovedale in the present day Eastern Cape, and the Catholic Marianhill of Natal) offered one of the few opportunities young *amakholwa* of any denomination had to achieve a higher education and its popularity grew rapidly. By the end of the 1890s, despite several expansions, the school began turning away large numbers of prospective students. Still its influence was expansive and its graduates, including John Dube and Albert Luthuli, would go on to form the core of the educated Christian elite in Natal; filling leadership positions not only in the church, but also in politics and business.

After a decade of false starts, Amanzimtoti Theological Seminary, located on the same grounds as the high school, finally opened its doors in 1874 with a class of ten students. Attendance held steady throughout the rest of the decade. While these men were deeply spiritual, they were rarely the top graduates of the high school and by 1885 the Americans were forced to admit that few Amanzimtoti graduates moved on to the theological school. Those that did, however, were the passionate few and the entrance requirements (*amakholwa* men simply needed to evidence a deep commitment to Christianity combined with a desire to preach the gospel) were kept low to insure that the most dedicated could quickly began their training. Because of this open door the proscribed courses at the Seminary were broad, although centered on the Bible. So while they studied history, geography, and English, they did so by examining Jewish history from the Bible, biblical geography, and the English lectures of some of the best preachers of the day.[83] The course of study was designed to provide seminarians, in three to four years, with definite ideas of the whole Bible and how best to employ these in spreading the Gospel. Students engaged in daily exercises in the Epistles and twice-weekly ones from the Old Testament. Seminarians also practiced the ceremonial functions of pastor, taking turns leading prayer services and daily chapel, writing their own sermons, and going out to the surrounding homesteads to preach on Sundays. It was purposefully a rigorous experience designed to produce theologically orthodox ministers, and a decade after its inception only eight had completed the full course, with twenty-five washing out. Even for those who finished, however, the prospects of assuming their own congregations were relatively grim, as the second generation of American missionaries proved reluctant to hand over control of the churches. So, by 1885, only four graduates were employed by the AZM as preachers, none as pastors and the rest waited for their opportunity or accepted positions with other societies.[84]

The mission matched the establishment of the boys' high school with an all girls' boarding school at Inanda four years later, in 1869. Like Amanzimtoti, enrollment at Inanda increased gradually with demand eventually outstripping availability. Unlike the boys' school, however, most of the girls who attended did so from the surrounding region, as families generally thought it unsafe for their girls to travel to and from the school during breaks. At Mapumulo, for example, only three girls had attended Inanda by 1885 and even those, all from Christian families, sent male relatives to accompany the girls along the length of the sixty mile trip.[85] The school also appears to have had a much higher percentage of girls from traditional homes attending, many against the wishes of their families as Inanda became something of a safe house for the "runaway" girls discussed in the previous chapter. The school provided a surprising (given the time and their gender) array of educational opportunities for the girls. Yes, the girls did learn to sew; they also paid for their education by running a laundry. But Mary Edwards, the principal of Inanda for virtually the entire period covered by this work, was deeply committed to *amakholwa* women becoming more than mere housekeepers.[86] In particular the girls at Inanda were encouraged to become teachers and the curriculum, at least as rigorous as that at Amanzimtoti, well prepared them for such employment.[87] But the high-minded principles of many AZM missionaries often clashed with Zulu gender expectations and much to the frustration of Edwards, many of the girls failed to finish their education, choosing instead to marry and raise a family. Perhaps not surprisingly, given the many competing pressures on young women at Inanda, the school became one of the primary sites of revival in 1896–1897.

BEING A CHRISTIAN WOMAN

In 1874 Umbalasi, the AZM's first convert, died of old age. Her funeral, attended by both *amakholwa* and *amabhinca*, was a grand affair fitting her renown. The sheer force of her personality must have been incredible, for she carved out a leading role both in the church and outside of it; she was highly regarded both as the widow of a chief and as a "mother in Israel."[88] In this she is remarkable, for unlike *amakholwa* men, who took plow to field and wagon to road, *amakholwa* women had little opportunity to shape their identity outside of church and home. Even Umbalasi, who was thought of as a women of "commanding influence" was remembered for her willingness to speak out on church matters and for having given birth to Ira Nembula, whose son John was the first *amakholwa* to receive a degree in higher education and was then studying in the United States to become a doctor.[89]

At least initially, some converts carved out identities beyond matrons of church and family. Christian women, who learned to sew under the tutelage of mission wives, put their new skills to use, creating independent businesses by buying bolts of cloth, cutting and sewing them, and selling the finished articles in Durban. Particularly successful women re-invested their profits by buying sewing machines, or set up their own laundries with washing soap and irons (all those new clothes needed to be clean). When cloth could not be obtained, particularly early on, *amakholwa* women improvised. Umvoti women made hats out of the palm leaves found all along the coast and wove them together so attractively that the women were able to do a brisk business among both the people of the station and the growing white population of Natal.[90] Later, after palm leaf hats went out of fashion, the women of Umvoti turned to baking bread and churning butter, both of which they sold to their white neighbors as a means to raise their own income.[91]

But in one key area, women lost ground. The advances offered by missionaries drew *amakholwa* men into the fields, and as plows tilled soil they also cut women away from the fields—one of the few sites women controlled in traditional society.[92] It is not that women stopped working the fields, they still planted, weeded, and helped harvest, but Christian men, armed with cow and plow, increasingly took possession of both the fields and what they produced. Some women responded by turning to another traditional site of women's wealth and empowerment in Zulu society, beer making. But here too they found their way blocked, for while *amakholwa* women certainly participated in the growing *utshwala* industry in Durban, this was circumscribed by their faith and the abstinence campaigns launched in the 1880s discussed in more detail in the chapter 3. This marginalization of women from household production was encouraged by missionary wives who encouraged their Zulu sisters toward a "civilized" existence spent "employed in house affairs."[93]

But even the grandest *amakholwa* house was quickly dealt with and boredom must have set in for many young women, the majority of whom must have been extraordinarily independent to have chosen the path they did. Perhaps it was this reason, as much as any other, that led Christian women to an inward focus on their faith and an increasing involvement in the churches. There they occupied the sacred spaces ignored by men in their pursuit of business opportunities. It would be a mistake to refer to the Christian church of Natal as a "women's church," but the groundwork for the startling gender imbalance that emerged a century later was laid at this time.[94] As early as 1849 Adams noted that at Umlazi one of the most important influences in promoting Christianity on the station was the weekly female prayer meeting "which has been instrumental, apparently, in bringing quite a number of females to a saving knowledge of the truth."[95] The women's prayer meeting, frequently led by missionary wives, but just as often by leading *amakholwa* women, became a staple on all the stations, translating readily into abstinence campaigns, central committees for hosting large events and other movements.[96] The establishment of Inanda further strengthened the power of these groups. New trends began at Inanda, such as "secret prayer," which spread from there to other stations by graduates teaching, or even, occasionally, by girls home on break. While men frequently participated in prayer sessions and Bible studies, these were rarely all-male affairs and not until the revival of 1896–1897 did men deliberately question both individual spiritual health and that of the community; something that had long concerned the women's prayer groups.[97]

While being Christian restricted, at least in theory, women to a "respectable" life, it also offered paths of power unavailable to those outside of the church. Certainly the constant stream of young women "escaping" to the missions suggests one such avenue.[98] But once inside the church, women found new idioms of autonomy available to them. For example, Sarah, a member of the church at Inanda, agreed to marry a young man in early 1888, but only under the condition that he, a station resident but no longer Christian, come into full communion with the church and give up beer.[99] The young man agreed, collected the cattle necessary in order to garner permission from her brother and proceeded with the courtship. But Sarah became agitated during a sermon by the Zulu preacher Jwili entitled "Be ye not unequally yoked together with unbelievers" and arose from her pew proclaiming that the Holy Spirit had informed her that she could never see the face of God in peace if she proceeded with the marriage. The church community rallied around and urged her to do as she needed as a Christian woman. Despite the furious insistence of her brother and the heartbroken pleadings of the young man, she refused to proceed with the wedding. Her faith had given her authority to stand her ground and in invoking it she gained the backing of the *amakholwa* community, regardless of her gender.

For those few women choosing independence, the mission offered few opportunities, but teaching was one of them and a handful of young Zulu women took up the call. Graduates of Inanda entered the profession in increasing numbers as the twentieth century approached. A few *amakholwa* women also sought "professional" jobs in the cities, most as housekeepers. An even smaller number sought to express their faith as missionaries. Throughout the nineteenth century a handful, from various stations, joined the ABM's efforts to the Ndebele. In 1891 several young women from Inanda volunteered to go to Inhambane, a much more remote work in southern Mozambique. Grace, the daughter of Jwili who had become the local station *induna* and Salina, the daughter of a preacher, received their parents' permission after hearing a call to service. The church held a service for the girls in which residents from several of the surrounding stations filled a chapel adorned with palm branches to overflowing. The seventy girls at Inanda packed the front of the stage and led the congregation in song. Miss Jones, an African American missionary who served for a short time in Natal before moving on to the Ndebele mission, sang and spoke of the importance for her of coming to the land of her ancestors, William Wilcox, the missionary leading the effort to Imhambane, noted its dangers, and several of the local *amakholwa* preachers offered up prayers. Grace then spoke of how she had been dedicated to the Lord in baptism and Salina noted that the Lord had urged her not to hide her talents, but free her light to all. Salina's father spoke, charging the girls to be the "iron to dig in

God's ground" and was followed by Jwili who drew an allusion to the past by reminding the audience how Shaka had regularly selected the best and fairest of girls in the country and brought them to him whether the parents were willing or not. God, Jwili felt confident, surely had a much stronger claim to the *amakholwa* community's best and brightest. The girls departed, although only for a year, on what surely must have appeared to other young women in attendance, after such a ceremony, as one of the most important and prestigious tasks a woman might perform.[100]

As the twentieth century neared, Christian women found their lives increasingly troubled. The *amakholwa* community, as we will see, was rent by issues that directly affected women, such as *utshwala*, and *lobola*, but also by splinter movements led by the men of their lives. These men also responded to new opportunities in the growing urban centers of southern Africa and *amakholwa* woman, like their traditional sisters, bore the costs of Randlords paying insufficient wages to black workers to support families left behind in rural areas.[101] While *amakholwa* men frequently occupied better paying jobs than other Zulu, *amakholwa* women needed to stretch this income further to meet the bourgeois lifestyle that came with Christianity. The need to provide for a household ran headlong into the restrictions placed on women as they sought to lead respectable lives. So women who sought work outside of the household did so at the risk of being seen by their community as morally questionable. Women could look in the churches for their identity, but what if the answers they found offered little relief?

An important note needs to be inserted here, however, for early conversion is often seen as a deeply gendered affair, with congregations dominated by women, and the only men in attendance serving in leadership as deacons, preachers, and pastors. This suggests that Zulu men were only interested in the church to the degree that they could access political power while the women were content with "softer" spiritual comforts. This is patently untrue for the AZM for many of the early converts were men and for whom reasons behind conversion were as multivaried as they were for women. And while the image of a "female" church is close to the reality for the early twentieth century institutions in many parts of Natal, the actual disparity was in reality offset by the Durban and Johannesburg churches, two of the larger congregations in the mission, which were almost exclusively composed of men—a matter of discussion in later chapters.

THE CHRISTIAN WALK

In 1860, *amakholwa* from across the stations of the AZM gathered together to attend their annual meeting and voted to sponsor, for the first time, one of their own as a missionary. Mbiyana Ngidi, the man they selected, was a "promising" man from Itafamasi, one of the smaller and poorer AZM stations. In response to their call Mbiyana uprooted himself and his family and the following year established a church alongside the Ihlimbiti, a remote river a healthy horseback ride from Mapumulo, itself one of the most far-flung of the AZM stations.[102] Ihlimbiti had no wagon access and there was little for Mbiyana to gain materially from the experience, but for him the calling of his faith was sufficient. His commitment to working for this faith was unique; other Christians had just begun profiting from their identity as middle men and were unwilling to devote themselves to evangelization. Yet his experience of the faith was similar to those of nearly every other convert. Like others, Mbiyana attended weekly prayer meetings and Bible studies, sang hymns in popular monthly concerts, and attended the Sabbath. The weekly sermon at the Sunday service provided Mbiyana and others with a roadmap with which *amakholwa* charted their Christian walk. At Itafamasi, as throughout the mission, converts also met prior to the Sunday service. Here, away from the traditionalists who, particularly during the earlier years, attended the primary service, converts gathered in celebration of their community, sharing prayer with each other.[103] It was moments like these, in the predawn stillness of brisk Natal Sunday mornings, in which *amakholwa* forged community.

For the earliest converts, life in the church was a daily affair. At Umvoti in 1846, station residents attended a nightly Bible study. Aldin Grout came to these with small fragments of scripture translated into Zulu, and the assembled group, twenty to thirty in all, listened as Grout read them and then revealed the kernel of doctrinal truth contained in each; not, however, without comment from the gathered, for much discussion frequently followed.[104] At Umlazi in 1849, converts attended daily prayer meetings, participation evidence that they had become "truly the Children of God."[105] At each of the early stations converts demonstrated a similar commitment to their spiritual lives, attending daily prayer meetings, biweekly catechism classes (in which they mulled over such subjects as "Christ's sermon on the Mount; What must I do to be saved?; Paul the doorkeeper; Is your head right?; The African servant; and The backslider") and Saturday gatherings designed to prepare their hearts for the Sabbath.[106] The creation of their faith permeated their daily lives.

Inevitably, the *amakholwa* community could not keep up such a vigorous pace of religious observance and by the middle of the 1850s the daily prayer meetings and Bible studies slowed into weekly, and on some stations, monthly events. Faith became routine, a part of their identity if not necessarily the central component.[107] At Umvoti, residents still gathered to expound on the scriptures, but by 1855 they did so once a week in each other's newly constructed homes, the delight and perhaps competition of hosting edging into ground once solely reserved for the spiritual. In place of the bi-weekly catechism classes a committee, elected by members of the church, rotated through the homes of each of the station residents and chatted with them about their Christian walk.[108] As the concerns of daily life intervened, individuals became less able, and even less willing, to devote the time they once had to their faith. We will return to the question of the centrality of faith when discussing the revival and the goals of those who led it.

As faith became more formalized and *amakholwa* became occupied by business interests off the station, Sunday became critical in knitting together the community. Throughout the nineteenth century, *amakholwa* met early, often at sunrise, to hold prayer meetings prior to the main service. These services, led by believers, were generally quiet affairs, filled with quiet prayers offered up by individuals for the community, each other, and themselves. They were meant to purify the heart for the coming service but they also acted as a unifying force, defining who belonged in the community and what their concerns might be. Christians offered up prayers for successful pregnancies, good crops, absolution of sins, and conversion of friends and family.[109] The primary service, often lasting several hours, took place in midmorning and in the early years missionaries frequently performed before packed houses of hundreds, with overflow audiences sitting on the floor, standing behind the lectern, and even straining to hear from outside the church doors under the shade of thorn trees.[110] As the novelty wore off, attendance dwindled to church members and those interested in becoming so, missionaries, and later Zulu preachers and pastors. The service remained largely the same through most of AZM history, centered on a sermon (designed to provide listeners with an understanding of God's expectations and how to meet them) and with hymns and formal prayers scattered throughout. Communion, usually a monthly affair, provided church members the opportunity to demonstrate their good standing publicly and it was treated with solemn respect. Over the course of the century the original Sunday school, held immediately after the service to reinforce the tenets learned that day, gave way to Sunday evening meetings in the homes of believers for prayer, tea, and coffee.[111]

As the *amakholwa* community reduced the daily exercise of faith into more manageable weekly meetings, the importance of large ceremonies in defining the identity of the community grew proportionately. Weddings, in particular, were occasions of great celebration with couples bound together in church, promising to lead "civilized and Christian lives," and raise Christian families.[112] In one of the first *amakholwa* marriages, the bride and groom held a relatively simple celebration in Umvoti's one room schoolhouse with eighty others, *amakholwa* and traditionalist, in attendance. After a brief service the missionary served a wedding cake made of corn meal and sweetened with raisins. The assembled drank gallons of coffee with their cake and went away happy.[113] By the end of the century *amakholwa* constructed weddings as both internal affairs, designed to bring the community together in celebration of their shared beliefs, and external events that demonstrated to traditionalists the benefits of Christian living. In a particularly elaborate affair in 1882, two couples shared a double wedding at Umsumduzi. The brides, dressed in blue and white Japanese silk dresses complete with veils and orange blossoms, entered into the church followed by little girls holding their trains.[114] Once the service, conducted by Josiah Tyler with assistance from Zulu preachers, was complete, the brides marched out of the chapel, itself decorated with flowers and greens, to the music of a concertina. After a feast of two oxen, goats, sweet potatoes, pumpkins, bread, and beer, in which the *amakholwa* community sat together at tables and chairs while their traditionalist neighbors gathered under the shade of nearby trees, the couples opened their wedding gifts. The presents, including a bedstead, bureau, metal teapot, and a table complete with chairs and a woven cover, further reinforced the couple's identity.[115]

Births which lead to baptisms, puberty which led to first communions, conversion which brought both bundled together—the passages of life were marked by official church events that were all occasions for the community to come together and celebrate itself. These private events were reinforced by the seasons of the church. Christ's birth was celebrated at Christmas, his death on Good Friday and resurrection at Easter; these occasions provided *amakholwa* with an opportunity to affirm and demonstrate their faith, and in doing so to affirm their identity as Zulu Christians. Other events, such as the opening of a new church at Umzumbe in 1870, were widely celebrated. The missionary at Umzumbe titled his sermon "The Lord is in this place" and the congregation demonstrated why, praying and singing to consecrate the brick and thatch structure as a house of God.[116] At Esidumbini in 1869, the church celebrated the end of the school year with a feast. The seventy-five children who had attended the day school received small hand-made presents at a celebration in which 175 others attended.[117] *Amakholwa*, fifty-nine in all, sat at properly set tables, eating, laughing and sharing boiled beef, corn, toast, and cake. For *amabhinca* in attendance, a large ox was provided and they sat in the nearby grass, watching their *amakholwa* neighbors break bread together.

Death provided one final opportunity for individual *amakholwa* to demonstrate their faith and for the community to close ranks and honor their own. When Ukalo, a member of the Umvoti congregation, finally succumbed to a long illness, those *amakholwa* with him at his passing noted at his funeral that he was prepared for death, that he spoke of his trust in Christ, and that death held no terrors for him because of his faith that death simply removed him from a world of sin and transformed "him into a state of spotless purity and happiness." When death finally overtook him he "quietly yielded his life to God who gave it."[118] This Christian interpretation of death attracted Zulu not just for the self, but also for the hope that the community of believers was translated into an afterlife.

In December of 1851, nearly a hundred Zulu Christians from the AZM gathered at Ifumi, to celebrate the anniversary of the first missionaries landing in Natal.[119] Perhaps more importantly, the occasion allowed *amakholwa* from stations across the colony to convene and celebrate their community. The gathering lasted from Thursday to Sunday and members from all the stations arrived to take part. Friday included prayer services and *amakholwa* going out, two by two, among the surrounding *amabhinca* to invite them to the Sunday service. Christians then met on Saturday for a long meeting in which they prayed for the presence and refreshment of God's spirit. On Sunday morning, Christians gathered together before sunrise and marched around to every house on the station to pray for and with its residents; the long, snaking column of *amakholwa* growing with each stop. The Sunday service, attended by some 700 participants (most of them curious traditionalists) was addressed by the station missionary, who referred to the assembled crowd as "the largest and most interesting congregation I had yet seen in Africa." When the service ended and the *amabhinca* departed, *amakholwa* gathered for communion; the shared bread and wine serving as one of the strongest symbols of faith and community for the gathered, much as it had for centuries of Christians everywhere.

In 1862, a decade later, the Native Annual Meeting (NAM) as it came to be known, had evolved from the initial simple service into a more formalized event. Rotating through stations able to handle the strain of hosting the multi-day affair (it was rarely held on any but the largest of the stations), Ifumi once again rolled out the red carpet. This time 150 *amakholwa* attended. Once again a Friday prayer meeting was held, although without the evangelization campaign of a decade earlier. The following day was given over to the business of the community. In particular much discussion accompanied the Native Home Missionary Society (NHMS) established at the previous year's NAM by *amakholwa* eager to formalize their responsibility to spread the faith, and for whose operation £50 had been raised. With this fund the NHMS intended to sponsor two *amakholwa* missionaries at £2 a month, although, at least initially, only Mbiyana Ngidi volunteered. I would argue that the founding of the NHMS, part of a sense of the religious obligation to proselytize, also signified a significant shift in *amakholwa* society away from a sense of personal obligation to spread the word. Previously, as seen in the earliest NAM and on occasion at many of the mission stations, Zulu Christians had felt obligated to preach to their traditionalist neighbors. In formalizing this process through the establishment of the NHMS, *amakholwa* translated this duty into financial support for "their" missionary. This effectively released them from evangelical expectations and freed up time to attend to more profitable ventures.[120]

The 1862 NAM, like its predecessor, was very much an African affair, American missionaries stayed in the shadows, offering up a few sermons but otherwise left the event to *amakholwa* preachers who led both the sacred and secular meetings. Little changed in the following years and the NAM only grew in importance through the years of this work, one of the few occasions *amakholwa* gathered together from throughout Natal (and beyond) to celebrate their community and to conduct business. It also offered an opportunity for *amakholwa* to police the borders of their community, clarifying what it meant to Zulu Christians in the churches of the AZM even as, by the end of the century, they became far less heterogeneous.

Given the costs of doing so it is perhaps surprising that those who hosted the event often did so with enthusiasm. When the NAM was finally held at Umtwalume in 1881, for example, the community there spent three months preparing for it.[121] Residents bought wood from an American sailing vessel marooned off the nearby coast and built fifteen new homes for fear that the old ones were too small to hold all the guests or too dilapidated to entertain properly. Christian craftsmen turned left-over lumber into doors and larger tables. And sixty American chairs were purchased to insure that every Christian guest could sit at these newly fashioned tables. Larders were stocked with tea, coffee, flour, sugar, and curries. On several occasions, *amakholwa* women made the 150-mile trek to Durban to purchase cloth that they then turned into sashes for windows, banners for the church, and fine new clothing. When guests finally arrived they found Umtwalumi transformed, a model Christian village filled with model Christians, their clothes, their homes, their expression of faith all speaking to their choice of identity. But constructing this ideal came at a cost, nearly impoverishing the residents of Umtwalume, creating doubts as to the purpose, and raising indignation that after demonstrating their capability they remained under mission control.

WHOSE COMMUNITY?

In 1884 Ntoyi, an older girl from the location surrounding Inanda, ran away from the home of her parents to join the Inanda boarding school for girls. Her parents, horrified by this development, met with Mary Edwards to protest, but to no avail and Ntoyi spent the school year at Inanda. She proved to be an exceptional student, one of the brightest at Inanda and, after declaring her conversion during the year, one of the most devout. Still, Edwards was nervous about her returning home during the summer break, knowing that many girls failed to return for a second year after succumbing to family pressures or losing interest. Edwards, more than most missionaries, understood the instability of the early *amakholwa* identity; that belief ebbed and waned and that a sense of familial responsibility tugged at the heart of even the most dedicated Christians. She needn't have worried about Ntoyi howerver, who returned for a second year as committed to her new faith as ever. Later Edwards heard that the *amakholwa* preacher/teacher stationed near Ntoyi's home had been asked if her friends and family had opposed her conversion and her return to Inanda for a second year: "O they can't any longer," he explained, "They have been overcome for a longtime."[122]

By the middle of the 1880s it seems reasonable to apply this comment, meant as an explanation for Ntoyi's return to Inanda, to the entire *amakholwa-amabhinca* relationship; antipathy toward *amakholwa* had dissipated. This shift represented a significant step from earlier comments disparaging their prospects, "in adopting such a course they must always be poor, despised starving people," or their confused identity: "Did they not know that they were black men?"[123] The assumption made by most was that only whites could live as *amakholwa* proposed to do—that Zulu culture and identity were inseparable from the color of their skin, their language, their heritage, their identity. For years the perception of *amakholwa* as poor, pitiable, confused, and perhaps even insane held.

But with success in the Colonial world came an image transformed, grudging respect, and even admiration. Not surprisingly this occurred first at Umvoti where, as early as 1857, *amabhinca* interacting with *amakholwa* from the mission reserve often referred to them as "*amakhosi.*"[124] Grout attributed this shift in traditionalist attitudes to the ability of *amakholwa* to adapt to the new economic reality of Natal, noting that they "now see that a man with oxen and plow are able to cultivate more than a man with several wives and this makes him wealthier, and that a man with a wagon can bring his goods right to the best markets." Here again one finds a correlation drawn by missionaries between civilization and Christianity, between the idea that Christianity allowed one to access civilization just as civilization was a necessary component of a Christian identity. It is not surprising that, given this persistent emphasis, *amakholwa* came to view the acquisition of the "things" of civilization as a necessary, and at times sufficient condition of Christianity. Indeed, in 1861 the AZM proudly proclaimed that those outside of the church could see that those who have "forsaken all for Christ do receive manifold more in this present time."[125] This thought was reinforced by the increased social and economic flexibility evidenced by *amakholwa* during bad times, such as the drought that struck Mapumulo in 1867, during which Christians avoided famine by employing plows to plant much larger areas—and then were able to profit from the plight of their traditionalist neighbors by hauling in foodstuff for sale from unaffected lands.[126]

But material wealth alone did not mitigate traditionalist judgment of the *amakholwa* community, something missionaries in their rush to equate Christianity with civilization misunderstood. Just as important to this process was the ability of traditionalist and *amakholwa* to work out where this new community was located within the intricate web of relationships that structured Zulu society. Traditionalists initially reacted angrily to family members converting, at least in part because doing so created gaps in the Zulu social chain; losing a son or brother, a daughter or sister, a friend, created reverberations felt by all. Homestead heads, as already seen, felt great frustration at their converted children's loss of respect, occasionally worried about the loss of labor from their sons, and despaired over what conversion meant for the *lobola* prospects of their daughters. But this was only the beginning, for mothers needed to worry about loss of seniority if children abandoned them.[127] Brothers feared that a Christian sibling would refuse his responsibility to marry one's widowed wives (and thus ensure the wellbeing of both the women and their children) should one pass away. And losing a friend to the mission station could mean losing the support of an individual in the same age-regiment as oneself, weakening the strategic alliances built up along generational lines.

The uncertainty of how these individuals, who were seemingly lost but still occupied visible ground, fit or did not fit into the social web undoubtedly generated considerable anxiety. But as each side began to resolve the liminal status of the *amakholwa* community, allowing many *amakholwa* to translate their newfound wealth into respectable positions within traditionalist society, this angst lessened. Missionaries came close to understanding this when, in 1861, they noted that traditionalist hostility to the Christian message had diminished only after Zulu realized that Christians did not renounce their friends and family after conversion and instead simply avoided some of their customs.[128]

Part of this shift is also attributable to *amabhinca* accepting *amakholwa* as uniquely positioned to serve as intermediaries to the western world. After the first decade, traditionalists sought out believers, not missionaries, when they wanted western medicine, needed to change money, or wanted to sell chickens, produce, and other products.[129] Recognizing the advantages of the plow, traditionalists hired Christians to turn over their fields and, as we have already seen, sold their crops to *amakholwa* traders. Later, as the benefits of education became clear, local chiefs hired *amakholwa* teachers for higher salaries than those paid by the mission. One such chief, some twenty miles from the nearest mission station, hired a Christian teacher and then sent along two of his sons to continue their education when the Christian returned home.[130] Both *amakholwa* and *amabhinca* also came to believe that Christians held a responsibility to act as Zulu representatives to the Natal government. In the early 1880s an *inkosi* near Umzumbe called on his Christian brother and the local missionary to help him secure his land against white settlers; the sort of task *amakholwa* increasingly found themselves called on to perform.[131] The net result of these interactions was that by the middle of the 1880s, a missionary reported that the "fear of friends or family becoming Christian—is mostly a thing of the past."[132]

For *amakholwa* the anxiety of this relationship was a trickier issue, for they were expected to maintain a certain level of "civilization" as part of their Christianity. Marriages and other ceremonies proved to be particularly perilous occasions when dancing and drinking were expected of all participants not only for the enjoyment of it, but also as a way to bring the blessing of the ancestors down on the new household. Even everyday interactions could be fraught occasions; one *amakholwa* asked his missionary,

> What shall I do when I am out, for instance, on a journey among the people, and they offer such food as they have, perhaps the flesh of an animal which has been slaughtered in honor of the *amadhlozi*? If I eat it they will say: 'See there, he is a believer in our religion; he partakes with us of the meat offered to our gods.' And if I do not eat, they will say, 'See there, he is a believer in the existence and power of our gods, else why does he hesitate to eat of the meat which we have slaughtered to them?'[133]

Amakholwa negotiated their way through such difficult problems by compromising. At Umzumbe, in 1852, *amakholwa* went to feasts, received meat from the slaughtered sacrifice, but did not publicly thank the *amadhlozi*, instead praising God "in their hearts."[134]

But, in attempting to balance a new belief with continued family relations, *amakholwa* frequently found they faced far more troubling challenges. In 1862 the poor family of a deathly sick man asked one of his sons, a Christian resident of Esidumbini who had done relatively well for himself, to contribute a cow that would then be sacrificed by an *isanusi* in the search for a cure.[135] The traditionalist family was shocked by the son's initial refusal to contribute the animal and raised the question of what others would say if his father died after he had refused to help. Here Christian faith bumped directly into traditional belief and made negotiation between the two nearly impossible. The son recognized that either way he acted someone would question his standing and ultimately chose blood over spirit by providing the sacrificial beast.

The breadth of Zulu kinship meant that even second and third generation *amakholwa* were not free of difficult familial expectations. At Umsumduzi one Christian couple, he the son of Christian parents and she the daughter of one of the church's first converts, found themselves under increasing pressure from their extended kin after three of their four children died in infancy. Death, relatives suggested to the young couple, was tied to the station and unless they moved away they should expect their remaining child to pass away as well. The couple stayed, but risked complete rejection by traditionalist relatives if their son had died.[136] That the relationship with *amabhinca* took much longer, and proved much more difficult, for *amakholwa* to resolve is evidenced by Jwili's sermon (discussed above in the case of Sarah,) in which he admonished his fellow Christians "Be ye not unequally yoked together with unbelievers."[137] A marital message that, for most *amakholwa*, likely resonated across many aspects of their lives.

The difficulties Zulu believers experienced in their relationship with traditionalists were replicated in their efforts to integrate into settler society. It is fairly clear that early *amakholwa* did not expect full acceptance into an English identity, or even a white settler in Natal one; their relationships, at work, in the church, and at home, continued to be largely with other Zulu and for this reason the politics of settler Natal seem to have concerned them very little during the formative years of the community.[138] But, as we will explore further in the following chapter, as the twentieth century approached many of their hard won symbols of Westernization; land ownership, exemptions from native law, tax breaks, freedom from *isibhalo*, were slowly stripped away by the white settler community. The granting of responsible government to Natal in 1893 went far towards making untenable the slender claim *amakholwa* staked out for membership in the "civilized" community.

Not that *amakholwa* always sought such inclusion. The early white settlers were themselves a rough lot and missionaries regularly characterized them as drunken womanizers, greedy for African land and, in particular, jealous of the successes regularly achieved by African Christians. Missionaries worried that residents from stations located near large populations of white settlers, such as Inanda, Table Mountain, and Umvoti, suffered from "the evils of such proximity."[139] For their part, *amakholwa* found the name of the religion they professed smeared by whites who professed the faith but did not live by its tenants; *amabhinca* were quick to note that white settlers got drunk, lied, stole, swore, and broke the Sabbath and still called themselves Christian. Particularly troubling for *amakholwa*, was when these same settlers reacted with hostility towards their efforts to advance themselves. When the government proposed building the sugar mill at Umvoti, residents there hoped that their industriousness would demonstrate the value of their Christianity to the economic development of Natal. But angry letters appeared in the Durban paper condemning the proposal and demanding that no special aid be given to Zulu Christians.[140]

The general hostility towards *amakholwa* grew over the course of the century. In 1894 a missionary recently arrived from America stood dumbfounded when a white neighbor at Umzumbe confidently asserted: "You must admit that they have no souls."[141] The roots of this hostility ran deep into the "scientific racism" that underlay almost all official discourse emanating from white South Africa about the "native question."[142] But several other factors should not be discounted. Particularly, as mentioned above, *amakholwa* offered significant competition to white farmers. Both outproducing them and being able to move in and out of Western and traditionalist worlds, the years leading up to the Anglo-Zulu war saw *amakholwa* generate wealth at a rate that angered their white neighbors. *Amakholwa* also did not readily fit into the paternalistic model settlers assumed, for they were educated, Christian, at times wealthy, and demanded more respect than the majority of whites were prepared to offer any blacks. A letter titled "Our Blight" in the Natal Mercury captures the frustration of this unrealized paternalism:

> I wish again to call attention to the misery all classes of white people are enduring through the chronic and useless attempts to Christianize their native servants. This training thoroughly unfits them for honest hard work and the natives become, as a rule, a despicable, treacherous, drunken, cowardly, immoral worthless lot and if this course is pursued by a few misguided beings, the gaol accommodations will have to be increased for their proselytes.[143]

This rejection by "civilized" society chafed *amakholwa* sensibility, but it was later efforts by the Natal government to cut away the few privileges they enjoyed which neatly dismantled their sense of "belonging" in Western society and which provoked a crises of identity that led *amakholwa* to reexamine the nature of their faith during the revivals held at the turn of twentieth century.

The inclusion *amakholwa* sought, and failed to find, from the white community of Natal was gladly taken from another, unlikely source; the world body of believers they found themselves in communion with. Joining the church at Umvoti or Inanda, or even the furthest outstations of Umsumduzi or Mapumulo, meant converts became part of something much larger than their own local mission station, or even the American Zulu Mission— a global community that believed in much the same truths as they. Learning to read and write signified one's Christianity, but putting pen to paper and claiming a place alongside Christians the world over provided *amakholwa* with a surprisingly powerful affirmation of their new identity. So, in the middle of the nineteenth century, members of the Umvoti congregation heard of the ABM mission in Gabon and sought to reach out to their brothers in Christ. The letter, opening with a note informing the congregation that the residents of Umvoti had donated £3 towards the work in Gabon, moved on quickly to establishing the place of *amakholwa* in the wider Christian world, asking the people of Gabon how many believers were in their body and describing their own history and the particulars of their church. "Have you sickness?" the letter continued, attempting to determine how these people, like them, but not, fit into their world view, what did they eat, wear, learn? The letter concluded by asking that the Gabon congregation respond and appealed to their shared faith by concluding: "May ye be happy and adhere constantly to God, it be to the end, it be in the end ye enter heaven."[144]

Where *amabhinca* depended on age-regiments as sources of support beyond kinship, *amakholwa* turned to their faith to provide connections well beyond their home congregations. Members of one station visiting another were received with open arms and outright moves from station to station were not infrequent. More importantly being part of a larger body of believers known as "Protestants" allowed members of the AZM to settle on stations run by other denominations and vice versa, and the churches frequently recorded new members entering in good standing from the other mission bodies of Natal.[145] Their faith also provided *amakholwa* with an easy means of organizing themselves for security and support. Christians from the AZM working in Durban, and later Johannesburg, organized themselves into congregations well before the mission responded to their calls for such action. These urban churches drew their membership from across the stations of the AZM and other mission bodies, and put them in the same pews together singing hymns that proclaimed their shared faith.

This sense of being part of something larger often lay lightly over the *amakholwa* community. While local issues certainly dominated their concerns, events that connected them with the worldwide body of believers drew dramatic responses from *amakholwa*. Prior to the Weavers revivals, one of the most fervent religious experiences within the AZM was the "World's Prayer Meeting." It was first proposed by "brethren in Northern India" as a week of prayer in which Christians from every corner of the globe prayed for the "conversion of the world." The first such event, held in 1860, captured the *amakholwa* imagination and stirred many toward previously unfelt depths of religious conviction. For a half a decade this week of prayer held every January became a central event on all the stations; with twice daily prayer meetings, confession of sins, and prayers offered up not just for each other and their church, but for "all of Christ's church on earth" and for all who had yet to believe, whether they be in Zululand or Turkey.[146] The World's Prayer Meeting produced such a sharp burst of religious fervor because, like the revival to follow, it captured the imagination of the community by placing them within a movement in which the one aspect of their community that held together all the strands of their identity, their faith, stood paramount. For one intense week, *amakholwa* became an integral part of a worldwide body of believers, their participation evidence of their universal Christian identity.

After a decade, however, the initial fervor attached to the World's Prayer Meeting faded. For nearly two decades, this annual event limped along before being abandoned altogether. But for the next forty years Africans and missionaries alike sought without success to replicate the intense emotions aroused by the World's Prayer Meeting. As the churches of the AZM slid into a decade's long funk, these efforts became more urgent. But missionaries proved ignorant of their own fault in this growing malaise. Their insistence on morally "pure" congregations in particular, lay at the heart of the troubles and not until the revivals at the end of the century did *amakholwa* engage with their faith with the same fervor.

NOTES

1. This is the same Ntaba Luthuli mentioned in the previous chapter who struggled with the message for two months after hearing a sermon by Grout. Untaba's early Christian life is pieced together from various sources. See, particularly, ABM 175/67 L. Grout to Anderson, June 22, 1846; ABM 175/859, L. Grout to Anderson, March 1, 1847; ABM 175/871-2, L. Grout to Anderson, April 24, 1848.

2. These are frequently referred to as "upright" homes in the mission correspondence; presumably less because those who lived in them were expected to live "upright" lives than that the frame of the house stood straight-up, vertical to the ground unlike traditional Zulu homes which used interlacing staves planted in the ground at one end and curved until they could be planted again at their terminus.

3. Luthuli, teaching in conjunction with Grout, worked with a class ranging from twenty-five to seventy children a day, depending on the weather, the depth of the nearby river, and the state of the crops. Under the shade of a large thorn tree he conducted reading and spelling exercises for the better part of a year. *Amakholwa*

later built a small school and two other teachers took his place. ABM 175/859, A. Grout to Anderson, March 1, 1847.

4. Mofokeng, "Black Christians" 34; Jean and John Comaroff, *Revelation and Revolution*. See, particularly, chapter 6, in which they elaborate on what they mean by "colonization of consciousness."

5. Gerald West, "Mapping African Biblical Interpretation," 51.

6. Benjamin Pine, the lieutenant governor of Natal, issued a directive in 1854 declaring that all natives entering or living in Durban, Pietermaritzburg or Ladysmith, and all those appearing before any of the colony's magistrates, were required to be clothed "from shoulder to knee" in blanket, shirt or other material. Despite this law it remained a common assumption by colonists, even into the next century, that dressed Zulu were Christian. Later, missionaries frequently cautioned that a crime committed by a clothed Zulu did not necessarily implicate an *amakholwa*. ABM 175/506, copy of proclamation by Benjamin Pine, February 8, 1854.

7. Understandably, losing articles of clothing often signified a return to "heathenism." A young man at Ifumi, who had shown great promise as a catechist, brought William Ireland to grief when, before returning home to visit a sick relative, he chose to remove his Western clothing and dress "in the native style." Ireland believed, probably correctly, that this meant he was unlikely to return. ABM 175/1079, Ireland to Anderson, January 1, 1852.

8. ABM 175/653, Adams to Anderson, October 1, 1847.

9. ABM 175/27, Adams to Anderson, September 28, 1846.

10. ABM 177/180, Umtwalumi station report, 1866–67.

11. Although even then, during the early years, the process did not always extend outside of the church walls. Aldin Grout happily reported in 1848 that seventy five people had recently appeared at Sunday service "clad very decently" and that those same people *usually* dressed while working during the day. ABM 176/928, A. Grout to Anderson, September 12, 1848.

12. ABM 175/27, Adams to Anderson September 28, 1846; ABM 185–805, Wilder to Means, August 7, 1881. Not to be outdone, young *amakholwa* women began wearing skirts fashioned after the kilts of the Scottish regiments involved in the Zululand campaigns.

13. ABM 178/470, L. Grout to Anderson, April 10, 1860. One missionary, in defending his congregation's dress, noted that while there were instances of "foolish and ostentatious" displays, in his estimation the remarks made against the clothing worn by *amakholwa* represented more of an attack on contemporary Western civilization than a legitimate concern about the conduct of the Zulu Christians. ABM 184/327, Harris to Smith, March 28, 1889.

14. As at least one account of the event goes, it was the Afrikaner ignorance of Zulu stick-fighting prowess that cost Retief and his men their lives. When they arrived at Dingane's kraal he ordered them to be killed, but warned his council, "I shall not order the men to carry assegais in case the Boers become suspicious. They must carry dancing shields (*amahau*), and not war shields (*izihlangu*), and also *izikwili* sticks." C. Webb and J. B. Wright, (eds.), *The James Stuart Archive of Recorded Oral Evidence Relating to the History of the Zulu and Neighbouring Peoples Volume V* (Pietermaritzburg: University of Natal Press, 2001), 7.

15. Thanks to Benedict Carton for clarifying the rather opaque rules and nature of stick-fighting for this section.

16. The sobering of *amakholwa* clothing is most evident in the pictures from this period. See, for example, AZM A/4/57, picture of students from Amanzimtoti; *Missionary Herald*, "The Zulu in South Africa," February 1902, 61–62; *Missionary Herald*, "The Zulus; Welcome to the American Board's Deputation," September 1903, 389–92.

17. In the first decade of the mission, there are a handful of scattered references to "family altars" built within *amakholwa* homes. It is difficult to say, however, if these were emulations of spaces *amakholwa* observed in mission households, places where Bibles were stored and crosses hung, or if they were a conscious attempt by Zulu Christians to take an aspect of traditional faith and adapt it to their new lives. Most likely, of course, it was both.

18. ABM 175/653, Adams to Anderson, October 1, 1847. In later years, on rare occasions, Christian women, married to traditional men, convinced them to move onto stations and then into the church. But, particularly before the Anglo-Zulu war, this process was a one-sided affair involving *amakholwa* men and traditional women.

19. ABM 178/435, AZM annual report, 1867–68. However, with sixty-eight western style homes, Umvoti was significantly ahead of any of the other stations. There is a clear link between the number of houses on a station and its relative wealth. Those stations closest to Durban, such as Inanda, Umvoti and Amanzimtoti, where economic opportunities were both more diversified and easier to access, had the greatest number of upright houses in the 1868 count. *Amakholwa* located on the peripheral stations, particularly those in southern Natal, evidenced their relative poverty in the lack of these homes. Only six homes had been constructed at Ifafa, eleven at Amahlongwa and none at Umzumbe. At Mapumulo, the northernmost station of the AZM, nearly eighteen years passed between the construction of the first and the sixth. ABM 177/315, Mapumulo annual report, 1866–67.

20. Webb and Wright, *James Stuart Archive Volume 3*, 229, 232.

21. ABM 188/88, Groutville station report, 1890–91.

22. ABM 177/179, Umtwalumi station report, 1866–67.

23. Lewis Grout, *Zululand, or, Life Among the Kaffirs*, 99.

24. ABM 176/318, L. Grout to Anderson, September 2, 1852.

25. ABM 176/928, A. Grout to Anderson, September 12, 1848; ABM 177/472, Wilder to Anderson, June 13, 1853.

26. In particular *amakholwa* did not hesitate to write to missionaries who were on leave or retired in America, in order to update them on events and gossip, or even to complain about treatment at the hands of newly arrived missionaries. For their part the early missionaries, filled with a paternalistic sense of ownership over "their" stations, occasionally passed on complaints from *amakholwa* to the Secretary of the American Board. This developing connection into the wider world through the medium of their faith is an important aspect of the development of an *amakholwa* identity discussed in more detail later in this chapter.

27. ABM 184/683, Kilbon to Means, August 11, 1881.

28. Jeff Guy, "The Destruction and Reconstruction of Zulu Society," in Shula Marks and Richard Rathbone (eds.), *Industrialisation and Social Change in South*

Africa: African Class Formation, Culture and Consciousness, 1870–1930 (New York: Longman, 1982), 189–190; Lewis Grout, *Zululand*, 97–98.

29. ABM 177/172, Umtwalumi station report 1859–60. Not only was food scanty, but also grimly routine. Christians at Umtwalume found that their choice to clothe themselves left them unable to afford meat or milk and put sugar and tea, a staple of many Christian households, into the realm of unrealized longing.

30. ABM 177/206, Umsumduzi station report, 1866–67; ABM 177/182 Umtwalumi station report, 1866–67; ABM 179/520, Pixley to Anderson, June 14, 1864.

31. ABM 184/246, A. Grout to Smith, October 12, 1886.

32. ABM 175/67, A. Grout to Anderson, June 22, 1846; ABM 175/653, Adams to Anderson, October 1, 1847.

33. ABM 176/928, A. Grout to Anderson, September 12, 1848.

34. ABM 175/517–18, AZM annual letter 1855–56. Shortly after this census, lungsickness broke out in Natal, killing fifty of the community's trained oxen.

35. Keletso Atkins has argued for an early adoption of English money by Zulu, noting, I think significantly, that the lungsickness epidemic of 1855 opened the door for many to rethink the primacy of cattle as the "big note" in the Zulu economy. She has, however, overstated the depth, both geographically and culturally, of this shift. Certainly as late as the end of the nineteenth century, young men continued to contract their labor out in return for payments made in cattle. Instead it seems likely that the combination of rinderpest and Johannesburg dealt the most serious blow to the primacy of cattle in the traditional household economy. Atkins, *The Moon is Dead*, 95–97.

36. This was no small matter, as a wagon, the oxen to pull it, and the accompanying tack, could run upwards of £90. The sheer cost encouraged many *amakholwa* to pool their resources, and many of the carts and wagons on the mission stations during its first half-decade were owned cooperatively.

37. C. B. Webb and J. B. Wright, *The James Stuart Archive of Oral Evidence Relating to the History of the Zulu and Neighbouring Peoples, volume II*, (Pietermaritzburg: University of Natal Press, 1979), 8, 207–209.

38. Charles Ballard, "A Reproach to Civilisation": John Dunn and the Missionaries; 1879–1884," *South African Historical Journal* 9 (1977), 45.

39. For most of the nineteenth century, white farmers struggled to meet the needs of the growing colony and it was up to African and later Indian peasants to fill the gap. Charles Ballard and Giuseppe Lenta, "The Complex Nature of Agriculture in Colonial Natal: 1860–1909," and Joy Brain, "Indentured and Free Indians in the Economy of Colonial Natal," in Bill Guest and John Sellers (eds.) *Enterprise and Exploitation in a Victorian Colony: Aspects of the Economic and Social History of Colonial Natal* (Pietermaritzburg: University of Natal Press,1985).

40. ABM 177/366, Personal Interview with L. Grout, undated; ABM 178/462–463, 473, L. Grout to Anderson, April 10, 1860. In a ceremony to mark his daughter's leaving Natal on a missionary trip to Inhambane (now Moputo, Mozambique), Maziana, a local preacher at Inanda, recalled his own trip to Inhambane as a trader, his first (and seemingly most memorable) trip by sea during which he became so sea-sick that he was sure he, and everyone else on board, would perish. He took

comfort in prayer, arrived alive, and went about his business. ABM 191/483, Ransom to Smith, April 28, 1891.

41. ABM 178/462–63, 473, L. Grout to Anderson, April 10, 1860. Grout penned a scathing critique of some of his fellow missionaries who, he complained, had become little more than middlemen in this trade, lending *amakholwa* money, securing lines of credit for goods, and even, in one case, providing ivory amulets for Christians to trade; all "to be paid, perhaps, in cattle, when the native returns from his expedition to KwaZulu or Emanpondweni."

42. I explore this development within *amakholwa* society in greater depth in my thesis, "Constructing an AmaKholwa Community: Cattle and the Creation of a Zulu Christianity," University of Wisconsin-Madison, 1998. There, I map out the willingness of *amakholwa* to employ cattle in new ways by manipulating both the symbolic and economic aspects of cattle. This use of cattle proved a difficult balance for most to maintain and, as we will see, the temptation to use them to reintegrate fully back into Zulu society as wealthy patrons complete with the polygamous benefits that this entailed proved difficult for many to ignore.

43. ABM 176/545, Umvoti Station Report, June 1858. Competition from large sugar plantations (worked by indentured Indian labor) brought diminishing returns and by the time the government sold the mill twenty years later, the venture had lost some £50,000. The three Umvoti residents who purchased it struggled without success to turn a profit for the latter half of the nineteenth century. Other cash crop projects also came to naught. At Umtwalume the government offered plows at cost to any *amakholwa* who agreed to raise cotton for three years. Three young men took up the offer, but the plants never took and the project died an early death. Attempts to establish arrowroot, tea, and coffee suffered similar fates, victims of bad soil, bad management, and uncooperative markets. ABM 175/987, A. Grout to Anderson, June 3, 1857; ABM 177/68, AZM annual letter, 1862–63; ABM 177/172, Umtwalumi station report, 1860–61; ABM 177/298, Umvoti station report, 1862–63; ABM 178/612, J. Tyler to Clark, April 10, 1876; ABM 188/88, Groutville station report, 1890–91; ABM 190/386–87, Bunker to Friends, January 4, 1897.

44. ABM 175/1089, Ifumi station report, 1853–54; ABM 179/492, M. Pinkerton to Clark, November 10, 1871.

45. ABM 178/462, L. Grout to Anderson, April 10, 1860.

46. ABM 175/975, A. Grout to Anderson, August 24, 1856; ABM 177/294, Umvoti station report, 1860–61; ABM 177/112, Joint Letter of AZM, March 7, 1864. The effects of lungsickness, much more so than the rinderpest plague to follow, were spotty, with some areas of Natal suffering through severe mortality rates while others remained relatively untouched. Still, seven years after the epidemic, missionaries reported that the effects of the disease lingered throughout the colony, with oxen and cows costing 150–300 percent more than they had prior to the outbreak.

47. ABM 180/42, AZM Annual Report for 1868. Two of the residents did so well for themselves that, by 1864, they had each accumulated property worth £1000. In reporting this figure Grout, one of the fiercest promoters of the links between prosperity, civilization, and Christianity, worried that he might soon be called on to

preach against worldliness, although he was then "not yet anxious to do so." ABM 177/301, Station Report for Umvoti, May 1864.

48. Here, of course, I am succumbing to yet another pithy phrase from Norman Etherington, who writes about Frere, "When a bully with a black hat and a moustache is caught with a smoking gun in his hand, posses and juries don't ask very penetrating questions. Frere was the sort of villain cinema audiences love to hate, a sanctimonious, pig-headed, officious, self-righteous, ambitious city slicker from out of town. One hundred years after the event there is no reason to revise this estimate and award him a retrospective white hat and a shave." Norman Etherington, "Anglo-Zulu Relations, 1856–1878" in A. Duminy and C. Ballard (eds.), *The Anglo-Zulu War: New Perspectives* (Pietermaritzburg: University of Natal Press, 1981), 13–14.

49. ABM 183/320, AZM Joint Letter: "Some remarks on Mr. Wilcox's paper on self-support," undated; ABM 212/33, Mrs. Bridgeman to Friends, May 24, 1879. Mrs. Bridgeman voiced her concern that *amakholwa* were spending their sudden wealth on "personal self-indulgences" and not on the spread of the gospel.

50. ABM 177/315, Mapumulo station report, 1866–67.

51. ABM 175/1089, Ireland to Anderson, June 1854.

52. ABM 177/69, AZM annual letter, 1862–63. The previous year so many *amakholwa* were away from Amanzimtoti cutting timber and hauling it into Durban, that the missionary there had been forced to suspend the daily prayer meetings for the first time. ABM 179/325, McKinney to Anderson, March 1, 1862.

53. ABM 184/96, Goodenough to Means, March 31, 1883. The deep financial problems faced by Natal during this period were, for *amakholwa*, exacerbated by interest rates on the wagons they had so recently purchased of up to 60 percent.

54. ABM 188/233, Mapumulo station report, 1893–94. The lure of the rapidly expanding Witwatersrand gold fields provided fresh fodder for missionaries to rail against. As early as 1885 the missionary at Mapumulo preached against the lure of gold wealth. Using Numbers 23:10 he expounded on the story of Balaam who, although commanded by God to have nothing to do with the Moabites, was so enticed by their gold that he fell out of honor and into a life of sin. Pounding the point home he then used Revelation 21:8 to demonstrate the awful results of choosing such a path. ABM 184/382, Holbrook to Smith, February 20, 1885.

55. ABM 175, tabular view for 1853. In 1863 the residents of Umvoti paid the staggering sum of $300 (£75) to hire a private white teacher from Durban. Later, after the boom had gone bust, they paid out the highest salary of any of the churches, £3 per month, to a *amakholwa* graduate of Amanzimtoti. For their part, the residents of Amanzimtoti were able to pay the son of a Scottish Presbyterian £50 for his services during the early 1860s. ABM 177/68, AZM annual letter, 1862–63; ABM 177/74, AZM annual letter, 1863–64.

56. ABM 178/484, L. Grout to Anderson, April 10, 1860. Grout noted elsewhere, that none of the seventeen young men "of faith" previously targeted by Aldin Grout as promising possibilities for the future leadership of Umvoti, had taken up work as either teachers or preachers. ABM 177/366, personal interview with Lewis Grout, undated.

57. ABM 180/40, AZM annual letter 1867–68. The mission reported fourteen *amakholwa* teachers in twenty-one of its day schools. Remarkably, particularly in light of future developments in the last decades of the century, the mission needed to hire eight white teachers from Natal in addition to their own workers from America.

58. ABM 177/318, report of Umbiana's station, 1866–67.

59. ABM 181/206, Amanzimtoti seminary report 1876–77.

60. ABM 184/96, Goodenough to Means, March 31, 1883. In 1883, during the height of the depression, the number of pupils in the primary schools of the AZM dropped sharply and a recommendation was made, but not followed, that the mission establish a discretionary fund to assist *amakholwa* children whose families could not afford to pay the fees.

61. ABM 185/550, tabular view for 1889. While there were teachers and preachers who only performed the one function, such as female teachers or those employed in the schools of the mission glebe churches where missionaries conducted services, generally, those employed as preachers also taught, a dual role that often also provided them with a dual income just sufficient enough to eke out a living.

62. ABM 212/170–71, Edwards to Orcult, July 15, 1881.

63. ABM 184/728, Kilbon to Means, June 19, 1883. Kilbon wrote enthusiastically of the Institute, judging it a "real success."

64. ABM 177/62, AZM annual letter, May 1861.

65. ABM 176/192, L. Grout to Anderson, September 1851.

66. For the figures used in this paragraph please see the tabular views found in ABM 175, 177, and 183.

67. ABM 175/1032, A. Grout to Anderson, June 1859.

68. 175/1032, A. Grout to Anderson, June 1859; ABM 176/545, Mellen to Anderson, June 1858.

69. ABM 175/380, Bryant to Anderson, May 16, 1849.

70. ABM 177/84, AZM annual letter, 1864–65.

71. While there were never sufficient government grants to meet the needs of the schools (in 1868 the total disbursement to the AZM was £409), the AZM slowly, almost inevitably, became addicted to the money. Not until 1903 did the AZM turn down one of these grants. ABM 180/40–42, AZM annual letter, 1867–68.

72. ABM 177/178, Umtwalumi station report, 1866–67.

73. ABM 180/29, AZM annual letter, 1867–68.

74. ABM 175/379, Bryant to Anderson, May 16, 1849.

75. Lewis Grout, *Zululand*, 223.

76. ABM 177/85, AZM Annual Letter, June 1865. The mission press shut down in 1875 as work could be sourced to presses in Durban for much less than the missionaries could do it themselves.

77. ABM 176/186, L. Grout to Anderson, September 1851.

78. ABM 175/500, annual letter of AZM, 1854–55.

79. The majority of the young men (and it was only young men) who were taught at Amanzimtoti during its early years were in their early teens, however a significant number were slightly older. Many of these were accepted less for their

educational record than their spiritual one and the mission hoped they would provide a "leavening" influence over the younger students.

80. ABM 177/228–29, Amanzimtoti Annual Report, May 1869. Ireland reported in May of 1869 that two of his students from the previous term had returned home "beyond the Umzimkulu" the previous Christmas break and not been heard from again. The missionary at Umtwalumi, on the far southern fringe of Natal, expressed a great deal of pride when, in 1867, two of his students decided to attend the high school.

81. By 1888 over 1200 students attended twenty-six schools, a decade earlier barely half this number attended AZM institutions. ABM 183/547, AZM tabular view for 1888.

82. ABM 181/205, Amanzimtoti seminary annual report, 1876–77.

83. ABM 183/287, Schedule of classes for Amanzimtoti Seminary, June 1887, ABM 183/350, Robbins to Smith, February 5, 1885.

84. Ibid.

85. ABM 184/391, Holbrook to Smith, February 20, 1885. Like Amanzimtoti the boarding school took Christians from other denominations, particularly from the Wesleyans, the Church of England, and the Scottish Presbyterians.

86. It has become commonplace to view mission institutions set up for African women as mere "finishing" schools preparing young women to become wives for Christian men, or well-trained servants for white settlers. Benedict Carton, for instance, argues "By the beginning of the twentieth century, some missions were transformed into virtual placement agencies, becoming intermediaries for girls seeking domestic employment and, possibly, a monogamous union with an African convert husband." Implicit in this charge is the notion that missionaries sought to replicate the gender roles of home in southern Africa. Certainly Inanda was not an institution of liberation but, at least in the case of the AZM, this theory fails to take into account that the girls' schools were almost always run by women and women who were often proud and belligerent enough to stand up to pressure from their male peers. Gertrude Hance, an early American teacher at Inanda, argued successfully for a female principal (who would become Mary Edwards) for the school by employing missionary rhetoric against those who argued that only a man could best run the school. Noting her certainty that America could provide a woman who would fill the position better than any man she commented that: "We don't want the natives here to think we are falling into their ways of looking at woman's work." ABM 184/267, Hance to Means, April 8, 1883. Heather Hughes vacillates on this point but ultimately comes to a similar conclusion, noting that while missionaries wanted Inanda to produce women that looked like mission wives, it "did not educate African women for economic subservience . . . " Carton, *Blood From Your Children: The Colonial Origins of Generational Conflict in South Africa* (Charlottesville: University of Virginia, 2000), 75; Hughes, "A Lighthouse for African Womanhood: Inanda Seminary, 1869–1945," in Cheryl Walker (ed.) *Women and Gender in Southern Africa to 1945* (Cape Town: David Philips, 1990), 197.

87. Like Amazimtoti, the AZM at Inanda employed several of the early graduates to great effect. At Inanda Talitha Hawes became something of an institution following her employment in 1876. She was later joined by Dalita Isaac who would, as we will see, play an important role in the later revivals. For a fuller account of these two

Zulu women who played such a critical role in shaping the nature of Christianity in southern Africa see, Meghan Healy, "'Like a Family': Global Models, Familial Bonds, and the Making of an American School for Zulu Girls," *Journal of South African and American Studies* 12 (2010).

88. ABM 181/577–78, Ireland to Clark, January 21, 1874. Lewis Grout, *Zululand*, 215.

89. After graduating, Dr. Nembula returned to South Africa, working first at Lovedale and then at Amanzimtoti. Despite his desire to work with the mission, the AZM could not afford to pay him and he instead became a district surgeon at Umsinga in KwaZulu until his death in 1896 which cut short the life of one of the most gifted members to pass through the mission of any nationality. Briggs and Wing, *The Harvest and the Hope*, 131.

90. ABM 176/928, A. Grout to Anderson, September 12, 1848.

91. 177/301, Station report for Umvoti, May 1863.

92. John Wright, "Control of Women's Labour in the Zulu Kingdom," in J. B. Peires (ed.), *Before and After Shaka: Papers in Nguni History* (Grahamstown: Institute of Social and Economic Research, Rhodes University, 1981).

93. ABM 178/200, Lindley to Anderson, Inanda February 3, 1864.

94. ABM 185/351, Robbins to Means, December 18, 1882.

95. ABM 175/662, Adams to Anderson, September 20, 1849.

96. ABM 184/245, Author unknown to Means, early 1880s.

97. For an insightful account of women's prayer groups see, Deborah Gaitskell, "'Wailing for Purity': Prayer Unions, African Mothers and Adolescent Daughters, 1912–40," in Shula Marks and Richard Rathbone (eds.), *Industrialisation and Social Change in South Africa* (New York: Longman, 1983).

98. Some of these have been discussed in the previous chapter. It should be noted here, however, that the relationship between girl, family, and missionary, created by these instances, was more nuanced than a passing glance might indicate. Missionaries frequently presented these stories as heroic ones involving great anger and fear on the part of all involved. But Mary Edwards, the principal of Inanda, provided a candid glimpse into these encounters when, in 1885, she wrote that not only did she say little when parents arrived at the girls' boarding school attempting to convince their daughters to return, simply warning them not to use violence, but she occasionally advised the same girls to return home, particularly those who were "really needed" for family responsibilities. ABM 185/286, Inanda Annual Report, February 28, 1885.

99. ABM 183/877, Edwards to Smith, August 27, 1888.

100. ABM 191/482, Ransom to Smith, April 28, 1891.

101. Cherryl Walker, "Gender and the Development of the Migrant Labour System c. 1850–1930: An Overview," in Cherryl Walker (ed.), *Women and Gender*, 168–196.

102. ABM 177/61, AZM annual letter, 1860–61.

103. The number of *amabhinca* attending Sunday services dwindled steadily through the middle of the nineteenth century. Still, many continued to participate at least sporadically, drawn by curiosity, by the potential festivity of the occasion, and for a few, by interest in the message being delivered.

104. ABM 175/26, Diary of A. Grout, September 1846. Examples of the sort of questions offered by curious Zulu are found in the previous chapter.

105. ABM 175/662, Adams to Anderson, September 20, 1849.

106. ABM 180/29, AZM Annual Letter, June 1868.

107. Of course, as Weber points out, without such routinization stable social systems cannot emerge. Indeed, daily prayer meetings work against the sort of economic life that must develop and while charismatic leaders can hold a core group of followers to nontraditional practices for a time, eventually even they must step back. Max Weber, *The Theory of Social and Economic Organization* (New York: 1947), 363–369.

108. Discussion of the private faith lives of individual *amakholwa* is largely absent from the missionary literature. This certainly does not mean it did not exist, but it seems clear that public expressions of faith carried more weight both for *amakholwa* and missionaries. The revival, as it did across a wide spectrum of their faith, altered how *amakholwa* thought of private prayer, emphasizing it as a necessary component.

109. ABM 176/545, Umvoti station report, 1857–58; ABM 177/171, Umtwalumi station report, 1860–61.

110. ABM 177/293, Umvoti station report, 1860–61.

111. ABM 175/964, A. Grout to Anderson, June 20, 1855; ABM 176/545, Umvoti station report, 1857–58; ABM 177/171, Umtwalumi station report, 1860–61.

112. ABM 176/163, L. Grout to Anderson, September 1850.

113. ABM 175/27, A. Grout to Anderson, September 28, 1846.

114. ABM 212/674–75, N. Tyler to Friends, September 20, 1882. There is a relatively well-known photo of a double wedding, quite probably this occasion, which historians have employed to suggest the incredible lengths *amakholwa* underwent to demonstrate their Westernization. Converts not only felt obligated to demonstrate their "civilization" to whites, but, more importantly, their Christianity to both traditionalists and to themselves. This celebration, attended by relatively few whites went far less towards demonstrating civilization than it did towards *amakholwa* demarcating their religious and social borders.

115. Although I have made the argument here that this ceremony helped mark a Christian identity, Benedict Carton has suggested in personal correspondence an alternative reading in which *amakholwa* were deliberately echoing the Zulu royal house's *umkhosi* celebration. This "First Fruits" festival both allowed the Zulu community to celebrate the impending harvest, and reinforced the patronage relationship of crown to subject. If Zulu Christians harbored any such grand aspirations as part of this wedding it is not hinted at in any of the primary sources.

116. ABM 189/149, J. Tyler to Clark, June 23, 1870.

117. ABM 180/133, J. Tyler to Clark, January 13, 1869.

118. ABM 178/166, A. Grout to Anderson, October 24, 1864. Deathbed affirmations of faith were favorite narratives of missionaries. That is not to say that they did not resonate within the *amakholwa* community. Those who claimed to feel the "presence of Christ" in their final moments as they headed to a place where "there is no more death, sorrow nor pain" reaffirmed the essential promise of *amakholwa* faith and as the stories passed from lip to lip they brought a sense of conviction to those who shared them. ABM 177/178, Umtwalumi station report, 1866–67.

119. ABM 175/1078, Ireland to Anderson, January 1, 1852; ABM 175/519, AZM Annual Letter, June 1856.

120. Revival, as we will see, reversed this once again and imbued *amakholwa* with a strong sense of obligation to spread the faith.

121. ABM 185/805, Wilder to Means, August 7, 1881.

122. ABM 185/286, Edwards to Smith, February 28, 1885.

123. ABM 175/987, A. Grout to Anderson, June 3, 1857.

124. Ibid.

125. ABM 177/61, AZM annual letter, 1860–61.

126. ABM 177/315, Mapumulo station report, 1866–67.

127. Thanks to Benedict Carton for suggesting this possibility.

128. ABM 177/61, AZM annual letter, 1860–61. The mission wrote: "It is also seen that when a person renounces heathenism, he does not renounce his friends. He has the same affections for them as before, although he can no longer unite with them in their evil customs. It is pleasing in the eyes of the heathen, to see a son supporting his aged parents and caring for his brothers and sisters."

129. ABM 176/316, L. Grout to Anderson, September 2, 1852.

130. ABM 177/75, AZM annual letter, 1863–64.

131. AZM A/1/2, minutes of special meeting, July 28–29, 1885. Despite Dinizulu expressing "great eagerness" the immediate aim of their discussion, to establish a school run either by American or *amakholwa* missionaries, came to naught. But the discussion made it possible, later that decade, for Christians affiliated with the AZM to establish an independent Christian village in KwaZulu at Impapala, just across the border from Mapumulo. Later, the *amakholwa* community led a systematic effort to legitimize the authority of Prince Solomon ka Dinizulu in the hopes that he might act as their spokesmen. The romance attached to the Zulu regency by Christians was not new. As early as 1885 John Hlonono, a prominent Christian of the AZM, met with Soloman's father, Dinizulu during a trading trip across KwaZulu and the two discussed establishing ties between the Zulu monarch, the AZM, and the NHMS.

132. ABM 183/363, Rood to J. Means, June 6, 1883.

133. Lewis Grout, *Zululand*, 89.

134. ABM 176/317, L. Grout to Anderson, September 2, 1852. A tactic the missionary feared would lead *amabhinca* to believe that *amakholwa* continued to believe in the spirits.

135. ABM 181/76, J. Tyler to Anderson, June 29, 1862.

136. ABM 176/612, J. Tyler to Clark, April 10, 1876.

137. ABM 183/877, Edwards to Smith, August 27, 1888.

138. Here, perhaps more than anywhere, I feel somewhat constrained by my mission-based sources which while allowing me to delve deeply into how Zulu naturalized Christianity are much shakier when it comes to the pre-Anglo Zulu war political concerns of the *amakholwa* community.

139. ABM 175/462, AZM annual report, 1851–52. The land hunger of white settlers even led one American to note the moral failings of his own people: "The Anglo-Saxons are notorious for their greed of land, and we have known for years that there has been a feeling among some colonists that the natives have possession

of some lands which should be obtained for the occupation of the white population, lands which are not very distant from towns, or which are rich soil and are thought too valuable for the natives." ABM 185/442, Rood to Smith, November 8, 1886.

140. ABM 176/317, L. Grout to Anderson, September 2, 1852; *Natal Mercury*, Letter to Editor signed "An Observer," July 5, 1860; ABM 177/69, AZM annual letter, 1862–63.

141. ABM 190/66, A. Bigelow to Smith, March 27, 1894.

142. Paul Rich, "Race, Science, and the Legitimization of White Supremacy in South Africa, 1902–1940," *The International Journal of African Historical Studies* 23 (1990): 674. Although American missionaries seem to have been free of the most virulent racism of many white settlers in Natal, Benedict Carton has argued that the Americans were willing to make skin color a marker of civilization. Benedict Carton, "Awaken *Nkulunkulu*," 137–140.

143. Natal Mercury letter quoted in ABM 190/66, A. Bigelow to Anderson, March 27, 1894.

144. ABM 175/480, Letter from the Umvoti Congregation to the Congregation in Gabon.

145. See, for example, ABM 177/171, Umtwalumi station report, 1859–60; ABM 177/187, Pixley to Anderson, November 8, 1866.

146. ABM 177/171, Station Report for Umtwalumi, May 1860; ABM 177/202, Station Report for Ifumi, June 1861; ABM 178/143, A. Grout to Anderson, January 13, 1863.

3

Conflicting Identities

Entering the last decades of the nineteenth century *amakholwa* seemed at peace with the nature of their community. They practiced a muscular Christianity, one in which work and education played an equally important role alongside worship. Using this drive, they carved out a small but lucrative role in the Natal economy, assumed mission responsibilities through the Native Home Missionary Society, and aggressively pursued educational opportunities for themselves and their children. With the profits from their successful businesses, they acquired the things they believed demonstrated their faith, homes, clothes, and the like. Zulu Christians attending church in the 1870s simply needed to glance down the pew at those sitting alongside to know that their neighbors were like them, that they shared a commitment and belief in a world view that made them special in God's eyes. Theirs was an identity to be proud of and to hold dear. But in the last decades of the nineteenth century a variety of forces shattered this carefully constructed identity and the *amakholwa* community was left reeling, wondering what it meant to be Christian and Zulu at a time it seemed increasingly difficult to be both.

This process began internally. A new generation of missionaries called into question the "purity" of the congregations, and in so doing challenged the *amakholwa* perception of themselves as God's chosen people in Natal. In the years following the Anglo-Zulu war, missionaries demanded that Zulu Christians live by a more tightly defined moral code and many who considered themselves believers suddenly found themselves excluded from the churches for practices that had previously gone unpunished if not even unmentioned. The rules by which many had entered into their faith seemingly no longer applied and *amakholwa*, on whom respectability weighed heavily, faced difficult decisions between new moral laws and a desire to maintain cultural practices suddenly deemed immoral. Inevitably some left the church while others chose to follow the new stricter guidelines. For most of the community, however, the final decades of the nineteenth century were a much more ambiguous time, when *amakholwa* searched for a balance between church rules, the old ways, and new desires.

But altered rules alone do not account for the scandals that shook Christians of the AZM at this time. Durban and Johannesburg attracted many of the most ambitious men and women throughout South Africa and industrious *amakholwa* left the stations in droves to make their fortunes elsewhere. For lengthy periods they left behind their fields, families, and churches, each absence a small spark of instability. The cities also pulled an entire generation of *amakholwa* from the classroom, their skills underdeveloped yet increasingly demanded by the colonial economy. At the same time, a new type of Christian emerged. Converted in the cities, these new believers did not make their home on the mission station but instead returned to live with their families, breaking the previous pattern of Christian consolidation. Missionaries responded by opening "out-stations," sites of worship that were rarely more than wattle and daub huts. Ill-clothed and continuing to live in traditional style homes, they represented a rapidly growing *amakholwa* population that could neither be easily counted nor readily integrated into the old mission churches. Early Zulu Christians had represented a readily identifiable middle ground between traditional and western society, but over time a wide, often puzzling array of Zulu "Christians" emerged in Natal.[1] *Amakholwa* must have realized that the small, cohesive community represented by the early NAMs was doomed to extinction, but as the body of believers grew, spread, and differentiated, it still must have been a bitter pill for the once tightly knit community to swallow.

In addition to these internal stresses, the *amakholwa* community suffered a series of short, sharp blows beginning in 1893. That year Natal received "responsible government" (that is a semi-independent status that allowed colonies to set many of their own policies) from the British, placing the fate of Africans in the hands of the colony's settler population. The same settlers had long expressed open envy of *amakholwa*, hungrily eyeing the mission stations while muttering about missionaries "spoiling" Zulu for hard labor. This might not have been troublesome to Christians if missionaries, who had long championed their interests, had not suddenly abandoned them. After years of negotiation the mission agreed to hand over control of the reserves to the government. *Amakholwa*, understandably worried about what this might entail, urged the AZM to sell them the glebe plots they rented before finalizing the transfer. The mission refused and added insult to injury by collecting rents on the land for the very first time.

Then, at this darkest hour, even God seemed to turn on them, as for over a year one natural disaster followed the other. During the summer of 1895–96 a plague of locusts that were described as being as big as a fist descended upon Natal, stripping fields across the country and leaving many *amakholwa* destitute and hungry. But as the community recovered from the insects an even more terrible plague lurked over the horizon. From the middle of 1896 forward word slowly trickled back to the mission stations from Christian transport riders of an even more calamitous event about to befall all of southern Africa. Rinderpest, a cattle disease of such ferocity that it had devoured entire herds in under a week as it marched inexorably across Africa, was, by 1896, hovering just outside of the colony and each passing week brought reports of another, ever closer outbreak to Natal.

EXCLUDING THE SINNER

The earliest fissures in the community of AZM *amakholwa* occurred as a result of the very financial benefits brought by their lives as believers. The approaching winter months of 1879 found the residents of Umvoti Mission Station flush with the financial windfall of the ongoing Anglo-Zulu war, the culmination of a decade of growing prosperity for *amakholwa* everywhere. Residents, particularly those with wagons, had worked hard over the previous half-year, generating unprecedented profits from moving goods for the British army. Some used this wealth to acquire additional trappings of Christian life: nice suits and dresses, top hats and bonnets, brick homes, store-bought furniture, place settings of china and silver tea servings. Others bought additional wagons and teams of oxen, positioning themselves to make even more money as the English army hunted King Cetshwayo across Zululand.[2]

A few even bought additional plots of land, extending their holdings at a time *amakholwa* on other stations sought the right to do the same. As part of the original vision of the AZM, missionaries had planned Umvoti as a middle-American farming community and divided the Mission Reserve lands into a central village surrounded by agricultural plots. The small village lots attracted, at that time, relatively little attention. But the fifteen-acre "garden" lots of Umvoti were situated on ideal sugar growing land and wealthy residents began buying up additional lands, often consolidating existing small holdings into larger, more profitable, properties.[3]

In the late fall and early winter of 1879, however, it came to light that several Umvoti men had invested their newfound wealth in other, more traditional ways. Men such as Umakabeni and Umyokana, two of the earliest participants in Aldin Grout's home school, took their earnings, purchased cattle, and then used them to clandestinely marry second wives.[4] In doing so they sought to translate their success as *amakholwa* into a traditional vernacular. For while the material goods that filled their homes held relevance to their fellow Christians, but *amabhinca* continued to mark status by the size of one's herds and the size of one's family. It seems that despite their impressive brick homes and ability to read, many of the newly wealthy *amakholwa* felt the sting of being thought of as members of an impoverished community.[5]

Cattle reproduced relatively quickly, offering an excellent return for anyone in Natal prosperous enough to assemble a few head for breeding. But while Umvoti, like most of the other mission stations, offered a communal grazing area, neither it nor the small agricultural plots could support the sizable herds the wealthiest residents of Umvoti began amassing in early 1879. In response, these men established *inhlonhla*, secondary cattle posts long used for alternate season grazing, on location lands removed from the missions.[6] There, away from fellow *amakholwa*, men like Umakabeni and Umyokana managed their herds. As these grew so did their position in Zulu society and they attempted to discreetly trade in on their fortune, acquiring second and even third wives that they settled in *imizi* off of the stations.

When their actions came to light, the congregation of Umvoti expelled the newly polygamous men from the church. But, much to the annoyance of the resident missionary, this proved to be the extent of the penalties imposed. Umakabeni, Umyokana and nearly a half-dozen other of Umvoti's once leading citizens, could not be removed from the station as they owned the titles to their homes outright. Elsewhere, churches administered harsher punishments. At Umsunduze, a Christian man took a second wife and moved off the station to live with her, leaving his disabled first wife and their children behind in the Western-style home he had built. The church made an example of him by removing his entire family from their home, one of the nicest on the station, and giving it to another church member. The polygamous man came to the missionary, complaining bitterly: "I can't see why my children need to be deprived of all this on my account. Why should they be punished for my sin?"[7]

He appealed to the wrong power, for according to Congregational usage it was churches that voted on and imposed punishments. Missionaries headed the disciplinary committees formed to investigate wrongdoings and suggested penalties they thought appropriate, but by the 1880s congregations of the AZM voted on a broad range of issues affecting the community, including matters of discipline. Like other South African missions, the first

American missionaries ran the mission reserves as their own personal fief-doms, however subsequent missionaries sought to bring the Zulu churches more closely in line with their American model, and the AZM slowly became more democratic as congregations voted on everything from the acceptance of probationary candidates to church finances.[8] The penalties imposed on polygamists than, represented to at least a degree the desire by *amakholwa* to define who belonged within the borders of their community and under what circumstances.

Certainly those who chose polygamy understood it was a "sin" with severe consequences. From the earliest, the doctrine of the church forbade polygamy and male converts understood that to be Christian was to take only one wife. Women living in polygamy prior to their conversion were in a much more liminal position, but unmarried Christian women also under-stood that for them marrying into polygamy could not be an option. Some half-heartedly invoked the Old Testament to justify their actions, but un-like subsequent issues such as *lobola* and *utshwala*, which most *amakholwa* regarded as unfairly imposed, few Christians questioned the theological or cultural validity of monogamy.[9]

Men such as Umakabeni and Umyokana understood the border they were transgressing, and they hid their actions as long as possible. Even after their denunciation and expulsion from the community their actions speak to their full comprehension of Christian doctrine. Unlike traditional society, where ancillary brides built their homes next to those already es-tablished by senior wives, the two men kept their secondary wives off of the stations even after they were revealed. At Umvoti, of the eight converts who took additional wives following the Anglo-Zulu war, none brought them onto the station. Public sentiment proved "so strong against the courses of these apostate Christians, that they have not cared to defy it." And public pressure was matched by personal guilt. The polygamist from Umsunduze referred to his "sin" and only objected that the punishment also affected his innocent children.

While polygamous men occupied the majority of mission angst, the ac-tions of their first wives are equally interesting. For while most stayed on the mission stations in their old homes raising their children as Christians, and missionaries referred to them as "among the best" Christians on the stations, they often remained married to their wayward husbands. Indeed, contrary to missionary characterizations of them as "cast aside" or "scorned" these women maintained active roles in the lives of their husbands. One missionary bitterly complained that polygamist husbands returned to the stations on occasion and claimed the "privileges in the family same as if they had not sinned." Yet these women did not abandon the church to join their husbands off the stations, instead they retained a careful balance between the expectations of their faith and their deeply imbedded roles as Zulu wives.[10]

Off of the stations, disgraced *amakholwa* found that despite their wealth, *amabhinca* continued to view them as outsiders. Stated one: "We laugh at those who come back in this way, saying, 'Are you not well, that you go and say you will do the work of *Nkulunlulu*, [God] and now you are throwing it all up? If you go in for a thing you should stick to it.'"[11] Such derision, combined with guilt and dissatisfaction with their new traditional lives, drove some back. One reported that his new "heathen" wife and kraal had "disgusted" him. At Esidumbini, where a Zulu preacher pursued a second wife in the 1880s, traditionalists later spoke of him as one "who did not forsake what the missionaries called sin" yet still wore clothes, lived in a square house, and aspired to be a station *induna*.[12] When even *amabhinca* noted the trouble with transgressing the moral boundaries of this new community, wandering Christians stood very little chance of discreetly living dual lives. Another polygamist, Joel Hawes from Inanda, returned to the church, "humbly confessing his sins" after his second wife, a woman who became a "thorn in his side," left him. During his remaining years he lived a "godly" life and died a "member of the faithful" after raising several sons, Benjamin and Thomas, who served as leaders in the AZM.[13]

Others never returned, too bound up in the web of kinship and responsibility that accompanied additional marriages. A decade later enough of these men stood outside of the church wanting to return on their own terms that they provided the backbone for an unsuccessful independence movement launched by Mbiyana Ngidi (discussed in more detail below.) But in the early 1880s this was still not the case, and these men found themselves unhappily caught in-between, excluded from church membership, often banned from the stations, and scorned by both *amabhinca* and *amakholwa*.

Still, while *amakholwa* identity withstood this initial assault, the community itself was weakened. By 1880 many churches in the AZM had excluded some of their wealthiest and most prominent members; men who had shown the greatest initiative in pursuing "modernity" and were leaders not just in financial, but also religious matters. The NHMS, led by a committee of twelve, lost a majority of its executive in 1880 when the scandal broke.[14] Umvoti, the AZM's crown jewel, and the station hit hardest by the episode, slid into a long torpor. In 1884 the missionary in charge almost wistfully called the recent deaths of two polygamists "impressive providences" that might allow the station to recover its former glory.[15] But no recovery followed and by the late 1880s the station that had once offered handsome wages to teachers could no longer pay its bills. The financial problems were accompanied by spiritual ones, and at the NAM of 1895, George Nxaba, a preacher at Umvoti, felt called to defend his station, noting that while the feeling in the rest of the AZM was that the work "does not prosper" at Umvoti it was "better than it used to be." This was a less than stirring accounting, and not until the following year, when revival stirred the station, did they throw off this lethargy.[16]

PURITY

In the middle of 1884, six months after the last member had put on the blue ribbon marking their abstinence from beer, the congregation of Umzumbe met on the Sabbath for a sunrise prayer service. Their righteousness that morning angered Boshi, an evangelist leading the services for Mabuda Cele, the regular preacher who was away at the NAM. After prayer and song Boshi stood to deliver his message. Beginning on familiar ground he urged the assembled to give their all in serving God, a common theme with which those gathered were familiar and responded positively. But Boshi continued and what he said next called into question the very basis of *amakholwa* identity, that in the act of accepting Christ, Zulu Christians created a unique community whose walls of faith separated them from the surrounding traditionalists. The congregation, he warned, should not congratulate itself for getting rid of beer, and certainly should not speak as if they were better than the traditionalists around them, for, he charged:

> We are very much like the heathen in many things. We are all very much under the power of the *amadhlozi*. Who is there among us who would be willing to go into a neighbors' house and take *amasi* [sour milk] there? Why? Because we believe that the *amadhlozi* are in the milk, and many other things we would not do for fear of the spirits. Now can God, who is a jealous God, give us his blessing while we thus regard the spirits? How can we call ourselves better than other people when this is so?"[17]

Boshi's comments caused a sensation within the church and some scolded him for speaking openly about such things, angered, no doubt, that he had removed their thin veil of respectability.

The resident missionary, Henry Bridgman, stunned by this development so soon after celebrating the recent abstinence victory, spoke with Boshi about his remarks. Boshi affirmed his comments and noted that the practices he spoke of were as common at Umzumbe as they were among Christians of all churches. Moreover, he maintained, church members engaged in a whole host of other "heathen" activities, particularly those in connection with marriage, healing, and *ukuzila* (taboos connected with the *amadhlozi* and requiring women to withdraw from normal routines.)[18] In response Bridgman called a meeting attended by the entire congregation. Over the course of several hours the members filled in the details of their non-Christian beliefs. It was acknowledged that Christian women and girls, like their traditionalist friends and family, would never drink *amasi* in another homestead for fear of angering the spirits and thus killing the calves of that herd. In the same way Christian wives still practiced *hlonipha*, the avoidance of speaking the name of one's father-in-law, for fear that doing so would bring doom upon one's own children. The congregation also acknowledged that upon the death of either a child or husband, residents in the affected household still sprinkled the gall of a slaughtered ox on their persons in order to avert future loss. Finally, the congregation discussed the celebrations held for a bride's engagement that typically involved butchering a cow. Suspicious missionaries had previously been told that these were simply occasions to share the family's good fortune (and a bit of meat) with neighbors. But now *amakholwa* at Umzumbe acknowledged for the first time that the cow slaughtered on such occasions still served as an offering of thanks to the *amadhlozi* and Christians feared that failing to do so might anger the spirits, brining ruin down upon the newlywed's household.

From July to October of 1884 the congregation held a series of twice-weekly meetings at which these and other practices were discussed, and votes were taken whether they ought to be forbidden or not. Cele, Boshi, and Joseph (another Umzumbe evangelist), led the meetings and moderated what were frequently very lively discussions. Each practice had its defender and church members argued that while they frequently participated in certain customs, they had no real regard for the spirits, doing so only because the traditions had been passed down from their fathers. Some issues stirred more debate than others; an entire day was spent on the matter of sour milk. Most of the women in the church had grown up observing this rule and found it difficult to disengage from it, the observance a habit they argued, not a belief in the *amadhlozi*. In the end they were won over by readings from Colossians 2:8–20 showing that they needed to give up the practice or bring shame upon Christianity.[19] Another afternoon was spent on the question of native medicine. Here a compromise was reached and *amakholwa* agreed that they would not go to the kraals of traditionalists for treatment, but that if medicines must be had, they should be used in their own homes.

The use of traditional medicine fell into liminal moral ground that neither the mission nor its converts quite knew how to resolve. While teaching at Inanda in 1883, John Dube was struck down by severe pains in his head, shoulders and elsewhere. Dube, whose father, a pastor and *induna* at Inanda was considered a shining example of the AZM, tried Western medicine to no avail and eventually accepted the invitation of a nearby chief who was also a close friend of the family, to receive treatment from a Zulu *inyanga*. Later, Dube expressed shock at the missionary criticism he faced; unaware that receiving traditional medicine was a "heathen doing." He had been willing to participate, he noted, "because I was sick and I thought that through my Saviour's help I will get well and go home. I did not trust in their medicines at all, but I always prayed to the Lord that through his help they may do me good." Besides, he commented, he had brought his testament with him and spent his time reading, praying, and preaching to the women and girls of the kraal, telling them that the "snakes and other human customs will not save them."[20]

As the congregation of Umzumbe slowly separated from all that might be mistaken for traditional belief, they sharpened the lines dividing them from those outside the church. In the end, a committee of four, two men and two women, gathered together for two days to finalize the congregation's conclusions, eventually producing three pages of rules for the *amakholwa* of Umzumbe to live by. In addition to forbidding *amakholwa* participation in many practices associated with *amadhlozi*, the document also included a ban on *lobola* and abstinence from all forms of alcohol. The text, along with the Umsunduze Rules presented four years earlier by the American missionaries, became a central creed for all the AZM churches.

The rules, while written down by the congregation of Umzumbe, represented the culmination of several decades of increasing pressure on *amakholwa* to purify their lives according to the moral ideals of missionaries just then entering the field. This campaign had crystallized around two issues: the taking of cattle by Christian fathers upon the marriage of their daughters, or *lobola*, and the drinking of *utshwala*, the Zulu beer traditionally derived from fermented millet. For a decade the churches of the AZM were embroiled in a fierce debate as members struggled to reconcile newly shifting boundaries of their faith.

The longest and fiercest of the debates involved the question of *lobola*.[21] In 1880, when missionaries meeting at Umsunduze formally made the taking of cattle for daughters a disciplinable offense, it culminated a decades long debate. As early as the second NAM, held at Ifumi in 1852, missionaries had raised the issue with *amakholwa*, who acknowledged problems with the practice, but refused to forbid it. The first generation of missionaries did not press them on the matter.[22] Only when younger missionaries began entering the field in the 1860s did internal discussion over the issue heat up. This second generation of missionaries, men and women who grew up as abolitionists, readily compared *lobola* with slavery and they passionately spoke out against it, going so far as to set up an "underground railroad" in which women "sold" into slavery with "old polygamists" were whisked away to safety.[23]

Amakholwa fiercely defended *lobola*. For most, it represented an important opportunity to maintain social connections and build status with traditionalist friends and family without sacrificing their Christian identity, as they would in the case of polygamy. To missionary charges that they were selling their sisters and daughters into slavery, *amakholwa* responded with a host of counter-arguments. They noted that the language surrounding *lobola* could not be commercial as it could not be construed as a commercial transaction and only represented the recognition of the loss a daughter represented to a father's household. They also claimed that *umfazi*, or wife, could not be translated to mean slave or servant just as *indoda*, or husband, could not be translated as master.[24]

More trenchantly, *amakholwa* argued that the lack of *lobola* jeopardized the purity of their sisters and daughters, for the moral character of a woman was factored into the exchange. A bride of questionable repute brought far fewer cattle, so fathers and brothers had a special interest in protecting women's purity.[25] *Amakholwa* argued further that in refusing cattle they disparaged their daughters' purity and reinforced the view of some traditionalists that the stations were hotbeds of immorality.[26] Women who felt their honor slighted by the refusal of their fathers to demand cattle, or grooms who wouldn't pay beasts for them, further undermined the missionaries' argument. At Umvoti, at least one husband, whose wife had no surviving male relatives, transferred cattle into her hands just to silence her constant complaints over his having failed to exchange any cattle for her; this alone, Grout noted, "could remove the disgrace."[27]

Zulu Christians also defended the practice because they feared losing their carefully carved out "middlemen" positions. In attacking *lobola* what missionaries failed to recognize, and to what *amakholwa* were fully attuned, was that *lobola* acted as the social thread weaving together Zulu individuals, families, and entire communities into an intricate web of relationships and social obligations. Unlike polygamy, or even the worship of the *amadhlozi*, participation in this practice was critical if Zulu Christians wished to maintain these connections. *Amakholwa* rightly interpreted the move by American missionaries as a threat to their economic well being, and for a time they successfully maneuvered to exclude it from the missionary conceptualization of sin. They accomplished this by both cajoling and threatening; warned one Zulu preacher in 1867, "if you take men out of the church for this practice you will cause great trouble in our churches, many will go out, I myself will probably go out."[28] In a rare moment Nathanial Clark, the secretary of the ABM during the early years of this dispute, tried to intervene on behalf of *amakholwa* when, in 1868 he admonished the younger members of the AZM: "Your work is not to make American but Zulu Christians."[29] Unfortunately his warning did not carry the day.

In 1878 the *amakholwa* community lost the last American defender of *lobola* when Andrew Abraham finally retired, returning to the States after nearly thirty years in southern Africa. With Abraham gone, the new generation of missionaries moved quickly, meeting at Umsunduze in 1880 and adopting a new standard of purity by which *amakholwa* would be judged worthy of taking communion—the ultimate symbolic act of demonstrating one's Christianity. These "Umsunduze Rules" as they became known, centered on polygamy, beer-drinking, *isangu* (hemp) smoking, and *lobola*, making each a disciplinable offense.[30] The mission quickly set an example by punishing several preachers for breaking the *lobola* regulation and the slow but steady growth the mission had experienced the previous decade halted. At Amanzimtoti, the second largest of the stations at the time, membership had grown or remained flat almost every year to 1879, when it stood at 106. Two years later, after the Umsumduze Rules had gone into effect, membership fell to 100 before recovering back to 105 shortly after.[31] Of the new laws passed at Umsunduze, the restrictions on *lobola* proved the most difficult for *amakholwa*.[32] At Emutshane for example, many willingly gave up beer, but in 1890 only nine members, less than half of the congregation, took part in communion; the rest had been excluded for *lobola* offenses.[33]

That a larger exodus did not occur is attributable less to the willingness of *amakholwa* to obey the new restrictions, so much as in their cleverness in finding ways around them. Zulu Christians effectively laundered their cattle by diverting *lobola* to non-believing relatives, held a number of celebrations (such as *ukugana* the party held for the "choosing" of the bride by the groom, *ukwemula* the ceremony held for a daughter who had reached marriageable age, and *abayeni* the bridegroom's gathering) at which "gifts" of cattle were given to the bride's father. And eventually they even began accepting cash.[34] But sneaking around the law gutted the sense of moral certainty that previously imbued the *amakholwa* community and the vigorous Christianity practiced by participants in the World's Day of Prayer seemed a long way off from the cowed congregations that followed the implementation of the Umsunduze rules.

Like *lobola*, the question of *utshwala* simmered for several decades. The AZM consistently forbade liquor (to the point of worrying over the planting of sugar cane on the stations) but for several decades they tolerated *utshwala*, a thin, sour millet or corn mash, generally more filling than intoxicating. While not defending it, early missionaries had noted that though much merriment and noise accompanied the drinking of beer, actual drunkenness rarely followed.[35] But following the Anglo-Zulu war, newly arrived missionaries carried the message of America's fledgling temperance movement with them to South Africa. Once in Natal they came to believe that "beer-drinks" were inherently conducive to immorality.[36]

As in the United States, churchwomen (in this case missionary wives) launched the movement and proved its driving force. Unlike the States, however, local women did not always rally to the cause. *Utshwala* production had long rested in the hands of Zulu women, and *amakholwa* women, already deprived of much of the control they had previously exercised over the fields, proved reluctant to surrender this important contribution to their household economy. After several years of frustration, during which Christians gathering for "women's meetings" successfully resisted the urgings of female missionaries, the American women turned their attention to the *amakholwa* leadership, urging pastors and preachers to sign a pledge promising to abandon the use of beer in their homes.

To their surprise, temperance leaders encountered resistance behind the pulpit as well. Pastors, preachers, evangelists, and seminary students all partook of *utshwala* and some offered an impassioned defense of it, noting, in particular, its nutritious benefits.[37] For his part, Jeremiah Mali, a respected teacher at Amanzimtoti, refused to translate an article that appeared in an international Christian weekly heralding the denunciation of beer by Khama, the Christian king of the Tswana. He did, however, take the article with him to the following NAM, held at Umzumbe in 1878. There, *amakholwa* discussed the matter and searched for a compromise, one that would allow them to continue drinking *utshwala* while maintaining their own claim to salvation. After the NAM, *amakholwa* participants reported their conclusions. "There could be no harm in drinking a little, but that they were not to get drunk or to attend heathen beer drinks."[38]

In the course of a year, from 1877–1878, only Maduba Cele, a recent graduate of the Theological Seminary working at Umzumbe under Bridgman (whose wife led the temperance campaign) signed the pledge. Cele made his decision during that year's "Week of Prayer" (one of the last) and wrote down his declaration. The note is worth quoting at length:

> I am happy to write a few words about this matter which has for a long time tied me up, and for many years. A matter also, from which I have for a long time had not thought of separating. And yet today I choose to separate from Utywala because I have been a lover of Utywala. Very much now I want to be a lover of giving up Utywala. Very much, for a long time, I have been hearing that it disagrees with the way of God. Also, as for myself at times, it almost finished [sic]. I wish to give it up. Also I would be happy if these words might be heard by many of our brethren and that they endeavor to give it up, because of our faith and also because we are the light, we are the kingdom of Christ. Also for a long time I have been hoping that I would see another, who is a believer like myself, giving it up first, before me. But I do not see him. It would seem therefore, as though, perhaps, I should be the first to give it up. Friend, let us endeavor to give it up![39]

Cele's letter, reflecting the rhetoric of the mission but cast in his own words, reveals several fears; a personal one, over both his soul and his standing among his neighbors, and a larger one concerning the state of the community. Of particular note was his grudging acceptance of the temperance movement's conclusion that the *amakholwa* community had a responsibility because "we are the light" to give up beer and lead traditionalists by example. Failing to do so meant placing themselves outside of the kingdom of believers. Cele's pledge did not hold long. Later that year, during a bout of illness, Cele's Christian sister came to Umzumbe to watch over her brother and declared: "Such a thing was unheard of that a sick man should drink only water!" and nursed him back to health on a diet heavy in beer.[40]

Having failed to bring either women or church leaders into line with the new morality, temperance advocates refocused their strategy. Following the lead of the first missionaries they turned to the schools and launched the first "Blue Ribbon" campaigns among children. The first occurred at Umzumbe in late 1878 and the occasion was marked by much festivity; a picnic was held at the nearby river and children marched there through the village waving blue flags and banners bestowed with abstinence slogans. Afterwards they marched back into the church which was adorned for the occasion with flowers, palms, flags, and temperance banners. Speeches, singing, and short skits followed that demonstrated the "foolishness and deceitfulness of the drink."[41] For children used to the daily drudgery of classes, the occasion must have seemed a delightful diversion and they promised not to drink beer in the future in return for a bit of blue cloth pinned to their jackets. Half of the school made the pledge and returned home that evening, the small strip of blue acting as reminders to reluctant parents of their own moral failings.[42] Over the course of the next year the children repeated the festivity every other month until, eventually, they all wore the ribbons. Their parents slowly followed and by 1884, six years after the first abstinence pledge, all thirty-odd church members, even those women who stood to be most affected, wore the blue ribbon first put on by their children.

As part of the Umsunduze Rules, drinking *utshwala* became a gatekeeper offense; potential converts needed to renounce its use before being admitted into the church, and those already in could be disciplined for its consumption. But most missionaries proved understandably reluctant to fully enforce this edict, doing so would have meant expelling entire congregations. Instead they turned to the Umzumbe model and the abstinence campaigns spread to the other stations.[43] The successes slowly mounted and in 1883 Zulu preachers met to discuss the matter once again, this time agreeing on the need to abstain from beer and forbid its drinking in their homes.[44] In 1890 Mapumulo, the last of the stations to do so, held a temperance campaign, insuring that nearly every AZM church member had heard the anti-*utshwala* message.

But hearing a message and taking it to heart proved two very different matters. It is clear from mission letters that many *amakholwa*, even those who wore the blue ribbon, continued to drink *utshwala*.[45] Some *amakholwa* responded by attempting to find ways around the rules. By 1894 *isibebe*, a weaker form of *utshwala*, became a popular social lubricant. When this was banned *amaheu*, known as the "calf of the cow" (the cow being *utshwala*) took its place. Missionaries argued that these "light" beers were simply the rafts that "took people out to the big ship of *utshwala*."[46] But the abstinence campaigns successfully mobilized at least a part of the church against drinking. And where converts had previously neither viewed *utshwala* as sinful, nor bothered to inform missionaries of the indulgences of others, now scandals and recriminations shook the small community of believers. In a series of purges that lasted the better part of a decade, many offending members were trimmed from the roles of the mission for "unchristian" acts. Every station was affected and those not disciplined for *lobola* offenses often ran afoul of *utshwala* regulations. At Umtwalume the recently elected station headman, a widely respected deacon in the church, refused to give up his beer and was removed.[47] At Noodsberg a half-dozen of those living in "aweful vice" were expelled or suspended.[48] Many in the Mapumulo congregation had "fallen into sin" and were forced out of the church.[49] At Inanda the church roles were reduced by a third . . . and so it went, each of the churches suffering a loss of membership, both from the purges, and from being unable to replace losses with new members.[50]

The story of Hobiana, an old man who had slowly come around to Christianity, is typical in this regard. During the 1880s, Hobiana had carefully explored the messages of the Bible with *amakholwa* and a local missionary. What he found appealed to him and he prepared for conversion by cutting off his headring, buying clothes, and dismissing his second and third wives. But Hobiana found he could not give up his beer: "I am old." He declared. "My teeth are gone: I have never been intoxicated; I do not go to beer drinks; I have given up my heathen customs; I have cut off my headring; I have given up my wives; but how can I give up this little cup of beer." For some time Hobiana held out, and the missionaries worried among themselves about forcing this old man to give up his beer, believing that he had otherwise fully demonstrated his commitment to Christianity and wondering if an exception ought to be made. After a year, however, Hobiana relieved them of their difficult choice by putting on the blue ribbon and joining the congregation at Umzumbe.

Amakholwa complained that missionaries took away everything from them in the way of small pleasures, leaving nothing in their place. But the

AZM argued that it was within reach of all its members to keep themselves supplied with tea, coffee, and sugar, provided they were industrious. Some did just that, stocking their ladders with the goods of Christian respectability; others simply left the churches, abandoning the mission station, their homes, and *amakholwa* neighbors for a life outside of the community. For many who left, however, this did not mean abandoning their beliefs, and gradually an expatriate Christian community grew across Natal.[51]

UNDERMINING THE FAITHFUL

In the years leading to the revival, *amakholwa* identity shifted perceptibly. Prior to 1879 *amakholwa* viewed themselves as the elect, God's chosen people. Their actions, whether in matters of business, or religion, bespoke a confidence of place and purpose and they believed themselves bonded together both by their acceptance of Jesus' resurrection, but also by their commitment to "civilization." But a second generation of missionaries arrived in Natal, determined to alter this equation, convinced that the former had led Zulu Christians astray. Suddenly *amakholwa* identity seemed far less certain and from this point forward, many sought alternative versions of what it meant to be a Christian. Indeed, the Umsumduze Rules so muddied the water that, a decade long identity crises gripped *amakholwa* as they struggled with what it meant to be Christian and Zulu; to be members of the church, educated, "civilized," and yet still marginalized.[52]

Particularly damaging to *amakholwa* identity was the emphasis of the second generation of missionaries on the sinfulness of converts.[53] Prior to 1879 "sinner" had meant traditionalist and by converting and living "civilized" lives *amakholwa* understood themselves freed from the taint of such a label. But in the decades following the Anglo-Zulu war, missionaries shifted this category to include members of the *amakholwa* community. In 1885 the mission wrote that the "trouble is that the majority of those in our churches have not enough *moral earnestness*."[54] Missionaries meant this, and certainly Zulu Christians understood it, as a judgment of practices not previously regarded as immoral. In 1887 members of the congregation at Noodsberg must have wondered who he spoke of when their newly arrived missionary, a much younger man than many of them, warned that: "Christ was disgraced by the lives of some of the members of that church, who while preaching to others were themselves following greedily the lusts of the flesh." And then suggested that the nature of the Christianity they practiced was inadequate because it was not in "making fine prayers and professing but *living* in *real love* to God which constituted a Christian."[55] A missionary at Amanzimtoti warned his congregation in 1894 that wedding feasts on the station had become a "disgrace to the community."[56] The general letter of 1896 bemoaned: "Our native Christians are far below the standard we hoped they would reach after so many years of instruction. It cannot be said that they have made the best use of the advantages that have been given them. One sometimes wonders when they will rise to a higher standard of mankind, self denial, industry and purity."[57]

The problem for *amakholwa* was twofold. As material goods, large and small, infiltrated traditional society, their symbolic power inevitably waned. The first generation of *amakholwa*, as we have seen, demonstrated their faith through outward acts, pulling on pants, building upright homes, buying plows, etc. But for missionaries arriving in Natal in the last decades of the nineteenth century, these gestures were inconclusive evidence of faith for everyone seemed to have indulged in these items. Younger missionaries stripped buying plows and wearing clothes of their religious significance. A missionary at Umsunduze, for example, reported that while pleased that many traditionalists had come to him requesting clothes "this does not always mean much" and by the 1890s Zulu returning from working in Johannesburg and Durban "even tho not Christians" were using their wages to build Western style homes.[58] This was a fitfully articulated process, but it left *amakholwa* wondering what made them Christian and why, for they had built their identity partially in opposition to what it meant to be traditionalist.[59]

Perhaps unsurprisingly, a malaise settled over the congregations of the AZM during the two decades following. At Amanzimtoti the spirit of the church was reported as being so low in 1890 that only a few were left who did "not seem to have lost their first love" for the church.[60] Some responded to the attacks of younger missionaries by rejecting their right to judge certain Zulu traditions. The most dramatic moment in this reaction was when Mbiyana Ngidi, the preacher who had earlier refused to pursue riches away from the church, left the AZM to establish an oppositional church that allowed its members to partake in both *lobola* and *utshwala*. That it failed speaks in part to the control missionaries maintained over church property, in particular the church itself which gave them a great deal of sacred and secular legitimacy, and perhaps says less about Mbiyana's rejection of the Umsumduze Rules.

Still, as one of the first church leaders to separate from the AZM Ngidi has received perhaps more attention from historians than his actual influence merits. Missionaries feared that he might persuade many *amakholwa* to follow him when he established his Uhlanga Church, but despite initial success, Ngidi ultimately failed to build a sufficient following in Natal and soon moved to the less competitive waters of kwaZulu. While most have seen this schism as a precursor to the political ambitions of late nineteenth century Ethiopian movements, it is Michael Mahoney's more nuanced account that makes the important link between Mbiyana's theological stance and the movement of those who had been disciplined for beer and polygamy into his church. Mahoney is correct when he notes that Ngidi's conflict was with the American missionaries, not Europeans in general, but he errs when he argues that patronage from a local chief and nearby Norwegian missionaries was sufficient to win broad popular support from *amakholwa* for Ngidi. It was not, and as Mahoney notes, "Given the situation, it is surprising that so many Africans at Noodsberg stayed with the AZM." I would argue that Ngidi failed to secure legitimacy for his claim of sacred authority and while the Norwegian missionaries supported him in his own personal spiritual quests (getting married in the church and receiving an exemption from the practice of traditional law) this certainly did not translate into legitimacy in the eyes of other *amakholwa* for whom rites of the church held import.[61]

Others shifted the other direction and embraced the mission's connection of certain Zulu customs with moral depravity. One Zulu preacher emphasized the differences between *amakholwa* and traditionalists by noting: "Go up to a kraal and find a few hungry children trying to get a breakfast; ask them where their father and mother, 'Oh they have gone to a beerdrink.' Go in the evening and the miserable children are still alone, the father and mother not yet returned from the almost endless carousel."[62]

This *amakholwa* project to redefine their understanding of what it meant to be Christian took center-stage at the 1895 NAM held at Mapumulo. John Hlonono, a recent Seminary graduate, preached on the nature of their Christianity while Usidumuku and Cetewayo conducted temperance meetings. Ceteywayo's message attempted to reclaim those who felt left out of the church by the Umsunduze Rules, condemning their actions and urging them to recognize that their faith came with many responsibilities. Derived from Galatians 5:1, Ephesians 6:20 and 1 Corinthians 9:25, he noted that a hunter going hunting with a good, well-loaded gun, will still fail if he has no cap for the gun. Likewise, he argued, temperance is a "small part of the armor of God, but no Christian can succeed without it."[63] During the NAM, as at Umzumbe a decade earlier, participants carefully examined a host of customs, debated their relative merits and attempting to reconcile Christian beliefs with practices they were being told were no longer allowable. In one of the keynote sermons, Maduba Cele preached against drinking, dancing, "witch" medicines, charms, and *lobola*. But Cele's sermon, closely aligned with the mission vision of a "pure" church, did not meet with full agreement and a vigorous discussion followed. One participant noted that he did not see any difference between Zulu medicines and ones taken by whites. "When they are sick they like medicine and their medicine does not come from heaven, it is dug up from the ground, like that of the natives and where is the difference?" Two decades after the Umsunduze Rules, *amakholwa* could not agree on who they were, or who they were to become.[64]

THE CHANGING FACE OF *AMAKHOLWA*

In 1886 Yedwana, a strapping young man, hoisted onto his back the heavy copper church bell he had purchased and hauled it from Isipingo to his home at Kwahlulwana, one of the remotest corners of the colony.[65] He marched a hundred miles, over the hills of southern Natal along increasingly desolate roads, until reaching Kwahlulwana, where he had only recently returned from a period of migrant work in Durban. He, and the other two young men from his village who accompanied him, had attended both Sabbath services and night school at the AZM chapel in the city. There the three learned to read, converted, and returned home determined to live faithfully and spread the word. Instead of cattle, they pooled their earnings and bought two Bibles, several New Testaments, hymnbooks, and later, the bell. They had no knowledge of carpentry; Yedwana had worked as a kitchen boy and the other two were likely employed as unskilled laborers, but they built a roughly hewn church nevertheless. To legitimize the entire structure, to make it identifiable in their eyes at least, Yedwana lugged the bell some 100 miles and hung it outside. Inside the converts cobbled together fifteen benches and an altar made from felled trees, crafted a door out of an old wooden crate, draped cloth over the altar and hung a paraffin lantern for evening services.

For three years the young men toiled in anonymity, their presence unknown to any American missionaries. Then, in 1889, having gathered around them several candidates for baptism, they called on Umzumbe, the nearest of the AZM stations, to provide someone to serve as both preacher and teacher. Arriving at Kwahlulwana to investigate the community, Laura Smith was astonished by the level of commitment and passion exhibited by the small congregation. Yedwana, unmarried and still living in his father's hut, had nevertheless emerged as the spiritual leader of this community. The congregation he had gathered was rough, but their prayers were articulate, their singing passionate, and while Smith doubted they could afford the salary of a teacher/preacher, she was deeply impressed that the faithful had maintained both theological and moral standards advocated by the mission (and often found wanting in many of the old churches).

Yedwana and the congregation at Kwahlulwana exemplify the evolution of what it meant to be Christian in late nineteenth century Natal. No longer were there clearly defined borders between believer and non-believer.

Yedwana lived in the kraal of his traditional father, had not purchased a plow, and spent little money on any of the material goods that had helped define previous generations of *amakholwa*. Yedwana practiced his Christianity far from the mission reserves. Not surprisingly, missionaries came to see such examples as demonstrating a genuine vitality of the faith and example of what could be accomplished if only *amakholwa* on the reserves would devote themselves to the spread of the message.[66]

Outstations began blossoming around the main churches of the AZM in the years following the Anglo-Zulu war. Initially this was part of a deliberate expansion, planned by the mission as a way to extend the reach of their message across their mission reserves. During the first decades of the mission, Americans went out on regular preaching circuits, stopping at kraals within easy rides of the central stations to preach, pray, and read the gospels. In the 1870s some of these sites began requesting regular contact, particularly in the form of schools. The mission, already overstretched, could not meet these demands and instead filled these positions with *amakholwa* paid to serve as both preacher and teacher. During the 1880s some of these developed into their own congregations, building their own churches and calling their own pastors.[67]

The pace of outstation growth quickened following the end of the Anglo-Zulu war. *Amakholwa*, who had previously spurned the low pay of teachers and preacher, welcomed the opportunity for steady and respectable employment as the economy began to deteriorate. But the real spur came from men like Yedwana, individuals returning from Durban (and later Johannesburg) to some of the remotest corners of Natal and carrying with them the essence of their newly acquired Christian faith.[68] Few of these believers were baptized and fewer still held official appointments from the church, but they still considered themselves united to Congregationalists in belief and practice. Squatting on settler land, living on locations or in KwaZulu, these young men and women lived lives of faith in places often far removed from the nearest of the old churches. But these Christians did their best to reproduce the religious lives they had lived in the cities. Unlike their mission reserve brothers, for these Christians being *amakholwa* had little to do with living as part of an agrarian community. In the cities, religious life occurred within the walls of the churches and provided escape from the difficulties of urban life.

In this way, for example, three new outstations opened up around Amanzimtoti in 1890. At Kwatunguzi, a young man returned from the city and began preaching in his family's large kraal to a growing audience. At Ngahatyahatya, a woman "dreamed a remarkable dream" opening the way for her to hold services in her kraal. They proved such a success that those in attendance later requested a chapel and school from the AZM.[69] At

Golokodo, a ravine difficult to access and nearly cut off from the surrounding world, Frank and James returned in 1890 after attending Amanzimtoti.
They begin preaching and as at Kwahlulwana, the mission was surprised
when they returned years later, looking for help with the large congregation
they had gathered.[70] A few years later James and John returned as converts
from Johannesburg and used their wages to build a church at Entinyane.
The building, a wattle and daub structure roofed in iron, could seat 100, an
ambitious goal for the relatively remote site.[71]

In response to this growth, the AZM requested a young missionary be
sent out by the ABM in 1892 whose sole duty would be to visit the "many
persons who were once identified with our churches who are at present
scattered here and there in Natal, having no privileges of Gospel ordinances
or influences within their reach."[72] By 1896 the mission was forced to admit
that so many small congregations had emerged in the previous few years
that they had no way of keeping up with them all. The impetus of mission
had shifted out of their hands.[73]

This process occurred throughout Natal and even further afield. In 1894
a group from Mapumulo, feeling the time was ripe to return, moved back
across the Thukela River, purchased land and established a small settlement at Impapala. *Amakholwa* from several different denominations joined
together in this project, built a school, hired a teacher, and raised up four
different churches, one of which they called the "American Church." The
following year the members of this congregation approached the AZM,
asking that the mission supply them with a native preacher. Remarkably,
the mission resisted this *fait accompli*, having reached an agreement with
other missions, particularly the Norwegians, to stay out of Zululand. They
advised the Impapala people on the best methods of organizing themselves along Congregational lines and instead formed a loose affiliation
with the church.[74]

While missionaries rarely expressed anything but pleasure at these developments, they did acknowledge the potential problems inherent in the
growth of "unsupervised" Christian congregations. Particularly troubling
was the potential for *izifuni*, or seekers, to mix "Biblical truths" with the
"innumerable superstitions of the people" producing a syncretic Christianity.[75] The 1885 Natal Missionary Conference had warned against just
this potential, noting that many Zulu were becoming Christian without
an extensive knowledge of the scriptures. They were, participants agreed:
"Christ's children, but very weak and needed nursing."[76] In response, the
conference recommended that the "best" *amakholwa* teach classes throughout Natal and missionaries endeavor to bring Christian settlers into a more
regular discourse with catechists.

Despite these warnings, missionaries of the AZM, the same ones who were then considering making tobacco use a disciplinable offense, proved surprisingly willing to overlook some particularly sticky moral dilemmas that members of these new congregations brought into the churches. A deacon who put away his old wives and married an entirely new one, women in polygamous relationships, and a chief with eight wives who made a deathbed conversion; all found their way into the new churches.[77] But in these remote congregations, where years could drift by without a qualified preacher arriving to administer either communion or baptism, *izifuni* did not need to hurry into such life-altering decisions.

While missionaries embraced this movement and the congregations it produced, *amakholwa* from the established stations reacted more ambivalently to these new Christians. At the very least *amakholwa* understood that the growth of outstations cut into their own church membership, reducing the financial base upon which they could draw on to pay their own teachers, preachers, and pastors. When Ellingham called its own preacher in 1896 it became the fourth such outstation in a decade to do so in the area around Ifafa. Its weekly collections that had once flowed into Ifafa's coffers instead stayed to pay the new church's own expenses.[78] But the ambivalence ran deeper, a result of the threat outstations posed to the unique identity *amakholwa* had carved out. When ragged congregations from distant corners of the colony began calling themselves believers without acquiring the accompanying objects of civilization, members of the established congregations looked on suspiciously. At Umvoti in 1896, the congregation voted that all who did not contribute at least 1 shilling per quarter would not be allowed to receive communion—a financial hurdle for those, mostly in the church's outstations, who believed but simply did not possess the resources of those on the mission station.[79] But by then, being *amakholwa* no longer meant wearing clothes, building square homes, engaging in the new economy, living on the stations, or worshipping in an impressive brick church. In less than a decade, the borders of the *amakholwa* community dissolved under the weight of believers who didn't acquire the material symbols of Christianity and traditionalists who did.

One instance serves to illustrate the anxiety felt by mission station *amakholwa* over this process. In the late 1880s an old woman from an outstation of Amanzimtoti went before that church's examining committee to seek approval for baptism. The committee, as the missionary recalled later, pressed her hard. But the old woman, a recent believer, was unfamiliar with the standard vocabulary of belief and could not provide her inquisitors with the expected answers. The committee, composed of "old disciplinarians," prepared to reject her, but the resident missionary interfered at the last moment and asked "Mama, do you love Jesus?" This gave her the words she needed and she declared her faith with conviction. Members of the committee, thrown for a moment, tried to renew the attack, but were fended off by her replies of: "I love Jesus, I love Jesus" and she was eventually admitted.[80]

TROUBLE WITH THE URBAN

In March of 1890 John Mdiwa, a *amakholwa* who had most recently taught courses at Amanzimtoti, accepted an appointment as an AZM teacher and preacher in Durban.[81] While the appointment paid relatively well (he received one of the highest salaries the mission offered its Zulu workers) it came with a host of difficulties. For one, there was no church he could call his own, merely a rotation of four different preaching places. The Americans had only sustained a sporadic presence in the city, despite the urgings of *amakholwa* eager to maintain their spiritual life while there.[82] This lack of permanency amplified Mdiwa's second problem, the diverse nature of the Durban congregation. Participants in the *amaconto amakula* (main Sabbath meetings) could be fully vested *amakholwa* working in the city, traditionalists attracted by the spectacle of service on a quiet Sunday, or catechists, attempting to follow a path into a new life by learning to read at night school, and learning to pray during morning services. For Mdiwa, used to the comparatively advanced abilities of those at Amanzimtoti, the scattershot nature of those in his congregation occasionally drove him to despair of their abilities: "Some of these seem to be in earnest, some seldom come to these meetings, a great majority come not knowing what they come for, only that they use the words "ngi y im ketu uJesus" (I choose Jesus)." Most of Mdiwa's scattered flock was also ephemeral, working as seasonal migrants and rotating between Durban and their homes.[83] Finally, the recent gold strikes on the Witwatersrand also troubled Mdiwa, attracting many of his leading men to Johannesburg.

But Mdiwa was never without Zulu eager to hear his message. The prayer services he ran every Wednesday and Friday were well attended and so many came on the Sabbath that he held two separate afternoon gatherings. For those exploring baptism, Mdiwa ran a popular Wednesday evening catechism class, the gathered praying over the condition of their souls. Likewise, the night school found an eager audience as students packed into the meager building seeking the brass ring of literacy.[84] Even here, however, Mdiwa felt the problems of running an urban mission, for while attendance was always high, the class was never composed of the same faces;

the demands of work often kept participants away just as did the freedom of town life.

Despite these disadvantages, Mdiwa was successful and the Durban church grew. The AZM worked hurriedly to capitalize on this urban trend, and in 1891 they acquired two lots in Beatrice Street, centrally located not far from the train-station, the homes of whites nestled into hills ringing Durban where many *amakholwa* worked as servants, and "The Point," with its docks and numerous barracks housing thousands of Africans.[85] The following year, with an overflow crowd of 300 in attendance, the Durban church, a modest building whose cost had largely been covered by *amakholwa* contributions, opened its doors.[86] Those who wished to formally join the Durban congregation (entitling them to vote on issues affecting the church) needed to present a letter of release from their home congregation indicating their good standing. Within the first year forty-five had done so.[87] Once rooted, the work grew rapidly; by the middle of 1896 the Beatrice Street church maintained twenty-four preaching places across Durban, held several services on Sunday to accommodate all those who wished to attend, and already planned an expansion. For *amakholwa* in the city it represented a victory and one of the Zulu preachers in charge of the work reported with satisfaction "the healthy nature of the church now that people coming to Durban to work have a common place of worship."[88]

The success of the Durban church highlights the puzzling question as to why the AZM had failed to establish an earlier church in the city. Certainly it was not from lack of need; as seen in Rufus Anderson's narrative, many Christians had lived and worked in the port town from its earliest days. Cost certainly mattered, for unlike the grants of land the mission received for the reserves, land in Durban did not come free or even cheap. In addition, the transitory nature of Zulu working in Durban, particularly prior to the end of the century, did not lend itself to building a congregation. But perhaps most importantly, the mission avoided establishing a permanent church in Durban for fear of encouraging the growth of an urban *amakholwa* community.

As already discussed, the AZM envisioned *amakholwa* communities as small, self contained, agriculturally based settlements, and for much of the nineteenth century they loudly warned believers against the moral dangers inherent in city life.[89] The cities were "universities of vice," cautioned missionaries, and *amakholwa* needed to be wary of imitating the morally degraded habits of some Europeans or risk being "smeared with the worst that the twentieth century has to offer."[90] *Amakholwa*, missionaries emphasized throughout the nineteenth century, were rural farmers, not rickshaw pullers and dockworkers in Durban, or shaft drillers in Johannesburg.

But agriculture could not support everyone on the stations; the material goods of "civilization" were expensive to acquire[91] and *amakholwa* men and women[92] who had pursued other economic opportunities, did not hesitate to seek their fortunes in the rapidly expanding metropolises of South Africa. When they did go, they found their services in high demand. As educated and comfortable with English, they filled a specialized niche, particularly in Johannesburg, and were employed in comparatively well-paying positions as interpreters, overseers, and clerks.[93] By 1895 the urban labor market across southern Africa took in all those *amakholwa* who sought work off of the stations even as the prosperity that came with gold enriched all corners of the colony.[94]

As in Durban, the initiative to form an AZM Church in Johannesburg fell to *amakholwa* working there. Congregationalist Zulu worked on the Witwatersrand at least as early as 1890 and two years later their numbers had grown significantly.[95] Initially many joined the Presbyterian Church, theologically akin to the AZM and already established in the city. But the Presbyterians, a white congregation, encouraged them to go their own way and in early 1892 they wrote the AZM, requesting recognition as a Congregational church and asking that the mission send a pastor to minister to their needs.[96] The mission, hoping to avoid being extended into another urban setting, asked the Congregational Union (the assembly of white Congregational churches in South Africa) to take up this work. But *amakholwa* persisted, and unhappy with the Union's proposal to place a Xhosa preacher over them, they flooded the AZM with "complaints and pleadings" until the mission capitulated.[97] The Johannesburg Christians promised to match the funds spent by the AZM in buying land and building the church, and the mission voted in early 1893 to send Benjamin Hawes, one of their "best and most experienced" native preachers to the city.[98]

Yet, while *amakholwa* in the city sought to stabilize their lives by immersing themselves in the traditions of the church, their very act of working in the city threatened the identity of the *amakholwa* communities they left behind. Not surprisingly, the Christian home suffered under the strain of fathers, sons, and daughters seeking their fortune in the cities. But certainly life in the mission reserve churches also suffered from this urban migration. Across the mission, during the first half decade of the 1890s, Sunday schools shut down for a lack of participants, weekly prayer meetings held for generations ended, preachers and evangelists resigned before heading to the city and, as at Mapumulo, preachers reported that so few church members remained on the stations that they could no longer hold Sabbath services.[99] Young *amakholwa*, those who had infused the Zulu Christianity with much of its vibrancy, left the stations in droves for the cities.[100] For many *amakholwa* parents this was one of the greatest blows, for even when their children returned home wearing the blue ribbons of an abstinence campaign they did not believe in, *amakholwa* maintained a zealous commitment to education. But now relatively large salaries and the lure of urban life threatened this pillar of *amakholwa* identity. An entire generation threatened to grow up off of the stations, away from home and out of the schools.

By 1895 the depth of the crisis was clear and the mission attempted to fend off the attraction of the urban by raising the wages it paid its best teachers to £40 per year, hoping that this might induce students to complete their educations.[101] This did little to stem the hemorrhage and two years later the mission considered closing Amanzimtoti Seminary, its empty desks and spiraling debt an indictment on their insistence on a rural *amakholwa* identity. The principal of the Seminary bemoaned this development, noting that even if the school could attract sufficient students the question became how to keep them for an entire term, let alone their entire secondary education, when they could earn £13 per month in the city.[102] But salary alone does not tell the full story of *amakholwa* disillusionment with education. Many, quite correctly, questioned the value of a higher degree. A minimal (standard six) education was more than most Zulu possessed and sufficient for most employers. Indeed, in the increasingly racialized environment of turn-of-the-twentieth-century South Africa, few careers, outside of low paying teaching positions, called for the higher degrees encouraged by the mission. Missionaries and *amakholwa* leaders appealed for children to continue "for the elevation of their race and the advancement of the cause of Christ."[103] But the sense of shared purpose, of Christian mission and commitment to a progressive elevation of the *amakholwa* community, had eroded dramatically in the previous decade—a situation furthered by the fights over *lobola, utshwala,* and the Umsunduze rules.[104]

Student flight was not the only problem. Youth returning from the cities placed new stresses upon Zulu society, stresses magnified on the mission reserves, where their activities upon returning home (gambling, drinking, and various sexual improprieties were common complaints), threatened to undermine *amakholwa* claims of moral superiority.[105] Both church members and missionaries attempted to rein in what they perceived as a morally degenerate generation, but the youth proved difficult to control and station residents did their best to merely quiet them at inopportune times. When the NAM was held at Esidumbini in 1894, for example, the station residents insured that: "Overdress, beerdrinking, horseracing and the overpowering influence of a rabble-babble of irreligious young people" was notable for its absence.[106] Indeed, while the previous generation had fought for their right to engage in certain customs, such as *lobola,* while remaining part of the church, for some young *amakholwa* their experiences in the cities led them to reject Christianity entirely. At Umzumbe in 1892, the congregation called several young men, born Christian but behaving badly after recently returning from the goldfields, to appear before the church so that they might "show them the error of their ways." The young men, however, could not be convinced, and a shocked congregation listened silently as they proclaimed: "We do not have the resolve to believe in Christ."[107] *Amakholwa* and missionaries understandably feared that they had lost a generation.

DESPAIR OVER LAND

In late December of 1893, Mfanfile Kuzwayo, one of the most prosperous *amakholwa* of Mapumulo wrote the AZM:

> Some of us who are on the Glebe request to buy our land. This is because all of the areas around the Glebe are full and small now. And those who are already on the Glebe have spent a lot of money trying to beautify the area and have planted trees and built beautiful houses at their own expense. So we are making this request because we are tired of living like birds who always wander the sky without a fixed place to stay. We want to make it clear that we are not happy to stay in these places because we know quite well that they do not belong to us. May the grace of our Lord Jesus Christ be with you if you approve our request.[108]

Kuzwayo had written a similar letter several years earlier, but as the recently elected headman of the *amakholwa* of Mapumulo he felt called to press the mission once again on the matter.[109] He took the document to the station church, where, after Sunday service, twelve other *amakholwa* men, home owners, planters of crops, plow owners, wagon drivers, and church members, signed their names. The *amakholwa* residents of Mapumulo were not alone in their desire to purchase land. Across the mission, Christians who believed that they had met the expectations embodied in "Christianity" and "civilization," wrote the mission expecting to make the natural last step embodied in the very idea of the "village model": freehold titles.

That the number and urgency of these requests increased in the early years of the 1890s is not surprising, for Natal's imminent transition to responsible government, which would give the colony effective control over internal matters, loomed and a dread over the intentions of the settler government seeped into every corner of the mission. Missionary and *amakholwa* both understood that this was a reasonable fear. As early as 1886 the Natal Legislative Council had sent a letter to the AZM stating its intention of canceling the Mission Reserve grants and asking the Americans to sign away the rights to certain properties after a commission appointed by the legislature in 1884 found that stations from several missions, including the AZM's Table Mountain, were "underutilized."[110] Without power, the Council could not act at this time, but this vague threat hung ominously over the mission during the next decade.[111] In response both to this threat and the scattered requests of *amakholwa*, the mission came close, in the late 1880s, to allowing converts to purchase land on the reserves. At a special meeting in 1885, called to discuss a petition for ownership made by *amakholwa* at Ifafa, members of the mission argued for the necessity of Zulu Christians "buying land on the reserves and securing inalienable titles to land" as soon as possible.[112] But the problem of title-wielding polygamists at Umvoti had spooked the mission, and, despite the pleadings of the *amakholwa* community, the AZM came to no consensus and refused to act.[113] By late December of 1893, when the petition from the residents of Mapumulo arrived, the mission had definitively concluded that freehold tenure would not be granted, and Kuzwayo's request was politely, but firmly, turned down.[114]

This was not all. Much to their chagrin, *amakholwa* found their appeal for freehold tenure not only rebuffed but new rents attached to their continued residence on the mission reserves as the AZM sought to alleviate the strains of an ABM budget shortfall.[115] In late 1888 notice went out to all reserve residents that as of May 1890 the mission would charge five shillings per acre to plant on mission land, ten per acre if the crop was sugarcane.[116] For *amakholwa* families already resident this was affordable, for their newly converted outstation brethren it often was not and it became that much more difficult for these Christians to relocate and join their brethren—further damaging the preferred ideal of *amakholwa* as a tight-knit, semi-exclusive community. Worse, the rents also coincided with increasing land pressures on all Africans as Crown lands were sold off by the government and settlers began turning off squatters to make their own use of the land.[117] For *amakholwa* on the stations, the rents also appeared disarmingly similar to those white landlords charged their traditionalists serving as another reminder of the crumbling edifice of their supposed "special" identity. Over the next decade, the mission drew substantial revenues from these rents, but did so at a severe cost, embittering feelings already damaged by the cultural battles and engendering a lasting distrust among converts.[118]

Still, the granting of responsible government to Natal in 1893 gave *amakholwa* far more cause for concern. A year passed after this event before the Natal government turned its attention to the mission reserve question. On December 17, 1894 the attorney general and the secretary for native affairs called representatives from the largest missions to a meeting at which they outlined the basis for government action. Using the 1884 commission, the attorney general explained that the government felt the missions had failed to follow the original intention of the reserves to create "civilized" natives, had assumed administrative powers not originally conferred, and that the population on mission lands was far sparser than it could be.[119] Further, he charged, the collecting of rents violated the spirit of the original grant and suggested that the only way to settle the matter was to place the reserves under a government oversight body, the Natal Native Trust.[120] Missionaries mounted a defense, noting that the revenue from the rents went to schools, churches, roads, and other "civilizing" improvements, and suggested that reserves be made an exclusive residence for *amakholwa*.[121] Two additional meetings brought no real compromise and in March of that year the attorney general surprised the missions by offering a bill to the new Natal Legislature advocating unilateral action.

In response, the missions notified the attorney general that they would refuse to cooperate in any handover unless alterations were made. In particular the missionaries wanted to insure that "exempted" *amakholwa* would continue to be allowed to reside on the reserves; requested that the former Mission Reserve Trustees be allowed to suggest rules and regulations by which those on the reserves would be expected to live; wanted a clause added that nothing in the bill would "impair the original intent of the Trust"; and asked that the bill be held over until the next session.[122] The attorney general responded by declaring to the assembly that because the missionaries had "withdrawn from taking an active part in making the bill a good measure, it devolves on the House to make a good bill." The AZM, recognizing this threat for what it was, protested once again to the attorney general: "We fear the existence of our Mission will, in the event of an unsympathetic Government taking office be imperiled, should the Bill become law. . ." But they clearly understood that they did not argue from a position of strength.

Amakholwa, fearing that they might lose their land to whites, renewed their efforts to obtain freehold title. Now, however, they not only took their case to the missionaries, but also directly to the government, asking the Natal legislature to insure that all "Christian and Civilized residents" would be able to own their own land and act as farmers to "become a contented civilized peasantry" within the colony.[123] The government gave this little consideration when the bill ultimately became law as Act No. 25, 1895 in early August.[124]

For the government, Act 25 was seen as speeding along the process of incorporating residents of the mission reserves into the larger structure of Natal Native Affairs. Everyone on the reserves was now expected to register with the government and pay taxes, a burden their traditionalist neighbors had long borne but from which Christians had been sheltered. The bill also granted the Natal government power over the sale and rental of land, appropriation of pasture and commonage, all matters to do with roads, fences, woods, and waterways and gave the government power to decide who was allowed onto the stations and who could be removed from them. The government also assumed power to insure the "preservation of health" and the "observation of decency" on the stations, two dangerously broad powers.[125] *Amakholwa* found little to appease them in the provision that a portion of the mission reserves could be alienated for their exclusive occupation, on which all traditional customs, rites and ceremonies not consistent with the tenets of the attached religious body would be prohibited. The smaller glebes already accomplished this and it was, after all, missionaries who most fervently desired that practices such as *lobola* be banned. Worse, a rider was attached to the bill proclaiming that the "Supreme Chief" (the SNA) could send "any tribe, portion of a tribe or native" to the mission reserves now that they were fully incorporated into the colony.[126] The reserves seemed poised to become a holding ground for Africans being squeezed off of lands elsewhere.

Left to the "mercy of an intensely hostile colonial sentiment" *amakholwa* were, by December of 1895, "already counting on the early sale of the reserve lands" to colonialists.[127] *Amakholwa* representatives appealed to the AZM and the mission agreed to oppose the switch from Mission Reserve Trust to Natal Native Trust, even going so far as to appeal to the British Colonial Office for protection.[128] Crippled by the AZM's refusal to cooperate, the law lay in limbo for a year. But the mission did not collect rents during this time and their ambivalent legal status worried the mission as legal problems mounted. After a year the mission folded and voted in the middle of 1896 to cooperate with the government in carrying out the new law.[129] For *amakholwa* the decision reeked of betrayal and underscored a growing conviction that the AZM could no longer be trusted to represent their best interests. Ironically by this time the law had become a dead letter and the Natal government, as we will examine in the final chapter, waited another half-decade before pressing again for control. The intervening years were ones of great confusion, as no one was quite sure who wielded authority over a whole host of issues dealing with the reserves, from granting approval for plowing on communal land, to collecting rents, transferring titles, and appointing Christian headmen.[130]

While the battle over mission lands raged, *amakholwa* also fought against the new Natal government's plan to stop granting exemptions from native law to Christian Africans. These exemptions, which the colonial government had first approved in 1865, allowed for educated, propertied (although this meant goods not land) Zulu Christians to petition the SNA to be placed under English laws. Exempted *amakholwa*, who wore silver or bronze medals to demonstrate their status, swore an oath of allegiance to Queen Victoria and in so doing removed themselves from the power of their previous chiefs.[131] Initially, the percentage of *amakholwa* exempted was rather small, but, perhaps as a reward for services rendered, their numbers jumped dramatically following the Anglo-Zulu war, and throughout the next decade many Christians sought and were granted the exemption.[132] From 1894 on, however, the SNA reduced the number of exemptions granted to a mere trickle by imposing increasingly stringent demands (such as a requirement for English literacy) on applicants and halting the practice of automatically extending the exemption to children of the exempted.[133] The granting of exemptions was halted because the new colonial government feared that they offered a door to enfranchisement and the government wanted to bring all natives, Christian or not, under the control of the SNA. Finally colonialists generally found intolerable the *amakholwa* belief that in achieving exemption they acquired the full legal standing of Europeans.[134]

Across Natal, the settler government sought to dismantle *amakholwa* aspirations.[135] In 1896 twenty Christian men from Umtwalume were called out to work on nearby public roads. These pressgangs, long a hated reality of life for traditionalists, were a new experience for *amakholwa* and while they performed "cheerfully," they also protested against any future inclusion in Natal's forced labor system.[136] Elsewhere resident magistrates, those charged with overseeing the colony's local affairs, began ruling against *amakholwa* in several small, but symbolically important ways; allowing fines by chiefs to stand, despite evidence that the fines had been imposed as a deterrent for choosing Christianity, refusing to license marriages between Christians without the payment of *lobola*, and preventing *amakholwa* preachers from moving to Zululand.[137] This last issue, in which the SNA sought to impose restrictions on where Christians, particularly those already exempted, were allowed to live, became entangled in the efforts of the Natal government to craft a "native law" based on loosely interpreted traditions and co-opted chiefs.

For much of the nineteenth century, colonial Natal attempted to administer its African population cheaply by employing chiefly legitimacy in their favor.[138] But exempted *amakholwa*, free from chiefly rule, had long been the fly in this ointment and agitation over the status of *amakholwa* was not new; the colonial government had long struggled with the question of just where the Christian community fit into administration of the colony. Theoretically, exemptions were meant to sort out these difficulties, so, for example, when Chief Swaimana lodged a complaint in 1892 against Thomas Hawes, an exempted AZM preacher, for moving onto land under his control without his permission and against his wishes, the SNA backed the chief and forced Hawes to move precisely because he was exempted and therefore not really a "native" and thus not allowed to live on location land without special permission, a permission he had not been granted.[139] After 1894 the new government was not only concerned that exempted *amakholwa* undermined the powers of the native administration, but also wanted to be rid such distinctions altogether. To accomplish this Natal tried reincorporating *amakholwa* into the chiefdoms surrounding the mission reserves. Under a law passed in 1896 which laid down exact boundaries for chiefs, (previously "tribes" had less to do with geography and more with declared loyalty) the Natal legislature stipulated that these lines of chiefly control did not stop at the borders of the mission reserves, but would be drawn "in continuation of boundaries on contiguous locations and the natives on reserved missionary land shall be bound by a boundary thereon in the same way as a location native is herby made subject to a location boundary."[140] Everyone was given two years to adjust to the new system. Christians at Esidumbini petitioned instead to create a self-governing council of those not wanting to be incorporated into "tribes," but the SNA responded that those wishing not to live under certain chiefs known to be hostile to their faith should engage in land swaps to remove themselves elsewhere.[141] In a single stroke, the Natal government had potentially incorporated large numbers of Christians under the power of chiefs, and thus, under native administration.[142]

The law exacerbated what had become a growing problem on the stations, the extension of factionalism into church affairs. While Christians in some communities, such as Mapumulo, considered themselves separated from the surrounding chiefs and established *amakholwa* headmen in their place, elsewhere, such as at Inanda, Umtwalume, and Amanzimtoti the mission reserves were surrounded by powerful chieftaincies that retained loyal Christian subjects. In the early days of the Christian community there were few divided loyalties. Believers were first and foremost members of the church, brothers and sisters in Christ who had given up their past lives to, literally, wear the new clothes of their faith. But in the late 1880s and early 1890s, as the initial identity they had constructed began to collapse under the weight of the forces discussed, their Christian community lost ground to older political loyalties. Land disputes and cattle raids highlighted factionalism off the mission reserves, but on reserves disputes most often centered on matters of church policy: invitations for baptism, the allocation of church funds, the appointment of station *induna*, and, most heatedly, the calling of Zulu pastors and preachers, which, because of the democratic nature of Congregationalism, involved potentially divisive elections.[143]

The most heated of these disputes occurred at Inanda in 1895, when the church voted nearly equally for the pastoral candidacies of John Dube and Cetywayo Goba.[144] Both were, by the standards of the mission, equally fit for the position.[145] But in reviewing the ballots the mission found numerous irregularities and concluded that the vote had broken along political, not spiritual lines; Dube was a favored nephew of Mqawe, a powerful local chief, while Goba was the second son of an independent *induna*.[146] In reaction the mission declared the whole process null and void, called the church together, and gave a sermon on the "principles of brotherliness that Congregational usage and Christ's church require—oneness of spirit—harmonious meetings—united contributions towards one purse—independence of tribal distinctions or other outside relationships in all church matters." But resolution was slow in coming and the following year the church voted again with similar results. The mission advised both candidates to retire and Goba withdrew his name, but not Dube, whose faction insisted that he had won the elections (he had by a handful of votes) and threatened to build their own chapel, splitting the church, if their man was not given the appointment. The AZM held firm but was surprised when Dube left for America, his supporters having raised sufficient funds for him to travel to the United States.[147] The split appeared irreconcilable to all involved, but one year later, following the revival at Inanda, the two sides united to call their own pastor.

UNDOING BINDING TIES

In the middle of 1895 AZM congregations across Natal received a letter from America, which appeared to signal a remarkable shift in mission policy.[148] The letter, from the Conference of Foreign Missions, an umbrella organization to which the ABM belonged, called on native churches across the globe to assume responsibility for their own faith by supporting themselves both financially and spiritually. The AZM, which received the letter in early 1895, translated and circulated the document with the hopes that it might inspire increased tithing. But in translating the idea of "to take charge of"—as in to be accountable for—the American's used the Zulu *ukuziphatha*, in a way that allowed *amakholwa* to read the idea as "to be in command of" and many came to believe that the Board intended to transfer all authority and responsibility into the hands' of the congregations—including, naturally, the titles to the mission reserve lands.

Read this way the letter, which called on churches to aggressively pursue their own pastorate, seemed to offer a step-by-step guide to autonomy and congregations across the mission were stirred to action. The congregation at Amahlongwa wrote the mission mere weeks after receiving the letter, requesting that Simon be named their pastor: "We understand that you are willing to accede to such a request as this, if the church assumes the whole support of its preacher. This the church has agreed to do. We think the time has come when we should move in this matter."[149] Inanda, Umtwalume, Mapumulo, Johannesburg, Umzumbe, and Esidumbini all made similar requests. When *amakholwa* gathered for the NAM held at Mapumulo that year, many arrived expecting the mission representative to detail this handover. But the mission, apparently unaware of their considerable blunder, reacted clumsily when confronted and informed those gathered that they should not misinterpret the letter as meaning that every church should now call its own pastors "after the same manner of the American churches" but rather that after sixty-some years, the Zulu churches should no longer expect "generous aid from abroad." The time had come, the mission argued, for the churches to pay for themselves and the mission suggested contributing to a common purse controlled by a group of six *amakholwa* and missionaries known as the *Isitupa*.[150]

The disappointment of *amakholwa* was palpable, particularly in light of missionary intransigence in promoting the cause of Zulu leadership. As the number of outstations expanded during the last decades of the nineteenth century, the mission refused to fill the churches with Zulu pastors, calling instead on the ABM for new missionaries to fill growing gaps in coverage.[151] But the Board, overextended and facing an impending financial collapse, offered no relief. Initially the mission responded by increasing the number of stations under watch of each missionary, David Harris, for example, was assigned a vast swath of lower Natal, including Ifumi, Amahlongwa, Ifafa and Umtwalume and reported that it required a great deal of traveling to reach all the stations even occasionally. So while he was based out of Umtwalume, his schedule kept him away and the weekly duties of the church fell to a Zulu preacher. Indeed, the AZM maintained a permanent presence during the 1890s only at Umvoti for the prestige, Inanda because of the political troubles, and Amanzimtoti where two missionaries ran the high school and theological seminary. Despite this reality, resistance to surrendering control was fierce. When Smith encouraged the mission to accept a transition to Zulu leadership one of the missionaries argued that it made little sense for the congregations to pursue such action: "No man, of whatever color he may be, will chose what seems to him to be an inferior article which he has to pay a high price for when he can get a *better* article *for nothing*."[152]

This reluctance to appoint pastors (those responsible for ecclesiastical oversight of their own churches as opposed to preachers who had no formal claim of authority over the congregations they worked with) was linked to the moral troubles of several *amakholwa* pastors during the 1870s. Missionaries had a long institutional memory for these matters and cited them when pressed to surrender control.[153] For his part, Charles Kilbon offered a more sophisticated argument when he suggested that too often the congregations still equated pastors with chiefs and that youthful pastors stood the risk of clashing with the Zulu ideal of seniority—it would be difficult, he thought, for older men to be taught by their juniors. This was, he believed, changing with the newer generation and therefore in the coming years it might be possible to again appoint Zulu pastors. It is noteworthy, of course, that he did not seem to consider if elderly Zulu Christians did not notice his own youth; race, as always in Natal, trumping age.[154]

For over a decade, during which time several preachers waited their opportunity to lead, the mission did not employ a single Zulu pastor.[155] But the financial difficulties of the Board weighed heavily and from the mid-1880s to 1895 both the number of missionaries and the financial contributions from the Board fell. The AZM reacted, as we have seen, in part by imposing a rent, but also by interpreting the increasingly urgent suggestions of Judson Smith, the ABM secretary, that they should devolve control to the churches, by suggesting that the churches should pay the entirety of salaries for Zulu clergy.[156] The mission planned on having these preachers operate on circuits, relocating every three years to avoid business entanglements that had led to the downfall of previous Zulu pastors. They would also be expected to minutely detail the progress of their work, recording the number of Sabbaths preached, kraals visited, and donations collected; preachers, it was argued "should not become too independent."[157] This plan promised to be onerous for both congregations and Zulu preachers and met with little acceptance either in Natal or the Board's Boston headquarters.

By 1894, after a decade of distrust, antagonism, and denied opportunity, resentment finally coalesced into anger. At that year's NAM in Esidumbini, the mood was thick with suspicion, choking out the religiosity of the event as participants closely questioned the missionary representatives over AZM handling of church contributions.[158] But the enmity between mission and *amakholwa* ran deeper than simple bookkeeping. The mission's refusal to sell land, their decision to charge rents, and their questioning of *amakholwa* morality and thus their Christian identity, all undermined the relationship between mission and congregation. of their congregations ate away at the relationship. By 1895 *amakholwa* had even come to regard the theological school graduates with suspicion, fearing that they had "gone over to the missionaries."[159] So when the ABM offered them autonomy, they did not hesitate to seize the moment; doing so not only meant administering their own church affairs, but also securing their land and, importantly, asserting their Christianity.

The mission, pressed on all sides to begin divesting authority, agreed only grudgingly to the process, and a special committee formed to investigate candidates recommended moving forward slowly in the ordination of three *amakholwa*.[160] Within a year the number installed reached four, as those churches that agreed to fully support their nominees were granted permission to call their own pastors.[161] But as requests for similar consideration from other congregations, both large and small, flooded the mission, their resolve stiffened against further ordinations. Bolstered by the Dube/Goba dispute at Inanda, the AZM "settled down into the belief that the churches of the Zulu mission are not prepared to select their own pastors" and recommended instead that the American Board send a follow-up letter to the churches recommending a standing committee which would have responsibility to chose pastors for the churches and regulate their time of service and whose membership would be shared between Zulu and the AZM.[162] It was not a popular compromise, however, for it essentially stripped the churches of the very independence of action promised in Congregationalism. The Board refused and congregations continued to claim their right to call their own leadership.

Perhaps surprisingly, the most strident demands for autonomy came from the recently formed congregation at Johannesburg. In their original request, these *amakholwa* had specifically asked for a black preacher and the mission, after some prodding, had agreed to send Benjamin Hawes. But members of the mission questioned the wisdom of handing over responsibility to a Zulu of what was quickly becoming a key post:

> Place a white man there from the start and don't begin it until you do so. The native would get into no end of trouble very likely with these men or get us, perhaps. They like to take things in their own hands and they are not very wise yet—And too far [a]way to be helped by our advice.[163]

In 1894 the AZM sent Herbert Goodenough to run the Johannesburg church. While the Johannesburg congregation did not initially object to this development, there was friction between themselves and Goodenough from the start and they were one of the first to respond to the self-support circular, calling Umvakwendhlu to be their pastor. By the time their letter arrived, however, Umvakwedhlu had already agreed to lead Esidumbini and the congregation's discontent festered until April of 1895, when they gathered secretly to write a letter to the AZM detailing their grievances.

Their letter reveals a community anxious over its connection to the mission, its place in the urban world, and its Christian legitimacy. Strikingly, the Johannesburg congregation charged Goodenough with failing to uphold the moral standard of the mission by operating an apartment house near the church that he rented out to "Cape coloureds" (Afrikaans-speaking people of mixed race) working in the city. They argued that among these residents were many who engaged in adultery and other licentious acts that brought shame upon their church. They also believed it was not right to teach children born out of wedlock to these people in the church school, arguing, "they should be refused and thereby the parents be taught to be married."[164] It angered them that because Zulu Christians could not afford this housing, morally deficient but wealthier "coloreds" moved in next to the church. Goodenough, they argued, had thrown their entire congregation into disrepute. Finally, the *amakholwa* community wanted an account given of where the money from the weekly collections was going. They did not want it spent on Goodenough's properties or the education of the colored children, but rather on the expansion of the Johannesburg mission and toward paying the salary of Fokoti, the recently appointed Zulu preacher to Johannesburg and the man the congregation intended to become their pastor. As we will see later, the mission's response to their concerns was far less than the Johannesburg church had hoped for, again leaving *amakholwa* with the impression that the mission did not respect their own spiritual and temporal authority, perhaps because the AZM regarded them as somehow not fully Christian.[165]

THE YEAR OF PLAGUES

In 1895 the women of Esidumbini mission stayed home. In previous years many had gone to Durban at this time to sell goods, but in early 1895 hordes of locusts darkened the skies and descended upon the ripening fields of Natal. Larger than a man's fist, the red locust is, alone, capable of impressive consumption. In swarms the insects can strip a maize field in hours, finishing a season's production and threatening starvation for the affected household.[166] Beginning in early 1895 great swaths of land were consumed and women, in particular, spent all day in the fields, rising early and going to bed late to fight a campaign against the inevitable.[167] The plague spanned two growing seasons and many of those on the mission stations lost their crops in 1895 and 1896, leading at least one missionary to allude to the "second of Pharaoh's plagues" and call 1895–1896 the "locust year."[168]

While attendance at Sunday services, prayer meetings, and other regular gatherings declined dramatically, Christians did gather for several special sessions, crying out for relief. At the height of the outbreak, the residents of Mapumulo gathered twice daily in this way for a week before the swarm finally moved on, having stripped their fields clean.[169] William Wilcox, hoping to fend off the hunger to follow, worked closely with Mfanefile Kuzwayo, the elected Christian *induna* for the station, to import corn from America, distributing grain at cost to those suffering from "extreme famine."[170] Many other stations and outstations suffered similarly and even those who had resisted going to the newly urban areas of southern Africa had little choice but to seek outside employment in the face of starvation. The remaining ties that bound *amakholwa* together threatened to come undone when Itafamasi, crippled by food shortages in the face of the plague, announced at the last moment that it could not host the 1896 NAM. The organizing committee responsible for the NAM (composed of both *amakholwa* and missionaries) urgently searched for a replacement site, but the conference taxed its hosts under the best of circumstances and one by one the stations declined. Faced with the alarming possibility of losing the one event in which their own voice was preeminent, the *amakholwa* of Inanda, who had suffered less than others, volunteered, and hosted a stripped down meeting at great financial hardship.[171]

Not surprisingly the year of tribulation brought spiritual responses. One missionary wrote:

> The plagues and calamities which have overshadowed the whole of South Africa are quite as likely to prepare the way for a more spiritual era, as the plagues on Egypt helped to build the road of redemption for God's people. Whatever shadow therefore a local report may fling, we would not have it obscure the prophetic assurance of our souls of the glorious days about to dawn.[172]

As in previous years, an itinerant white evangelist was brought in with the hopes of exciting religious renewal, but it was Johannes, a blind *amakholwa* preacher speaking about the blessings of the Holy Spirit, who caused a brief "outpouring" of the spirit.[173] Any hope of respite resulting from this worship vanished, however, as reports of a more terrifying plague began trickling in. Rinderpest, *amakholwa* transport riders returning from long hauls across southern Africa warned, would bring doom to them all.

Early in the year these stories were little but vague rumors, but in March of 1896 rinderpest, a cattle epidemic of staggering proportions, broke out across the Zambezi River, the last major natural barrier to its spread across the southern African subcontinent. The disease, originating in the steppes of Asia, had been introduced into sub-Saharan Africa almost a decade earlier when, in 1889, Italians imported Black Sea cattle to feed their armies during their unsuccessful Ethiopian campaign.[174] Once introduced, the epizootic swept through Africa, working its way both south and west, and destroying herd never before exposed at rates up to 90 to 95 percent.[175] In Kenya, Uganda, Tanzania, and Mali, Africans experienced similar tales of woe, as the disease devoured their herds, leaving many susceptible to famine, other diseases, enslavement, and ultimately conquest.[176] The disease itself, which also attacked varieties of wild game, progressed rapidly through its host and death could occur as quickly as thirty hours after the initial appearance of the disease, but generally took from four to seven days. Cattle initially developed a broken cough, their eyes went red and watery and soon they became listless, disinclined to rise from the ground as their temperature soared, they passed bloody diarrhea and their mouths and nostrils became covered in bloody foam. Shortly before the end, an animal's temperature plummeted precipitously and it became semi-comatose, uttering low moans while its muscles twitched uncontrollably. Save for a few stragglers, an entire herd of hundreds of animals could be gone in less than a week.[177]

Despite receiving warning as early as 1892, the various colonial governments of southern Africa remained ill-prepared for its arrival.[178] Worse, the warnings and recommendations of various agricultural commissioners were drowned out by the Ndebele uprising in Zimbabwe in early 1896, itself sparked in part by the clumsy efforts of the British South Africa Company to control recent outbreaks of the disease.[179] The revolt helped spread the plague by increasing the amount of wagon-traffic in and out of infected areas just when such traffic needed to be shut down. Belatedly, at an April conference held in Mafeking, agricultural officials from Natal, the South African Republic (SAR), the Orange Free State (OFS), and the Cape Colony agreed, after touring an infected herd and seeing the devastating results of the epidemic firsthand, to a series of measures designed to quarantine southern Africa from the rest of the continent. They also reluctantly agreed that the only way to stop the plague was to pursue a "stamping out" policy in which all animals with the disease and all animals that came into contact with the infected beasts would be immediately destroyed. Recognizing that this would be an unpopular approach (with all farmers white and black) the commission agreed that compensation should be paid to owners of healthy cattle killed.[180]

But their efforts were too late and while, as popularly told, the Afrikaner Volksraad debated imposing these measures, a rinderpest-ridden beast collapsed in the streets outside of the parliament building in Pretoria that May.[181] Natal promptly closed its borders with the Transvaal, stranding scores of *amakholwa* transport riders who failed to make it back home after risking recent events in a gamble to secure one last trade.[182] From August on the *Natal Mercury* began running regular updates of the plague's steady march toward the colony, reporting the utter hopelessness of stopping it for, "the disease was carried under some circumstances by birds, by flies, and even by the wind. As these could not be fenced out, the colony needed to face the very real prospect that the disease would break in."[183] If these developments weren't disturbing enough, the Natal government wanted to drive home to Africans the danger the colony faced, and sent the Under Secretary for Native Affairs (USNA) S.O. Samuelson to the locations and mission stations located along the colony's borders with the message that rinderpest was "like a fire which carries everything before it . . ." "It could" he noted frighteningly, "be carried in one's clothes; horses, dogs and vultures could communicate it." He related a case where calves licked the harness of a horse ridden by a man traveling from an infected area, killing off the entire herd.[184] From September 28 to October 1, Samuelson visited with traditional chiefs and *amakholwa* leaders at Mapumulo, delivering his blood-curdling message, informing them that they needed to discontinue the practice of *siasing* cattle, report suspicious deaths to the government, be aware of dogs and vultures and, if (although the implication was more when) the rinderpest struck, to bury all carcasses.[185] By October, rinderpest had become a central concern in the native press, one Xhosa language newspaper reported:

> Rinderpest is now the all-absorbing topic. Traveling south through Africa sweeping "every hoof of cattle to ruination"—and if the country had been blessed with lynx-eyed or far-seeing and capable ministers of agriculture during the past year or two, a stand against the pest might have been made before it had crossed the Zambezi, reports of it having filtered down here while it was in Blantyre. But there can be no question that the country's outlook is becoming dark and lowering with every day that passes, owing to the dogged march of the ghastly monster.[186]

The Zulu language newspaper *Inkanyiso Yase Natal*, in one of its last editions, warned as early as June against the coming of the cattle plague and a Christian from Mapumulo wrote the *Natal Mercury* to ask the government to convene a meeting of all the native chiefs in Durban: "Seeing that we are on the eve of being visited and totally robbed of all our earthly and dearest possession—our cattle—it is high time that we also voiced our wishes to government before it is too late to mend." Remarkably, Natal managed to remain disease free for another half year, but for Zulu Christians this proved the tipping point in a long string of crises. It is not surprising that several months after the USNA met with Mapumulo leaders, including Mfanefile Kuzwayo, *amakholwa*, staggered by a decade of events that had slowly torn apart their initial identity, enthusiastically re-embraced their Christianity. Rinderpest, migrant labor, the collapse of their agrarian "civilized" identity, and various other maladies added up to a moral emergency that demanded a moral response. Their community, born in faith, returned to its roots, seeking not just a revival of faith, but also of identity.

NOTES

1. Michael Mahoney makes this point nicely in, "The Millennium Comes to Mapumulo: Popular Christianity in Rural Natal, 1866–1906," *Journal of Southern African Studies* 25 (1999).

2. Cetshwayo evaded the British army on several occasions before finally being captured the end of August 1880. KwaZulu was then divided into thirteen principalities that were eventually reduced to a state of civil war when Cetshwayo was brought back from British imposed exile. See Jeff Guy, *The Destruction of the Zulu Kingdom: The Civil War in Zululand, 1879–1884* (Pietermaritzburg: University of Natal Press, 1994).

3. Many of those who bought additional lots created a stir in 1894 when some thirteen Indians were leased lots of 3–15 acres each at a rate of 10 shillings per acre. The mission objected, of course, but so too did several *amakholwa* who protested against *iCoolie ikula* working on the Sabbath. SNA 2966/1896, resolutions passed by Lower Tugela Association re: Indians on mission reserves; AZM A/2/10, Imina Sojuba to AZM, November 30, 1896.

4. ABM 212/216, Hance to Means, May 15, 1879. Over the course of the next several years, cases of polygamy from throughout the mission came to light. The greatest number, and the most dramatic cases, however, came from Umvoti. These were not the first instances of polygamy to occur on the mission. Previously, however, it had been a sporadic phenomenon and one attributed to a lack of "true" conversion. Missionaries also attempted to dismiss the 1879 polygamists as having "apparently never understood anything at all what it is to be born again." But the depth of involvement of these men in the lives of the churches makes this argument difficult to sustain.

5. Although there is no direct evidence, it is reasonable to speculate that a correlation exists between the participation of Umvoti residents as transport-riders in the Anglo-Zulu war, and their attempts following the conflict to shore up their status among traditionalists. Unlike the Edendale *amakholwa*, for example, who formed their own military unit, the Edendale Light Horse, and served in an active military role, those Zulu Christians who made money from the war as transport riders received little recognition outside of payment. Indeed, most must have suffered the indignities of being treated as the hired black help by the infamously brusque quarter-masters of the British army. So, while the members of the Edendale Light Horse returned to their station as war heroes, with church bells tolling, the transport riders of Umvoti returned home even more cognizant of their second class citizenship in the white world. Pursuing connections among traditionalists than seems a perfectly reasonable response, despite its risks.

6. C. Webb and J. B. Wright (eds.), *The James Stuart Archive of Recorded Oral Evidence Relating to the History of the Zulu and Neighboring Peoples, Volume IV* (Pietermartizburg: University of Natal Press, 1983), 34.

7. ABM 212/615–16, J. Tyler to Friends, November 14, 1876.

8. James Cooper Jr., "Enthusiasts or Democrats? Separatism, Church Government, and the Great Awakening in Massachusetts," *The New England Quarterly* 65

(1992), 277; Stephen Foster, "A Connecticut Separate Church: Strict Congregationalism in Cornwall, 1780–1809," *The New England Quarterly* 39 (1966).

9. ABM 185/815, Wilder to Means, April 6, 1882. In the early 1880s missionaries, knowing many *amakholwa* believed that the AZM had deliberately withheld the publication of the Old Testament out of fear that it would strengthen arguments for *lobola* and polygamy, discussed the need to carefully establish orthodox understandings of the work as the date for its release neared. Their strategy centered on the need to familiarize congregations with the theology of the Old Testament within the context of the gospels and to then reinforce this by teaching the history of the Christian Church. The lack of the Old Testament did not prevent at least some *amakholwa* from bringing up Old Testament comparisons. During a polygamy trail at Umsumduzi in 1876, at least one church member, "less educated than the others" spoke out for leniency, asking whether David and Abraham were not in heaven despite their multiple marriages. But the majority present, presumably more thoroughly instructed in the expectations of contemporary Christianity, "unhesitatingly" condemned "the disgraceful course," and recommended "prompt and decisive action" suspending the polygamist from the church. ABM 182/612–14, J. Tyler to Clark, April 10, 1876.

10. AZM A/3/49, Goodenough to SNA, June 25, 1894. ABM 183/359, Rood to Means, June 6, 1883.

11. C. Webb and J. B. Wright (eds.), *The James Stuart Archive*, Volume IV, 14.

12. AZM A/3/41, Esidumbini station report, 1890–91.

13. AZM A/3/41, Lindley (Inanda) station report, 1896–97.

14. ABM 185/905–07, Wilder to Smith, June 1, 1899

15. AZM A/1/2, 49th Annual Meeting of AZM, June 4–11, 1884.

16. AZM A/1/7, Report of NAM at Mapumulo, 1895. As will be seen later in this chapter, the polygamy scandals also killed efforts by *amakholwa* outside of Umvoti to obtain freehold tenure. The AZM, spooked by their failure to remove the polygamous men from Umvoti, could not agree on plans to sell land on the other stations until it was too late. After the events at Umvoti, Christians from the AZM were forced to fill their land hunger with expensive properties off of the stations, slowly draining the wealth and energies of even the best *amakholwa*. Nicholas Cope, "The Zulu Petit Bourgeoisie and Zulu Nationalism in the 1920s: Origins of Inkatha," *Journal of Southern African Studies* 16 (1990): 435–37; Norman Etherington, "Mission Station Melting Pots as a Factor in the Rise of South African Black Nationalism," *The International Journal of African Historical Studies* 9 (1976); and C. Tsheloane Keto, "Race Relations, Land and the Changing Missionary Role in South Africa: A Case Study of the American Zulu Mission, 1850–1910," *The International Journal of African Historical Studies*, 10 (1977).

17. The story of that meeting and subsequent events are reconstructed from two sources. ABM 183/310, history of the Umzumbe Church, undated; AZM A/4/59, Manuscript Reminiscences of Mrs. L.B. Bridgeman [Amy Cowles].

18. For a particularly interesting discussion of how rinderpest affected the abilities of households, both Christian and traditionalist, to perform *ukuzila*, see Benedict Carton, "'We Are Made Quiet by This Annihilation': Historicizing Concepts of

Bodily Pollution and Dangerous Sexuality in South Africa," *The International Journal of African Historical Studies* 39 (2006).

19. Colossians 2:8, 17: Beware lest any man spoil you through philosophy and vain deceit, after the tradition of men, after the rudiments of the world, and not after Christ. . . . Let no man therefore judge you in meat, or in drink, or in respect of an holyday, or of the new moon, or of the Sabbath days: Which are a shadow of things to come; but the body is of Christ.

20. ABM 212/87–88, J. Dube to Bradly, January 26, 1884.

21. So fierce were these debates, in fact, that most of the other missionary bodies showed little appetite, despite their own reservations, in pursuing the matter. Only the Roman Catholics joined the AZM in making *lobola* a disciplinable offense. For their part, *amakholwa* in other missions believed that the practice had undergone a dangerous evolution by the end of the century and recommended the custom be regulated "so as to be in accordance with Christian propriety." Etherington, *Preachers, Peasants and Politics*, 139.

22. ABM 175/1078, Ireland to Anderson, January 1, 1852.

23. ABM 179/417, W. Mellen to R. Anderson, November 26, 1860; ABM 177/667–68, H. Bridgeman to N. Clark; ABM 179/483, W. Mellen to N. Clark, June 10, 1870; ABM 191/303, Mrs. C. Goodenough, February 11, 1890. Arthur Christofersen has noted that the American Civil War imbued an entire generation of theological students and missionaries with an inflexibility of thought, a moral certainty that stretched from small daily affairs to matters dealing with the church. Arthur Christofersen, *Adventuring With God: The Story of the American Board Mission in South Africa* (Durban: 1967), 67.

24. ABM 177/198, A. Abraham to N. Clark, March 2, 1868; ABM 177/139–40, D. Rood to N. Clark, November 25, 1867. Because of the connotations it acquired in the brothels of Johannesburg, *umfazi*, became a derogatory term that is now replaced with *inkosikazi*.

25. ABM 177/494–95, A. Abraham to N. Clark, November 19, 1867. At least one missionary agreed and argued that: "Such is the state of society here that if that [*lobola*] is done away our girls will stand unprotected morally and the women will be treated like slaves." ABM 177/465–64, C. Lloyd to her mother and father, 1868. Catherine Lloyd, whose husband Charles died shortly after their arrival in Natal (she would later marry one of Daniel Lindley's sons), served without payment until 1878. She was the most perceptive of the AZM missionaries and her few letters that remain are filled with keen observations. She attributed this to a role in the mission that allowed her time to mingle with the people, "hearing them talk more than others." Of *lobola*, she wrote: "To any one hearing of a Christian man as marrying his daughter for a certain number of cows, it seems terrible and unchristian, but is one of those things that distance makes worse than the reality. It is true that those of our mission who are so strong in saying "women are slaves" and "the mission shall be broken up and go home before this custom is allowed" these can bring up a few solitary cases that seem very horrible—just as I can tell of cases in America where daughters were forced to marry against their will an old and rich man instead of someone they loved who was poor."

26. C. Webb and J. B. Wright (eds.), *The James Stuart Archive Volume IV*, 14.

27. ABM 178/223, A. Grout to R. Anderson, November 4, 1867. The Anglican dean of Pietermaritzburg noted that young women were not willing to give it up for fear that it would lessen their husbands' respect for them. *Inkanyiso Yase Natal,* "Report of the Provincial Missionary Conference" April 24, 1896.

28. ABM 177/152, D. Rood to N. Clark, November 25, 1867.

29. ABM 177/467–71, N. Clark to Zulu Mission, June 2, 1868.

30. ABM 181/71, W. Ireland to N. Clark, May 27, 1880.

31. ABM 181 & 183, AZM tabular views.

32. Although this could be a gendered argument, as women suffered more economically from *utshwala* restrictions.

33. AZM A/3/46, AZM annual report, 1889–90.

34. ABM 188/407, C. Bridgman to J. Smith, June 1896. AZM A/1/2, AZM annual letter, 1884–85.

35. ABM 183/360, Rood to Means, June 6, 1883. In traditional society these events, particularly those connected with marriage, brought together members of both sexes to drink and dance, share stories, trade insults, and tell ribald jokes. While Christian engagement parties were tamer affairs, *amakholwa* frequently attended the celebrations of *amabhinca* friends and family and often partook with everyone else from the large clay *utshwala* brewing pots.

36. ABM 185, J. Tyler to Means, Oct 16, 1882. Reporting from Umsumduzi Tyler noted that wedding celebrations on the station had become "altogether too noisy and conducive to immorality" and he proposed, in a series of regulations, to forbid the brewing and consumption of beer on mission land. Wallace Mills has pointed out, however, that among Xhosa Christians in the Cape Colony, *utshwala* was steadily replaced at beer drinks by harder liquor such as brandy. There, unlike among Zulu Christians, Xhosa (both traditionalists and believers) supported prohibitions being set in place. Mills, "The Roots of African Nationalism in the Cape Colony: Temperance, 1866–1898," *The International Journal of African Historical Studies* 13 (1980).

37. AZM A/4/59, manuscript reminiscences of Mrs. L.B Bridgman (A. Cowles).

38. Ibid.

39. AZM A/4/51, pledge of Mabuda Cele, Umzumbe, January 1878.

40. AZM A/4/59, manuscript reminiscences of Mrs. L.B Bridgman.

41. Ibid.

42. Of course the contemporary analogy here might be sexual abstinence campaigns advocated by the American President George W. Bush's administration in the early 2000s. Recent research suggests that such an approach hasn't been particularly effective today, and one wonders if alcohol abstinence campaigns were any more so in the late 19th century. Elise Rosenbaum, "Patient Teenagers? A Comparison of the Sexual Behavior of Virginity Pledgers and Matched Nonpledgers," *Pediatrics,* 123:1 (2009), 110–120.

43. The Umzumbe temperance campaign remained a potent and widely used model for several decades. Organizers of a teachers' workshop held at Adams in 1907, staged a temperance meeting in which 200 children, dressed in white and wearing blue ribbons, marched up and down the station roads. Proceeded by a giant drum keeping beat, the children sang rousing temperance songs and carried

brightly colored banners and flags before entering the church for an afternoon of lectures, songs, "drama" and catechism. The event concluded with a recitation of the temperance pledge and signing the temperance oath. The organizers encouraged Zulu teachers in attendance, most who had participated in similar affairs in their childhood, to reproduce the event at their own schools. AZM A/4/59, A. Cowles to Friends, September 3, 1907. Leaping ahead a century, it is remarkable how closely a form of contemporary AIDS abstinence education known as "Virginity Testing" is in some of its practices to the AZM's earlier temperance movement—right down to public performances designed to not only reinforce the participants morality, but also that of the community as whole. See, Fiona Scorgie, "Virginity Testing and the Politics of Sexual Responsibility: Implications for AIDS Intervention," *African Studies* 61 (2002).

44. ABM 184/728, Kilbon to Means, June 19, 1883. AZM A/1/2, Minutes of Annual Meeting, May 29th, 1883.

45. Of course *amakholwa* women continued to brew the stuff, if more surreptitiously then before.

46. AZM A/4/59, A. Cowles, "Wets and Drys in Africa," undated. AZM A/3/41, Ifafa station report, 1893–94. The missionary at Ifafa acknowledged that his congregation's concern deserved consideration.

47. AZM A/3/41, Umtwalume station report, 1894–95.

48. ABM 184/382–384, Holbrook to Smith, April 19, 1887.

49. AZM A/3/46, AZM annual report, 1889–90.

50. Gertrude Hance "The Story of Hobiana," *Congregational Church Magazine*, September 1892.

51. The increasing number of excommunicated Zulu Christians further complicated the question of *amakholwa* identity. Were these men and women *amakholwa*, or not? Christian theology demanded that those who confessed their sins be welcomed back, but a distinct sense of a "fall from grace" imbues their subsequent narratives. And there was a limit to how many times the AZM welcomed returning sinners. Noziwawa, one of the first converts at Amanzimtoti, was suspended or excommunicated nearly a half dozen times from 1854 to 1886, for offenses ranging from drinking beer, to polygamy to receiving *lobola*. Late in the 1880s he was once again removed, this time for adultery. Several years later he married the woman with whom he had the affair, sought to be readmitted into the church and was shocked when the resident missionary railed against him, proclaiming that the outcast *amakholwa* had caused enough harm to the cause of the church. Christian friends of the man, scandalized by the missionary's refusal, appealed by asking "does not the Bible say that we should forgive seventy times seven?" But the missionary was unmoved and Noziwawa attended services without being in full membershi AZM A/4/59, Bunker to Friends, January 1, 1898.

52. While this work focuses on the *amakholwa* of the AZM, it is clear that a similar moral crisis gripped Christians of other denominations. The Anglican Bishop of Zululand, writing in the Zulu newspaper *Inkanyiso Yase Natal*, noted in 1895: "We cannot, perhaps, expect a very high standard of spiritual life amongst the greater number of our people, but we must try and make it as high as we can. At any rate we must not be in a hurry. A cheap Christianity is worse than no Christianity and

this for the sake of those who may be admitted into the Christian covenant as well as for those outside." *Inkanyiso Yase Natal*, "Cheap Christianity," February 8, 1895.

53. The dialogue of "sin" played an increasingly important role during this time. In 1890 those attending the annual ABM gathering were reminded that they had become missionaries because they were "convicted of the sinfulness of heathen" and that millions faced certain damnation without their ministry. In 1894, the director of Amanzimtoti Theological Seminary reported that the paramount aim of that institution was to make its pupils "personally and deeply realize the sinfulness of sin and the richness of grace and to be humbled by the one and inspired by the other to work for the redemption of men and the honour of Christ in this land." ABM pamphlet, "Missionary Motives" presented October 9, 1890 by Rev. Edward Alden; AZM A/3/41, Report of the Theological School, 1894.

54. ABM 183/417–18, AZM annual letter, 1884–85. Original emphasis

55. ABM 184/382–84, Holbrook to Smith, April 19, 1887. Original emphasis.

56. ABM 188/217–18, Amanzimtoti station report, 1893–94.

57. AZM A/3/46, AZM annual letter, 1895–96.

58. AZM A/4/59, Bunker to Friends, July 21, 1899.

59. Only by the early 1900s did wearing clothing lose its symbolic power—as one missionary noted: "In the old days it was almost a mark of conversion for a man to don a shirt over his *mutya* of skins. That action has lost its significance, for most of the heathen men adopt that much civilization, and thousands who are not rich in other marks of spiritual growth dress in full and often elaborate European costume." AZM A/4/59, J. D. Taylor writing in the *Southern Workman*, June 1909.

60. AZM A/3/46, Amanzimtoti station report, 1889–90.

61. See Norman Etherington, *Preachers, Peasants and Politics*, 158–162; Mahoney, "The Millennium Comes to Mapumulo," 383–85; and Les Switzer, "The Problems of an African Mission in a White-Dominated, Multi-Racial Society: the American Zulu Mission in South Africa, 1885–1910," PhD dissertation (University of Natal: 1971), 374–76.

62. AZM A/4/56, "From the African Correspondent of our Seminary," *Advances, Chicago Theological Seminary Newspaper*, May 7, 1892. The Zulu preacher extended the metaphor of heathen/uncivilized vs. Christian further, noting that a recent Christian convert said of his traditionalist wife, "She is more than a man, she is a tiger" and that drink had made her "such a brute."

63. AZM A/3/41, report of the 1895 Native Annual Meeting at Mapumulo, June 1896.

64. Even those preachers and pastors closely aligned with the mission cringed at the idea, floated in a separate meeting in 1895, that tobacco use be made illegal among Zulu teachers. The mission had previously informed the ABM that they wanted no missionaries sent to them who used the leaf, and had strongly discouraged its use among preachers. The mission wanted to ban its use among teachers, a move Zulu leaders understood as a prelude to implementing a mission-wide prohibition. The Zulu preachers and pastors responded carefully: "We disapprove in principle of the use of tobacco by a Christian teacher but do not think that a fixed law can yet be wisely made that in no case shall one using tobacco be appointed a preacher [teacher]." AZM A/1/7, Native Agency Committee, 1895.

65. The following is from AZM A/4/56, L. Smith to Friends, March 14, 1889.

66. On several occasions the mission had pushed hard for *amakholwa* to go off of the stations to preach the Word among traditionalists. This had met with very little success. So frustrated did the AZM become by this that they stressed the issue at the Native Institute of 1871, pointing out that biblical passages such as 2 John 10–11 and Rom 1:14–15, called on believers to enter into fellowship with unbelievers and do all in their power to "give the Gospel to all classes and conditions of men without distinction." AZM A/1/7, Report of Native Institute, July 27–August 7, 1871. Occasionally such exhortations took root, such as when a young couple from Mapumulo settled among traditionalists in order to preach and teach to them while making their own way financially. But this was an exception worth noting. AZM A/3/41, Mapumulo station report, 1890–91.

67. The celebration at Empusheni, previously an outstation of Inanda, on June 4th, 1883, provides a fine example. The Sunday was broken into two events, the Organization of the Church and the Ordination of the Pastor. The celebration covering the formation of the church began with a formal invocation, followed by singing and a statement by the mission moderator. In the heart of the service the congregation recited the articles of faith, the covenant and the rules by which the new church would abide (these included a commitment to the Umsumduze Rules and a promise to pay their Zulu pastor £3 per month.) The ceremony installing Nqumbe as pastor came later that afternoon. It involved a public examination of the candidate, much singing and praying, and the formal extension of the "right hand of fellowship" by the congregation. Six years later Nqumbe became the head of another outstation turned church when he accepted an invitation from Noodsberg, outside of Mapumulo, to head their newly formed congregation. AZM A/1/2, minutes of semi-annual meeting, April 18–20, 1883.

68. Patrick Harries cites several examples of migrant workers from southern Mozambique returning home from the goldmines as committed Christians and founding churches. Quite unexpectedly the AZM also found itself with congregations near Maputo when a converts returned to the area after attending one of the Congregational missions near Johannesburg. Harries, *Work, Culture, and Identity: Migrant Laborers in Mozambique and South Africa, c. 1860–1910* (Portsmouth: 1994), 105–8; *ABM Herald*, November 1907, 533–34.

69. AZM A/3/46, Amanzimtoti station report, 1890–91.

70. AZM A/4/59, Bunker to Friends, July 21, 1899.

71. Ibid.

72. AZM A/1/7, Native Agency Committee, 1892. This request was not granted and for a short time the mission used one of its own for this purpose. After the revival, when the need was particularly acute, the mission hired several *amakholwa* for the task.

73. AZM A/3/46, AZM annual letter, 1895–96. The mission noted that they did not need to build "proper" churches at these sites as "Houses such as they can erect are sufficient for all practical purposes to began with."

74. AZM A/1/7, Report of 1895 NAM at Mapumulo, 1896. ABM 188/310–11, Mapumulo Station Report, 1895

75. Hance, "The Story of Hobiana," *Congregational Church Magazine*, September 1892.

76. ABM 183/582–83, report of the 1885 Natal Missionary Conference. Several years later the AZM worried that Zulu preachers and pastors at outstations, perhaps in an effort to quickly raise up viable congregations, were "admitting members to church fellowship without due probation and instruction" and noted that: "Our work, as missionaries, will be to keep this in check. " AZM A/3/46, AZM annual report, 1895–96.

77. AZM A/4/50, Bunker to Friends, July 21, 1899; AZM A/1/7, report of Polela work, February 4, 1895; ABM 185/549, J. Tyler to Means, October 16, 1882.

78. AZM A/3/41, Ifafa station report, 1895–96.

79. AZM A/3/41, Umvoti station report, 1895–96. The missionary in charge, recognizing this for what it was, attempted to block this legislation.

80. AZM A/4/59, Bunker to Friends, July 21, 1899. Bunker was happy to note that the old woman had proven her love by walking a "good walk" since that trying moment.

81. The following is from AZM A/3/46, Amanzimtoti station report, 1889–90.

82. For a time the AZM attempted to meet these worship needs through an association with the white Congregational Church (English) of Durban. This arrangement appears to have fallen through, however, when the Durban Congregationalists failed to meet their pledge of financial support for the work. Later, the AZM battled white residents of Durban who sought to keep black churches from their neighborhoods. AZM A/1/2, AZM semi-annual meeting, Jan. 29–30, 1885.

83. A few held skilled positions and lived in Durban the entire year, like Joseph Mngoma, a Christian from Esidumbini who worked as a harness maker. SNA I/1/222 1896, exemption petition of Joseph Mngoma.

84. Mdiwa expressed frustration with the young men from the mission stations who, despite making blunders while reading the Bible during church services, eschewed the night schools as below them.

85. There were barracks scattered throughout Durban, but the Point (a strip of land extending out into Durban harbor) held the greatest concentration of the long, low corrugated iron buildings packed with bunks and used to house the thousands of workers needed to unload the steamers docking at Durban.

86. AZM A/1/7, committee on Durban work, 1892.

87. Ibid. This is a reasonable estimate, than, of the number of AZM members living permanently in the city, as few migrant laborers bothered to obtain the necessary paperwork releasing them outright. The mission also informed its pastors and preachers throughout Natal that the Durban church would look into any "straying sheep" that they wanted checked on in the city.

88. AZM A/1/8, report of the 1895 NAM at Mapumulo, 1896.

89. Only in the next century would the mission fully embrace an urban mission—acknowledging the easy evangelistic opportunities they offered for all of southern Africa. AZM A/4/59, "The Passing of a Great Missionary—Frederick Bridgman, DD," C. Patton, 1924.

90. ABM 183, 582–83, Report of the Natal Missionary Conference 1890; AZM A/4/59, "Point of Contact," paper presented by J.D. Taylor at Natal Missionary Conference, 1902. Taylor complained that white men visited the African workers' barracks with rum and cards, spreading "evil" habits in this way. He also connected the rise of "layita" (*amalaita*) gangs, the semi-military organizations blamed for much of the crime in Durban at the turn of the century, on the influence of white men who used rickshaw pullers to take them from barroom to barroom, and then to the town's brothels. For more on Durban's *amalaita* see Paul La Hausse, "'The Cows of Nongoloza': Youth, Crime and Amalaita Gangs in Durban, 1900–1936," *Journal of Southern African Studies* 16 (1990).

91. Missionaries acknowledged the paradox of being Christian without sufficient money to express belief. The missionary at Inanda realized that many of his congregation found jobs in the cities to pay for the *amakholwa* lifestyle: "To wear the garb of civilization they must have money to buy clothing and to meet the wants of their new life." A/3/41, Lindley [Inanda] station report, 1890–91.

92. In 1895 the AZM built the "Women's Durban Lodging House" for *amakholwa* women visiting the city. It operated with success for a short period, but missionaries placed the project in the hands of the Durban businessmen who had originally contributed to its opening and within a few years the house was closed. This was not from lack of need, however, for even when fully funded the mission estimated the house could only take in 1 in 100 of the women in town. Several prominent *amakholwa* men, including Dr. Nembula, urged the mission to move Mary Edwards from her post as principal of Inanda to the house, presumably believing that her talents were more urgently needed in Durban watching over the purity of *amakholwa* women. AZM A/1/2, minutes volume VII, semi-annual meeting, Feb 2–7, 1895; AZM A/3/46, annual letter, 1895–96, AZM A/1/6, report of the Durban work, 1896

93. AZM A/3/41, Amanzimtoti annual report, 1891–92. H. Marwick, the Natal SNA representative in Johannesburg, noted in 1896 that the bulk of exempted Christians in the Witwatersrand worked as traders, transport riders, gardeners, and general servants. He also noted that they were, with few exceptions a very upstanding and respectable group, including in which he cited Fokoti Makanya, an AZM preacher discussed in more detail in Chapter 6. SNA 131/1896, Letter from H. Marwick, May 14, 1896.

94. AZM A/1/7, self-support committee, July 1895. See also, Bill Guest, "The New Economy," in Duminey and Guest, *Natal and Zululand*, 302–314.

95. While there were no doubt others, we know that Bryant Xletwa began working as a messenger for the Pretoria police department in 1890. By 1892 the number of *amakholwa* working in Johannesburg had risen to as many as two hundred, although the number of these baptized as Congregationalists is unclear. AZM A/4/62, Survey of former Jubilee students engaged in Johannesburg, 1906.

96. AZM A/1/7, committee on mission work among the Zulu of Johannesburg, 1892.

97. AZM A/1/7, committee on Johannesburg work, 1893.

98. AZM A/1/2, minutes of volume VII, semi-annual meeting, February 1, 1893.

99. ABM 188/233, Mapumulo station report, 1893–94; AZM A/3/41, Ifume station report 1891–92.

100. At Amanzimtoti, in 1890, a recently commenced Christian Endeavor Society ended abruptly when all but one of its members left the station to work in either Durban or Johannesburg.

101. AZM A/1/8, Minutes Volume VII, annual meeting, June 28–July 6, 1895. Previously, few teachers had made as much as £30 per year and many had earned less than £20 for their services.

102. AZM A/3/41, Amanzimtoti Seminary report, 1896–97.

103. Ibid.

104. The banning of *lobola*, for example, presented young adults with difficult decisions over loyalties. Some of their elders advocated either openly disobeying the law or surreptitiously skirting it, while others demanded they stay fully in-line with the church's teaching. It is little wonder that older *amakholwa* complained bitterly over the actions of their juniors, or that it was these very same children who became the shock troops of the revival.

105. Not surprisingly, the specter of young men returning from migrant work empowered by their hard-earned wages hung heavily over traditional society as well. These youths only grudgingly gave over wages to homestead heads and often used some of this money to buy prestige goods that boosted their own perceived standing over that of their elders. See Benedict Carton, *Blood From Your Children*, 63–65.

106. AZM A/3/41, Esidumbini station report, 1894–95.

107. AZM A/3/41, Umzumbe station report, 1891–92. The missionary in charge reported: "I have had fewer sadder experiences than these frank confessions of a total eclipse of faith."

108. AZM A/2/10, Mfanefile Kuzwayo to AZM, Dec 27, 1893.

109. AZM A/2/10, Mfanefile Kuzwayo to AZM, October 22, 1890. In the first letter Kuzwayo had written: "We are embarrassed for staying in a place that is not ours," after the mission began requesting rents on acreage used for crops. He proposed rectifying the problem by buying the land from the mission. Kuzwayo wrote several more times without success.

110. AZM A/1/2, Minutes Volume VII, special meeting called to address demands of the Legislative Council, October 9–10, 1884; ABM 185/443–445, Rood to Smith, November 8, 1886. The vague language in the original Mission Reserve grants made action by all sides difficult, lending itself to arguments both for and against various proposals.

111. ABM 185/464, Rood to Smith, September 11, 1888.

112. AZM A/1/2, Minutes Volume VII, special meeting, July 28th, 1885.

113. Ibid. This despite the pro-ownership faction of the mission attaching a rider to their support which allowed for the "inalienable" right to land to be stripped if the owner should become a polygamist.

114. AZM A/1/8, Minutes Volume VII, semi-annual meeting, January 30—February 2, 1894.

115. The collection of rents was also an attempt by the mission to control *who* settled on the reserves, an issue with which they found themselves at odds with local chiefs who frequently assigned land on the reserves to followers, Christian or not, without consulting the mission. The AZM wanted to limit its land to *amakholwa*,

but increasingly came into conflict with the SNA (which enviously viewed the mission reserve lands as an outlet for its own overcrowded locations) who supported the rights of chiefs to assign even mission reserve lands. AZM A/1/7, Committee on Rights and Privileges of Reserve Trustees, 1893.

116. AZM A/1/2, Minutes Volume VII, semi-annual meeting, November 27, 1888. As part of this lease, farmers agreed not to grow objectionable crops such as tobacco or Indian hemp. In charging rents, it should be noted, the Americans merely followed the lead of many of the other missions in Natal who had long levied small charges.

117. John Lambert, *Betrayed Trust: Africans and the State in Colonial Natal* (Pietermaritzburg: 1995), 105. At Iduma, an outstation of Umtwalume, the land was sold to Europeans in 1891, forcing the people in the area to leave and abandon their church. AZM A/3/46, AZM annual report, 1890–91. At Newtonville, a small outstation where the mission had purchased a few acres for the church and school, the congregation crowded onto a tiny plot after the land next to the station was appropriated for white settlement. AZM A/3/41, Netwonville station report, 1894–95.

118. AZM A/3/42, report of the Johannesburg work, 1899. The mission attempted to disconnect themselves from the image as rent collectors by hiring outside agents to do the work.

119. AZM A/3/46, Record of the proceedings of the meeting held for the purpose of inquiring into the question of Mission Reserve lands, December 17, 1894.

120. Several decades earlier the missions originally granted mission reserves by the British government had formed a joint Mission Reserves Trustee to handle questions pertaining to the management of these bodies, the government proposed to dissolve this body in favor of its own.

121. The SNA expertly deflected these points, noting that several of the native reserves were already overcrowded and that traditionalists living there would convert without meaning if they believed this would bring them onto the stations—just as nonbelievers on the stations would convert to avoid being turned off.

122. AZM A/1/7, Reserve Trustees report, 1894–95. The following exchange is taken from the same.

123. *Ikanyiso Yase Natal*, editorial on the Mission Reserve Bill, July 12, 1895. The editorial also criticized missionaries for a failure to provide industrial training and for using the mission reserves as a "rent-producing medium, much after the fashion of the ordinary Native farming of the Colony."

124. AZM A/2/24, Act No. 25, To Regulate the Use of the Mission Reserves, August 8, 1895.

125. Ibid.

126. Ibid.

127. HAZM, Bunker to Friends, Dec 3, 1895; AZM A/3/49, Goodenough to SNA, June 25, 1894. AZM A/3/49, AZM to members of the Ministry, October 12, 1895. AZM A/3/46, Conclusions from studying the trust deed of AZM reserves, 1895.

128. AZM A/3/49, AZM to members of the Ministry, October 12, 1895; AZM A/3/46, Conclusions from studying the trust deed of AZM reserves, 1895.

129. AZM A/1/8, Minutes Volume VII, annual meeting, June 26–July 11, 1896; AZM A/1/8, report of reserve trustees, 1896.

130. SNA 381/1896, application for transfer of Umvoti land from Shampiyana to Hagu; SNA 8282/1896, Esidumbini magistrate report. In October 1896, an American missionary, feeling at a loss, filed a complaint with the SNA over the actions of a young man who had built his house on common grazing land at Inanda. The SNA decided to take no action and rather gleefully responded that had the AZM participated earlier in the formation of the Natal Native Trust this would not have occurred. SNA 1730/1896, complaints from Dr. Bridgman over problems on Adams M.S.

131. The metal badges, no larger than a quarter and complete with ring and brooch, were issued in 1891 in response to *amakholwa* complaints that their original exemption letters, which they were required to carry and display on demand, had become worn from use. The silver medal could be had for nine shillings, the bronze for five. SNA 509/1895, application on behalf of Ntombi Pakati, exempted native, for a badge.

132. SNA 390/1895, list of natives exempted from the operation of Native Law.

133. Lambert, *Betrayed Trust*, 167.

134. Welsh, *The Roots of Segregation*, 242–44; SNA 3002/1897, August Hlamini petitions to be removed from Native Law.

135. As Welsh notes: "Among the *amakholwa* class the fundamental grievance was the refusal of the Government to admit them to anything remotely approaching equality with whites." Welsh, *The Roots of Segregation*, 295.

136. AZM A/3/46, AZM annual letter, 1895–96. The mission was assured that this was an error, not a switch in policy, but the "error" was repeated on several subsequent occasions on other stations.

137. The cattle fine levied on Ugubana, a recent *amakholwa* convert near Zwaart-kop, caused one American missionary to write that Natal was now the only place in the British Empire where there was no freedom of religion. Letter from Rev. F. Bunker, *Natal Witness*, November 19, 1895; AZM A/3/41, Umvoti annual report, 1895–96.

138. This began to change at the turn of the century when chiefs became embroiled in land disputes, tax collection, and the colonial criminal judicial system. See Lambert, *Betrayed Trust*, 128, 135; Carton, *Blood From Your Children*, 91–102.

139. SNA 375/1892, complaint by Chief Swaimana. After much debate, the government eventually granted Hawes permission, although the fears of the chief "that Thomas Hawes is a man who creates trouble wherever he goes" were later borne out and the AZM removed Hawes after his actions divided the Noodsberg congregation.

140. SNA 526/1896, changes to the Code of Native Law, Bill #27, 1896. This was an extension of a ruling the previous year in which the SNA had refused to allow Christians in outstations to be placed under the rule of Christian headman in non-contiguous stations. SNA 481/1895, petition by certain residents of Ipolela and Lions River Location to be placed under Stephen Mini.

141. SNA 8282/1896, Local Magistrate Report Esidumbini. The *amakholwa*, who were looking to create a council of elders, made their own claim to traditionalism, noting "they were guided by former practice amongst Natives where the 'Bhandhla' dealt with matters of all kinds."

142. Although on several AZM stations, Christians had already appointed "headmen" as part of an earlier effort to improve the position of the community prior to 1893.

143. AZM A/3/41, Esidumbini station report, 1890–91; AZM A/3/46, Amanzimtoti station report, 1893–94; AZM A/3/41, Umtwalumi station report, June 1894–95; AZM A/2/10, members of congregation of Umtwalumi to Goodenough, April 25, 1895.

144. The following is taken from several sources, including: AZM A/1/8, Minutes Volume VII, annual meeting, June 1895; ABM Pixley to Smith, September 8, 1896; ABM Pixley to Leitch, March, 1899. A similar incident occurred at Mapumulo the following year, but was settled without the high drama that ensued at Inanda. AZM A/3/41, Mapumulo annual report, 1895–96.

145. Dube, in addition to being well educated and having served as a preacher and teacher, was also the son of the late Rev. James Dube. The elder Dube was an energetic, extremely intelligent and faithful man of royal heritage who became one of the first Zulu pastors in 1870 when he took over leadership of the Inanda church. Many in the mission viewed him as the man to whom they would pass over the reins of leadership and they mourned his early passing from dysentery in 1877. ABM 182/375–77, Pixley to Clark, November 10, 1877.

146. Goba's father had recently been appointed as an *induna* and while his constituency wasn't as numerous as Mqawe's it contained a greater percentage of *amakholwa*.

147. We will return to Dube's American trip in chapter 6.

148. The following is from AZM A/2/17, Conference of Representatives of Foreign Mission Board in the US and Canada; AZM A/1/7, self-support committee report, July 1, 1895; AZM A/1/8, Minutes Volume VII, annual meeting, 1895; ABM 189/642, AZM annual letter, 1896–97; ABM 188/565–67, AZM annual letter, 1897–98.

149. AZM A/2/10, church of Amahlongwa to AZM, June 24, 1895. Inanda, Umtwalumi, Mapumulo, Johannesburg, Umzumbe, and Esidumbini all made similar requests.

150. AZM A/1/7, self support committee Report, July 1, 1895.

151. AZM A/1/2, special meeting, March 20–21, 1888. The following year the AZM closed an annual missionary meeting "truly remarkable and pitiable from the smallness of numbers and the poor health of at least half the brethren present." The report concluded with the dramatic cry: "Cannot someone come to the rescue of our mission?" AZM A/1/2, AZM annual meeting, July 26–July 2, 1889.

152. ABM 184/411, Holbrook to Smith, March 9, 1889. Original emphasis.

153. Charles Holbrook warned against the immediate appointment of native pastors in 1889 by suggesting that "half of those ordained lose their mental balance and so conduct themselves as to forfeit the respect of both the missionaries and the Christian natives alike (cf Paul in I Tim 3:6.)" Holbrook to Smith, October 23, 1889.

154. ABM 184/892, Kilbon to Smith, March 2, 1889.

155. Rufus Anderson, became pastor at Umzumbe on May 29, 1870, and was followed by Msingaphansi Nyuswa at Imfume in June and James Dube at Inanda

in December of that same year. They were followed in 1872 by Benjamin Hawes at Itafamsi and Ira Nembula at Amanzimtoti. The mission ordained Umbiana Ngidi in 1873 after which only two other *amakholwa* were ordained until 1896.

156. AZM A/1/2, Annual Meeting, June 26–July 2, 1889. The plan was: "That each church of the Zulu mission now assume the whole or part of the support of a native licentiate who by the Spirit and by nature and attainment is qualified to assist the missionary in the labors of the circuit."

157. AZM A/1/7, committee on the appointment of preachers, 1891; AZM A/1/2, Annual Meeting, June 26–July 9, 1891. It does appear that many of the preachers of the AZM sought to supplement their meager salaries. For example, the preacher in charge of Emutshane, an outstation of Mapumulo, spent much of his time attending to his sugarcane crop at Umvoti. This meant frequent absence from the small church for weeks at a time and he often only returned on a Friday or Saturday to preach before leaving again on Monday. AZM A/3/41, Mapumulo station report, 1890–91.

158. AZM A/1/7, report on 1894 NAM, 1895. The committee attributed this hostility to the "natural suspicion of the Native Character, sharpened by education and contact with Europeans" but still recommended that two members of the churches be asked to assist in book-keeping to dispel future doubts.

159. AZM A/3/41, Theological school report, 1894–95. With six graduates, that year's class was the largest yet produced by the AZM. But the *amakholwa* community largely ignored the public ceremony, a showy affair complete with speeches, songs, and diplomas adorned with red ribbons.

160. AZM A/1/7, Committee on the ordination of Zulu pastors, 1895.

161. The four called were Umvakwendhlu at Esidumbini, Simon at Amahlongwa, Sunguza at Umtwalume and Mabuda at Umzumbe. The reluctance of the mission to move this far is evidenced in their lukewarm reporting of the matter in the Annual letter for the year: "It will take time to prove whether we have acted wisely in ordaining so many men in so short a time; but we trust that these four of whose ordination I have spoken, will in no way disappoint our expectations." AZM A/3/46, AZM annual report, 1895–96.

162. AZM A/1/8, Minutes Volume VII, semi-annual meeting, February 5–7, 1896; ABM 192/327, Pixley to Smith, September 8, 1896. Pixley, the senior member of the mission, stated flatly that the churches were not ready to choose their own pastors because they made their decisions not on who was the best spiritual fit, but on who troubled them the least over purity questions and would be able to intervene on their behalf with the government.

163. AZM A/3/41 & A/2/29, J.C. Dorward to Kilbon, October 16, 1893.

164. AZM A/1/7, report of the Johannesburg committee, June 1895.

165. The mission did, however, closely question Goodenough over the matters raised by the Johannesburg congregation. He maintained that he carefully screened those who lived in the tenement, always asked for marriage certificates, and threw out the few cases that demonstrated immorality. He also noted that while he built the boarding house for *amakholwa*, he had planned the residence for families and that few Zulu in the congregation took their wives and children with them to the city. The mission, hoping to address the congregation's concerns over the weekly collection, suggested that the church appoint a treasurer to work in consultation

with Goodenough and that the collections go to pay both Fokoti's salary and the expansion of the work into Germiston, a rapidly growing black township of Johannesburg (Goodenough had used some of it to pay down the church's debt, giving credence to the congregation's argument that it was, in fact, their church.) AZM A/1/7, report of the Johannesburg committee, June 1895; AZM A/1/8, Minutes Volume VII, semi-annual meeting, February 1896.

166. Charles Ballard, "A Year of Scarcity: The 1896 Locust Plague in Natal and Zululand," *South African Historical Journal* 15 (1983): 34–52.

167. AZM A/3/41, Amahlongwa station report, 1894–95.

168. ABM 188/345–46, Amanzimtoti station report, 1895–96. The missionary at Amanzimtoti hoped that the station's sweet potato crop, which had escaped destruction, would save the people from actual famine.

169. AZM A/3/41, AZM annual report, 1895–96.

170. *Natal Mercury*, "Missionaries and Mealies," May 8, 1896. Wilcox, responding to an earlier letter accusing the "missionary of Mapumulo" of spending more time selling food than preaching, detailed his "at cost" philanthropy and noted, "I know this is not agreeable to those who want to make from 100 to 300 percent on mealies . . . "

171. AZM A/1/8, report of the NAM, July 22–28, 1896. The plague made many *amakholwa* noticeably poorer and contributions to the work of the NHMS at the 1896 NAM were down by half from the previous year. Missionaries worried that this material impoverishment would drive many into a spiritual one. ABM 188/322, AZM annual report, June 1895–96.

172. AZM A/1/8, report of the NAM, July 22–28, 1896.

173. Johannes is a fascinating figure who appears intermittently in both government and mission sources over the next several years. The mission initially welcomed his presence but grew weary of his call for radical purity. The government, as I detail above, came to see all evangelism by African Christians as potentially subversive and Blind Johannes was jailed for a short time before being eventually banned from Natal. For more on Johannes see Carton, "'We Are Made Quiet by This Annihilation,'" 101–102.

174. John Ford, *The Role of Trypanosomiases in African Ecology*, (London: Oxford University Press, 1971), 394. While the Italian origin is the dominant theory, the French believed the disease was introduced by the British into the Sahel in 1884 during their effort to relieve Gordon in Khartoum.

175. *The Natal Mercury*, "Rinderpest Restrictions," April 11, 1896.

176. Although the dramatic impact of rinderpest on many African societies is an inescapable reality of early colonial history, it has gone surprisingly understudied. Part of the problem, of course, is that it passed through areas free of European administration and thus went unrecorded. Once rinderpest crossed the Zambezi River in 1896, it became a preoccupation of white settlers in southern Africa and documentation, and thus historical analysis, are more readily available. For some of the better works see, Charles Ballard, "The Repercussions of Rinderpest: Cattle Plague and Peasant Decline in Colonial Natal," *The International Journal of African Historical Studies* 19 (1986); Charles van Onselen, "Reactions to Rinderpest in Southern Africa, 1896–97," *The Journal of African History* 13 (1972); Pule

Phoofolo, "Epidemics and Revolutions: The Rinderpest Epidemic in Late Nine-teenth-Century Southern Africa," *Past and Present* 138 (1993). For a particularly compelling history that places the social effects of rinderpest within the wider context of the continent, see Jan-Bart Gewald, *Herero Heroes: A Socio-Political History of the Herero of Namibia, 1890–1923* (Athens: Ohio University Press, 1999), 110–140; Karen Brown, "Tropical Medicine and Animal Diseases: Onderstepoort and the Development of Veterinary Science in South Africa, 1908–1950," *Journal of Southern African Studies*, 31 (2005), 513–29.

177. SNA 229/1896, report of the Commissioner of Agriculture, Natal.

178. Monica Wilson and Leonard Thompson (eds.), *The Oxford History of South Africa* (New York: Oxford University Press, 1971), 116.

179. T. O. Ranger, *Revolt in Southern Rhodesia, 1896–97: A Study in African Resistance* (Chicago: Northwestern University Press, 1967).

180. In limiting compensation to healthy cattle, the commissioners created a dangerous climate in which those with obviously infected beasts had little incentive to report outbreaks. Worse, many chose to hide diseased beasts in the hope that some might survive. SNA 229/1896, Report of the Commissioner of Agriculture, Natal.

181. This was a story related to me twice during my stay in South Africa, but for which I found no evidence.

182. Those trapped were eventually allowed to strip to take their tack and their wagons across the border by hand. Their oxen, however, were left to their fate at collection points and *amakholwa* had little choice but to sell them at a great loss, as the SAR charged them exorbitant rates to pasture the beasts. SNA 423/1896, William Gumede and thiry-six others write that they and their wagons and oxen spans are detained at Standerton; SNA 1793/1896, Request to release oxen of Mordecai Ndebe; SNA 1869/1896, Request of Joseph Kumalo and ten others to take material across Buffalo River.

183. *Natal Mercury*, "Rinderpest," September 29, 1896.

184. *Natal Mercury*, "Native Meeting at Newcastle," October 27, 1896.

185. SNA 1557/1896, "Measures for prevention of spread of rinderpest." For their part, Zulu leaders took advantage of this relatively rare meeting with the USNA to express their concerns on a host of issues, not just cattle disease. So while they asked Samuelson to keep them informed of the progress of the epizootic and suggested that the SNA send out native representatives to the infected areas, they also discussed the state of affairs for migrant workers in the SAR, the performance of J. S. Marwick, the Natal native representative in Johannesburg, the evils of unrestrained alcohol sale at the goldfields, the powers of district headman, irrigation, the making of roads, and the continuing locust plague. *Natal Government Gazette* October 15, 1896.

186. *Umvo Neliso Lomzi*, "The Darkening Prospect," October 1, 1896; *Inkanyiso Yase Natal*, "I Rinderpest," June 2, 1896; *amakholwa* from Mapumulo *Natal Mercury*, "A Native's Views," October 9, 1896. The same author, writing under the penname J. Mapumulo, thanked the government for sending Samuelson around to native locations. *Natal Mercury*, "Appreciation of the Natives," October 22, 1896.

4

Revival

Shortly before sunrise, on the morning of September 22, 1896, the Holy Spirit descended upon Mbiya Kuzwayo.[1] The experience did not frighten him, for during the previous week he and a handful of others at Mapumulo had attended meetings with Elder George Weavers, an itinerant Holiness preacher from Iowa who spoke of their need to be filled by the Spirit, an experience he called "sanctification." The message delivered by Weavers, radical for the simplicity of the path it offered to salvation but demanding an intensely emotional faith, deeply impressed the young Zulu and he volunteered to act as Weavers' interpreter. Like others present, Kuzwayo had always considered himself a Christian. But now, despite inheriting his religion from his father, a preacher and *amakholwa* headman, he found himself questioning the depth of his faith. Shaken by this doubt, he eagerly pursued the transformative experience promised in Weavers' sermons by engaging in days of fasting and prayer. So prepared, he later recalled that instead of trembling with fear, his heart leapt for joy when the Spirit commanded him: "Go and tell Brother Weavers that this is a blessed day. No man or woman shall work. We shall have a whole day's service!"

Kuzwayo obeyed the Spirit's call and informed Weavers who moved the next meeting, previously planned as an informal gathering in the mission house, to the church in hopeful anticipation of the fulfillment of the Spirit's promise. Word of the fantastic prophecy spread through the narrow social confines of the mission reserve and curious *amakholwa* swelled the audience. The worship proved far different than normal Congregational services—long on spontaneous prayer and singing it lasted from late morning until early evening. But despite the intensity of the meeting, and the earnestness with which the congregation participated, the "Holy Rain" anticipated by Kuzwayo did not fall and he went to bed that evening moved, but unsatisfied by the day's events.

Any frustration he felt did not last long. The following day another large congregation gathered at the church. Deep in prayer the hours slipped by until, late that night, the Spirit seemed to strike down a young woman who loudly confessed her sins before the startled congregation. Afterwards, freed from her sense of burden, she leapt to her feet and ran through the church, clapping her hands and proclaiming the power of God. Her exaltations electrified the assembly, and shortly afterwards those in attendance felt the Holy Spirit descend upon them in mass, an experience that reminded Kuzwayo "of my Saviour's words in Luke 24:49 'Tarry ye in the city of Jerusalem, until ye be endowed from power from on high.'" Afterward forty to fifty *amakholwa* rose to their feet and, in a cacophony of religious ecstasy, began preaching, shouting, weeping, jumping, and even running about the little church. The missionary at Mapumulo reported: "In all my experiences I have never seen such a meeting."

Kuzwayo also felt the power of God descend and touched with this new power he began preaching:

> . . . in an unknown tongue, that is, English. That day I felt as if I could stand and preach in English to any congregation without fear. For God had taken all fear from me. Because what I spoke was not from my own experience, but what the Holy Ghost told me to utter.[7]

As the moment passed, Kuzwayo joined the men and women around him calling out: "*Halibongwa igama lika Jehova*" (May the name of God be praised) and "Allelujah! Glory to God! Lord!" Spent, the assembled finally began returning home well after midnight. But even in their exhaustion they could not contain their spiritual enthusiasm and as they made their way along the darkened paths of the mission reserve they clapped and sang, making the air ring with their "melodious voices." Awakened by the commotion, those who hadn't attended could only wonder what insanity had taken their friends and family. This ecstasy, I would argue, occurred as a result of both a personal transformation and sense of communal joy as Zulu embraced this new form of Christianity—one whose theological innovations they borrowed heavily from to craft a religion that better served the needs of their community.

Six months later the revival had spread to nearly every station and outstation of the mission, generating fervor across much of Natal, into Zululand, and even Johannesburg. For those who participated, even those missionaries who were veterans of such spiritual campaigns, the experience was astonishing. Wrote one AZM missionary: "I have never before seen such a powerful work of the spirit among our people or indeed anywhere."[3] Commented another: "In the entire history of the mission there has been no such awakening among the people."[4] Weavers, a solid Midwesterner little given to hyperbole and with decades of revival experience, recalled his months of preaching in Natal as "some of the grandest meetings" he had witnessed.[5]

For Congregationalist *amakholwa*, the revival came none too soon. Under the weight of economic misfortune, frustrated ambitions, threatening plagues, increasing government hostility, youthful rebellion, and seeming missionary indifference to these issues, the community, so carefully constructed in its early years, had begun to crumble. Perhaps even more troubling, missionaries continued to shift the terms of Christian identity, making purity increasingly important and casting the entire community under the dark shadow of "sin." All told it suggested a deep moral crisis, and *amakholwa* turned to their faith for a moral answer. The revival offered wayward sinners a new birth, a chance to approach Christ freshly cleansed and transformed. It also presented an opportunity for Zulu Christians to lay claim to their own churches in both a literal and figurative sense. For the theology of this revival, based in the Holiness ideas of sanctification and consecration, provided the *amakholwa* community with a legitimacy born of the Spirit—the sanctified could sin no more so the missionary's primary role as gatekeepers of the churches became irrelevant. For those who participated in revival, the experience was not only liberating, but also allowed them to claim autonomy from the missionaries of the AZM as they transformed their Christianity into something decidedly more local.

THE AMERICAN ORIGINS OF ZULU REVIVAL

The roots of the revival at Mapumulo stretch across the Atlantic into the Appalachian hills and American Midwestern frontier lands of the early nineteenth century. It was here that the Second Great Awakening took shape under large tents at nondescript gathering places such as Red River, Muddy Run, and most famously, Cane Ridge.[6] Presbyterian, Baptist, and Methodist preachers competed with each other to win souls in public, almost carnival-like events. Frontier living had given participants many reasons to respond to this call, and the revivals met with enthusiastic audiences who reacted by weeping, shaking, jerking, laughing, collapsing into comas, writhing on the ground, and even barking—all as part of an experience of what was called a "rebirth"; an experience that "saved" participants from their past sins.[7] Their success sparked similar efforts up and down the frontier and preachers used the revivals as an effective tool to first create and then grow new congregations. By the 1830s these camp meetings had evolved from their chaotic emotional roots, into more carefully planned affairs, events at which practiced circuit revivalists effectively managed their audiences to an emotional peak without the fervor spilling over.[8]

Charles Grandison Finney, a lawyer turned Presbyterian minister, became one of the most successful practitioners of this art and brought the camp meeting indoors, first touring churches in upstate New York and then, after a dramatically successful year of revival in Rochester from 1830–1831, turning his attention to the bigger cities of the United States.[9] Finney's services were notable for their breaks with the staid traditions of denominations such as the Congregationalists. While maintaining the high religious emotions of earlier revivals, Finney also introduced a number of innovations: at all-night meetings, prayer was offered up for sinners who sat up front on deliberately uncomfortable "anxious benches," women openly participated, congregations addressed God in a familiar manner, and, on occasion, audience members fainted while in the grip of religious ecstasy and convulsions.[10] Finney's critics, mainly Congregationalists and Presbyterians, worried that the revivals were rife with the "excessive emotionalism" stirred up by Methodists and Baptists at camp meetings, but for Finney they represented the natural path of God's work. Writing a half decade after Rochester, Finney explained: "God has found it necessary to take advantage of the excitability there is in mankind, to produce powerful excitements among them, before he can lead them to obey."[11] The service he rendered was not a miracle, Finney believed, but rather an intentional action, for it was up to humans to save souls and to free the world of sin. Faced with this responsibility, Finney recruited local lay ministers to lead prayer meetings in the months before his arrival and then to meet with converts following his departure. This marked a final step in an American journey away from the Calvinist theology of predestination begun nearly a century earlier by Jonathan Edwards. By the beginning of the Civil War few American theologians would argue that a person's salvation rested anywhere but in his own hands.

The appeal of Finney's revivals eventually waned and he responded by accepting a position in 1835 as professor of theology at Oberlin.[12] Once there, Finney and the institution's first president, Asa Mahan, explored the idea of perfectionism, a doctrine with roots in the writings of John Wesley.[13] Wesley held that humans were capable of perfect obedience to God's will, and that when they were filled with His love, they could be released from all intentional sin. For Methodists this was a two-step process of "justification" followed by "sanctification." In the first, God saved one from one's past sins and a person was "born again" as a Christian. Sanctification followed justification and, in Wesley's view, was a gradual process by which a person grew in Holiness, emptying the heart of sin and replacing it with love. In sanctification's final step, the Holy Spirit entered the cleansed soul, empowering and enabling converts to live lives free of sin. After studying Wesley's writings, both Finney and Mahan underwent their own sanctification experience. Inspired, Mahan wrote several popular works detailing his belief that by accepting Jesus Christ into their hearts, Christians could win a complete victory over sin.[14]

Mahan and Finney were not alone in advocating this radical doctrine. In New York, Phoebe Palmer, a Methodist evangelist, began holding her "Tuesday Meeting" in 1837, shortly after her own experience of sanctification. Building upon Mahan, Palmer subtly altered Wesley's theology, advocating an experience of "entire" sanctification by which the Holy Spirit immediately entered an individual and rendered them holy; an instantaneous gift from God, no matter how new to the faith a believer might be.[15] To accomplish this, Palmer believed one needed to have "naked" faith in Jesus Christ and lay their entire being on his "altar" in an act of "entire consecration."[16] The simplicity of her message won a significant following and her "Tuesday Meeting" became a model for similar gatherings throughout the country. She also edited a journal devoted to sanctification and wrote one of the most influential works on the doctrine in 1843, *The Way of Holiness.* The popular urban revivals of 1857–58, centered in New York but occurring throughout the country, gave Palmer's message an even wider audience and she began touring the United States, establishing small communities of sanctified individuals in her wake, believers who embraced this new gospel of Holiness.

The American Civil War interrupted Palmer's efforts to promote Holiness, and it wasn't until after the war that this youthful theology became truly popular when it linked with a growing "camp meeting" movement. In 1867, a group of Methodist preachers gathered at Vineland, New Jersey to take part in a Holiness revival and found the experience so life-altering that they agreed to devote themselves to conducting itinerant Holiness revivals throughout the country.[17] They organized themselves under the rather unwieldy name of the National Camp-Meeting Association for the Promotion of Holiness and the following year reconvened for an assembly at Manheim, Pennsylvania. Upwards of 25,000 attended this gathering and it made headlines in newspapers throughout the country, including a two-page pictorial in *Harper's Weekly.*[18] The association, emboldened by this success, expanded its work, and by the middle of the 1870s, held meetings in nearly every state and territory of the nation in addition to a fledgling international presence in India and Australia.

As the National Camp-Meeting Association grew and many Methodists embraced its Holiness theology, a backlash developed against the theology within the Methodist church. Advocates of Holiness were passed over for promotion or reassigned, the ecumenicalism and emotionalism of the camp meetings was questioned and most notably the church supported theological critiques of Holiness that argued against its fundamental belief in instantaneous sanctification.[19] Angered, what began as a slow trickle in the late 1870s turned into a tidal wave of defections the following decade as Holiness followers left to establish independent congregations. Many of these defections occurred in the recently settled lands of the American Midwest, the sort of social milieu in which Methodism had succeeded so dramatically nearly a century earlier. It was here that the Holiness call to live "[i]n the world but not of the world" rang most clearly and those who split from the Methodist church referred angrily to unwelcome "church machinists" in New York mandating the smallest details in far-away congregations.[20] By the 1890s this spirit of "come-outism" had run its course; the Methodist church survived, albeit greatly reduced, and a bewildering array of Holiness churches dotted the American religious landscape.

"ONLY FOR SOULS":
WEAVERS AND THE HEPHZIBAH FAITH ASSOCIATION

On December 29, 1862, Private George Weavers was shot in the face while fighting in the battle of Chickasaw Bayou.[21] The battle, a disaster for the Union forces led by William Tecumseh Sherman, was meant to take Vicksburg, a city whose strategic location overlooking a sharp bend in the Mississippi River allowed Confederate artillery to block Union use of the waterway south of that point.[22] The original Union battle plan called for Sherman's attacks north of the city to distract the defenders while Ulysses S. Grant sneaked in from the east. Grant was delayed, however, and after several days of unsuccessful maneuvering in the marshes, Sherman attempted a frontal assault on the heavily fortified rebel defenses that sat astride Walnut Hills.[23] Weaver's unit, company A of the fourth Iowa Regiment, slogged through the swamp and hacked clear of the thick underbrush under heavy artillery fire before charging up the bluff. They managed to break through the first line of defense before finding, as so often occurred during the war, a communication breakdown had left them isolated and without reinforcement. Under intense fire from three sides they withdrew, fighting as they retreated while suffering heavy casualties.[24] Sometime during this engagement, a ball struck Weavers in the face, shattering his lower jaw and knocking him out of the war.

For five months Weavers lay near death in a field hospital. The mortality rate for such wounds was appalling, and several surgeons prepared the young soldier for the worst, informing him that he had little hope. Indeed, when his throat swelled shut the best they could offer to prevent strangulation was a small bottle of oil that he used to keep his airway greased open. Somehow he survived, and in June of 1863 the Army transferred him to St. John's hospital in Kentucky. He remained there for over a year, undergoing five operations before the ball that felled him was extracted along with eleven pieces of his jaw. By August of 1864 he had recovered sufficiently to be discharged, first from the hospital and then from military service. He made his way home to southeastern Iowa, where he married Susanna Hill the following December, settling down with her on a 369-acre farm "of fine land" to raise crops and children.[25]

But while struggling to breathe in the army hospital, Weavers had promised God that he would "walk in the light" should he live, and on his return to Iowa he joined the Sydney Baptist Church and became a lay minister. Here he found his calling, for despite a poor education he had an obvious gift for preaching and within two years a neighboring Baptist congregation invited him to be their pastor.[26] Over the next twenty years he worked in several different churches, honing his skills in the small farming towns that speckled the plains of Iowa and Nebraska. He remained, however, vaguely dissatisfied with his own faith and in 1875 he returned to his spiritual roots, holding the first revival camp meeting of what would be many to follow. The skills that made him a very good preacher made him an outstanding revivalist and his services, which he conducted throughout the region, drew large crowds.[27] It was during one of these, in the early 1880s, that Weavers met Sister Elwell and Sister Townsend, two Holiness women who successfully brought him to an experience of "entire sanctification." Weavers spent time reading Holiness texts and examining the Bible looking for scriptural support for this new theology. Satisfied with what he uncovered, he withdrew from the Baptist denomination in 1886, taking with him many members of nearby Baptist churches.[28]

Like other Holiness churches, the new congregation sought to weed out all "man-made" organization from their church, adopting only those rules they believed the Bible commanded them to follow for fear of falling into "denominationalism," and even avoided taking an official name before eventually calling themselves the Church of Christ.[29] For several years they met in each other's homes, their church the living rooms and parlors of members. Weavers, for his part, came to believe that as part of the spirit of consecration God called him to give up his possessions, and he sold his cattle, two mules, the machinery he used to farm and the land he tilled. With part of this money he bought a "tabernacle" (in this case a very large canvas tent), and beginning in 1888 Holiness people began holding week-long camp meetings under it at a place they called Mount Zion, a bluff overlooking the Missouri River a few miles south of Tabor, a small town in far southwestern Iowa. Each year the assembly increased, with Weavers' skills as a revivalist attracting participants from throughout the Midwest.[30] One of those who attended was L.B. Worcester, a young man of consider-able skill who met and married his wife, Georgia, George Weaver's eldest daughter, at one of these early gatherings.

By 1892, the Holiness congregation had outgrown the living rooms of the area, and Weavers, with the assistance of Worcester, purchased the opera house in Glenwood, Iowa to serve as the new church. When this too became crowded the following year, they turned their attention once more to Tabor, where forty acres were purchased as part of an ambitious plan to expand the work.[31] More than a church, Weavers and Worcester envisioned the newly named Hephzibah Faith Home Association as a center for the propagation of Holiness throughout the world.[32] To this end they built a dormitory and schoolhouse for elementary and high school students, an orphanage, a seminary for the training of Holiness missionaries, and purchased a print shop. Long before any missionaries ventured forth, the printing press became their agent of outreach. Weavers served as editor of *The Sent of God* (*SOG*) when it first began in 1891 as a sporadically issued chronicler of Holiness life. By 1893, with their own dedicated press and a more capable editor, the Hephzibah faithful issued the *SOG* as a bi-monthly newspaper to a subscription base of nearly 4,000 readers.[33] The essence of the theology Weavers carried to South Africa can be gleaned from the pages of the *SOG*. Not only did the newspaper print excerpts from many of his sermons, but it also featured a series of articles in which Weavers sought to establish the biblical foundations of his newly established church. From these, several themes stand out as particularly important, both because they encapsulated key tenants of Holiness but also because it was these that *amakholwa* eagerly accepted during the revivals of 1896–1901.

BECOMING HOLY, DIVINE HEALING, & "THIS PRESENT EVIL WORLD"[34]

The message *amakholwa* repeatedly heard from Weavers was that to be counted a Christian one needed to enter into a state of Holiness by un-dergoing "consecration" and "sanctification." Radical in its simplicity, the message suggested to audiences that it was they, not outside arbitrators such as church officials and missionaries, who determined their own mem-bership in Christ's church. In comparison to the expectations missionaries had placed on catechists (even that word implies a level of intermediacy of belief that Weavers abhorred) this theology had the appeal of presenting a direct route to God. While the AZM envisioned a path into the churches that led through schools, Western-style homes, clothes, and above all their own gate-keeping, Weavers believed education was good only so far as it served God, and that the acquisition of material goods in pursuit of "civilization" was not only unnecessary but ultimately even damaging to one's relationship with Christ. [35]

Freeing oneself from one's possessions was just part of the process called "consecration," the central feature of which was the realization by the sinner of his sinful nature, and a necessary step in the achievement of Holiness.[36] "Repent," he commanded, "and be converted, that your sins may be blotted out. . . . "[37] Raising this awareness was one of the primary motivations for revival, and those being put under conviction to feel the "deep, malignant, hateful nature of your depravity" were offered a confessional lifeline for "God always saves the moment true faith is exercised."[38] But Weavers believed that salvation was dependent on "complete consecration" that is the revealing of all sins in a purging of past evils. Speaking from Proverbs 28:13, Weavers warned: "He that coverth his sins shall not prosper but whoso confesseth and forsaketh them shall have mercy."[39]

Nor was consecration merely an ephemeral experience. Sin was the work of demons, evil spirits that worked their wicked ways in man through emotions such as lust and greed, but also by taking tangible forms in material objects such as tobacco and whiskey.[40] For *amakholwa* this rang immediately familiar as traditional Zulu cosmology argued for agents of evil actively meddling in everyday life. Better yet, it suggested that missionary charges of impurity against the *amakholwa* community ignored the spiritual battle waging around them when it held individuals to blame for their faults. Undergoing consecration meant casting these demons out of the body where they would otherwise stay and feed upon both the soul and the flesh of the unconsecrated and unsaved. To fully free oneself from the bondage of sin, the sinner also needed to "surrender everything for Christ," particularly those things that kept them from enacting His will in their lives, as well as their "soul, body, time, and talents."[41] The ambiguous nature of this idea yielded varied responses; in Natal, as we will see, *amakholwa* interpreted it as bringing to the altar those items they connected to their past "sinful" lives—beer pots, pipes, traditional medicines, and even stolen goods. But it could also mean giving up all material goods, (as Weavers did), separating from unbelieving husbands and wives, or leaving jobs for lives as itinerant preachers.

While emotionally and spiritually wrenching, the good news for those who endured consecration was that sanctification waited as their reward.

As with ideas of perfection current at the time, the Hephzibah faithful understood Matthew 1:21, "And thou shalt call his name Jesus, for he shall
save his people from their sins" as promising a literal state of absolution by
which those who accepted this gift lived lives free from sin.[42] Consecration
prepared the soul by cutting away "the poisonous leaves and branches,"
purifying the heart and making room for the Holy Spirit that, with sanctification, dwelled within and "puts heaven down in us."[43] Sanctification
allowed *amakholwa* to "live a holy life while here on earth," a life free of
sin and the troubling emotions, such as hatred, guilt, and despair, that
were connected with man's disconnection from God.[44] This was a powerful
theology for those living on the boundaries of society, and not surprisingly
many of those attracted to the Holiness message, such as Weavers himself,
had lived hardscrabble lives on frontiers. For Zulu Christians who lived in
the cultural, social, and economic margins of southern Africa the theology
offered much.

Being "cleansed of all sin," "pure of heart," and a vessel for the Holy
Ghost carried with it weighty moral expectations for those *amakholwa* undergoing sanctification. The faithful needed to lead lives of social purity
and yielding to sin became not just a step backwards, as in the mainline
denominations, but evidence that the Spirit of God no longer resided in
the offender's soul.[45] If this were to occur, the sinner had little choice but
to again undergo the process of consecration, clearing out the impurities
missed the first time. Still, while sanctified swore "eternal allegiance to
God" and promised "never to yield the contest, but to fight for Him till
death ends the conflict" the act also offered great power—over sin, but also
in the gifts of the Holy Spirit imbued in the individual.[46] Citing Luke 24:49,
Weavers highlighted this pledge "And behold, I send the promise of my
Father upon you: but tarry ye in the city of Jerusalem, until ye be endued
with power from on high."[47]

Not surprisingly, considering his own miraculous recovery, Weavers
passionately believed in the power of divine healing. Like other Holiness churches, the Hephzibah congregation viewed healing as one of the
primary gifts of the Holy Spirit and one all sanctified could benefit from.
Weavers wrote of it often and carefully backed his faith in divine healing
with biblical references to Jesus healing everything from leprosy, blind-
ness, and infirmity, to palsy, dropsy, and undiagnosed "issues of blood."[48]
He also turned to James 5:14–15 for clear-cut directions in performing
these miracles: "Is any sick among you? Let him call for the elders of the
church; and let them pray over him, anointing him with oil in the name
of the Lord: And the prayer of faith shall save the sick, and the Lord shall
raise him up."[49] Nor did Weavers and other Holiness members hesitate to
act on this faith. When participants at the annual camp-meeting fell ill, the

sanctified gathered around, singing, "The Great Physician now is near, the sympathizing Jesus," and anointed the sick with oil and prayer.[50] When a woman at a revival service fell down and broke her arm in the summer of 1893, Weavers and others gathered over her to pray and "the bones were set by the power of God."[51] These incidents led Weavers to believe that not only was divine healing possible, but that use of human medicines evidenced a lack of trust in the daily and active power of the Holy Spirit in one's life. Divine healing became an article of faith at Hephzibah, and while it may have proven a difficult test of membership for some, it found a readier audience among *amakholwa* congregations, many of whom held much more diverse views of health and healing than their Western educated AZM missionaries.

Although Weavers promoted a type of communalism at Hephzibah, his intense hostility towards denominationalism reflected a fierce individualism. He railed against popes, bishops, superintendents, and any other hierarchical structures he believed stood in the way of a personal relationship with Jesus. To the question "To what church do you belong" Weavers suggested answering: "The saints of God are not church property, but belong to Christ. The church is Christ's church."[52] In writing of the requirement of all sanctified to follow the Word of God, Weavers noted, "the Spirit will guide us into all truth, yet I have heard men say, 'I will go wherever the Bishop or chairman sends me.' This is putting the Bishop or chairman in the place of the Holy Ghost. The Lord says, 'Thou shalt go to all that I shall send thee'" (Jer. 1:7). Even the sanctified needed to be wary, for he believed many revivalists were little better than "ecclesiastical soul hunters" who were ready to "put bands, rules, and straps on them" all for the sake of counting a membership higher than the next church or worse, filling up their coffers.[53]

Weavers' near pathological abhorrence of "man-made authority" eventually led him into disagreement with his own Church of Christ when they adopted rules he believed would not withstand the "judgment fire."[54] When the Faith Home was formed, the leadership gathered as a council to discuss every proposed rule and rule change, not accepting the validity of any regulation until its biblical basis had been well documented. And while Weavers and Worcester were the driving force behind Hephzibah, the input of others was frequently sought and welcomed; indeed both men went off on long missions, leaving the running of the association in the hands of others. Symbols of hierarchy were avoided, but the few who fully committed themselves to the workings of the church were honored for their dedication with the appellation "Elder"; other sanctified addressed each other as "brother" and "sister." Brought to Natal, this philosophy of individual empowerment served *amakholwa* well. In late 1896, the AZM had only recently begun to allow Zulu Christians into positions of authority within their own churches. Weavers' message of God's expectation that *all* sanctified serve as leaders of the church, provided *amakholwa* with legitimacy to press their own claims of spiritual authority.

The Civil War brought a darkening of the American national consciousness and an end to the golden age of postmillennialism, a doctrine that held that Christ would return only after the millennium, a thousand-year period of peace described in Revelation. According to this creed, if Jesus was to return only after the millennium it was beholden on Christians to work toward the perfection of humanity by ending slavery, war, poverty, and a host of other troubling social conditions.[55] Most if not all of the AZM missionaries who arrived in South Africa prior to the turn of the century, came believing that their activities contributed to bringing about the millennium. In addition to preaching the Gospel, they taught schools, encouraged participation in the capitalist economy, and passed on their own faith in the inevitable progress of mankind to *amakholwa* congregations.

Premillenarians like Weavers had no illusions about progress. Their doctrine held that the millennium would occur only after the return of Christ, who would carry away all true believers and leave behind the unworthy majority to endure a period of tribulation. This eschatology stripped away the activist impulse of social responsibility that had accompanied postmillennialism, leaving in its wake a prophetic conviction in the corruption of the world. If Christ could (and most likely would) appear at any moment, it was far more important for the premillenarian missionary to spread the Word to as many people as possible than to dawdle in one spot setting up schools and other impermanent institutions. Leaving little doubt where he stood, Weavers preached:

> All things point to his near coming. It is midnight now. The last hour! The last hour! Awake, the world is in darkness! You ought to be ready. It is high time. The lamps are going out. Oh, my God! Let the Holy Spirit come, or you will be left to go through that awful tribulation.[56]

For *amakholwa* undergoing the many traumas of the late nineteenth century, Weavers' words must have rung true, just as the promise of AZM missionaries that their hard work would be rewarded by their acceptance into the "civilized" societies of the world must have appeared increasingly hollow.

Indeed *amakholwa* were not alone in their growing discontent with the rallying cry of "Commerce and Civilization" advanced by the AZM, David Livingstone, and any number of other mid-nineteenth century missionaries. Indeed some converts elsewhere in Africa, like John Chilembwe, a Baptist pastor who led a revolt against British planters in colonial Malawi during the First World War, came to regard the economic axis of this philosophy as little better than another form of slavery.[57] The revivals of 1896–97 were certainly not a form of violent millenarianism like those that followed in central Africa or those that had come before such as that of Nongqawuse, a Xhosa girl who borrowed from Christianity to offer a prophecy that promised if the people would only kill all their cattle the world would be made anew.[58] Instead millenarianism simply informed the revivals, giving participants a sense of urgency and providing a further wedge between the theology of the AZM missionaries, and the faith *amakholwa* were piecing together from any number of sources.

Like other premillenarians, Weavers advocated for a radical disconnect from the surrounding world; yet Hephzibah upheld the duty of all sanctified to engage in missions to that world. Women of the Hephzibah congregation refrained from making themselves attractive, adopted simple hairstyles, and wore dresses without bright colors or fanciful patterns. Men wore no neckties and both sexes wore no jewelry. Rings, pins, gold watches, cufflinks, and chains were sold and the proceeds donated to the cause of missions. The sanctified spoke of this humbling of self as "taking the way," sacrifices that brought them closer to God.[59] The Hephzibah community also took seriously Christ's warning about heaven, rich men, camels, and the eye of a needle; Weavers suggested a Christian consider: "Do my riches hinder my Christian progress? Where your treasures are there will your heart be also. Ye cannot serve God and mammon."[60] Even in tiny Tabor, with its radical roots, the Holiness community became almost a world apart from locals, who flippantly referred to the Hephzibah grounds as "Sankytown." Because sanctification did not exclude the sanctified from temptation, Holiness members avoided many of the local celebrations that integrated the rest of the community; dances, ballgames, traveling circuses, and the like all represented Satan's snares.

Yet God did not permit total disengagement from the surrounding world, and all Hephzibah felt called to evangelism, in part because their sanctification served as an immediate commission for missionary work. As a man whose only training occurred on the job, Weavers disparaged the educated refinement of preachers and missionaries who "are first sent to colleges that teach church theology, and when their education is finished they go out and preach what they have learned—they preach to suit their hearers rather than preach Christ. The more worldliness, the less of Christ is preached, and the farther they get away from God, until both pulpit and pew are lost in worldliness."[61]

For the sanctified, no special education or appointment by a mission body was necessary, for they received the gifts of the Holy Spirit when they were filled with his presence. Christ, Weavers noted from Mark 6:7-13, called the apostles and bestowed upon them "power over unclean spirits, and commanded them that they should take nothing for their journey, save a staff only; no scrip, no bread, no money in their purse. . . . and they went out and preached that men should repent. And they cast out many devils, and anointed with oil many that were sick, and healed them."[62] The Hephzibah community maintained that no less should be expected from the contemporary apostles in their midst, even if the demons were now rum and tobacco. In this manner "souls that are convicted and sanctified by the Holy Ghost become soldiers for Christ right away,"[63] a commission many *amakholwa* eagerly accepted.

HEPHZIBAH MISSIONS

In October of 1894 the Hephzibah leadership changed the name of the association to the Hephzibah Faith Missionary Association, reflecting a shift in focus; the dissemination of the Holiness message in *foreign* lands would now take precedence. The motivation for this shift probably came from L.B. Worcester, who heard a revivalist speak of the need for new workers to step forward and fill up the ranks of those missionaries who died in the field.[64] But the visit of R. L. Marsh, from Wichita, Kansas, in May of that year provided the final impetus. Marsh, a Holiness preacher who had left the Congregational church, spoke over the course of a week about his intention to establish a Christian colony in Africa. Marsh, *SOG* reported, "has a real missionary spirit and said in his last sermon that since the call is so general, to go into the world to preach the Gospel, those who are fully consecrated to God will need special light to enable them to stay at home and still obey God."[65] Shortly after, William Worcester, L.B.'s younger brother, received a "Pentecostal fire" inspiring him to prepare for his own mission trip to Africa.[66] Weavers and the elder Worcester felt similar callings and spent several months touring the Midwest, raising support for foreign missions. That summer L.B. and his wife Georgia left Tabor in a buggy. Holding revival services as they went, they slowly made their way westward across the United States, living from donation to donation until, nearly a year later, they finally boarded a ship bound for Japan. Other Holiness members followed, many selling off their worldly possessions to fund mission trips to India, China, Haiti and elsewhere.[67]

Around that time, Weavers and William Worcester decided on South Africa as the destination for their evangelical efforts. Why South Africa? Perhaps a story printed in *SOG* the previous year influenced the selection. In it Thomas Cook, a Wesleyan evangelist among the Xhosa, described how entire audiences had broken down weeping and offered to take Christ as their Savior when he had preached the story of the cross; they were, he believed, a people ripe for salvation if only sufficient harvesters could be found.[68] Holiness had also found converts in Natal, and the Hephzibah missionaries expected friendly assistance upon their arrival. Regardless, in the middle of November 1895, a "grand" send-off was held for Weavers as he left Tabor. A number of former missionaries came and gave accounts of their own experiences, and Weavers preached a farewell sermon noting that just over thirty years ago he had bade farewell to friends and family from the same spot when going off to fight a different type of war. All gathered around and laid their hands upon him, praying for his safety and the success of his endeavor.[69] In what must have been a spectacle to behold, the crowd made its way to the train station, singing and praying along the way before seeing Weavers off to Chicago.[70]

Weavers did not proceed directly to South Africa. Once in Chicago he met with Henry O'Neill, an African working for the Holiness journal *The Fire-Brand*, and together they traveled to Waverly, New York where, over the course of a month, they held a series of two-a-day revival meetings.[71] Warmed up, Weavers sailed for England and made his way to Cambridgeshire, his birthplace. It was an unhappy return, for Weavers experienced considerably less success in England than anywhere else he preached. In his first three months he attended every church in the city without seeing "one soul saved at these places yet. They need the Holy Ghost but they will not accept him."[72] The English, he came to believe, had become a "fallen" people "whom the gods of this world have blinded," the working class little better than "white slaves," and their church services "more like political gatherings" than worship.[73] Despite the successes of the Keswick convention, the Holiness message had seemingly not penetrated this particular area and Weavers found that the locals "do not believe it is possible to live without sin (1 John 3:9) nor be sanctified (John 17:17) nor be healed (James 5:14–15)."[74]

After a few initial opportunities, invitations to preach dried up and no churches welcomed him or his message. Indeed, one minister made a pointed reference to Weavers' plain, uneducated style:

> I heard a man preach who said he was led by the Holy Ghost, that the Holy Ghost told him what to say. I thought if he was led by the Holy Ghost, I do not want him to lead me. Why, he made so many blunders, even the children came to me and said his grammar was not correct. I feel if lawyers and doctors and businessmen need to be educated surely ministers ought to be.[75]

For Weavers, who sarcastically referred to highly educated yet unsanctified ministers as "professors," this critique further illustrated the degenerative state of the English churches and he responded by striking out on his own.[76]

In his last months in England, Weavers began attending both the market and the local horse fair, where he would kneel down and pray before engaging in that venerable English tradition of standing on a soapbox and preaching. He attracted large audiences in this way, managed to hand out large numbers of religious tracts, and even convinced a few that they should give up card playing, tobacco, and drink.

William Worcester and his wife Ida joined Weavers in England in July, and together they sailed for South Africa, arriving in Cape Town in mid-August before being "called" to Durban, where they disembarked on August 22, 1896.[77] The network of connections that Holiness made available to them soon became evident. Not only were they met by members of the local Holiness community, but at the end of the dock's gangway where he handed out Holiness tracts to disembarking passengers they unexpectedly ran into "Brother" Keyes, a young man they had met the previous winter at a revival in Guthrie, Oklahoma. Within a fortnight, the Worcesters had accepted an invitation from William Wilcox, the AZM missionary running Groutville, to stay with him while they learned Zulu and prepared for their lives as missionaries. For his part, Wilcox probably extended the invitation at the behest of the Weisses, a Holiness couple from Iowa who had volunteered to assist Wilcox at Mapumulo the previous year and who knew Weavers, if not personally at least from his writings in the *SOG*.[78] The Worcesters accepted the invitation, and a short time later, in mid-September of 1896, Weavers made his way to visit the Weisses at Mapumulo where, at a small gathering in the mission house, he stood up to speak a few words to those few *amakholwa* who had gathered to welcome him.

A VOICE IN THE DESERT:
"BUT THERE SHALL COME ONE MIGHTIER THAN I . . . "[79]

Weavers was not the first revivalist to work among *amakholwa* of the AZM. In 1875, Major Malan, an evangelist who had resigned his British army commission to become a missionary in South Africa, visit Umsumduzi as part of a larger tour of the country. His exhortations had earlier touched off "a work of grace" among Sotho Christians, but had little effect among the *amakholwa* of the AZM. The American missionary at Umsumduzi, fearing that this reflected badly on his church, urged readers back home to "pray, dear brethren, *for a revival among the Zulus.*"[80] The World Day of Prayer, as mentioned previously, offered some of the spiritual excitement missionaries often found wanting among their congregations, but the effect was static. It offered, as I have suggested, an opportunity to reaffirm, not revolutionize, the nature of the *amakholwa* community and the faith they practiced.

It was a graduate of Oberlin, William Wilcox, who made the first determined efforts to bring "modern" revival to the AZM. Wilcox had hoped to establish a mission near Maputo, but Portuguese resistance to the American effort frustrated Wilcox's attempt. In 1891, without his own reserve to manage, he began extensive evangelical efforts throughout the AZM. On one occasion he focused on Durban and conducted evangelistic services with two local white ministers, the Revs. Russell and Fernie, at which "Christians were strengthened" and others "were led to accept Christ as a personal Saviour."[81] For the next half-decade both of these ministers conducted services throughout the AZM and became frequent speakers at the Native Annual Meeting, occasions that always sparked heightened "interest" from *amakholwa* participants, but were apparently accompanied by no real spiritual fire and produced no substantial changes in *amakholwa* Christianity. Indeed, one *amakholwa* recalled that when Weavers began preaching at Mapumulo he worried that this would be another mission-sponsored event that resulted in little change: "Still I thought it would be like all the revivals which were being held every time by the other *abafundisi*, [teacher/preacher] but the work was carried on."[82] It was not.

The other source of early evangelism came from a few dedicated *amakholwa* preachers. For while the Americans proved unwilling to hand over control of the churches to Zulu pastors, they did encourage the activities of evangelists. Missionaries occasionally hired *amakholwa* preachers to travel through local kraals, spreading the seeds of Christianity as they went. These efforts were inevitably successful, but they could seldom be sustained; the qualities that made individual evangelists successful also made them desirable elsewhere, and missionaries could not or would not meet the going rates. Prior to the revival, volunteer efforts by Zulu evangelists were sporadic at best. At the time of the World's Day of Prayer in 1893, "some of the best and most spiritual" residents of Inanda began holding bi-monthly meetings among traditionalists, inviting them forward during the service to receive prayer and discuss Christianity.[83] But no mention is made of these gatherings the following year and they likely faded away. Elsewhere, even this minimal effort was not made. That same year, the church at Umsumduzi brought in no new members and *amakholwa* there engaged in no evangelization efforts off of their station.[84] The missionary at Amaholongwa believed that there would be little need for white missionaries if only "all our converts [were] alive to their duty and responsibility with regard to the evangelizing of their heathen neighbors . . . "[85] He despaired of this occurring.

Yet the following year Johannes, the blind *amakholwa* preacher discussed in the previous chapter, heralded the start of a remarkable transformation in the churches of the AZM. A student of Amanzimtoti Theological Seminary, Johannes took advantage of the long summer break to tour several stations, preaching as he went and serving as the proverbial voice in the wilderness. Early 1896 found him at Ifume and there the community was so "shaken and awakened" under his preaching that it became one of the few mission stations to report a gain in church membership that year.[86] Impressed, the mission invited Johannes to speak at the NAM, held at Itafamasi July 22–28, 1896. The Rev. Walter Searle, a white South African preacher, acted as the official evangelist for the event, but Johannes stole the show. His exhortations moved the assembled *amakholwa*, and they responded with an "outpouring of the spirit" unprecedented in the mission to that point.[87] From the NAM, Johannes, whose vacation from the seminary was now permanent, made his way to Umzumbe where the missionary in charge of the station reported that his exhortations moved "all classes—backsliders, kraal people and Christians."[88] More importantly, many believed the meetings had prepared the ground for "what was to come." Those in attendance at the 1896 NAM had undergone an "awakening" that gave them a taste of what it meant to be revived. Johannes, the blind Zulu preacher, had shown them the path towards a faith whose form resonated far more deeply than that which they had engaged in for the previous fifty years.[89]

MAPUMULO, SEPTEMBER AND OCTOBER 1896

For the Christian residents of Mapumulo, the early spring of 1896 held little of the season's usual promise. Locusts had consumed much of the previous season's crops and their eggs lay thickly strewn across the land, waiting the first new rains before opening. Burning the land was an effective deterrent, but one that required a great deal of manpower, an increasingly scarce resource at Mapumulo and other mission stations as the Witwatersrand goldfields and the Durban docks drew away residents at a ferocious pace. The imminent threat of rinderpest also hung heavily over the station. *Amakholwa* participating in transport-riding had suffered when the border with the Transvaal was closed as a preventative effort that May. Even for those without wagons, however, attaching plows to cattle must have been an extremely grim activity that spring, for stories of the inexorable march of rinderpest had long since passed from lip to lip, rumors confirmed by increasingly apocalyptic reports in local newspapers.[90] Even the notoriously unresponsive Natal colonial government added to this trepidation when, as part of a larger tour, the Undersecretary for Native Affairs had scheduled a meeting for the first week of October to discuss rinderpest regulations with local chiefs and the *amakholwa* headman of Mapumulo.

External pressures were not the only problems troubling the Congregational community of Mapumulo. Young men and women returned from working in the cities and, empowered by their comparatively rich salaries, openly flaunted established rules. Christian leaders expressed helplessness as their youth squandered their earnings on garish clothing and drink, gambled what remained on horses and cards, and engaged in loud public brawls when they lost.[91] Just as many elders had troubled their families by choosing to become Christians, so did their children now trouble them by seeming to reject the faith of their fathers. Yet these families felt little inclined to turn for help to AZM missionaries, for many felt a deep sense of betrayal at the repeated refusal of the mission to allow them to purchase land on the mission reserves and worse, the imminent transfer of control of these lands to the feared Natal colonialist government. These feelings of injustice coincided with a growing perception among *amakholwa* that now was their time to assume leadership of the churches. This feeling crystallized around a letter sent out from the American Board that called on Zulu congregations to assume responsibility for their own affairs—a call refuted by missionaries who insisted on their continuing authority over *amakholwa* churches.

Worse, events within the church at Mapumulo (as elsewhere) seemed to vindicate the missionary position. In a nod to the wishes of the American Board, AZM missionaries had reluctantly encouraged a few churches to elect their own pastors. A tide of bitter factionalism subsequently split many of these congregations. At some locations these rifts grew strictly along political lines, with candidates backed solely by members of their own clans. At other churches, such as Mapumulo, jealousies tarnished the elections. Each *amakholwa* community that dissolved into quarrelling seemed to support missionary opinion that the time was not yet right to pass on control, and they urged the Board to send additional missionaries; not to supervise, but to directly run individual mission stations and churches.

Mapumulo had nominated two men, friends who, although neither had any formal training for the ministry, had spent time as evangelists preaching in the various outstations of the mission reserve. But the nomination of Mbiya Kuzwayo had attracted opposition not, it would seem, for any objections to his fitness for the post, but rather in an effort to check the influence of his father, Mfanefile Kuzwayo. A "shrewd businessman," the elder Kuzwayo had made his early fortune as a transport rider and translated this success into buying several farms across Natal and into Zululand, a general store on the reserve, and a ferry-service across the Thukela River. Unlike many of his contemporaries, Mfanefile did not use his wealth to reestablish himself within Zulu society in traditional, polygamous ways. Instead he won praise from the American missionaries for not hiding "his light under a bushel."[92] Wherever he went, in his years as a transport rider, he faithfully held morning and evening prayers and his businesses and farms doubled as preaching places, reaching out to the surrounding traditionalists. At Nogwaja, five miles east of Mapumulo, he built a church and school from scratch, complete with a congregation of some thirty members.

While he did not translate his achievements into the "sinful" symbols of a Zulu bigman, he welcomed the prestige that accompanied success, and in 1885 he began serving as an informal headman for the *amakholwa* residents of Mapumulo. Along with his authority, his duties remained relatively limited. Acting as a sort of "justice of the peace," he could employ little beyond persuasion in his efforts to maintain order. In April of 1896, perhaps frustrated with the moral state of the station and those returning from work in the cities, Mfanefile forwarded a petition to the SNA to formalize his power as the official *induna* at Mapumulo, a position that would give him authority, under Native Law, to try civil cases and collect taxes.[93] This was not an unprecedented move; Groutville, among other stations, had elected an *induna* in an effort to bridge the divide between their claim to being "exempted" Christians, and the increasing efforts of the Natal government to bring all Africans under the code of Native Law. The local Magistrate supported Kuzwayo's claim but the SNA expressed reservations, noting that since 1891, Mapumulo had been divided between three different chiefs to whom residents paid their taxes. Wilcox, the missionary in charge of the northern stations, supported the petition and pointed out that the move was not unprecedented; Christian headmen had already been established on other stations and under native code the move was permitted "where there are more than twenty families as on this station." After some initial wrangling with the SNA, Mfanefile received his appointment after the chiefs who stood to lose *amakholwa* from their control agreed to the move. Mfanefile submitted a second petition complete with twenty-six names of individuals who attested to their desire to be ruled by a *amakholwa* headman.[94] Their objections overcome, the SNA assented to Kuzwayo's appointment over the *amakholwa* residents of Mapumulo.

A man of impressive energy, the elder Kuzwayo continued to devote time to the church, and despite his considerable secular responsibilities, served as one of Mapumulo's preachers for many years. When the call came from the mission for the Mapumulo church to elect a permanent pastor, however, Mfanefile declined to stand for the post, likely because the mission held to an informal policy by which its pastors were expected to give up their outside interests and devote themselves to pastoral duties. In his place he urged his eldest son, Mbiya, to run. This, apparently, was too much for many of the *amakholwa* residents of Mapumulo, and the divide evidenced by the evenly split election could not be resolved, even by missionary intervention.[95] It is not surprising that missionary involvement did not help the matter. Besides jealousy at the Kuzwayo family's wealth and power, it is likely, despite Mfanefile's pestering of the mission over the question of land ownership, that the elder Kuzwayo's adherence to the mission's codes of purity won him little support among fellow *amakholwa*. In addition to his monogamous ways, Kuzwayo had also been the first to renounce *utshwala*, a step that must have frustrated many who had hoped to present a united front against this missionary imposition.[96] Finally, with a man as powerful as Kuzwayo remaining faithful to the mission, recent schisms elsewhere stood little chance of gaining a foothold at Mapumulo. The only safe place for dissenters to express their frustrations was within the church walls, and so they did. But when Mapumulo failed to elect a pastor, it also suffered the indignity of having a "guest" missionary (Weiss and his wife Ida who volunteered to assist the AZM) appointed to oversee the station.

So, when Weavers arrived at Mapumulo, he entered a church unsure of its moral fitness, torn by internal strife, angry with its leadership, embarrassed by its own failure to claim autonomy, and fearful for its future. As a veteran evangelist, he must have recognized these as conditions ripe for revival. During his first several days at Mapumulo the revivalist met with a small group of English speaking *amakholwa*, praying with and preaching to them in Weiss's mission house.[97] These services, conducted during the third week of September, were intense, emotional affairs and word of their power slowly spread. By the end of the week, the living room was full of *amakholwa* attracted by the unusual events. What they heard was that God expected more of them than simple conversion, and that their salvation depended on undergoing a second birth, one in which they would be born of the Spirit. To accomplish this they needed to first confess their sins and yield their will entirely to God in an experience of "consecration" that prepared them for "sanctification," the filling of the entirety of their lives by the Holy Spirit. Once the Spirit dwelled within them they were empowered to live free from sin, to be "Holy" men and women of the Lord.

Mbiya Kuzwayo was one of those listening intently in the crowded mission house and the young Zulu was so deeply moved by what he heard that he felt called by the Spirit into action. On Tuesday, September 22, Mbiya, following a command from on high, called for a day of rest so that all might gather in the church and receive a similar blessing. Many attended, although perhaps reflecting the recent dissent, many also stayed home and were undoubtedly surprised when friends and family returned late the following night, "drunk with the Spirit" and acting inexplicably. Groping to understand, they asked themselves: "Are these people mad, crazy, or possessed with evil spirits?"[98] But despite the skepticism, the meetings continued, and during the following days the revival congregation grew. Wilcox, responding to a letter informing him of the revival, traveled from Groutville to observe the events.[99] His first night at Mapumulo he watched in amazement as a Christian woman, long separated from God and the church following the death of several of her children, came "under conviction" and lost consciousness, falling into a Spirit-induced coma.[100] I will elaborate on these in greater detail in the following chapter, but one is struck here by the connections between Holiness and traditional Zulu forms of worship that both allowed for such dramatic expressions of faith. Possession, as Harriet Ngubane makes clear, was not an uncommon event in Natal, but for Congregationalists until 1896 it was a simply unheard of act within the churches. This created a serious disjunction between how many *amakholwa* understood faith to be practiced, and how they had publicly lived their Christianity. Holiness freed them to express their Christianity within "normal" Zulu idioms.

As for the possessed woman, members prayed for her, but when the meeting finally came to a conclusion late that evening she remained kneeling, lost to the world and "still struggling with an unseen enemy." Weavers and several of those who had received an earlier blessing remained, and as they prayed great streams of sweat rolled down her, forming a puddle of perspiration at her knees. Suddenly, she came to herself, crying and shaking. The revivalists pointed her to the cross hanging over the altar, and in her ecstasy she looked up at the roof, searching for holes she feared she might float through.[101]

Her experience broke the last opposition and several days later, after Weavers took a short break to climb a nearby hill for "secret prayer," the entire *amakholwa* community of Mapumulo gathered at dusk to pray for their own consecration experience. Weavers preached once more, the assembled sang and prayed and then, as before, several in attendance came under conviction, falling to the floor as they struggled with the agony of their sins. One, a girl, went into a trance and remained unconscious for two hours before regaining her senses and confessing not only her own sins, but also those of many others in the church "which God had revealed to her."[102] Stunned and perhaps frightened, those in attendance who had yet to experience conviction also began confessing. Adultery, fornication, theft, drunkenness, witchcraft, and even a murder all came to light. Hours and then days passed in this manner, with the members of the church purging themselves, going home exhausted, and returning in the morning to do it all again. When the process was complete later that week, all but four of the churches members had confessed sins Wilcox believed worthy of expulsion.[103]

Mbiya believed that events justified his earlier urging to follow the call of the Spirit and with relish he compared the reactions of those *amakholwa* who had at first doubted to those of the bystanders of Pentecost in Acts 2: "For those who thought the Spirit to be the devil's now realized that God has come by his Holy Spirit on us, and means something, even to the saving of lost souls. Glory to God!"[104] The whole of the community, having undergone consecration and become thoroughly convinced of the presence of the Holy Spirit, now began the process of sanctification—making themselves Holy unto God to live lives free of sin. Christians paid off long forgotten debts, met previously unfulfilled church pledges, resolved personal feuds, and heaped a mound of items they feared might keep them from living sanctified lives upon the church altar; snuff boxes, pipes, beer pots, a concertina, witchcraft medicines, and items of traditional attire such as feathers, skins, beads, and even two headrings, were all give up to God.

In the end, consecrated and now sanctified, the congregation came together as one, united by both the mutual pain they had shared in confession and the pure joy they now felt as the Holy Spirit filled them with the power of God's love. So empowered by the experience were they that for the first time in the history of the AZM an entire church community, not just a few individuals, felt burdened to share their faith. Small groups of *amakholwa* took their message to the outstations, preaching, with breathless ecstasy, of the power of the Holy Spirit in their lives. A young man, sent to pick up mail in a nearby town, arrived at the post office and began preaching to several loitering native policemen.[105] The officers listened with amusement at first, but as the young man became "drunk with the spirit" and began behaving oddly, they became alarmed and threw the revivalist into jail. Undeterred, he continued to preach, pray, and praise God, rattling the cell with his shouts of "Hallelujah!" Unnerved, they soon released him with a warning that he must never return to fetch the mail and should promptly see a doctor for his illness. He returned to the mission reserve, preaching and praising God to those he met along the road.

"THE BILLOW OF FLAME ROLLS ACROSS THE LAND . . ."[106]

Shortly after Weavers left Mapumulo for Umvoti, on November 1, twelve Zulu revivalists followed him, led by Mbiya Kuzwayo these young men and women who were eager to share their own experience of sanctification with other *amakholwa*.[107] They traveled the thirty-five miles between the two stations slowly, praising God and holding prayer meetings along the way with any who listened. Arriving at Umvoti shortly after Weavers, but before he started preaching, they entered the church and spent the day inside fasting and praying. Unsettled by this group of firebrands and having heard of the events at Mapumulo, several of the Umvoti residents fled, determined not to endure the madness that had gripped their sister station.[108] But most stayed, and accompanied by the Mapumulo band, and with Mbiya Kuzwayo interpreting, Weavers began preaching the following day.

Unlike Mapumulo, the process of consecration began almost immediately. The first night of meetings went well into the following morning and those in attendance returned at daybreak to began again. The Umvoti congregation was moved, not just by Weavers' words, but also by the "light and joy in the faces" of those from Mapumulo, who, when not in meetings, moved out into the bush and hills ringing Umvoti to hold "secret" prayer.[109] Their earnest exhortations for the souls of fellow *amakholwa* could be heard throughout the reserve. These prayers must have cut close, for the fears and troubles of the Umvoti community mirrored those of Mapumulo or were, if anything, even worse, for Groutville had become a shadow of its former self. Wilcox noted that those left over from the earlier boom years were in the "woeful condition of the poverty stricken descendents of a great house. They have a great reputation to sustain with nothing to do it with."[110]

That evening *amakholwa* filled the pews and those that arrived late stood, lining the walls of the church until no more could pack in. As at Mapumulo, the services began with prayer and singing before Weavers delivered a message in his usual calm, yet intense, tones. More prayers and singing followed before the assembled were urged to lay their sins on the altar and experience the miracle of perfect love available to them through consecration. One after another, over a hundred *amakholwa* came forward for confession, emptying their souls in a great community-wide purge. Prepped by the Mapumulo band, they also came prepared for sanctification, bringing along all that might keep them from God. The altar was soon covered with traditional medicines, pipes, snuffboxes, beer pots and other "sinful" items. One young man, who confessed to a murder, laid a suit of clothes he had stolen on the altar, others brought books, writing instruments, and long-forgotten items they had pilfered from the school while a separate pile was made of shovels, rakes, and the like swiped from Wilcox.[111]

As at Mapumulo, those Umvoti residents who underwent consecration and sanctification experienced an ecstasy that they felt compelled to share with others. After the Spirit descended upon one of the leading men of the station he hurried home, banged through the front door and raised such a ruckus that his startled wife cried out from their bed in alarm: "What is the matter!" "Matter," he replied breathlessly, "I have received the Holy Spirit and I want you to get Him!" The next morning she and their children followed him into the church and underwent their own sanctification, an experience that led the entire family to preach the message of revival with great zeal to all who would stop and listen.[112]

After several weeks at Umvoti, Weavers accompanied Wilcox to Impapala in Zululand, the last of the northern stations under Wilcox's care. Here, it should be noted, the conditions that made Mapumulo and Umvoti ripe for revival did not seem present. Like many of the newer outstations of the AZM, the Impapala congregation had gathered itself together and built its own church before voluntarily seeking affiliation with the AZM. Because of this they retained a greater degree of self-determination than the primary stations, and they lived on Crown land, so were little affected by the mission's decision to surrender control of the Trust Lands.[113] The church had also recently selected a new preacher without the internal antagonism that had plagued both Mapumulo and Groutville. Finally like other outstations, the church appeared morally fitter than the older stations and missionaries proved willing to forgive missteps, chalking them up to youth, while celebrating Impapala as a model of Christian development. But while Impapala appeared economically, morally, and spiritually healthier than the older stations of the AZM, it suffered its own troubles. The local chief was hostile to their presence and encouraged the activities of a local Ethiopian sect, going so far as to assist them in a brief takeover of the Impapala church. The local magistrate had interceded on behalf of the Congregationalists, restoring their church but bringing only an uneasy truce to the hostilities.[114] And while trade across the Thukela continued, it was clear that rinderpest would soon force the border's closure, crushing the economic lifeline of the district.

Finally, as elsewhere, many of the youth of the community returned from work in the cities and mines in open rebellion against the authority of their elders, a rebellion that also extended to their inherited faith. The concern expressed by elderly *amakholwa* for their children ran deeper than simple generational conflict, however, for many of the youth were clearly troubled by the lives they lived in the cities of southern Africa. In the opening weeks of revival, two young men had already confessed to murder. As there is no record of such violence at either station, they likely occurred in either Durban or Johannesburg, dramatically underlining the brutal and dehumanizing experience of urban colonial capitalism that stripped young Africans, Christian and traditionalist alike, of their humanity.[115] It is perhaps not a surprise than that so many youth participated in the revival, or that they became its driving force. In staying up all night wrestling with sins, young men and women revealed the perniciousness of the colonial economy; in embracing consecration and sanctification they declared that Christianity had a place in their lives because it was a nimble enough theology to address their troubles.

So it was also at Impapala. Like Umvoti, messengers from Mapumulo prepared the way for Weavers, and at the very first meeting the revival began in full force. A young woman emerged from a four-hour trance to confess to "a most disgraceful crime involving her nearest family relations." A young man, crying and wailing, awakened Weavers at 2 A.M. to confess; they prayed together, and after several hours he departed, his soul consecrated. The native pastor responded to consecration by jumping up and down, shouting out his joy.[116] It was also at Impapala that divine healing is first mentioned, an aspect of the revivals that grew increasingly important over the coming months and years. First an old *amakholwa* woman proclaimed that God had "healed" her of her desire for snuff, and then, more dramatically, the sanctified gathered to pray over a snakebite victim, who, it was happily noted, fully recovered.[117] After an intense week in Zululand, Weavers departed with fifteen snuffboxes, three pipes, a hemp horn, three headrings and six pence, which the preacher's wife offered in payment for a book she had long ago taken from Inanda.[118] Nearly all, Wilcox reported, had experienced "definite blessing."

THE CHILDREN OF ZION

As Weavers, accompanied by Kuzwayo and the other revivalists, traveled through the northern stations, news of the remarkable happenings at Mapumulo and elsewhere trickled out to other mission stations. By word of mouth and by letter, the news spread remarkably fast. At Inanda Seminary, teachers received several letters from revived women detailing the excitement of recent events and seeking to right past wrongs. One former pupil wrote from Mapumulo:

> The Lord is doing great wonders among us—men and women are confessing their adulteries (sins). We girls, too, who are in the church as well as those outside, we have been doing these sins and then we would just deny them and go and sit down at the table of the Lord, but now the Spirit has shown us how awful our sins are, we have confessed them and have forsaken them.[119]

Another commented on the great piles of items, including medicines, laid on the altar while a third wrote: "I have no words to tell you the great joy we are having here; we are saying 'Praise the Lord' we are not ashamed to speak his word before anyone. I have given myself now to be wholly His." From one letter emerged a shilling's worth of stamps along with a note confessing, "I was thinking in my heart that I should never pay you this money, but when the Spirit of the Lord came to me with power and showed me my sins, He showed me this too, this money of yours which I was keeping."[120] At Umzumbe Girls' school students returned from their year-end break eager to inquire into the workings of the Holy Spirit. Thirty-two participated in a study of Acts 2:39 and within weeks a revival broke out at this far southern station completely independent of Weavers or the band of revivalists promoting his message. Back at Inanda, girls from northern Natal had received letters from friends from the very start of the revival, and, desiring a "like blessing for themselves," they organized an inquirers class in search of the Holy Spirit.[121] As word of the revivals spread, religious excitement grew everywhere. At Amanzimtoti, Esidumbini, Umzumbe, Durban, and elsewhere, congregations voiced an interest in the workings of the Spirit and sought their own "quickening."[122]

One of those who must have received a letter was Dalita Isaac, an *amakholwa* teacher at Inanda who responded to the news from the north and the growing earnestness of her students by holding several Sabbath evening meetings with girls of the seminary. Following the model of consecration and sanctification, Isaac focused her preaching on the subject of sin, speaking with frankness to the "particular sins" which Zulu girls were prone to yield. Following the second of these gatherings, teachers found a group of students gathered alone in a classroom where a discussion of consecration had led to an intense bout of crying. "My sins, oh, my sins" the girls wailed as the American principal and *amakholwa* teachers offered to hear their confessions. There followed several weeks of "earnest seeking" after the gifts of the Holy Spirit. Emulating the actions of those on the northern stations, some fasted for days while others took advantage of every break from instruction and their regular duties to go into the surrounding bush for "secret prayer."[123]

After a second successful tour at Mapumulo, Weavers arrived at Inanda shortly before Christmas of 1896. There is no record of the Mapumulo band preceding this visit, but Kuzwayo accompanied him, serving as both translator and spiritual companion. The revivalists arrived at the invitation of the seminary staff and spent their early days with the girls. For the 180 students of the seminary, the Holiness preacher's presence intensified the experience of conviction begun earlier by Dalita Isaac. Weavers first met with them in a classroom, and as he preached the girls began crying, quietly at first, but with increasing volume until, twenty minutes later, not a voice could be heard above the din. The missionary teachers, their

Congregational sensibilities jarred by the commotion, expressed amazement at Weavers' reaction, for instead of trying to "steady the ark," he sat
down to pray, allowing the girls' emotion to run its course.[124] When the
crying finally subsided one of the teachers attempted to end the meeting,
but the girls refused to be dismissed and one after another they confessed
thier sins, dragging the meeting late into the night.

They repeated the scene during meetings the next day and when, the following night, girls lay in bed sobbing, the teachers gathered them together
and Weavers informed them: "We do have to die for our sins sometimes.
I cried over mine." But, he then warned, "This crying can never save you"
and outlined a path towards sanctification in terms, "so plainly that they
could not help but see." For the rest of the week, the last in the school year
before students scattered to their homes across Natal, the girls met with
Weavers in small groups of two or three. In the classrooms, the chapel, and
outdoors, they received instruction from him on achieving sanctification
for themselves, and consecration for others.[125]

After the girls departed, Weavers turned his attention to the Inanda congregation. A large church, with many outstations, the community at Inanda
had built a reputation nearly equaling Groutville's. Located near Durban,
the gardens of Inanda fed the city over the years, and *amakholwa* willing to
rise early enough could work in the city without experiencing the difficulties associated with being a migrant. When the question of autonomy arose,
the residents of Inanda could proudly point to their history as the first Zulu
church to call and support an *amakholwa* pastor, James Dube. But, as elsewhere, serious troubles bubbled below the surface. The bitter dispute over
Dube's successor to the pastorship was traced in the previous chapter, and
the church endured both the bitterness that this bred and the indignity of
having an AZM missionary placed over them while the quarrel continued.
The community also suffered from a rapid erosion in their fortunes. Overcrowding, a plight that would blight nearly all of the mission stations in the
coming years, struck Inanda first, and by the end of 1896 Indian farmers
had already undercut the trade of *amakholwa* gardeners in supplying the
markets of Durban.[126]

During the last week of 1896, the people of Inanda gathered to hear the
message of the revivalists. They sought salvation as individuals and as a
community and what they found, what they created together, was a new
way of expressing their faith that must have been remarkably fulfilling, for
they participated in it with forceful enthusiasm. Meetings were held twice
daily and from the very first they were spiritually and emotionally powerful
experiences. Crying was followed by confession, some became comatose
for hours, others felt struck down by an invisible force that only freed them
when they arose to confess, and all believed themselves compelled by the

Spirit to divulge their darkest secrets.[127] Pixley, who had recently taken over Inanda but was the longest serving American missionary in Natal, wavered between wonder and dismay at what he saw. He worried that the congregation had hidden from him sins unsurpassed "since Paul and the Corinthians" but also commenting that "I am sure we never have known in our missionary experience such a fervency of spirit and so much pleading with God in prayer as we have witnessed in the progress of this work at Inanda."[128] Following the lead of the northern stations, the Inanda congregation participated in prayer meetings that lasted twenty-four hours, fasted to the point of collapse, and engaged in prayers so loud that the pews shook with the force of them. The desire for sanctification produced a mountain items sacrificed on the altar that the congregation feared led them into sin. At week's end, the revivalists led the church down to the nearby Msunduze River, where a ceremony was held and a bonfire of snuffboxes, pipes, ornaments, medicines, and even musical instruments were set alight. Potions that wouldn't burn were dumped into the Msunduze, the river carrying off the evil to the nearby Indian Ocean.

As elsewhere, the revival experience transformed the relation of the congregation to the church, to each other, and to their faith. At the end of the week, over fifty men and women, some who had long been members of the church but believed, after undergoing revival, that they had been Christian in name only, stood and declared their eagerness to witness for Jesus.[129] The demands of consecration and sanctification also moved the church toward reconciliation. A day after loudly receiving the Holy Spirit, Dalita Isaac stood and spoke: "Yes, my friends, the Lord has blessed me and filled me with His Spirit, but I have something to confess before you. I have confessed some things but now I have this to say. I have been believing foolish and wicked stories about this brother and this one [pointing to them] and ask their forgiveness for it."[130] Earlier, she had gone to their homes and, finding the men away, begged forgiveness from their wives. Now she confessed publicly, noting that the stories she referred to were known by many and therefore the men's forgiveness should be publicly sought. The men exonerated her, pushing forward the process of healing the division with the Inanda church.

Leaving Inanda, the revivalists arrived at Esidumbini, located between Inanda and Mapumulo, on the first day of the New Year, 1897. As at Impapala, the congregation of Esidumbini appeared less in need of revival than elsewhere. A growing church, they had recently called Umvakwendhulu, a graduate of Adams Theological School, to be their pastor with no notable dissent. During Umvakwendhulu's installation ceremony, the congregation participated with hushed awe, some even crying with joy at the sight of a Zulu pastor assuming the reigns of their church.[131] Yet this community of *amakholwa* also suffered from the troubles of the times; plagues, economic troubles, the dislocation of urban employment, fears over government intentions, and particularly a deep unease with the nature of their Christian identity—all of which provided fertile ground for the revival message.

Unlike elsewhere, the first meeting at Esidumbini, held on a fiercely hot Sunday afternoon, provided few dramatic moments. Weavers preached from Joel 2:23 and the church pastor, Umvakwendhulu, received "a blessing."[132] But otherwise the first day proved more a day of anticipation than participation. The revival began in earnest, however, early the following morning when *amakholwa* packed the church at daybreak. Weavers preached extensively from John 14, in which Jesus promised the Holy Spirit to his followers and afterwards, as the heat was broken by a fierce thunderstorm, the congregation underwent consecration, the sound of their cries and shouts mingling with the echoes of thunder to apocalyptic effect. Meetings that lasted all day, crying, fainting spells, fasting, and fervent expressions of faith followed over the course of the next week. Weavers preached several times from Romans 12:1–2 (NIV 1984), "Therefore, I urge you, brothers, in view of God's mercy, to offer your bodies as living sacrifices, holy and pleasing to God—this is your spiritual act of worship. Do not conform any longer to the pattern of this world, but be transformed by the renewing of your mind. Then you will be able to test and approve what God's will is— his good, pleasing and perfect will," and as the Esidumbini congregation grasped this message, they turned to sanctification, giving up beer, placing those items they believed kept them from God on the altar and pulling each other aside to right past wrongs. The congregation also became larger each day as outstation *amakholwa* braved the persistent rains and made their way over the surrounding hills to participate. As they crowded together, services became bedlams of simultaneous consecration and sanctification and each meeting saw large numbers come forward to confess. Weavers recorded the growing crowds of *amakholwa* seeking the blessings of the Spirit in his diary: on January the fifth "many" approached the altar to confess, on the sixth, during a "grand meeting" "many hard ones go to God," on the morning of the seventh nearly forty came forward and in the afternoon over a hundred approached the altar, kneeled down and asked the Holy Spirit to enter them in their last act before sanctification.[133]

By January 10, one week after the revivals began, there was no longer room in the church for all who wished to participate, and with the skies suddenly clear the congregation gathered instead under a nearby orange grove. "The people," Weavers wrote in his diary, "are wonderful stired [sic] up about there [sic] souls." Indeed the missionary overseeing Esidumbini reported that the experience had brought many hardened hearts to repentance, awakened backsliders and lukewarm Christians alike, and led all those in the area on the verge of conversion into full communion. In one of his last services at Esidumbini, Weavers preached from John 4:35–36 and Acts 2:1–4, drawing comparisons between the assembled and the early apostles.[134]

Toward the end of Weavers' stay, the newly revived community at Esidumbini gathered to celebrate their sanctification by offering up their testimonies. In the Holiness vernacular, testimonies were personal narratives of sinful lives saved by revival, and *amakholwa* told theirs with relish, explaining all that Lord had done for them, including, in the case of one outstation preacher, the healing of his diseased body. The accounts went on into the early morning, as each savored his or her opportunity to relate what had come to pass: a confirmation of their individual salvation, the rebirth of their community, and their awakening into a faith that now felt more firmly their own.

Two days later, the revivalists departed Esidumbini for Noodsberg. One of the first outstations of the AZM to form itself into its own church, the *amakholwa* community at Noodsberg had been torn asunder the previous decade when its preacher, Mbiyana Ngidi, left the AZM to form his own church. His actions, motivated by an interest in securing his own freedom of action and the belief that the prohibitions placed on *lobola* and *utshwala* were wrong, attracted a substantial following at Noodsberg and elsewhere. For years the two sides battled for control of the area, Ngidi's faction going so far as to occupy the church during at least one occasion.[135] Following Ngidi's death in 1894, however, most of the Noodsberg *amakholwa* returned to the American Congregational church, and by the summer of 1897, the worst of the conflict had passed. Indeed the congregation was just finishing construction of a new stone church when the revivalists arrived; the building serving as a visible symbol of their reconciliation.

Noodsberg lay not far from Mapumulo and it seems probable that faithful from the northern station had sowed the seeds of revival well before Weavers arrival, for on the first night of meetings, January 14, a large crowd gathered in the old church and the revival kicked off with a bang.[136] Crying, fainting, shouts of joy, and other physical expressions of consecration filled the night air, along with confessions of the assembled. As a hard rain poured down, *amakholwa* also underwent sanctification and two of their number claimed to be healed of serious ailments. The next morning the crowd proved too large for the old church and the congregation opened up the new stone structure for the first time, giving Weavers the honor of inaugurating it with a "powerful meeting" at which over a hundred came forward to seek the Holy Spirit. That afternoon Weavers sought out high ground for prayer, climbing, as he often did while in South Africa, the nearest available peak to be closer to God.[137] For several days, Weavers had felt that God was calling him back to America, and after prayer that afternoon he was sure of it. So, after one last meeting the following day, he wrapped up his brief campaign in Noodsberg and returned with the other revivalists to Esidumbini.

Several more days of meetings at Esidumbini followed, although their tenor had clearly changed; less revival than celebration, the people gathered to confirm their own sanctification, their place as people of faith, and their renewed Christian identity. The mood even infected Weavers, a somber man, who noted in his diary on January 17 . . . "This has been one of the best days for me in South Africa." While most in attendance had already claimed sanctification, some continued to undergo consecration. Emulating the earliest days of the Natal missions, a local traditionalist chief came to one of the meetings, bringing his people with him. The well-dressed chief sat near the front, but despite Weavers' urgings he refused to kneel and offer up his sins. The following day he returned, however, again bringing his people some of whom converted in one of the few moments of the revival in which traditionalists played a dramatic role.

The day before Weavers left Esidumbini he publicly passed the torch of revival to Mbiya Kuzwayo, the man through whom nearly all his sermons in South Africa had flowed. Weavers asked Mbiya to lead the morning meeting and the young Zulu delivered a stirring sermon, proving his ability to Weavers who noted with approval: "He is filled with the Spirit of God." By this point Weavers referred to Kuzwayo as "Elder Mbiya," an honorific he bestowed on only a faithful few committed to spreading Holiness, and befitting the apostolic brotherhood their travels had engendered, Mbiya spoke of the Iowan as "Brother Weavers." In his diary that day, Weavers appreciatively remarked of Kuzwayo: "He a lone [sic] has paid me by been [sic] filled with the Spirit for coming over to Africa." Later, Kuzwayo, giving thanks to God for the miracle of the recent meetings, called for a special collection at which £4 was taken up for Weavers.

On the 20th of January Weavers and Kuzwayo parted ways, Kuzwayo returned to Mapumulo while Weavers went on to Umsumduzi to preach an evening service.[138] Returning to Inanda the following day, the old revivalist spent several days fasting and going up onto a local hill for prayer. He then conducted a series of meetings on divine healing. Preaching from Exodus 15:25-26, Matthew 10:8 and 15:22-28, and Revelation 22:1-2, among others, he made a case for the power of God over temporal illness and troubles.[139] His message of spiritual power met with a receptive audience for whom active engagement in the "civilized" world was producing rapidly diminishing results. Practicing what he preached, he spent much of his free time during this second stay at Inanda praying with small groups of *amakholwa* over their sick friends and family. He also met with the American missionaries, who were holding their semi-annual meeting at Inanda. Weavers showed a particular interest in spreading Holiness among the Americans, and after one prayer session he noted with pleasure that "some were saved." Indeed, when he arrived back in Tabor, Weavers gave a lecture on his work in Natal at which he bragged that the "first work he did was to convert several missionaries who came over to convert the heathen but were badly in need of conversion themselves."[140] He was disappointed, however, that the missionaries spoke out so strongly against the practice of divine healing, a disagreement that, as we will see, later engendered hostility between the AZM and the Holiness message.

Weavers spent his final days at Inanda, January 31–February 2, holding meetings with the *amakholwa* congregation. The number interested in attending these meetings, from the Inanda congregation and its outstations, threatened to overwhelm the church and instead, taking advantage of fine weather, Weavers held these services on Inanda Mount, a nearby tabletop hill located next to the Umgeni River.[141] The Iowan preached extensively from Acts 2 and Acts 11, and like his last days at Esidumbini, the services at Inanda allowed the assembled to witness to their past lives of sin and rejoice in their newly won sanctification. At their last meeting, church members gave thanks to God for sending Weavers and offered him £8 to return home with and two elaborately carved walking sticks to remember them by.[142] When he departed, on February 3, the entire community assembled along the river, singing to him and waving their hats as he was rowed across the Umgeni.

By his last month in Natal, Weavers' fame had spread well beyond the AZM, and he received appeals for his services from other mission denominations and even white congregations in Durban and Pietermaritzburg.[143] He was, however, so sure of God's command to return to Tabor that he declined these invitations and bought a ticket for home.[144] Weavers spent his last days in Natal working in Durban, holding services in a Baptist church and traveling with Ransom throughout the city. They made brief stops at various outstations and preaching points of the AZM's city mission, each its own small success. On the 6th of February, Weavers sailed first for Cape Town and after a few days on to America. Once in the United States, he made his way back to Iowa and arrived home at the end of April, 1897. All told, he had spent just over a half of a year in Natal, but he left behind *amakholwa* congregations more fully engaged with their faith than any in the previous fifty years of Zulu Christianity. All across Natal, Zulu revivalists eagerly took up the message of Holiness and carried it from church to church, sweeping away with it any questions AZM missionaries could raise over *amakholwa* commitment to their faith even as they employed this new theology to rebuild the very nature of their Christianity.

NOTES

1. The following account of the first days of the revival at Mapumulo is pieced together from the following sources: *The Sent of God*, December 3, 1896, letter from Mbiya Kuzwayo dated September 30, 1896, and letter from Frank Weiss dated October 7, 1896; AZM A/3/41, Mapumulo and Groutville Annual Report, 1896–97; ABM 192/424–30, Price to Smith, February 11, 1897.

2. Kuzwayo's claim to understanding "an unknown tongue" is an odd one. As a onetime student at Amanzimtoti Boys Seminary he received several years of English training. When Weavers first arrived at Mapumulo he conducted the first meetings in the mission house without an interpreter, a role that Mbiya took over shortly before the Wednesday gathering. It is possible that Mbiya is claiming the gift of tongues as told in Acts 2:1–13 as part of his sanctification experience and as such is claiming legitimacy for his ability to translate from Weavers' English into his native Zulu.

3. ABM 192/424–30, Price to Smith, February 11, 1897.

4. *Missionary Herald*, "The Wonderful Revival," August 1897, 320–23.

5. *The Sent of God*, Notice on Weavers return to Iowa, May 6, 1897

6. Kenneth Brown, *Indian Springs Holiness Camp Meeting: A History of "The Greatest Camp Meeting in the South"* (Hazelton: Holiness Archives, 2000). The location and timing of the Second Great Awakening is a matter of some debate among American historians, with some arguing for an earlier origin in eastern cities.

7. Christopher Waldrep, "The Making of a Border Society: James McGready, the Great Revival, and the Prosecution of Profanity in Kentucky," *The American Historical Review* 99 (1994). For a perceptive work on these revivals see Ellen Eslinger, *Citizens of Zion: The Social Origins of Camp Meeting Revivalism* (Nashville: University of Tenessee Press, 1999). Eslinger carefully pulls apart the view that revivals represented a wild pioneer religion for a people suffering under severe hardship and austerity. Instead, she argues, camp meetings offered participants an opportunity both to reintegrate into an American society that had changed dramatically following the end of the Revolutionary War, and to establish a common identity at a time when the area had begun to create settled communities. Like the American frontier, southern Africa of the late 1800s was a land of significant upheaval where individuals sought the reassurance of tightly bounded communities, something revival accomplished supremely well.

8. Charles Johnson, "The Frontier Camp Meetings: Contemporary Appraisals, 1805–1840," *The Mississippi Valley Review* 37 (1950), 81–110.

9. For more on the Rochester revivals see Paul E. Johnson, *A Shopkeeper's Millennium: Society and Revivals in Rochester, New York, 1815–1837* (New York: Farrar, Straus, & Giroux, 1978).

10. William McLoughlin, *Revivals, Awakenings, and Reforms* (Chicago: University of Chicago Press, 1978), 124.

11. Charles Grandison Finney, *Lectures on Revivals of Religion* (Cambridge: Harvard University Press, 1960).

12. Oberlin was born out of the frustration a group of Congregational theology students from Cincinnati felt when they were prohibited from publicly advocating

abolition. Led by Theodore Weld, who had attended a Finney revival in 1825, the students helped found Oberlin in 1833 as a center for both revival and abolition. Finney fit in well with this activism, for in addition to his revivalism, Finney also maintained that slavery was sinful, refused to baptize slave-owners and actively supported abolition causes. For more on Oberlin see Robert Abzug, *Passionate Liberator: Theodore Dwight Weld and the Dilemma of Reform* (New York: Oxford University Press, 1980).

13. Wesley apparently found his inspiration during a conversation with Moravian missionaries during his failed effort to bring the Gospel to American Indians in 1735. "Saving faith" they informed him, "brought with it both dominion over sin and true peace of mind—both Holiness and happiness." Vinson Synan, *The Holiness-Pentecostal Movement in the United States* (Grand Rapids: Eerdmans, 1971), 14.

14. Timothy L. Smith, "Righteousness and Hope: Christian Holiness and the Millennial Vision in America, 1800–1900," *American Quarterly* 31 (1979), 26–28.

15. Charles Edward White, *The Beauty of Holiness* (Grand Rapids: Eerdmans, 1986).

16. Gregory Schneider, "A Conflict of Associations: The National Camp-Meeting Association for the Promotion of Holiness versus the Methodist Episcopal Church," *Church History*, 66 (1997), 272.

17. Kenneth Brown, *Indian Springs*, 9.

18. Ibid.

19. Melvin Dieter, *The Holiness Revival of the Nineteenth Century* (Metuchen: Scarecrow Press, 1980). Orthodox Methodist belief on sanctification is that the process is a gradual one, often taking a lifetime to fully achieve.

20. Gregory Schneider, "A Conflict of Associations," 280.

21. The following account of Weavers' early life and the establishment of the Holiness church is, unless otherwise noted, taken from the following: *History of Freemont County* Iowa Historical Company (Des Moines: 1881) 485–86; *Tabor Beacon*, April 30, 1914, "The Close of a Notable Life: Obituary for Reverend George Weavers"; *Mills County Tribune*, April 30, 1914, "Obituary for Reverend George Weavers"; and Paul Worcester, *The Master Key* (Kansas City: Nazarene Publishing House, 1966).

22. James McPherson, *Battle Cry of Freedom* (New York: 1989), 576–78.

23. For a fuller account of this action and the entire Vicksburg campaign see, Winston Groom, *Vicksburg, 1863* (New York: 2010), 221–236.

24. The 4th Iowa was an experienced regiment, called up at the very beginning of the war and had, in addition to seeing several small actions in Missouri, already engaged in the major battle of Pea Ridge, Arkansas; where they fought through a near disaster to carry the day.

25. Born in England in 1840, he emigrated with his family in 1849. They settled in Ohio but moved west, first to Illinois and then Iowa in 1861. Despite attending his first revival in 1856, Weavers later believed that he had "got into darkness" in his time before the war and that his injury sent him on the right path.

26. Weavers was never a fiery speaker in the classic revival mold, but he clearly possessed a charismatic gift of projecting to his audience the immediacy of the Holy Ghost in their midst, a sensation that frequently generated emotional responses.

One member of a small congregation in Nebraska, reporting on a Weavers-led revival held there, noted: "the Spirit of God was upon Elder Weavers as he talked to the little flock, commending them to God and the word of his grace; this was a grand time of rejoicing, leaping and dancing. It seemed a cloud of glory hung over the congregation; soon the scene changed from rejoicing to that of weeping for the lost; one after another fell under the power, burdened for a soul that had been rejecting the Spirit: his own sister while agonizing, offered her life for his soul, and God gave her the assurance that he would save him. [sic] Another brother came to the altar and was delivered from the appetite of tobacco. The Holy Ghost got hold of the meeting and we could not close the meeting till 1 o'clock in the morning." *The Sent of God*, July 30, 1893.

27. However not everyone was eager to host these revivals. After residents lodged a complaint against him, the authorities in one small town arrested Weavers for disturbing the peace. The prosecutor maintained that Weavers had caused the town's residents undue agony by his preaching, a charge Weavers successfully defended himself against. In the end, the case generated a great deal of local publicity and helped popularize Weavers' meetings.

28. *Tabor Beacon*, February 2, 1900.

29. *The Sent of God*, March 21, 1895. Those outside of the church, with no denominational reference point to work from, took to calling the congregation "Holy Baptists," "Weaverites" and eventually "the Holiness people."

30. The gathering occasionally attracted rougher frontier types looking for entertainment at the expense of the faithful. In one instance a drunken cowboy rode into the tabernacle on his horse as dinner was being served. After spilling several of the tables, the rider only beat a hasty retreat when a large man, who had yet to undergo the experience of consecration and sanctification, threatened to thrash him.

31. Tabor was a historically auspicious choice for the Holiness folks, for several disciples of Charles Finney founded the town in 1851. From Oberlin, they brought with them a deep commitment to perfectionism and the social gospel ideals that accompanied Finney's teaching. Early on they established the optimistically named "Tabor Literary Society," where neither sex nor race was made condition of membership.

32. The name Hephzibah is taken from Isaiah chapter 62 and refers to the delight God feels for those who proclaim the Gospel. It also happened to be the name of one of Weavers' sisters and his daughter. Sidney Newton, *Thanks, Tabor, for the Memories*, (Council Bluffs: Midwest Publishing, 1990).

33. By 1895 *The Sent of God* had a circulation of 6,500 and was mailed to every state and territory as well as internationally. The press also printed numerous tracts and a book on Holiness. *Tabor Beacon*, September 6, 1895.

34. Weavers writing from England shortly before he made his way to South Africa noted: "I praise God for salvation, and forever leading me to the Rock that is higher than I, who gave himself for our sins, that he might deliver us from this present evil world." *The Sent of God*, March 4, 1896.

35. The Faith Association operated as a Christian commune; no one received salaries, and labor and goods were pooled. When particular items were needed

they were prayed for, and the *Sent of God* frequently listed items their readers had donated in response to these prayers.

36. *The Sent of God*, August 17, 1893. The way Weavers employs "consecration" it means much the same as the Methodist theology of "justification."

37. April 4, 1895.

38. *The Sent of God*, May 20, 1897.

39. *The Sent of God*, June 18, 1896.

40. *The Sent of God*, September 6, 1894.

41. *The Sent of God*, August 19, 1894; *The Sent of God* May 20, 1897.

42. *The Sent of God*, February 27, 1895.

43. *The Sent of God*, March 21, 1895.

44. *The Sent of God*, July 30, 1893. *The Sent of God* warned that state of Holiness did not remove Christians from temptation for "Jesus was perfectly holy, and yet he was tempted." *The Sent of God*, August 17, 1893.

45. The question of backsliders was a difficult one for Weavers and the Hephzibah leadership. They agreed that sanctification released sinners from sin and that it enabled believers to lead sinless lives. They also believed that they were not released from temptation, but yielding to that temptation implied that the sinner had never really been sanctified. Weavers later took a more decisive stand, preaching, "Those who backslide are not sanctified." This is, perhaps, the problem with "instantaneous sanctification" that Wesley sought to avoid by suggesting that the act was a lifelong process of growing more holy. *The Sent of God*, November 3, 1898.

46. *The Sent of God*, March 21, 1895.

47. *The Sent of God*, April 4, 1895. See the introduction to this chapter for Mbiya Kuzwayo's repetition of this quote when recalling his own sanctification.

48. *The Sent of God*, December 5, 1895.

49. *The Sent of God* printed this "prescription" for healing on every copy it sent out.

50. Paul Worcester, *The Master Key*, 48.

51. *The Sent of God*, July 6, 1893.

52. *The Sent of God*, June 15, 1893. Going much further, Weavers later wrote: "One of the greatest enemies of the cause of Christ today, is the sectarian devil which seeks to lead the young converts into these great sectarian, political, man-made organizations which are destitute of the power and presence of God. It is like putting a plant into an ice-house for a young believer to join one of these great sectarian bodies. It will soon chill all the spiritual life out of him, and leave him as dead and cold as themselves."

53. *The Sent of God* September 6, 1894.

54. After the church was formed, Weavers recalled, "We adopted a few simple rules. This was our first going into bondage. Next year we made rules for the Council. We lost power with God, when we took man's word instead of God's Word." He realized the error when the Lord commanded him to seek "the old paths where is the good way, and walk therein . . . " In response he fasted for two days and returned to the Bible to weed out corruptions that had crept into the church. *The Sent of God* March 21, 1895.

55. James H. Moorhead, "Between Progress and Apocalypse: A Reassessment of Millennialism in American Religious Thought, 1800–1880," *The Journal of American History* 71:3 (1984); Timothy L. Smith, *Revivalism and Social Reform: American Protestantism on the Eve of the Civil War* (New York: 1957), 151–57.

56. *The Sent of God*, Aug 1, 1895.

57. Landeg White, *Magomera: Portrait of an African Village*, (New York: Cambridge University Press, 1989), 130–135; Karin Fields, *Revival and Rebellion in Colonial Central Africa.*

58. See J. B. Peires, *The Dead Will Arise.*

59. Paul Worcester, *Master Key*, 47.

60. *The Sent of God*, July 20, 1893.

61. *The Sent of God*, June 15, 1893.

62. *The Sent of God*, April 19, 1895.

63. *The Sent of God*, December 3, 1896.

64. And whose favorite songs were the missionary hymns "Only for Souls" and "We'll Girdle the Globe with Salvation." "Only for Souls" eventually became the motto of the Hephzibah seminary.

65. *The Sent of God*, June 7, 1894.

66. *The Sent of God*, July 5, 1894.

67. *Tabor Beacon*, October 22, 1924, "Hephzibah Faith Home a Growing Congregation." In the span of just fifty years 125 missionaries traveled to all parts of the world from tiny Tabor.

68. *The Sent of God*, January 18, 1894. Although the influence could also have come from an ad that frequently ran in the local newspapers for Kaffir Kola Extract, "the Greatest Remedy and Cure of the 19th Century." Complete with a line drawing of a man who appears more classical Greek than Zulu, the ad claimed that for only a dollar a month the afflicted received "an extract made from the juice of the nut of the Sacred Kola tree of South Africa. Used by Kaffirs and Zulus in their tribes for many generations as a positive cure for all nervous diseases in man or women, from any cause; dyspepsia; constipation; kidney and bladder ailments, and diseased liver." Unsatisfied users needed only to return the empty bottle for a full refund. *Mills County Tribune*, July 23, 1896.

69. *The Sent of God*, November 21, 1895. The newspaper noted that "this was indeed a meeting of power" in which even the "hearts of strangers were touched by the presence of the spirit."

70. *Tabor Beacon*, November 16, 1895. Non-Holiness passengers found the experience less enthralling and complained of the overcrowding that resulted from "turning a depot into a meeting house." But the paper reminded these "few persons" that "just such jams on excursion and college days frequently occur, enlivened by the college 'yells' and everybody takes it all in good part. Consistency is indeed a jewel."

71. Ibid. O'Neill later returned to Africa as a missionary to Sierra Leone.

72. *The Sent of God*, March 4, 1896, letter from Weavers.

73. *The Sent of God*, February 20, 1896; *The Sent of God*, March 4, 1896; *The Sent of God*, July 2, 1896.

74. *The Sent of God*, July 2, 1896.

75. *The Sent of God* March 4, 1896.

76. The editors of *The Sent of God* must have worked hard to clean up his printed letters and sermons, for Weavers' lack of education is evident in his diaries. While he disdained those who valued education above their Christianity, he also felt called to improve himself and diligently read the Bible and other religious texts. His minimal education, Mary Price later noted, was a "sore thorn in the flesh." But, she hastened to add, he was "so deeply taught in the Word that his discourses in clearness of thought and reasoning, in forcible, well-chosen words, would do credit to any seminary graduate." ABM 192/424, Price to Smith, February 11, 1897.

77. *The Sent of God*, October 1, 1896.

78. ABM 190/77, A. Bigelow to Smith, April 4, 1895. Weavers apparently did not mind allowing some mystery swirling around his presence in South Africa, for several of the AZM missionaries reported that he had come on a whim, drawn first to Durban and later to Mapumulo merely at the Spirit's beckoning (they also referred to him as a Baptist preacher, a mistaken affiliation that no doubt made his presence more tolerable.) Over the years, Weavers' "miraculous" arrival at Mapumulo has become an important point of the story. Michael Mahoney writes: "The strange, arbitrary visit to Mapumulo by the unsponsored and uninvited (though not unwelcome) Weavers provoked a dramatic response among the Africans there." He is correct about the response but the "arbitrary" element of his arrival doesn't survive deeper scrutiny.

79. Luke 3:15–17 "And as the people were in expectation and all the men mused in their hearts of John, whether he were the Christ, or not; John answered, saying unto them all, I indeed baptize you with water; but one mightier than I cometh, the latchet of whose shoes I am not worthy to unloose: he shall baptize you with the Holy Ghost and with fire: Whose fan is in his hands, and he will thoroughly purge his floor, and will gather the wheat into his garner; but the chaff he will burn with fire unquenchable."

80. ABM 182/596–98, J. Tyler to Clark, February 1, 1875. Original Emphasis.

81. AZM A/3/46, Annual Letter of the AZM, 1891.

82. *The Sent of God*, November 4, 1897, undated letter from W.N.

83. AZM A/3/41, Inanda Station Report, 1892–93. The tenor of these meetings is noticeably different than the revivals to come. Calm "inquirers" and "seekers" came forward to be conversed with and prayed for. The dynamic presence of the Spirit, so prevalent in reports of the later revivals, does not figure in these gatherings.

84. AZM A/3/41, Umsumduze Station Report, 1892–93.

85. AZM A/3/41, Amahlongwa Station Report, 1894–95.

86. AZM A/3/46, Annual Letter of the AZM, 1895–96. At the very least he also visited Umsumduzi, where he had a "powerful influence" without attendant gains in membership AZM A/3/41, Umsumduzi Station Report, 1895–96.

87. AZM A/1/8, Report of the NAM Committee, 1896.

88. AZM A/3/41, Umzumbe Station Report, 1896–97.

89. *Amakholwa* were not the only ones craving revival. Wilcox returned from the NAM feeling that he had received a "blessing" and met with Weiss shortly after to pray for a revival in the churches. Missionaries from the AZM who attended the Natal Congregational Union (the Congregational association for Natal) in Ladysmith

the previous year, heard Rev. Russell read a paper on "The Revival We Need." He noted that in many previous cases around the world revival had begun with the visit of an outside evangelist. Not, he hastened to assure, that God was dependent on any particular man, but He used him as an instrument to demonstrate His presence and power. Russell believed that "in Natal just now there were most hopeful signs—a spirit of enquiry, Christians anxious to rise to greater Holiness, much prayer for revival and the devil was very busy leading people into strange delusions." AZM A/3/41, Mapumulo and Groutville Station Report, 1896–97; *Natal Mercury*, February 18, 1895.

90. The *Natal Mercury* reported on April 11, 1896, of a meeting between representatives of the Farmers' Conference and the Natal government and which one of the farmers grimly noted, "Experience had shown it was useless to attempt to keep out any disease. There were men who, for a few pounds, were willing to break any regulation. If that disease got fairly established on this side of the Zambesi, they would all be paupers within twelve months." A month later, after rinderpest had broken out in the Transvaal, the paper reported, "The enormous loss, in many cases amounting to absolute ruin, already sustained by farmers and transport-riders in the districts north of Bechuanaland, the rapid way in which the disease has spread, warrants the most active and stringent measures being taken in order to save this Colony from a calamity that would practically ruin the farming interests for some years to come . . . " *Natal Mercury*, "The Rinderpest Commission," May 6, 1896.

91. AZM Minutes Vol VIII, Semi-Annual Meeting, January 27–February 1, 1897.

92. For an account of Mfanefile's early life see, ABM 184/349–50 Holbrook to Smith, February 20, 1885 and ABM 188/310–11, Mapumulo Annual Report July 1891.

93. SNA 3786/1896 "From the Magistrate of Mapumulo the forwarded petition of 'Certain natives of Mapumulo Mission Station for the appointment of Mfanefile Kuzwayo as the headman of said station.'"

94. The list is instructive in several ways. Like missionaries and *amakholwa*, the Natal government still clearly counted Christians by outward, material signs. So when the SNA wanted to know how many potential Christians there might be under Kuzwayo, he asked the Mapumulo magistrate to count the number of square homes in the area. This despite the steady increase in the number of outstation Christians—who were unwilling to live in "civilized" homes. The second petition duly noted that twenty of those who signed lived in such structures and only three remained in huts. Also, all of the signatories were men and all but eight were married heads of households. Of those single, one was widowed, one divorced with two children and one lived with his mother. And while Mfanefile did not accumulate power in the traditional Zulu manner by marrying additional wives, he found other ways to express his authority for, besides two of his adult sons, two other *amakholwa* men were listed as living under his roof. Mbiya, listed as an exempted native in the petition, was not one of them, having recently built his own house for his young family.

95. AZM A/3/41, Mapumulo and Groutville Annual Report, June 1896–97.

96. ABM 188/310–11, Mapumulo Annual Report, July 1893–94.

97. ABM 192/424–30, Price to Smith, February 11, 1897.

98. *The Sent of God*, Dec 3, 1896 September 30, 1896 letter from Mbiya Kuzwayo.

99. *Tabor Beacon*, April 30, 1914 "Close of a Notable Life."

100. I will elaborate on these in greater detail in the following chapter, but one is struck by the connections between Holiness and traditional Zulu forms of worship that both allowed such dramatic expressions of faith. Possession, as Harriet Ngubane makes clear, was not an uncommon event in Natal, but for Congregationalists until 1896 it was a simply unheard of act within the churches. This created a serious disjunction between how many *amakholwa* understood practiced faith to be practiced, and how they had publicly lived their Christianity. Holiness freed them to express their Christianity within "normal" Zulu idioms. Harriet Ngubane, *Body and Mind in Zulu Medicine: An Ethnology of Health and Disease in Nyuswa-Zulu Thought and Practice* (London: Academic Press, 1977), 146–50.

101. AZM A/3/41, Mapumulo and Groutville Annual Report, 1896–97.

102. Ibid.

103. Ibid. Wilcox, unlike other missionaries, deemed the revival process sufficient evidence of God's work in a changed heart, and no expulsions occurred at Mapumulo.

104. *The Sent of God*, December 3, 1896, September 30, 1896, letter from Mbiya Kuzwayo.

105. *The Sent of God*, December 3, 1896, October 7, 1896, letter from Frank Weiss. The Mapumulo missionary, having heard of the young man's imprisonment, hurried toward the jail only to meet the recently released revivalist on the road. Together they knelt down and gave thanks at the power of God in effecting his freedom. The experience further confirmed the sense of connection revived *amakholwa* must have felt between their current religious experience and the post-Pentacostal lives of the apostles found in Acts.

106. AZM A/3/41 Mapumulo and Groutville Station Report, 1896–97.

107. The AZM had long encouraged the active participation of women in the churches, but in subordinate positions as "Bible women" or teachers, not preachers. The Hephzibah community, while upholding the subordination of woman to man in the household maintained that "in the service of God they are on an equality with their brethren to sin, pray, exhort, and preach. And for scholarship, piety, and zeal they frequently excel the brotherhood . . . " *The Sent of God*, October 19, 1893. Although there is no evidence that the *amakholwa* revivalists deliberately emulated the life of Christ, it seems more than mere coincidence that twelve of their number went to Umvoti.

108. *The Sent of God*, April 15, 1897, February 11, 1897, letter from M. E. Price.

109. AZM A/3/41, Mapumulo and Groutville Annual Report, 1896–97.

110. Ibid.

111. Ibid.

112. Ibid.

113. That said, many of the Impapala residents had moved to Zululand from the stations of the AZM, no doubt retained family and friends on them, and thus shared their angst in this matter. And Crown land later proved just as vulnerable, as Natal eventually sold the land out from under the Impapala community to the

Natal Land and Colonisation Company. Henry Slater, "Land, Labour and Capital in Natal: The Natal Land and Colonisation Company 1860–1948," *Journal of African History* 16:2, (1975), 275–76.

114. ABM 188/310–11, Mapumulo Station Report, 1893–94.

115. Keith Breckenridge, 'The Allure of Violence: Men, Race, and Masculinity on the South African Goldmines, 1900–1950', *Journal of Southern African Studies* 24:4, (1998); T. Dunbar Moodie, Vivienne Ndatshe and British Sibuyi, "Migrancy and Male Sexuality on the South African Gold Mines," *Journal of Southern African Studies* 14:2, (1988); Robert Morrell, "Of Boys and Men: Masculinity and Gender in Southern African Studies," *Journal of Southern African Studies* 24:4, (1998).

116. *The Sent of God*, April 15, 1897, February 11, 1897 Letter from M. E. Price.

117. AZM A/3/41, Mapumulo and Groutville Annual Report, 1896–97.

118. Ibid.

119. ABM 192/424–30, Price to Smith, February 11, 1897.

120. Ibid.

121. AZM A/3/47, Inanda Girls Seminary Report, 1896–97. "A little later some began to hear from their friends of the wonderful work of grace that was going on at Mapumulo under Elder Weavers' preaching and began to desire a like blessing for themselves." See also *Missionary Herald*, "Interest at Inanda," March 1897, 110–11.

122. AZM A/3/41, Esidumbini Station Report, 1897; Umzumbe Seminary Report 1897.

123. AZM A/3/47, Inanda Girls Seminary Report, 1897.

124. Ibid.

125. ABM 192/424–30, Price to Smith, February 11, 1897.

126. Bill Freund, "Indian Women and the Changing Character of the Working Class Indian Household in Natal, 1860–1900," *Journal of Southern African Studies* 17:3, (1991); Vishnu Padayachea and Robert Morrel, "Indian Merchants and Dukawallahs in the Natal Economy, c. 1875–1914," *Journal of Southern African Studies* 17:1 (1990).

127. AZM A/3/41, Lindley Station Report, 1897.

128. Ibid.

129. *Missionary Herald*, "A Widespread Revival," April 1897, 152–53.

130. ABM 192/424–30, Price to Smith, February 11, 1897. Dalita Isaac apparently believed that the two men practiced some form of harmful witchcraft. Price expressed shock at her statement not for the split in the church it represented, this fell easily within her expectations, but rather because it meant a belief in "superstitions" the missionary believed long since vanquished by Western education and Christian faith. But, she noted with pleasure, "What all her training had failed to do for her the Spirit did, as it were, in a moment."

131. *Missionary Herald*, "Esidumbini—An Ordination," November 1895, 460–62.

132. "Be glad then, ye children of Zion, and rejoice in the LORD your God: for He hath given you the former rain moderately, and he will cause to come down for you the rain, the former rain, and the latter rain in the first month." Weavers' 1897 diary, entry for January 3, 1897. The description of the Esidumbini meetings come from this diary and from AZM A/3/41, Esidumbini Station Report, 1897.

133. There were eighty-nine members in Esidumbini's congregation, but the mission also counted 600 "adherents," men and women who had expressed some degree of interest in the Word. AZM A/3/48, tabular view for 1896.

134. John 4:35–36, "Say not ye, There are yet four months, and then cometh harvest? behold, I say unto you, Lift up your eyes, and look on the fields; for they are white already to harvest. And he that reapeth receiveth wages, and gathereth fruit unto life eternal: that both he that soweth and he that reapeth may rejoice together." Acts 2:1–4, "And when the day of Pentecost was fully come, they were all with one accord in one place. And suddenly there came a sound from heaven as of a rushing mighty wind, and it filled all the house where they were sitting. And there appeared unto them cloven tongues like as of fire, and it sat upon each of them. And they were all filled with the Holy Ghost, and began to speak with other tongues, as the Spirit gave them utterance." The meanings behind these readings will be discussed in more detail in the following chapter.

135. ABM 188/52, Noodsberg Station Report, 1890–91. In this instance, the mission threatened to prosecute Mbiyana and his followers with trespassing and the dissident faction surrendered their claim. They maintained a presence on the station, however, and even collected funds in an unsuccessful attempt to build their own church.

136. Weavers' 1897 diary, entry for January 14, 1897. Information about the Noodsberg meeting is entirely derived from this source.

137. Weavers was deeply moved by the natural beauty of the area. On the return from Noodsberg the party stopped at the Inguye River waterfall to take lunch. Weavers, awed by the site, wrote in his diary "Oh how great the God of nature has made this world I praise him that he every [sic] brought me to this country. This is a beautiful country."

138. Not surprisingly, considering the esteem he held for Kuzwayo, Weavers complained that the interpreter at Umsumduzi was not very good, but he believed that the message got through nevertheless.

139. Exodus 15:22–26 (NIV 1984), "Then Moses led Israel from the Red Sea and they went into the Desert of Shur. For three days they traveled in the desert without finding water. When they came to Marah, they could not drink its water because it was bitter. (That is why the place is called Marah.) So the people grumbled against Moses, saying, 'What are we to drink?' Then Moses cried out to the Lord, and the Lord showed him a piece of wood. He threw it into the water, and the water became sweet. There the Lord made a decree and a law for them, and there he tested them. He said, 'If you listen carefully to the voice of the Lord your God and do what is right in his eyes, if you pay attention to his commands and keep all his decrees, I will not bring on you any of the diseases I brought on the Egyptians, for I am the Lord, who heals you.'"

Matthew 10:7–8 (NIV 1984), "As you go, preach this message: 'The kingdom of heaven is near.' Heal the sick, raise the dead, cleanse those who have leprosy, drive out demons. Freely you have received, freely give."

Matthew 15:22–28 (NIV 1984), "A Canaanite woman from that vicinity came to him, crying out, "Lord, Son of David, have mercy on me! My daughter is suffering terribly from demon-possession." Jesus did not answer a word. So his disciples came to him and urged him, 'Send her away, for she keeps crying out after us.' He answered, 'I was sent only to the lost sheep of Israel.' The woman came and knelt before him. 'Lord, help me!' she said. He replied, 'It is not right to take the children's bread and toss it to their dogs.' 'Yes, Lord,' she said, 'but even the dogs eat the crumbs that fall from their masters' table.' Then Jesus answered, 'Woman, you have great faith! Your request is granted.' And her daughter was healed from that very hour."

Revelation 22:1–2, "Then the angel showed me the river of the water of life, as clear as crystal, flowing from the throne of God and of the Lamb down the middle of the great street of the city. On each side of the river stood the tree of life, bearing twelve crops of fruit, yielding its fruit every month. And the leaves of the tree are for the healing of the nations."

140. *Mills County Tribune*, May 6, 1897.

141. The similarities between Weavers' preaching style, particularly his love of outdoor settings, and the practices of Isaiah Shembe, the founder of Natal's most influential African Initiated Church, are remarkable. Given that Shembe lived near the Inanda church and attracted several members of its congregation when he established the Nazareth Baptist Church in 1906, it seems likely that Weavers influenced Shembe who became renowned among Zulu for his healing powers. See Bengt Sundkler, *Bantu Prophets in South Africa* (Oxford: 1964), 110–11; Elizabeth Gunner, "Power House, Prison House: An Oral Genre and its Use in Isaiah Shembe's Nazareth Baptist Church," *Journal of Southern African Studies* 14:2, (1988), 205.

142. Probably to the delight of his *amakholwa* audiences who saw in it an emulation of their own custom, Weavers went everywhere with a walking staff—not from need, he was robust, but in apparent observance of Christ's command to the apostles found in Mark 6:7–8, "And he called unto him the twelve and began to send them forth by two and two; and gave them power over unclean spirits; and commanded them that they should take nothing for their journey save a staff only." *The Sent of God*, April 18, 1895.

143. ABM 192/424–30, Price to Smith, February 11, 1897.

144. Weavers' sense of urgency is probably connected to a bundle of papers he received from Tabor on January 10, which caused him to bemoan the loss of the Spirit back at the Hephzibah Home.

5

Naturalizing the Faith

The revivals would not have survived his departure if they could be credited solely to George Weavers' presence. *Amakholwa* ownership over the movement became increasingly evident in the months after he left southern Africa when revivalism actually gained strength across Natal and beyond. Zulu who had undergone sanctification sought to share it with others, at first only with other Christians, but increasingly with traditionalists as well. At Mapumulo, revivalists toured outstations for months after the initial meetings, educating all who would listen in the power of the Holy Spirit and urging participants to imbibe in spiritual gifts such as prophecy and divine healing. Wedding parities, gambling, and beer drinks gave way to preaching as groups of sanctified youth traveled from kraal to kraal, holding revival services, praying, and reading the Bible to those they wished to convert. Weiss expressed amazement that none stopped to ask "Who will pay me to preach or teach, but they go at it with all their heart in it."[1] Led by a young man named Banabas, a group of enthusiastic revivalists made the trek from Impapala to Mapumulo, where they bought up all the religious tracts, Bibles, and Zulu teaching materials the missionary had on hand. Motivated only by their zeal, they returned across the Thukela River, intent on preaching and teaching throughout southern Zululand.

Meanwhile, Kuzwayo returned to Mapumulo to lead the local band of revivalists. Met with enthusiasm but little organization, he sought to channel some of their passion into an orderly evangelism by establishing regular preaching circuits in the countryside for all and holding regular *imvuzelelo*, revivals or periods of awakening, at which interested Zulu could undergo their own consecration and sanctification. The mission rewarded his efforts by placing him on their list of approved preachers while the church at Mapumulo acknowledged his leadership and charisma by asking him to become their pastor, easily breaking the impasse that had earlier immobilized the church into inaction.[2] Remarkably, he declined the invitation, choosing instead to work with Worcester, Wilcox, and several *amakholwa* in spreading revival across southern Africa. A large tent sent from Tabor arrived in June of 1897, and from Mapumulo the revivalists set out across Natal, Zululand, and even Johannesburg, holding services under the great stretch of old canvas.[3]

A similar phenomenon was underway at Esidumbini, where a band of evangelists sought to fulfill the responsibility of mission that came with sanctification. From mid-February on, small groups of sanctified Christians went out among the surrounding kraals, preaching to traditionalists and spreading the radical message of almost instantaneous salvation. They also organized larger endeavors. On March 3, the entire congregation gathered for a day of fasting and prayer, and in April twenty revivalists led a weeklong campaign at both Esidumbini and one of her outstations. The week, which featured altar calls and personal testimonies, concluded with an impressive Sabbath service attended by 500-some eager participants. The previous day, groups of *amakholwa* had dispersed across the surrounding countryside, inviting all they met to attend the service.[4] So successful was this campaign that several months after the April revival, the church at Esidumbini established two new outstations and re-opened several others.[5]

At Inanda, the seminary girls' enthusiasm only grew after Weavers' departure. After spending their Christmas vacation delivering their testimonies to friends and family, the girls returned for the start of a new school year on the 17th of February.[6] Reunited at Inanda, they conceived a larger more organized project and went out in small groups to nearby outstations and kraals, preaching the revival message at each stop. The American missionaries, long used to the customary diffidence of young women, were amazed at the boldness of these girls; not only did they publicly address their elders, but they urged them to abandon sinful behavior and lead new lives guided by the Spirit. To a missionary, a young girl inducing old men into fits of tearful confession seemed little less than miraculous evidence of the work of the Holy Spirit in the movement.[7] Africans, of course, understood that their patriarchy wasn't as complete as it might outwardly appear for spirit possession and prophecy among young women was not uncommon. I have previously mentioned the Xhosa prophetess Nongawuse, but here too we must consider *amandiki* spirit possession that gripped any number of young Zulu women at this time. For several decades around the turn of the century those so possessed filled their audiences with a great deal of unease and while, as Julie Parle has demonstrated, many may have been confused with what to make of their behavior and proclamations, no one could ignore them.[8] Of course within the Christian context it cannot be forgotten that these young women did not claim possession by spirits, but instead claimed to be channeling *the* Spirit.

The girls also assumed responsibility for furthering revival on the central station. In the months following their return they led several larger meetings and numerous smaller ones in Inanda's church. At one such gathering, a very young, yet obviously spiritually powerful young girl commanded the packed congregation to find Christ through confession. Another girl recalled that her heart almost failed her when she saw her elders assembled expectantly, but that she looked up and quietly prayed "Jesus you know I have no power to speak before my elders. You must help me and speak through me."[9] The meeting continued with great success and there, as elsewhere, the congregation gleefully claimed the "fruits of the Holy Spirit" such as divine healing and divination. Several of the girls also gathered with the station women, who, after listening to the girls, added their own testimonies of sanctification and agreed to organize themselves into a band of workers for the Lord.[10]

In April of 1897, a group of Inanda girls made their way to Amanzimtoti, where they led the young men of the seminary in revival. The effect was electric, for the boys had expressed an interest in the workings of the Spirit the previous school year, had heard much about it elsewhere, and felt overripe for the experience.[11] Once the period of consecration began, the boys abandoned sleep to struggle with their sins, stayed up for several nights to pray, and publically confessed their sins. During the first night, concerned by the commotion emanating from the boys' rooms, the seminary's two principals spied on them through an open window and were shocked by what they witnessed. Some of the boys knelt on the wooden floor, a few lay prostrate, and others, with hands clasped behind their backs and heads down, paced the room. One boy knelt with his eyes fixed upwards, clapping his hands and laughing a deep, joyful laugh. The cumulative commotion, a babble of individual voices crying, confessing, praying, and praising, awed the missionaries. Sufficiently impressed, they left the boys to their struggle.[12]

Through fasting and prayer the boys strived for sanctification. A prayer meeting replaced the boys' favorite debating society, and instead of playing football (soccer) after dinner, the boys climbed the surrounding hills to seek out moments of "secret" prayer (in open emulation of Weavers). For weeks their urgent prayers echoed throughout the mission reserve; the booming voice of one large boy could be heard even in the midst of a thunderstorm that deafened all other sound. As elsewhere, the boys sought sanctification by surrendering that which they felt separated them from God. Medicines and charms that promised assistance in love and fortune piled up on the altar as the young men grappled with their Christianity, their Zuluness, and their places in the colonial world of turn-of-the-century Natal. To the great surprise of their principal, the sanctified youth also renounced tobacco. Asked why they had done so even though its prohibition was not official policy of the AZM, they responded: "God's Spirit could not dwell in a polluted temple."[13] This must have stung a number of missionaries given the recent internal debate the Americans had about their own use of the weed.

The few boys who felt disinclined to participate found little peace. Harangued by a fellow classmate who followed him from room to room while loudly praying for his salvation, one of the Amanzimtoti boys finally hid under his bed. This desperate attempt backfired, however, when he was discovered and a group of sanctified boys surrounded him, trapping him there while they wore away his defenses in a communal effort to lead him to salvation. Eventually he confessed his sins and a missionary noted that that he went on to become a leader of the movement. Of the sixty-eight boys then attending the seminary, all but six eventually claimed to have undergone consecration and counted themselves among the sanctified.

At Amanzimtoti, as elsewhere, revival also provided participants with a powerful means of patrolling the community's moral boundaries, a critical function for an *amakholwa* community shaken by internal divisions, accusations by missionaries of their inherent immorality, and what many must have felt as the heavy stain of their experience in the boomtowns of colonial southern Africa. Confession was obligatory for consecration, but when expected confessions did not materialize, those placed under the power of the Spirit could reveal the sins of others through visions that echoed the traditional practice of "smelling-out" witches. Indeed, like witches, "sinners" were perceived as harming not only themselves, but the larger community.[14] At Amanzimtoti, shortly after the revival commenced, eight shillings disappeared from a boy's locker. That evening another boy had a vision revealing the thief. His fellow students accepted this vision as the Spirit revealed truth and united in loudly praying for the suspected fellow to confess his sin. The accused at first proclaimed his innocence, but when the prayers continued he became enraged, grabbed a couple walking sticks and threatened to strike his foes. With every volley of angry shouts, the kneeling boys responded with an "Amen" until, battered into submission by prayer, the suspect collapsed to the floor, his staves lying uselessly beside his prostrate form.

At three shillings sixpence, the Zulu Bible represented a week's wages for the average *amakholwa*, and not surprisingly most of the boys at Amanzimtoti had been content to own a significantly less expensive English language Bible that many could barely read. But Weavers' preaching style, reliant as it was on quoting biblical passages in support of his arguments, permeated across Natal and the boys at Amanzimtoti, like *amakholwa* everywhere, came to rely on a rhetorical style that made extensive use of justification through biblical quotation. They wanted to not only own a Bible for the sake of owning one, but to understand the words contained within and employ its messages both for their sanctification and in spreading the revival. Employing Lamin Sanneh's idea of "translation" here, this becomes a critical moment in the naturalization of Christianity. It was no longer sufficient to own a Bible for the sake of owning the book, that is for the identifying marker its mere appearance conveyed, but now the power of its language and the expectant truths it could reveal became paramount and for that, only a work in Zulu was truly sufficient for most. The boys, recognizing this, quickly bought up the entire stock of Zulu language Bibles the school had on hand, and when this proved insufficient the missionaries established a waiting list. One boy, hugging a newly acquired Bible to his heart, exclaimed "Oh, this is the book for us now! We have had enough of other books. The Bible, Oh, only the Bible now!"

Once their own ranks had been secured, the young men clamored for permission to go on evangelistic trips to tell others of their changed lives "and induce them also to give up all for Christ." Every Sunday, more than half of the school scattered over the hills as small bands took the message to *amakholwa* and traditionalists alike. Some of the boys covered as much as thirty miles by setting off from Amanzimtoti by 4:00 in the morning and only returning as the twilight faded shortly before 8:00 in the evening. Not satisfied with the limitations of where a day could bring them, over thirty boys proposed a long preaching tour of "distant places" (although it is not clear if this meant Natal, Zululand, or even farther). They were, they proclaimed, "willing to endure any hardships, walk any distance and to eat what they can get, or sleep where they may." The missionaries, convinced of the continuing importance of education despite the obvious limits settler society imposed on African upward mobility, urged the boys to remain in class and prove their newfound fervor through "works" on the station. Later however, when five boys approached the missionaries begging permission for a week's absence to hold meetings among the people of their outstation fifty miles distant, the missionaries felt they had little choice but to relent, for the boys couched their request in the language of revival, declaring themselves "burdened" by the Spirit to answer this call.

The boys set off early in the morning, stopping once for a late evening prayer-meeting before pushing on through the darkness. Arriving unheralded, the boys entered the church before dawn and began ringing the bell. Alarmed, residents of the station stumbled out of their homes "wondering if the day of judgment had arrived," only to the young men taking turns testifying to their changed lives and the powers of the indwelling Spirit. Any initial anger quickly gave way to wonder, and a crowd gathered in the church. The residents of the outstation were moved not only by the boys' words, but by their actions, for the young men proved eager to act on their own message, seeking out those they had wronged or defamed in the past to offer apologies, seek forgiveness and make amends. Within days a full-fledged revival had begun. By the end of the week the church's altar was covered with snuffboxes, pipes, and traditional medicines as the congregation sought sanctification.

A group of Amanzimtoti youth also made their way to Imfume in late April, where a revival had begun shortly before their arrival. As at Groutville, several leading church members opposed the revival, but the wife of Samson, a preacher at Ifume, swept aside their resistance with her own eagerness to experience sanctification. At the first gathering, she stood up over and over, crying and confessing as each additional past fault came to mind. Her deep sorrow at having sinned against her Savior affected the others, and falling to their knees, they too confessed with downcast faces and voices breaking with emotion. As the morning meeting ran into evening, the missionary in charge of Ifume attempted to end the gathering by asking several members to close in prayer, but the congregation was not prepared to do so, and the "closing prayer" led to several additional hours of confession. Sins from many years past were revealed and confessed with "as vivid conviction and as deep contrition as those recently committed."[15] Weary, the missionary retired from the meeting at 8:00 that evening, but returned later when he could no longer ignore the great tumult emanating from the church. In writing of the experience he confessed that the moment he entered the chapel he had to revise his notions of religious propriety, for he found the congregation in a great uproar: "To the ears their commotion seemed Babel repeated, but as I listened I could hear one great harmonious cry to God for forgiveness 'Jesu Christu Sitetela,' Jesus Christ forgive us." As he stood back, awed, several of the participants began to sing and gradually others joined in, getting up from their knees to sway with the words. More songs followed before, spent, those gathered quietly made their way home. Theirs was the ecstasy of sanctification, but it was also the joy at having found a Christian message that united the community in a local manifestation of Christianity that clearly suited their needs better than the theological bundle offered them by the AZM alone.

The next day the congregation gathered again, and some fifty rose for confession. A husband admitted to "terrible wrong" done to his wife and asked her forgiveness. She granted it and confessed that she had allowed hatred for him to enter her heart. Another wife confessed that she had intended to kill herself and her children because of the whippings her husband administered her, a double-edged confession to be sure, but one that still led down the path of sanctification. Others confessed to using traditional medicines, drunkenness, and thefts. Members called each other out of the church to settle grievances and returned inside to acknowledge the wrongs they had done. Both men and women confessed sexual improprieties, "vilest habits," which shocked the missionary (and which was, although not specified, almost certainly connected to the Zulu premarital sexual practice of *ukuhlobonga*, a form of non-penetrative intimacy that involved a young man rubbing himself along his lover's thighs just outside of the vagina. Accepted as a necessary part of youthful sexuality among Zulu, it was an act which missionaries found almost incomprehensible at every level).[16] All spoke with great sorrow about their past wrongs and, claiming the power of sanctification, avowed to leave behind their past ways.

When the boys from Amanzimtoti joined the revival they gave their testimonies and the church reciprocated, each side delighting in relating how Jesus had forgiven their sins, how they had become filled with the Spirit, and how the peace of God now rested wonderfully upon them. The seminary boys urged the church not to keep the revival message to themselves, but rather, as was being done elsewhere, to scatter the it throughout the surrounding outstations and kraals. The congregation of Ifume responded enthusiastically, and within a month, bands of revivalists had inspired seventy-four traditionalists to seek entrance into the church.

Of all the revivals begun after Weavers' departure, perhaps the most astonishing was that at Umzumbe, in far southern Natal, for it was to be a revival begun entirely by young girls, few (if any) of whom had contact with events to the north. Just over sixty young women returned to Umzumbe girl's seminary for the start of the new school year, many already deeply interested in the workings of the Holy Spirit. Undoubtedly fired by the news filtering down from other stations, they began to study Acts. For weeks this excitement simmered until, on Friday March 19, the girls turned a morning Bible study under the shade of banana trees into a day of consecration.[17] As at Inanda, the girls confessed to a litany of sins, and when it was over their faces glowed with a religious ecstasy. During the following days, heavy rains descended upon Umzumbe, and the girls, trapped inside by floods, took advantage of the storms to first pray for sanctification, and then that the church of Umzumbe might undergo a similar experience.

During these prayers, God spoke to one of the girls, bidding her to take several of her classmates and bring the revival message to the station *amak-holwa*. When the rains relented the next day, a small band of Umzumbe girls made their way into the church where they began holding an impromptu service. Drawn by this strange occurrence, and likely having heard of events elsewhere, several men joined the girls and shortly into the girls' testimony they were put "under conviction" for their souls, crying out to Jesus for mercy. One of the men, a preacher, confessed that his life had become a lie, that he had been living in sin and was a lost man. He detailed his sin, confessed all, and expressed his elation with consecration, at the willingness of God to "abundantly pardon" and take him back into the fold. Others soon followed, searching for their own such experience. Wrote the principal of Umzumbe seminary: "It seemed like a great search light—thrown upon the hearts of the church members—that marvelous power of the Holy Ghost bringing out inequities and sins hidden for long years."

The revival gathered momentum, as first station and then outstation residents flocked to the church to confess their own sins and seek sanctification. Emboldened by their success, the girls asked for permission to spread the "Good News" throughout the area. The missionaries tried to dampen this enthusiasm, but soon small bands of girls made their way off of the station, first preaching to family and friends and later at outstations and kraals. Remarkable scenes accompanied these efforts as entire audiences, sometimes as few as a dozen in a hut or as many as a hundred in a chapel, were stricken by a deep sense of sin. Listening to the girls' testimonies, strong men fell to the floor and cried out, "What must I do to be saved?" while others merely swayed and rocked, stricken into a state of semi-consciousness as they struggled toward confession.

In a remarkable difference from the revival elsewhere, the girls of Umzumbe emphasized a premillennial message, warning as they began: "Repent, for the kingdom of Heaven is at hand." Certainly the conditions for the end of the world appeared ripe at Umzumbe that winter. Drought, locusts, and rinderpest all threatened, but these troubles, along with the gradual breakdown in the social conditions of the mission reserve, differed little from those elsewhere, so the emphasis on the imminent return of Christ perhaps speaks of the imprecise transmission of Holiness theology from what was originally presented by Weavers through Kuzwayo and then passed from *amakholwa* to *amakholwa* until its manifestation at Umzumbe as a question of immediate morality under the threat of an imminent apocalypse. Regardless of the theological discourse, Christians in the area not only repented, but also underwent the second baptism of the Spirit called for in revival teaching; undergoing a sanctification that left them morally pure and thus spiritually powerful. The girls, returning from their short missions, handed over snuffboxes, pipes, beer pots, and traditional medicines to their teachers who happily destroyed them.

At Umzumbe, as at Mapumulo, Groutville, Durban, Esidumbini, Inanda, and elsewhere, the fires of revival burned throughout the rest of the year. Small bands of *amakholwa* insured that the meaning and memory of sanctification would not quickly fade, as they made trip after trip to outstations, kraals, and even other churches as far away as Umtwalume and Johannesburg. Not until the following year did missionaries report that the excitement generated during these times had begun to pass. But after nearly a year of such intense religious interest, the groundwork for future revivals and future changes within the mission had been well laid, sometimes much to the chagrin of missionaries of the American Zulu Mission.

THE UNEASE OF "STAID CONGREGATIONALISTS"

While Weavers received near universal support from the mission, missionaries were at a loss with how to respond to and channel the zeal growing in his wake. Some, like Wilcox at Groutville and Price at Inanda, underwent their own "second birth" and found little alarming in the actions of *amakholwa* congregations. Others, however, openly worried about the nature of the celebrations underway and reacted to them with apprehension. Particularly troubling to many missionaries were the emotional physicality of revival. Pixley worried: "While God has been manifestly present in this work, there have not been lacking instances when it seems as though Satan himself was present to destroy all the good influences by noise and confusion."[18] The sound of an entire congregation engaged in loud prayer as the Spirit moved them, created "such a din, uproar and crying" that for the missionaries it was "startling to some of our old Conservative and Puritanic notions. So that we were inclined at first to refer it largely to an emotional or to something else rather than a purely spiritual movement."[19] A teacher at Inanda concurred, writing: "We staid Congregationalists do not altogether appreciate such violent demonstrations. Considering their excitable nature, we feared that many might be crying simply because others were doing so."[20]

This concern over "excess emotionalism" features prominently in missionary correspondence from this period and shaped their response to this *amakholwa* movement. At Amanzimtoti seminary, the principal warned that revivalists risked measuring their faith "by their feelings" in a manner that would eventually lead to disappointment. The work of the missionaries after the revival was, he believed, to bring order to this spiritual chaos, "to lead them step-by-step to give precept upon precept, to boost this one up a hill of difficulty, to prop up that one against a chilling blast, to show by lesson upon lesson that serving Christ is being faithful in hoeing and grinding and studying, by telling the truth, by observing the rule of love, not by feeling feelings."[21] Even where feasible, such as among the youth of Inanda, Amanzimtoti, and Umzumbe, missionaries found such a reigning in nearly impossible and revival progressed largely unchecked by a missionary desire to guard against the "untamed" emotions of their congregations.

Perhaps not surprisingly, missionary attitudes toward the revival were also marked by jealousy. Pixley, by then the oldest American missionary in Natal and a man who had spent his life for the cause, reported rather crankily of revival:

> it did not begin with his coming or cease with his departure though we all have much for which to thank Elder Weavers of his help in increasing the interest which was already apparent to some of us when he came and for pressing home upon the hearts of the people some of the same old truths of the Gospel which we have preached in the past years.[22]

An essential truth lies almost hidden, however, in Pixley's comment, for while the initial impetus for revival came from Weavers, the force that carried it forward was distinctly *amakholwa*. For it was in Kuzwayo's translations, in the letters relating the events, in the actions of the bands of revivalists from across the mission that the movement achieved its broad popular appeal. It was very much a movement of Zulu Christians awakening to the power of claiming their faith.

Weavers, Pixley also noted, while a man of faith was "wholly uneducated in the schools of theology," the implication being that the revivalist was not therefore really qualified for mission work.[23] But here again lies a clue to understanding the popularity of both Weavers and the message he brought. The well-educated missionaries of the AZM relied on scripted sermons heavy with historical allusions both to the times of Christ, but also to events within Protestant and American history. The theological underpinnings of their messages could be complex and difficult for *amakholwa* unfamiliar with biblical hermeneutics to fully grasp. In a classic example of Foucault's concept of power/knowledge, missionaries had long employed their own theological training both to guarantee their continued control over the churches, and as a hammer against those aspects of Zulu culture they found disagreeable.[24] For his part, Weavers relied on biblical exegesis within the context of extemporaneous preaching. He focused on a few biblical verses, unveiled their meaning to his audience, and then detailed how they might apply these scriptures to their own lives. For *amakholwa* this approach was deeply inclusive and they responded by embracing both his message and his style. Weavers also had little interest in the material goods of this world and his roughhewn yet Godly manner clearly captured the hearts of his Zulu audiences. There was little in his demeanor that suggested superiority, and for *amakholwa* long sensitive to demonstrating their Christianity through their dress and education, Weavers must have marked a refreshing change from the expectations of missionaries at a time when it was growing increasingly difficult to meet those expectations. And unlike Natal's white settlers, Weavers' unpolished exterior did not translate into a racist disdain for Africans. He called them "brother" and "sister," broke bread with them, obviously appreciated the talents of Mbiya Kuzwayo, and delivered a message that, should they choose to accept it, made them equals before God with all other Christians.[25]

Ultimately, of course, even those missionaries who expressed concern about the revival could not argue with the results and were therefore little inclined to suppress the movement. So when young men and women made requests to engage in evangelical trips they were generally allowed free reign, and when revival bands showed up at church doors, missionaries and congregations alike celebrated their arrival and welcomed them in. But even though missionaries may not have realized it, each band of revivalists represented a further claim by Zulu Christians to their own spiritual authority. For Christians of the AZM a tipping point had been reached, from this moment Christianity in Natal became more and more an indigenous institution and the impetus for its spread among Africans soon passed out of foreign hands.

"A MIGHTY PREACHING FORCE": WHAT REVIVAL WROUGHT

Writing to Weavers almost two months after he departed, Dalita Isaac joyfully reported on recent events at Inanda and across Natal:

> We hear of the wonderful works done by the Spirit in many places. Great and wonderful things are going on here. So you see brother the seed that the Lord sent you to plant in Africa is growing very fast; the fire of the Spirit is spreading. People are being scattered in many places to go out and preach. The heathen take Christ as their Saviour and everybody is talking of these wonderful things."[26]

As for herself, she noted that she very much enjoyed her new life in Christ, expressed concern over the continuing power of Satan around her, and took comfort in her belief that the Spirit now dwelled within her. She also happily reported a new development, station residents at Inanda, not just girls, now worked among the kraals seeking converts, an important reminder, she believed, of the "many yet to pray for." Dalita took the responsibility for the souls of the unsaved seriously, and later she stood before the Inanda congregation and articulated her concern. Noting that it was the duty of the saved to serve the Lord, "who had so richly blessed them of late," she urged parishioners to help those who had recently converted.[27]

Isaac's sense of exhilaration at the changes revival brought nicely captures the mood of the *amakholwa* community in the years to follow. From Mapumulo to Umsumduzi, those who participated in revival were gripped by a belief in the enormous potential of the Spirit acting in their lives; revivalists did not concern themselves with everyday needs while out preaching but prayed with the full expectation that their prayers would be answered and their needs met.[28] This transformation also extended into the public sphere, for revival revolutionized the way *amakholwa* interacted with missionaries, traditionalists, and each other.

Finally, and most importantly for the long term success of the religion in the area (and indeed on the continent) Holiness also allowed for Christianity to be partly unshackled from many of the hegemonic aspects of colonial fueled missionization. As discussed earlier, it effectively extended the translation of the Gospel into the very roots of the religion. Weavers called for a faith aggressively stripped of worldly matters and concerns, and while not fully condemning "progress," he held that there existed little need for the material in the development of the sacred. For *amakholwa* after revival, to be Christian was now more than to wear clothes, work in the Western economy, live in square brick homes and attend Sunday services, in other words, to a "respectable" life as dictated by missionaries. To be Christian now meant that the Spirit of God dwelled within, and this activated idioms of personal spiritual power familiar to Zulu while also carrying evangelistic responsibilities and expectations that those who had undergone sanctification felt obligated to fulfill. The souls of their friends, families, and neighbors cried out for salvation, and with Christ's imminent return it was imperative on the revived to spread the Good News. But Holiness was not merely about additional responsibilities; those who were already burdened by the difficulties that accompanied the arrival of the twentieth century would have had little long-term interest had this been so. No, sanctification also offered a moral high ground, an opportunity to declare loudly "I am a Christian" and expect, backed by the conviction that all were equal before God, that this declaration alone would carry the weight of spiritual authority.

Building Zulu Christianity

Several months after Weavers departed Natal, nearly half of the girls at Inanda Seminary confessed that while they had believed they were Christian before the revival, they now knew that they had not truly converted until their experience of consecration. A teacher at the school, unnerved by this admission, asked the girls what their mistake had been. Some reported: "I was trusting in a few good works and to leaving off some sins, but I did not see my sins as I do now." Others responded that they had not sufficiently trusted Jesus for their salvation, while more than twenty responded that they had trusted to their clothes, believing that donning them was sufficient evidence of faith.[29] The teacher protested the mission's innocence, claiming that the AZM had been clear that wearing clothes did not equal salvation.[30] But missionary words mattered little, for the girls believed what the *amakholwa* community had accepted as truth; that Christianity could be captured in a few symbolic gestures.

And certainly the mission, as discussed earlier, went far toward fostering the *amakholwa* perception that their Christianity came as the direct result of their non-spiritual actions. In the year prior to the revival, a missionary visiting a dying young woman at an outstation of Umsumduzi felt compelled to comment on her surroundings, noting that she had died in an "old-fashioned beehive hut . . . Her bed was a mat spread on the ground; her pillow, a block of wood; her covering, a dirty blanket; her companions, heathen; her earthly comforts, none." In such a setting, the missionary believed, the temptations to relapse must be severe for nothing buttressed one from the prevailing moral sentiment. Extending this thought, the missionary concluded: "Unless the converts can be brought into a Christian environment and under continuous Christian training, learning, if possible, to read the Bible for themselves, it would seem well nigh impossible for the Gospel to maintain its sovereignty over their hearts."[31]

Given this then, it is unsurprising that many *amakholwa* concluded that they had not been fully Christian prior to their moment of *uvuswa*, their rebirth.[32] At Groutville and Mapumulo, many expressed the belief that revival had meant for them a "genuine first conversion."[33] The year after revival, many of the sanctified at Esidumbini and Noodsberg celebrated the date of their "rebirth" as their first full year of Christian living.[34] At Umzumbe, *amakholwa* acknowledged that while prior to revival they had intellectually accepted Christian doctrine and attempted to conform to the standards expected of them, they had done so "to be *counted* a Christian."[35] William Ngidi, one of the original band that visited Groutville from Mapumulo, wrote to the *SOG* praising God for sending Elder Weavers:

I thought at first I was all right, but after all I was not right. I had not seen God's light. I was a Christian. I was going about telling sinners to repent. I was also reading in the Bible about the Holy Spirit and telling others about him; still I knew him not. I remember that on September 22, 1896 the Lord revealed

himself by the mighty power of the Holy Spirit. On that day the Lord showed
me that I was not right and I said Lord take me as I am and sanctify me. I laid
myself on the hands of the Lord to deal with me. Today I am delivered.[36]

With so many men and women like Ngidi undergoing revival, it became
that much easier for those who had become alienated from the *amakholwa*
community to return to the fold. For those who had compromised their
faith in the pursuit of wealth, had participated in the violence of the cities, or had been accused of sin during the mission's purity campaigns,
revival freed them of their most heinous sins, opened the door for personal renewal and offered reintegration into the Christian community. At
least one missionary expressed concern over the theology of consecration,
fearing that there was a "great danger of the people thinking that in some
way confession is a payment for their sin" and believed that it too closely
represented the "old heathen idea that when the fine imposed by the chief
is paid that all guilt is wiped from the conscience as a result." The consequences of sin, he argued, needed to be fully felt in order to dissuade the
sinner from repeating his crime.[37] Finally, the promise of living a sin-free
sanctified life provided a powerful theology for those daily exposed to the
"corruption" that surrounded them and it is little wonder that an increasingly marginalized people should embrace the promise of personal and
communal empowerment.

The Indwelling Spirit

Equally important to the success of revival was the emphasis in Holiness
on an ever present Holy Spirit whose powerful presence could be called on
at any moment and, importantly, was a constant presence in the lives of
believers. Here, at long last, was a theology that resonated with Zulu belief
in the active role of the *amadhlozi* in their lives. It is clear from the confessions of the *amakholwa* congregations that previously they had hedged their
bets, practicing their Christianity while maintaining casual connection with
the ancestors. Holiness theology allowed them to move away from that
because unlike Congregationalism, the revivals recognized an active spirit
world just beyond the horizon of this existence. It was not that Holiness
allowed syncretism, Weavers clearly forbade anything that interfered in a
close relationship with Christ, but one can sense a deep feeling of relief as
amakholwa enthusiastically adopted the doctrine of sanctification, abjuring
their charms and traditional medicines for the power of the Holy Spirit. Indeed for several years not a missionary report of the revivals passed without
mention of *amakholwa* giving up items connected to the *amadhlozi*, and missionaries grew accustomed to the sight of dozens of small, brightly colored

bags suspended from the pulpit rails in churches, the traditional medicines inside (which could be expensive to attain) sacrificed on the altar in recognition that they were no longer needed. Perhaps unintentionally, the act of laying these items on the altar replicated the sacrificial practice common in most traditional ceremonies. As Axel-Ivar Berglund has shown Zulu set aside special cuts of meat from a slaughtered animal for the enjoyment of the spirits—its disappearance the following morning being evidence that the *amadhlozi* had heard their prayers.[38]

Previously missionaries had taught that worship of the spirits was wrong, but they had provided nothing to replace this practice. Here, however, was the answer to this problem, and one that allowed *amakholwa* to fully claim their Christian identity. For Weavers, the Holy Ghost was not a mystical force operating in a historical past, but an active power able to protect, heal, and guide men and women who followed Christ. To the question; "Do I believe in being led by the Spirit of God?" Weavers taught that Christians needed to answer yes, for, "The Spirit itself maketh intercession for us with groanings, etc."[39] Here was a critical piece of theology necessary for the construction of a Zulu Christianity—without it, I would argue, Christianity was unlikely to have thrived.

Just as an active and ever-present Holy Spirit provided a viable alternative to the daily workings of the *amadhlozi*, so too did Holiness theology offer divine healing at a time when the mission offered little else for an individual's health. After the revival, smalls groups of *amakholwa* responded to illnesses in their midst by gathering together, laying their hands on the afflicted and praying. While fraught with the potential for failure, this approach to health and healing echoed traditional approaches and given the inefficiency of Western medicine at this time, it is no surprise that almost two years after the beginning of the revivals, missionaries reported widespread use of faith-healing among *amakholwa*.[40] A decade later, when Dr. James McCord arrived to rebuild the AZM's medical mission, he was taken aside and warned that Western medicine was not necessarily welcomed by many church members for Weavers'

> most unfortunate idiosyncrasy was his belief that he could heal the sick. True, there were some remarkable recoveries in cases where psychic treatment was all that was necessary. But his idea that taking medicine was a sin was a severe handicap to patients who needed it. If such patients failed to respond to their own and his prayers, the elder was certain that they were either still living in sin or lacked faith.[41]

But this new doctrine of divine healing must have greatly assisted in the spread of Christianity among traditionalists, for not only did it fill an important need, but it did so without the costs and fuss traditionalists underwent. Christians simply gathered together and prayed over the sick, with no need to call in a diviner and then a healer, sacrifice livestock and pay what could be rather steep fees—the Spirit alone now provided.

Weavers' emphasis on faith healing made most of the missionaries of the AZM uncomfortable, and they did their best to discourage the practice. But their efforts often proved fruitless, as a vivid story from Amanzimtoti illustrates. Following revival there, five young men went to the mission dispensary to look in on a sick friend. They prayed with her, urged her towards consecration, and when she claimed to have confessed all her sins, commanded her "in the name of Jesus, to arise." And arise she did, despite the concern of the missionary in charge that she keep still. The boys returned to the seminary believing God had granted them the gift of healing during their sanctification and regarded this as evidence of the power of the Spirit in their daily lives. The principal attempted to temper this claim with firm words of doubt, a doubt he believed justified when the woman's condition turned worse the following day, but her reversal did not dampen the boy's enthusiasm. The women, they noted, had quarreled with her husband after their departure, allowing Satan to return to her heart.[42]

Following revival, *amakholwa* actively sought to translate the symbolic marker of being "born-again" into their daily lives. For this, Weavers had armed them with an expectation of a rigorous daily maintenance of their faith that included Bible studies, small group meetings, and frequent rounds of revival. All this was necessary to preserve sanctification, for Holiness theology held that while an individual was free from sin following the entrance of the Spirit, the devil could slip back in without constant vigilance. Particularly important in this defense was prayer—the more the better and the more specific the likelier God would respond in a like manner. One missionary argued that the most remarkable aspect of the movement was the belief it engendered among *amakholwa* that God not only heard, but answered their prayers, and they took advantage of this to regale Him with a bevy of petitions ranging from the everyday wants of the body to the more ephemeral needs of the soul.[43] At Inanda, the missionary in charge favorably compared *amakholwa* revivalists to Paul's description of the Thessalonians, noting that they now lived lives of faith, even in their everyday tasks.[44]

Rebuilding the Community

Shortly after the revival, the residents of Mapumulo held a vote to determine their next pastor. A previous vote, marked by bitter feelings toward the elder Kuzwayo, had split the church in two and laid bare bitter feelings long harbored in the small Christian community. But revival provided them with an alternative approach to what many feared was an intractable problem, and when the congregation next gathered to vote they prayed beforehand, asking the Lord to reveal his choice. This was not a figurative plea, for the *amakholwa* felt empowered by what they had recently undergone and were certain that God would listen to their petition. The first man to vote, previously the bitterest opponent to Mbiya Kuzwayo's candidacy, stood and declared "The Lord shows me I must vote for Mbiya." One after another the members followed until Kuzwayo had been unanimously chosen. Afterward the congregation proclaimed the election a miracle, a further sign of the Lord's blessing.[45]

As part of the revival experience, *amakholwa* settled their feuds. Compelled by the experience of consecration, individuals first aired the animosities, jealousies, angers, and hatreds that had driven them apart. Then, motivated by the desire for sanctification, they sought out reconciliation. At Inanda, Dalita Isaac rose and apologized for believing in malicious rumors, and individuals in the Ifume congregation pulled each other out of the church during the middle of revival services to apologize, returning only when they could announce their reconciliation. At Groutville, a faction that controlled the church treasury had been angry that their candidate had lost the pastoral election and refused to hand over the new pastor's salary. But after revival the congregation quickly acted to right this wrong and voted overwhelming to restore his pay.[46] At a revival meeting at Itafamasi in 1898, Wilcox, Weiss, and Mbiya Kuzwayo set up Weavers' old tent, and under it two long-feuding parties, whose division had made it impossible for the church to continue with its normal affairs, made mutual confessions, announced their fault in the matter, and came together in reconciliation.[47]

At Inanda and elsewhere, communities attempted to maintain this newfound peace through special meetings where *amakholwa* confessed enmity toward each other. At these "Watch Meetings" they revived hoped to maintain their sanctification by patrolling their own spiritual borders as well as that of their community. Further signifying the success of this new theology in filling a spiritual hole *amakholwa* had found wanting in Christianity, believers brought witchcraft to give up to the Lord, and confessed their plans for the substances.[48] Most often these were love potions, medicines that, when applied to the face or hands, induced a girl who looked upon the wearer to fall under a spell and obey any command. But more malevolent concoctions, purchased because of jealousy or anger and designed to make rivals sick (sometimes to the point of death) when placed on the threshold of a door or in the footpath of an intended victim, were also handed over. Watch Meetings thus offered not only a way for revivalists to maintain moral purity, but also helped stabilize the community.

The revival also brought equilibrium to the relationship between the older central stations and their outstations. When Christians from both dated their "rebirth" from similar dates, there was little reason for *amakholwa* from the older churches to affect a sense of superiority. Indeed, revivalist philosophy made spiritual purity primary in counting a church's achievements, not location, material success, or history. This produced a new accountability, in which members of the outstations, regardless of their social position, could claim to be sent by God to rectify faults elsewhere. So, for example, claiming that the "Mother" church was in moral trouble, Qanda Mseleku, a hunchback preacher, led members from all the outstations of Umzumbe to hold an *Imvuzelelo* (awakening time) there in the early 1900s.[49] They came singing "*Vukani, bandhla, bonilaleni na?*" (Awake, people, why do you sleep?) at the top of their lungs, marching up and over the hills of the reserve and right up to the church door. Many who came were recent converts, men and women unable to read but who could already recite entire chapters from the Bible, and their presence electrified the church. At the service that followed, Qanda led the gathered in singing and prayer, and when the time for consecration came the outstation revivalists led their central station brethren up to the altar, where they knelt and prayed together.

The spiritual authority of the less cosmopolitan outstation members went unquestioned because revival empowered and compelled them to act when other Christians had obviously lapsed. No longer did *amakholwa* of the AZM mark each other's Christianity by a complex set of symbols from literacy, to clothes, occupation, and church membership. Instead affirmative answers to questions such as "Are you saved?" and "Do you have the Holy Spirit?" were sufficient to communicate a mutual affiliation.[50] Thus the poorest and least materially advantaged could claim salvation right alongside those who evidenced more success in the Western world. It took little more than a conscious conviction of faith to answer such queries, effectively throwing open the church doors to new members and later helping to launch a host of Zionist churches. This shift came none too soon, for the wealth that allowed *amakholwa* of previous generations to demonstrate their Christianity had proved ephemeral, and they could no longer expect to maintain a material advantage over traditionalists.

The intensely communal nature of the revival phenomenon also went a long ways towards restoring the battered *amakholwa* community. Individual lives were indelibly altered, but these transformations occurred in public and as part of a congregation-wide experience. This was significantly different from the conversion narratives of earlier generations, when individuals came to their faith only after undergoing a long journey of personal discovery, assisted, perhaps, by a few other *amakholwa* and a missionary. Revival, on the other hand, resembled earlier acts of community faith, like the World Week of Prayer and the NAM, which had found the most favor among Zulu Christians. And maintaining sanctification meant devoting an impressive number of hours each week in public communion. So at Groutville, for example, the sanctified met every morning for an early Bible and prayer meeting, held a separate Friday evening service, and organized evangelistic bands to go out every afternoon to hold meetings among the outstations.[51] A year after revival, with their pastor away for three months, the congregation at Esidumbini carefully maintained daily Bible studies and prayer meetings by selecting a number of lay preachers to fill the role from among their ranks.[52]

Flames of Fire

As noted earlier, *amakholwa* demonstrated little enthusiasm for evangelism prior to revival. Outside of a few cases of itinerant preaching and mission-financed endeavors, *amakholwa* had proven unwilling to sustain proselytizing efforts in the years leading up to the end of 1896. But revival generated an unprecedented eagerness to bring the Word to unbelievers, and members at every awakened church drove new evangelistic efforts. The wall between believer and traditionalist, always permeable, was now to be fully breached, torn down one soul at a time.

The passion *amakholwa* demonstrated for bringing the Gospel to others began as a largely unorganized reaction to a sense of obligation believers felt coming out of sanctification. Initially this effort was truly revival-based—that is to say the focus was on those who belonged to Christian churches. The Mapumulo revivalists, the girls of Inanda and Umzumbe, and the boys of Amanzimtoti, for example, all started by taking the revival message to other *amakholwa*. But they, like others, soon felt called to reach non-believers as well. This did not always prove easy. The teacher at Umzumbe worried about her young female charges and would only allow them to visit kraals accompanied by teachers. Even then they were often met with disdain, sullen hostility, or even open anger, but their passion wore down opposition and generated interested among traditionalists in this newly imagined African Christianity.

Others felt called to proselytize in distant places. Pumbile Ngobo left Natal for Johannesburg after undergoing revival intent on bringing sanctification to others. Making his way overland he cried the entire way, missing his friends and family and fearful of what he might find at the goldmines.

But he believed that he was now obligated to share the news of his rebirth in Christ and he persevered. "You know," he later mused, "if you find something of yours that has been lost you do not keep still and not tell others. Well, it is just so with the Word of God. Those who receive the Holy Spirit and forgiveness of sin cannot keep still and not tell others."[53] William Ngide also made his way to the Transvaal, "letting others know how I was delivered."[54] He enthusiastically reported: "I preach out in the mines, and the Lord's work is going on rapidly and the people confess their sins and are converted and give themselves to the Lord." He also urged Weavers to come to Johannesburg, noting that the revivalist was needed there "more than I can express."

Ngidi and Ngobo were not the only youth responding to the Spirit's call. At Umzumbe, men and women went out in small groups, praying and preaching among the kraals with remarkable effect, returning from these trips with snuff boxes, pipes, and other items they had gathered from repentant audiences.[55] At Inanda, Pixley wrote in amazement at how the people had awakened to a new sense of responsibility for the salvation of traditionalists:

> Hundreds are now every Sabbath and during the week going forth to talk, hold meetings and preach to the people in the kraals. There has suddenly sprung into existence a mighty preaching force which is telling day and night the story of Jesus and of his salvation. Some of these men and women baptized by the Holy Ghost have become flames of fire to preach the Gospel and proving that they have indeed imbibed the spirit of the early Christians and showing as we think that they are working in the spirit of the Holy Master.[56]

When asked why they went, these lay evangelists responded that they now worked "for Christ and for the salvation of others" and felt called by the "Inkosi" (God) to speak of their own experiences in sanctification. They traveled long distances and occasionally met with scorn, because they felt called to warn traditionalists that "time is short," doing so with a power that amazed Pixley.

The story of their salvation and their testimonies to what God had wrought in their lives was the central component of the message *amakholwa* delivered. But other aspects of Weavers' Holiness theology also found their way into the telling. Pumbile Ngobo, writing from Johannesburg, thanked and praised "the Lord my healer" for leading him to the city. He explained his choice of words:

> Some may think I speak of the healing of the body from the sickness of the flesh, but no; I speak of the healing of the soul from sin. When I was walking in sin, I was saying I am all right, but no; I was dead. I could not see; I was

blind. But now I live, I see. I also tell the people that the Lord has the power to heal without medicines. I know this; I have seen it. Bless the Lord! But we first must know that our sins are forgiven, and then the Lord will hear us when we pray.

Just as for *amakholwa*, the emphasis in Holiness on the works of the Spirit and the healing potential of the Christian faith must have attracted traditionalists to the message in greater numbers than the more conservative mainline theologies. Once armed with such powerful and resonant proselytizing tools, Zulu Christians found the responsibility significantly easier.

The "bands" of Christians spreading the revival message were part of a much more organized effort than at first appeared. In the immediate aftermath of revival, *amakholwa* responded individually to the Spirit's call to mission, but revival leaders soon began channeling these efforts into more effective approaches. They looked for inspiration to the only reference they believed necessary, the first chapter of Acts, and so they went out like the apostles of early Christendom in bands of two, three, and four preaching to all who might stop and listen. But without leadership, this too proved ineffective. So, in the early months of 1897, Mbiya Kuzwayo organized the revivalists at Mapumulo into a permanent lay preaching force of "young Christian workers who call themselves the Volunteers."[57] Probably through his own energetic endeavors, Kuzwayo's group became increasingly popular among *amakholwa* of the AZM and quickly became a mainstay of the spiritual life of the churches.

The inspiration for the *amavoluntiya*, as they called themselves, came from Kuzwayo's days at Amanzimtoti High School, where years earlier the principal in charge of the school had attempted to start a Christian Endeavor Society (CES).[58] The pastor of a Congregational church started the CES in Portland, Maine in 1881, when he sought to channel the fervor a recent revival generated among the church's youth into a life-long commitment to an active Christianity.[59] He invited them to a conference where they decided to form a group that focused on discipleship, service, and outreach. The model, encouraging youth to "volunteer" in the work of Christ, quickly became a national phenomenon and by 1890 there were 12,000 CES groups with some 700,000 members throughout the world. Two years earlier, Natal became one of the first international sites for CES when the missionary at Amanzimtoti started a chapter with the hope that it might "drive out the mischief Satan finds for unoccupied minds." But the Natal branch of the CES suffered from the appeal of the cities, and in 1890, when the last active member left for Johannesburg, the group folded.[60]

Like the CES, the *amavoluntiya* focused their efforts on both the internal and external development of Christianity. They were primarily interested in promoting the revival message within the churches, but the group also engaged in active mission work. At Mapumulo, the initial group of twelve revivalists grew several times over, and once organized they ranged across the Thukela River valley spreading the Gospel. The Groutville congregation evidenced a "missionary spirit from the pulpit to the pew and consecrated workers are continually going out to other parts."[61] At Esidumbini, the group gathered at sunrise every Thursday for prayer and Bible study before receiving that day's mission assignments.[62] In the afternoon they spread out into the surrounding hills and valleys, visiting the kraals of traditionalists in small groups. The following week they gathered again, and a leader from each group delivered a report on their successes and failures, recommended follow-up visits and suggested additional preaching sites. At Inanda thirty *amavoluntiya* lay-ministers made a similar effort, regularly visiting the kraals of traditionalists in an effort to spread the Word as widely as possible. Members of the group at Impapala went out on weekly proselytizing trips, and claimed average audiences in excess of 500.[63] As revivalists initiated *amavoluntiya* groups throughout the country, *amakholwa* openly embraced an evangelistic impulse they had previously avoided, rapidly speeding up the process of Christianizing Natal. While the era of the white missionary had not fully passed, *amavoluntiya* represented the future of evangelization in South Africa.[64]

As part of their commitment to spreading the Word, the members of *amavoluntiya* not only engaged in the high drama of proselytizing and leading revivals to neighboring congregations, but they also served the more mundane needs of the Church. The group's members frequently served on various committees and volunteered wherever they were needed; a service that prompted one grateful missionary to note of the *amavoluntiya*: "I never knew the Endeavor Society whose members were more faithful."[65] But the group also presented a challenge to the mission, which did its best to normalize the volunteers and bring them under missionary oversight. Beginning in 1898, the AZM handed out to the group's members "Certificates of Preaching" that demonstrated, for any that might care to check, that the bearer was a member of the AZM in "regular and good standing" and was "hereby approved as a lay evangelist" for the church whose name appeared in the blank.[66] The mission also organized an annual Preachers Institute; a weekend long event held in several different areas of Natal at which attendees could discuss biblical law, the nature of the gospels and criticize each other's short sermons. By 1903 there were so many unordained and unpaid preachers that the mission began holding two annual conferences solely for this remarkable force.[67]

In "consideration of the rapid changes in the conditions of the people," the mission also recommended that the Theological Seminary be reorganized to make it possible for those with little or no previous training in theology to enter the school and to provide a year long course for local evangelists.[68] As part of this training, the mission also began sending its theology students on evangelical tours. They believed this important not only as a means of keeping "theory and practice in partnership," but also to give the students a taste of the life of a revivalist preacher, presumably a life so filled with the spiritual rewards of large-scale conversions that the students would not mind the low pay. To further this work the mission happily accepted the revival tent sent by Hephzibah to further revival work in southern Africa. *Amavoluntiya* members reacted eagerly to these opportunities, but like the young men of Esidumbini and Noodsberg, who "would gladly remain at home to engage in the work for small salaries, forgoing the large wages of Johannesburg" few could afford to commit themselves this fully to the Christian effort without other means of supporting their families.[69] So the *amavoluntiya* remained a group of eager Christian workers largely outside of mission control—allowing its members to fulfill both their temporal and spiritual duties by providing an organized outlet for their evangelistic impulse.[70]

Revival, Legitimacy, and the Spirit of Independence

For *amakholwa*, one of the central attractions of the Holiness message lay in the purified nature of the self following sanctification. Weavers taught, and they eagerly accepted, that having undergone consecration and then sanctification, they had made themselves temples for an indwelling Holy Spirit. So blessed, they could, through careful vigilance, lead sinless lives, a state of grace that made all who underwent perfection equal before God. What is remarkable is that in this moment Zulu became the spiritual equals of the American missionaries, the white settlers, and Christians all over the globe. Indeed, in most cases, they could claim to be more fully people of faith than most of those around them, including the majority of AZM missionaries who, while encouraging the revival, had not experienced its blessings.

The *amavoluntiya* are one example of a newfound *amakholwa* confidence in the power of their own faith—both in their assumption of missionary responsibilities and in their willingness to bring revival to other stations, effectively remaking the spiritual landscape of the churches without missionary involvement. But the congregations also demonstrated a marked increase in their willingness to patrol their own spiritual borders; for while Congregationalism provided churches with a democratic structure for their own governance, Holiness gave them the spiritual authority to claim this right.

Under missionary oversight, church members had previously hid their sins with the knowledge that much was at risk should they be revealed. A marked feature of missionary letters home during the revival is the shock and dismay they felt at hearing details of previously unrevealed sins and their surprise at the ability of the community to keep these hidden. But *amakholwa* had needed to maintain this secrecy, for revealing these transgressions frequently lead to excommunication and *amakholwa* who willingly or unwillingly removed themselves from the Christian community faced difficulties reintegrating into traditional society.

The process of consecration, while an emotionally wrenching experience, provided a model for *amakholwa* who wished to reveal their sins without being spurned. Not only did it present a path for the sinner to remain within the community, but it was also a necessary step towards perfection. Consecration was a double-edged sword however, for congregations that had undergone revival now expected their members to maintain a certain purity; sin was allowed but sorrow for the sin was expected to follow.[71] And individuals who did not reveal their own sin could expect to have it revealed for them with the expectation that doing so would lead them to return to the fold. If, at that point, they chose not to, then they could expect to be disciplined. So at Dalibe, an outstation of Noodsberg, the missionary in charge of the area expressed amazement at the "frank unfearing way in which some of the Christians showed up the sins of those who tried to conceal them and the staunch manner in which they stood for the right."[72] Unused to this level of forthrightness, she did not realize that the church was in the process of making her presence unnecessary. Enforcement was the last step of churches in claiming internal authority and the rules of revival had given congregations the tools necessary to do so outside of the purview of the mission.

Just as consecration allowed sinners the freedom to reveal their sins, so too did sanctification provided *amakholwa* with the moral authority, the legitimacy, to patrol the moral borders of their own churches. They, not missionaries, would now decide who was allowed in and why. While the church at Impapala grew dramatically following the revival, it did not do so indiscriminately, and where the AZM had previously worried that the little church in Zululand suffered from the lack of any nearby missionaries, following revival the congregation appeared at ease with the responsibility for maintaining purity free from mission oversight. Holiness held that the body was a temple and the congregation, determined to live according to this stricture, prohibited not only alcohol and smoking for its members, but also snuff, a ban not favored by the AZM. When a visiting missionary gave his support to a candidate for membership, an old man who had cut off his headring, lived a "worthy" life, and given up all his previous habits except snuff, the church disagreed, noting their own hard-won purity: "Our church is clean from this habit now and we fear that if we admit this man it will be thought that we do not condemn the habit and it will be a temptation to some of us who have given it up. We think he would better wait and we will labor with him that God may give him strength to lay this aside also."[73] To the mission's fear that the rule might cost the church converts, members pointed to their own rapidly growing assembly while the nearby Norwegian Mission Society, which allowed beer drinking and smoking, lost members. The work of *amavoluntiya* armed with revival apparently offset the disadvantages of enforcing purity.

To this, missionaries had no response, nor could they; the church at Impapala, now sanctified, stood as a moral rock to which the Americans could legitimately offer little instruction. This is not to suggest that all the members of Impapala or the other revived congregations lived sinless lives, or that these churches maintained their lofty spiritual positions. But at this critical moment, by undergoing revival *amakholwa* had taken the moral high ground, a nearly unassailable position from which they claimed spiritual sovereignty over their own institutions and their own faith. Following an outbreak of dysentery at Amanzimtoti High School, a group of revivalists saw the disease as a sign from the Holy Ghost and declared that it was now apparent to them that it was God's will that they go and preach. The American principals disagreed, and fearing a mass exodus might ensue, forbade the boys' departure, threatening them with expulsion should they proceed. But the young men left anyway, filled, in the mission's assessment, with such "spiritual pride" that "they were sure they knew the Lord's will better than any or all of their teachers."[74] They were not alone in this opinion.

In late May of 1897, Nyuswa, the Zulu pastor at Umtwalume, wrote a letter to one of the American missionaries. I quote here the portion of the letter that the AZM translated and forwarded to the Board in Boston:

> Beloved minister I am asking you to answer the following questions:
>   Am I Mr. Harris's worker? [Harris being the missionary overseeing Umtwal-ume]
>   Am I not God's servant?
>   Why am I under Mr. Harris?
>   Who is a white minister under another white minister?
>   Why is it necessary that a minister from Umtwalume be reported to America since the American Board is no longer helping us a pin's worth?

Nyuswa's questions disturbed the missionaries and they regarded them as a sign of an serious impending break between the mission and its flock; the first frustrated expression of an educated African elite straining to break free of the constraints of a white mission leadership.[75]

But Nyuswa's inquiries go well beyond a question of temporal authority. The first part of his letter, which the AZM did not bother to translate,
explains much about his subsequent questions:

> The work here is going with power indeed. Most of the youth have repented
> here in our home station. The members of the congregation are 260, those
> who have just come in are 85 . . . Spiritually the church has been revived
> (*uvuswa*). There is a spiritual revival. It continues with power indeed.

> The work outside the station is growing rapidly. "The harvest is great but the
> workers are few." The good news is that there is consecration of sins, throwing
> away of alcohol, smoking, and snuff tobacco. The young people have been
> greatly revived and are preaching in many places.[76]

Read in the context of the revival underway at Umsumduzi, Nyuswa's subsequent questions take on a deeper meaning than mere political agitation.
He was claiming nothing less than the full spiritual power that sanctification provided; equality before God for himself and his congregation. So
Nyuswa asked: "Am I not God's Servant?" knowing that he had acquired
the spiritual legitimacy that came with sanctification and knowing that the
mission could now only answer in the affirmative.

Not surprisingly, this assumption of equality extended beyond Umsumduzi. At the first conference between missionaries and *amakholwa* pastors
that followed the revival, the pastors echoed Nyuswa, demanding an equal
voice in the running of the mission. They argued for their right to participate and vote in all AZM meetings, not just those the mission opened to
them, to have a say in all questions of mission policy, to become trustees
of the mission reserves, and to decide for themselves when Zulu pastors
would be transferred to new positions. And just as missionaries were referred to as *umfundisi*, so *amakholwa* pastors requested the same, pointing
out that their current title, *umalusi*, did not signify the position they had
achieved before God.[77]

The sanctified also carried this spirit of egalitarianism off the mission
reserve and into their interactions with the white settler community, where
it was not well received. For while Weavers' message led them to believe
that they were equal before God with all Christians, the Natal government
differed. It is difficult to measure the hostility that these new *amakholwa*
assumptions generated, but the number of complaints in local white newspapers over the "disrespectful" attitudes of mission-educated Africans rose
perceptibly at this time.[78] This did not, however, stop the sanctified from
pressing for justice and appealing to the government for equality based
on their shared Christianity. When Thomas Hawes was stopped and com-

manded by white border guards to disrobe and bathe in the foul-smelling disinfectant used against the spread of rinderpest, he asked the guards:

> "Do the white people wash also?" They said ,"They do not." I asked, "Why not?" They said, "Because you are a native, you were born here." I assented and told them I was born in Zulu country, and I continued "Nevertheless the Governor has exempted me from the Native Law; *I am just as you are.*" They said, "Thou it be so, you are a native" and they took my letters of exemption on which is written all of this.[79]

In writing the SNA over this matter, Hawes began by carefully showing his respect, addressing him as "my chief" and noting that he was not really worthy to write him. But then he raised their mutual Christianity and pressed his right to raise the matter based on what he perceived as their shared faith: "But the thing I am extending is the love of Christianity. I know you are one, you do not make it doubtful in any way, in truth I know that you are one." The SNA, showing no regard for their "brotherhood," dismissed Hawes' complaint, noting that the matter was no longer relevant, for disinfectant was no longer being used; the answer effectively avoided the primary thrust of Hawes' letter; that Christian natives deserved to be treated as equals.

In conjunction with agitation elsewhere, the mission feared that the sudden spirit of autonomy expressed by their pastorate signaled an early end to the AZM. But this was not the intent of either the churches or their leadership. Neither Umsumduzi nor *any* of the churches that underwent revival in 1896–1897 broke with the AZM, they had no need to for the experience left them confident in their own autonomy, their legitimacy confirmed in their sanctification, and they appreciated the benefits that a continued association with the Americans brought them. They simply needed the Americans to understand that the relationship between mission and missionized had changed.

Slowly, the American missionaries recognized the new reality. By 1899 even those missionaries who just a few years earlier had disparaged the Board's request that the mission hand over daily control of the churches to a Zulu pastorate, now admitted that their roles were irrevocably altered; the day of the missionary ruling over a station as his own personal fiefdom had passed and a reduced force of Americans would only act in the future as supervisors, advising, but not running the churches. One missionary wrote rather wistfully, "It is an open question whether the time has not arrived for the people to assume control of their own evangelistic and pastoral work, looking to the missionaries for advice only. My personal feeling is that it has come or is near."[80]

THE GROWTH OF THE CHURCHES

For the next twenty years the churches of the AZM enjoyed an unprecedented period of growth. Remembered fondly, even today, it was a time when church memberships increased dramatically, participation in prayer meetings and Bible studies was enthusiastically embraced, and congregations took it as their responsibility to evangelize those who did not yet believe. The statistical consequence of revival was felt immediately in both human and monetary terms, but carried an enduring echo that proved much more significant.

Some churches saw their congregations double immediately and increase exponentially from there. At Impapala, church membership grew from fourteen to forty-two in the six months following the first revival service, with another twelve candidates prepared for immediate admission in the following month.[81] Despite drought, locust, and rinderpest, church members found a way to not only pay their preacher, but to hire a teacher and build a school. At the same time, Groutville and Mapumulo welcomed seventy new members into their ranks, nearly doubling the next highest year for incoming congregants.[82] The following year, twenty-four catechists joined the church at Mapumulo alone while many more sought entrance. Meanwhile, those regularly attending the weekly prayer meeting at Groutville tripled, with sixty to seventy participants gathering in the church prior to dawn every Wednesday morning.[83] The congregations at both stations, despite the devastating blow they received from rinderpest during the summer of 1897–1898, tithed more than ever before, both to their home churches and to the coffers of the Native Home Missionary Society.[84]

Other stations undergoing revival noted similarly impressive gains. Within the first month of the revival at Umtwalume, eighty-five new members were received into fellowship, bringing the congregation to 260. At Esidumbini, where, as previously noted, the missionary in charge proved resistant to admitting new members, only some forty-odd Zulu were welcomed into full communion. The inquirers' class, however, ballooned in the immediate aftermath of revival, with over a hundred entering into the preparatory education required by the AZM before baptism.[85] The following year the enquirers' class was larger still, with 169 Zulu sitting down several nights a week to learn about the nature of God, his Son and the church.[86] A little over a year after the commencement of revival, the church at Inanda had grown by a quarter again its previous size, and in 1898 it welcomed sixty-one new members, bringing the congregation to 422.[87] At Amanzimtoti, eighty-eight new members were received into the central church and her outstations during the church year 1898–1899, while in Durban, seventy-one new members joined in the year following revival.[88] By 1898, Durban's inquirers' class had become so large that the missionary in charge found it necessary to break them into four separate groups, with deacons administering the lessons. By the following year, some 1,500 participants gathered every Sunday at the various AZM preaching sites located throughout Durban to hear the word of God brought to them by a host of Zulu preachers, pastors and deacons.[89] At the main church alone, built to house 250 worshippers, the mission found it necessary to hold four services every Sunday to meet demand. At the end of the mission's first fifty years, 728 *amakholwa* were counted as adherents of the churches; in 1900 alone, the AZM added over 500 new members and in the five years after the first revivals, church membership rose dramatically.

Finally, the years after revival also saw a jump in the number of Zulu youth seeking to attend the seminaries at Umzumbe, Inanda, and Amanzimtoti. These youth came, however, not so much for the education and the material benefits promised by that education, as for the spiritual power they expected to derive from their time in the schools. The seminaries were regarded, and quite rightly so, as centers of the revival and thus attracted to them those who wished to associate themselves with new found ways of Holiness. Demand for enrollment increased dramatically and in 1897, lacking sufficient room, the Inanda Girl's Seminary began turning away students for the first time in its history.[90] Of the thirty-six new pupils who joined that year, thirty-three were illiterate and responded when questioned that their desire to attend Inanda flowed from revival services, where the Spirit had aroused in them a desire to attend courses. The workings of the Holy Spirit also extended to the girls already attending Inanda, where, following revival, most believed that God had sent them to the school in order to learn to read His book. At Amanzimtoti, a similar mood infected the boys who not only bought up all the Zulu language Bibles, but also cleared the principal out of his stock of Bible studies, hymnals, and readers; essentially anything which might "put light generally on the grand old Word."[91]

ELDER MBIYA KUZWAYO

While still serving as Weavers' interpreter, Kuzwayo had a conversation with a teacher at Inanda Girls Seminary about his experience of sanctification. She was puzzled at the enthusiastic embrace of the revival message by *amakholwa*, many who claimed the experience as their first true commitment to their Christianity. In writing of the revival to the Board in Boston she related his diplomatic answer:

> He was a good Christian before, all ready to receive those truths, *but now says that he sees those things of God in such new light that it seems as if he had never*

known them before. He finds new power in the Word and has great joy in being so consciously led by the Spirit in his work for the people and in his preaching. He has been thinking of buying a wagon in order to make money, but he says that the Lord has shown him he must give himself wholly to his work.

Picking up his ever present Bible, Kuzwayo opened it and continued: "I shall never forget the time when the Lord himself spoke this word to me. 'Go thy way, for thou art a chosen vessel unto me, to bear my name among the Gentiles.'"[92]

After nearly a half a year, Kuzwayo parted ways with Weavers at Esidumbini and returned home to Mapumulo to organize the *amavoluntiya*. On arriving home, however, he faced the first real challenge to his new faith. His youngest daughter, a small child, had become deeply sick. Feverish and congested, she grew steadily worse after his return. Previously, Mbiya recalled, he would have given the child a dose of Santomine. "But" he asked "The Lord who cast out devils, can he not heal the child?"[93] The medicine was rejected in favor of prayer, but slowly the child's condition worsened. A week went by and with each day Kuzwayo's concern deepened. Doubts crept in and he later confessed, "It came like a trial on my part as I had been testifying that the Lord is all in all. He saves the soul, and heals the body, which is a standing test to those who trust him."

Mbiya's mother, a woman of faith herself but perhaps a grandmother first, finally took the child with her to the home of her husband, Mfanefile. There, the young girl at last received Western medicine, but the more of it the family administered, the sicker the child became. Mbiya's father, faithful to the AZM and sharing their general suspicion of divine healing, urged his son to write a distant doctor for a prescription arguing that the "Lord is not pleased if we don't try means to help ourselves." Mbiya resisted, answering, "It is no use to trust human aid any more, but to trust to God." Following Weavers' example, he quoted extensively from the Bible in support of his position, but his father persisted and in the end the letter was written. That same day Mbiya called for "those who know the power of prayer" to come pray for the child, and a group of sanctified, including "Brother" Weiss, "took the child into a private room where we anointed and prayed for it."

The revivalists believed the girl showed a marked improvement almost immediately, but at sunset the boy who had been sent to the doctor returned with medicine in hand and Mfanefile ordered it administered. Mbiya, torn between his faith, concern for his daughter and deference to patriarchal authority, helplessly stood aside. That night, the child grew worse and by morning "there was no hope for the child to live." Mbiya left his father's house, went across a nearby river, and sought out "secret" prayer. He asked God if it was his will to heal his daughter while receiving the medicines and the Lord answered, "No, if you don't stop them at once the child is going to die." Emboldened by this divine command, Mbiya returned to find his extended family gathered around the girl, praying for her and "just waiting for the soul to leave the body." He said to his wife, "If you are not careful the child is in danger, but if we trust the Lord and leave off these medicines he will help us." At this, she broke into tears and fled the room. She returned shortly and admitted that the Lord had also spoken to her, telling her to take the child home. She strapped her sick daughter to her back, ignored the warnings of those around her that the girl wouldn't last the trip, and marched out with Mbiya.

The child survived, and once home the couple again gathered with their Holiness friends to anoint and pray for the girl. She recovered, living evidence to those who doubted in the power of divine healing. *Amakholwa* gave "glory to our God for his wonderful care" and Mbiya was pleased to write that even as he sat down to pen the letter to Weavers, the child laughed and jumped about the room around him in full and happy health. As for other events, Mbiya noted that it would, "take a book to write of all the incidents that have occurred since you left." Many had been healed by the power of God alone and Kuzwayo had participated in revivals in other parts of Natal where, "Professors of religion got the true way of salvation by confessing and forsaking their sins just as you saw at our station." For *amakholwa* getting "the true way" meant not only finding their own personal path to heaven, but also claiming a spiritual position that offered legitimacy and power at a time when they were losing both.

NOTES

1. AZM A/4/59, Weiss to Smith, January 1897.

2. AZM A/4/62, AZM Annual Meeting June 16–29, July 6–9, 1897.

3. *The Sent of God*, September 2, 1897, letter from William Worcester dated July 14, 1897. While in Durban to collect the tent, Worcester was given a "first class" bike by a local businessman, complete with a lamp for night travel and tools for repairs. When he returned to Mapumulo the congregation gathered as he rode it around for their amusement. Moved by the Spirit, the congregation held an impromptu ceremony to give the bike over to God's use, crying out to Jesus in praise and thanks. Thus, in their own way, they insisted on the spiritual authority given to them by revival. The bike became not Worcester's, but rather a communal tool for spreading the Word.

4. AZM A/3/41, Esidumbini Station Report, 1897.

5. *Missionary Herald*, "The Religious Awakening," July 1897, 272–73.

6. ABM 192/424–30, Price to Smith, February 11, 1897. At one outstation a girl spent an entire Saturday alone in the chapel, praying and fasting for the souls of the

congregation. At the Sabbath service the following day she delivered her testimony, prompting a revival during which the outstation preacher "who had been going sadly wrong" first wept and then confessed the hatred that had grown in him toward many of those under his care.

7. AZM A/3/47, Inanda Girls Seminary Report, 1896–97. Although as Ngubane has noted, young Zulu women possessed by a spirit are generally considered dangerous both to themselves and their families. Harriet Ngubane, *Body and Mind in Zulu Medicine*, 142–48.

8. Julie Parle, "Witchcraft or Madness? The *Amandiki* of Zululand, 1894–1914," *Journal of Southern African Studies* 29 (2003), 108–112.

9. AZM A/3/47, Inanda Girls Seminary Report, 1896–97. Again, there are obvious parallels here between the powers revival participants felt when imbued with the Holy Spirit and those experienced by traditionalists, especially *inyanga*, when they underwent communion with the ancestors. See Axel-Ivar Berglund, *Zulu Thought-Patterns and Symbolism* (Bloomington: Indiana University Press, 1989), 197–98.

10. *Sent of God*, May 20, 1897, letter from Dalita Isaac dated March 29, 1897.

11. AZM A/3/41, Amanzimtoti Station Report, 1896–97.

12. The following account of the revival at Amanzimtoti is taken from; AZM A/4/59, Amanzimtoti Seminary Report, 1896–97 and *Missionary Herald*, "The Wonderful Revival," August 1897, 320–23.

13. The boys, probably knowingly, echoed Weavers, who warned that tobacco, like alcohol, defiled the body, which he called the "temple of God," and prevented the Holy Spirit from residing in such an unclean environment. *The Sent of God*, July 20, 1893.

14. Axel Iver Berglund, *Zulu Thought Patterns*, 300.

15. *Missionary Herald*, "The Wonderful Revival," August 1897, 320–23.

16. For a fuller discussion of other premarital Zulu sexual practices that this reference may be citing see, Carton, *Blood From Your Children*, 69–71. Peter Delius and Clive Glaser make the important point that "missionary Christianity undermined pre-existing forms of sexual socialisation" as full sexual intercourse replaced *ukuhlobonga* and *amaqhikiza*, older female chaperones, fell out of fashion. Delius and Glaser, "Sexual Socialisation in South Africa: A Historical Perspective," *African Studies* 61 (2002): 38.

17. The following account of the revival at Umzumbe is taken from: AZM A/3/41, Umzumbe School Report, 1897; AZM A/3/41, Umzumbe Station Report 1896–97; *Missionary Herald*, "Special Interest—Boy's School at Amanzimtoti, May 1897, 198–99 and "The Wonderful Revival," August 1897, 320–23.

18. ABM 192/338, Pixley to Smith, April 19, 1897.

19. AZM A/3/41, Lindley Station Report, 1896–97. Pixely acknowledged that he no longer felt this way, but rather saw in it the seeds of God's work.

20. *Missionary Herald*, "Interest at Inanda," March 1897, 110–11. Miss Phelps, the author, continued: "However, too much feeling is better than none at all, and it does seem as if in many cases the Holy Spirit was dealing with them."

21. AZM A/3/41, Amanzimtoti Seminary Report, 1896–97.

22. AZM A/3/41, Lindley Station Report, 1897. This was a theme Pixley had articulated earlier when he wrote of the ongoing revival at Inanda: "At some of the

stations it appeared to commence with the visit of Elder Weavers, a Baptist minister from the States. At this station I think the work had already commenced when he came among us." ABM 192/338, Pixley to Smith, April 19, 1897.

23. Ibid.

24. Michel Foucault, *The History of Sexuality, volume I*, (New York: Vintage, 1981), 92–94. Although this comment might seem to put me in agreement with the Co-maroffs, I would argue that missionaries were not successful in their efforts in large part because Christianity can be and historically has been, ultimately divorced from the culture it arrived with. Of course culture isn't static, so it shouldn't come as a surprise that Africans have successfully absorbed new belief systems and made them their own in any number of unique and local ways.

25. Weavers' egalitarianism is not surprising considering the radical nature of the social milieu from which he emerged. The students of Finney (himself an ardent abolitionist) who founded Tabor, backed their ideals in the years before the Civil War by first serving as a stop along the underground railroad ferrying slaves to Canada and later by providing John Brown with a base for his operations into Missouri. Eventually, fearing reprisals, the town asked Brown to leave, but kept a cannon hidden under a haystack all the same in case slave owners should make an appearance. Weavers was one of the first volunteers from Fremont county and later preached alongside black ministers at Holiness revivals in Missouri and, as previously noted, went on a revival tour to New York with a Henry O'Neill, a revivalist born in Africa. *History of Freemont County*, 577; David Reynolds, *John Brown, Abolitionist: The Man Who Killed Slavery, Sparked the Civil War, and Seeded Civil Rights*, (New York: Vintage, 2006).

26. *Sent of God*, May 20, 1897, letter from Dalita Isaac dated March 29, 1897.

27. AZM A/3/47, Inanda Girls Seminary Report, 1896–97.

28. AZM A/3/47, Inanda Girls Seminary Report, 1896–97.

29. AZM A/3/47, Inanda Girls Seminary Report, 1896–97.

30. Not all missionaries felt the same. A teacher at the Umzumbe Girl's school wondered if the missionaries were blameless for the "dead and corrupt state of the churches" as revealed by the revivals. At the very least, she believed, missionaries were responsible for missing the clues of degeneration. AZM A/3/41, Umzumbe School Report, 1896–97.

31. *Missionary Herald*, "Spiritual Quickening at Inanda," May 1895, 198–99.

32. AZM A/4/54, Report of Conference with Native Pastors June 20–23, 1901.

33. AZM A/3/41, Mapumulo and Groutville Station Report, 1896–97.

34. AZM A/3/42, Esidumbini Station Report, 1897–98.

35. AZM A/3/41, Umzumbe School Report, 1896–97. Original emphasis.

36. *Sent of God*, November 4, 1897, letter from W.N., undated. While it is possible that 'W.N.' is not William Ngidi, his presence at Mapumulo and his active involvement in the subsequent revival, second only to Mbiya Kuzwayo, makes it extremely likely that the two are one and the same.

37. ABM 190/407–08, Bunker to Friends, April 22, 1897.

38. Axel-Iver Berglund, *Zulu Thought-Patterns*, 308

39. *SOG*, July 20, 1893.

40. AZM A/3/42, Inanda Station Report, 1898–99.

41. James B. McCord, *My Patients Were Zulus* (New York: Rinehart, 1946), 42–44. When he first arrived one of the missionaries pulled the young doctor aside and warned him that he would have to live down the reputation of Weavers, "a wild and wooly character—with extreme ideas of Holiness," that sent "mission work here into turmoil for years after he left, the result of his influence on the natives."

42. AZM A/5/49, Amanzimtoti Seminary Report, 1897–98.

43. AZM A/3/47, Inanda Girls Seminary Report, 1896–97.

44. Ibid. In 1 Thessalonians Paul praises the Christians of Thessalonica for the good example they had set for Greece and the rest of the known world.

45. ABM 192/424–30, Price to Smith, February 11, 1897.

46. AZM A/3/42, Groutville and Mapumulo Station Report, 1896–97.

47. AZM A/3/42, Inanda Station Report, 1897–98.

48. *Missionary Herald*, "Progress of the Revival," September 1897, 352–53.

49. The following is from AZM A/4/59, "Death of a Faithful Disciple" undated.

50. Although, as with most revolutionary concepts, the egalitarian nature of revival lost its potency over time, the idea that salvation could be acquired through the simple acts of consecration and sanctification has retained a hold through today. Thus the poorest and least materially advantaged could claim salvation right alongside those who evidenced more success in the Western world.

51. AZM A/3/42, Groutville and Mapumulo Station Report, 1897–98.

52. AZM A/3/42, Esidumbini Station Report, 1897–98. Not surprisingly, this intense engagement with their faith led to prayers that were "deeper and more spiritual" than those offered up prior to revival.

53. *The Sent of God*, June 2, 1898, undated letter of Pumbile Ngobo.

54. *The Sent of God*, November 1, 1897, undated letter of W.N.

55. AZM A/3/41, Umzumbe Station Report, 1896–97. One of these bands also visited a Methodist station some ways distant from Umzumbe, where the Wesleyans welcomed them and eagerly participated in a three-day meeting of their own, at which all present renounced traditional customs.

56. AZM A/3/41, Lindley Station Report, 1896–97.

57. AZM A/3/41, Mapumulo and Groutville Station Report, 1896–97.

58. Deborah Gaitskell incorrectly suggests that the *amavoluntiya* did not begin until 1899, when a revivalist from Umtwalume took the name from British colonialists who were then volunteering for the Anglo-Boer War (Gaitskell identifies this revivalist as "Banda," who figured much more prominently in later mission correspondence under his more commonly spelled name Qanda Mseleku, the hunchbacked preacher mentioned earlier in this chapter.) The archival records make clear that the *amavoluntiya* began at Mapumulo in the early months of 1897 and members of the group's present successor, the Soldiers for Christ, credit Kuzwayo (albeit through Weavers not the CES, which is forgotten) as the movement's founder. Gaitskell is correct, however, in attributing to the group a prominent role in the spread of an indigenous Christianity throughout the area (although her focus is on *Isililo*, the organization for women that cleaved off from the *amavoluntiya*.)

59. Francis E. Clark, *Christian Endeavor in All Lands* (Philadelphia: 1906).

60. AZM A/3/46, Amanzimtoti Station Report, 1889–90. In 1896, the principal of Amanzimtoti hoped to organize the boys into a movement of Christian students

along the lines of the YMCA, a federation he hoped would bring both white and black students into Christian fellowship throughout Natal. When this proved unsuccessful, the missionary in charge attempted to relaunch the CES on the heels of a very brief visit to Amanzimtoti made by the group's founder, Rev. Francis E. Clark, in March of 1897. The missionary in charge of Johannesburg also hoped to begin a Christian Endeavor Society, but *amakholwa* clearly preferred the *amavoluntiya* groups and these thrived where the model for their inspiration did not. AZM A/3/41, Amanzimtoti Seminary Report, 1896–97; Amanzimtoti Station Report, 1896–97; AZM Minutes, volume VII, Semi-Annual Meeting, January 27–February 1, 1897.

61. *Sent of God,* December 16, 1897, letter from William Worcester, dated November 5, 1897.

62. AZM A/3/41, Esidumbini Station Report, 1896–97.

63. AZM A/3/41, Mapumulo and Groutville Station Report, 1896–97.

64. AZM A/3/42, Inanda Station Report, 1898–99. Indeed, as the power of the group steadily increased over the years, they came to wield a disproportionate influence in the Congregational churches. It became not uncommon for *amavoluntiya* to clash with both missionaries and Zulu pastors in their zeal to insure the purity of the churches and decades later they continued to employ Weavers' Holiness message in this quest. A half-century after revival, an American missionary noted that: "To many Volunteers, membership means a higher order of purity and dedication than church membership. This can mean that a member will pride himself on being 'better' than an ordinary church member. To this extent, an organization like the Volunteers may carry within it some unhealthy notions of meriting the Kingdom of Heaven." Arthur Christofersen, edited by Richard Sales, *Adventuring With God: The Story of the American Board Mission in South Africa* (Durban: Julia Rau Christofersen, 1967), 129–30. The tensions that the groups generated are still occasionally felt today between its contemporary, the "Soldiers for Christ," and other Congregational church members and leaders. Interview with Reverends Scott Couper and Susan Valiquette.

65. AZM A/3/41, Mapumulo and Groutville Station Report, 1896–97.

66. AZM A/1/7, Committee Report on Preaching Certificate, 1897; AZM Minutes Vol. VII, Annual Meeting, June 21–July 3, 1899; A/1/8, Report of Preachers Institute, 1898. The Missionary in charge of the institute noted that all but one of the official pastors and preachers of the mission attended the first institute held at Groutville along with "many lay preachers from Mapumulo and Groutville."

67. *Missionary Herald,* "Eager Bible Students," March 1903, 121.

68. AZM A/1/8, Committee on Theological School and Theological School Tours, 1897.

69. AZM A/3/42, Esidumbini and Noodsberg Station Report, 1897–98.

70. Exact figures for *amavoluntiya* membership are not available, but it is possible to estimate because the mission, when counting such unpaid and largely unsupervised workers for its annual statistical snapshot, put them in a catchall category of "Other Native Laborers." For the year 1901–02, for example, the AZM counted 301 such workers, nearly double that of the next closest mission of the American Board. While there were other evangelistic opportunities, the fledgling Christian Endeavor group at Amanzimtoti for example, the vast bulk of those counted in the "Other"

category would have come from among the ranks of the *amavoluntiya* who, by that time, appear to have chapters on nearly every station. *Missionary Herald*, January 1903, 9.

71. Weavers preached that, according to 2 Cor, 2:6–7, it was obligatory for Christians to forgive if the sinner repented, just as they must disassociate themselves from unrepentant men in such a way as to not count them as an enemy, but be able to admonish them toward righteousness as a brother. *SOG*, April 18, 1895.

72. Ibid. After failing to convince fourteen of its members to give up beer, the Dalibe church suspended their membership.

73. AZM A/3/41, Mapumulo and Groutville Station Report, 1896–97.

74. AZM A/4/59, Amanzimtoti Seminary Report, 1897–98. True to their word, the principals expelled the boys when they returned later in the school year.

75. ABM 189/642–43, AZM Annual Letter, 1896–97. Les Switzer, 'The Problems of an African Mission in a White-Dominated, Multi-Racial Society, the American Zulu Mission in South Africa, 1885–1910', PhD Dissertation (University of Natal: 1971).

76. AZM A/4/53, Letter from Nyuswa to Bunker, May 26th, 1897.

77. ABM 188/566, Annual Letter of the AZM, 1897–98. The mission agreed to take the matter under consideration and the subsequent crises is discussed in greater detail in the following chapter.

78. So frequent and bitter did these attacks become, that the mission felt compelled to respond. See AZM A/4/59, "Point of Contact," paper presented by J. D. Taylor at Natal Missionary Conference, 1902. See also the *Natal Mercury*, November 17, 1905, in which the principal of Amanzimtoti, A. E. Le Roy, presented the results of an informal survey he had conducted among Durban businesses who employed young men educated at his school. Hoping to dismiss "the oft-repeated statement that 'The missionaries spoil the native'" his poll indicated that the majority of employers were pleased with their mission-educated workers: "And yet we do not by any means consider the boys working in town as our best product." Firing another statistical broadside, Le Roy noted that the mission knew the histories of over 800 men who had attended Amanzimtoti in its first fifty years, and that of those only eleven had been convicted of any crimes. He estimated that some ten percent of those 800 no longer lived worthwhile Christian or industrial lives, while another 20 percent were good workers whose private lives had strayed from the Gospel. "Of these figures," he asked, "need we be ashamed?"

79. SNA 1897/1614, Thomas Hawes to SNA, August 8, 1897. Emphasis added.

80. ABM 190/450–51, Bunker to Smith, March 9, 1899. "It is an open question whether the time has not arrived for the people to assume control of their own evangelistic and pastoral work, looking to the missionaries for advice only. My personal feeling is that it has come or is near."

81. AZM A/3/41, Mapumulo and Groutville Station Report, 1896–97; *Missionary Herald*, "Remarkable Work at Mapumulo and Umvoti," October 1897, 395.

82. Ibid.

83. AZM A/3/42, Groutville and Mapumulo Station Report, 1897–98.

84. Ibid.

85. AZM A/3/41, Esidumbini Station Report 1897–98.

86. AZM A/3/42, Esidumbini Station Report 1898–99. The missionary in charge noted with some dismay, that the majority of those who made up the inquirer's class at Esidumbini were women and children. But while it is true that women constituted a growing majority of those attending the station churches, it should also be noted that the churches in Durban and Johannesburg were almost exclusively filled with men. While these city churches did not entirely offset an overall gender disparity, they go far toward providing a sufficient explanation for the disproportionate number of women in the Esidumbini inquirers' class. This rise of a "women's church" is also likely to have occurred on stations further afield, such as Mapumulo and Umtwalume, where *amakholwa* men spent longer periods off of the reserves.

87. AZM A/3/42, Inanda Station Report, 1897–98

88. AZM A/3/42, Amanzimtoti Station Report, 1898–99 and AZM A/3/42, Durban Station Report, 1897–98.

89. AZM A/3/42, Durban Station Report 1898–99.

90. AZM A/3/47, Inanda Girls' Seminary Report, 1896–97.

91. AZM A/3/41, Amanzimtoti Station Report, 1896–97. For a more detailed discussion of this event see, Robert Houle, "Mbiya Kuzwayo's Christianity: Revival, Reformation and the Surprising Viability of Mainline Churches in South Africa," *Journal of Religion in Africa*, 38 (2008), 141–70.

92. ABM 190/424–30, Price to Smith, February 11, 1897. Emphasis added.

93. The following account is from *Sent of God*, November 4, 1897; letter from M.M. Kuzwayo to Weavers dated August 2, 1897.

6

A Zulu Church

Arriving at Table Mountain Mission Reserve in late May of 1897, William Wilcox set up the Hephzibah-donated tabernacle and began holding revival services. To his consternation, but not surprise, unlike everywhere else in the mission revival did not take at Table Mountain. Simungu Shibe, the station's preacher for over a decade, had recently refused reassignment by the AZM to another parish and his congregation supported him in this act of disobedience. The dispute that followed, covered in more detail below, had, by Wilcox's arrival, reached the point that Shibe and his congregation all but considered themselves independent from the mission. They had, not surprisingly, little interest in bearing their souls to one of the American missionaries.

The AZM, after several failed attempts to reign in Shibe, turned to revival as a tool to resolve the conflict. Wilcox, troubled by his own belief that the schismatic preacher had been treated unfairly, at first declined to go to Table Mountain, only relenting after insisting that he would not discuss who lay at fault in the dispute.[1] Regardless of his sympathies for their plight, the disgruntled congregation began holding their own ceremonies in opposition to his own shortly after he arrived and drew away most of the audience he had hoped to reach.[2]

Matters quickly turned, however, after Mbiya Kuzwayo's arrival. The young Zulu preacher had spent the previous months either leading his own revivals across the colony with *amavoluntiya*, or assisting Wilcox and William Worcester with larger services. Despite having just returned home to Mapumulo, Kuzwayo responded to Wilcox's call for help at Table Mountain. Arriving on the station he did not join Wilcox, but rather began attending the opposition services, listening to their complaints, praying with them, and speaking with them about the power of consecration and sanctification. Soon his gentle persuasion paid dividends and the opposition services came to an end as Shibe's congregation began attending the AZM sponsored revival.[3]

From that point, the revival at Table Mountain proceeded like those elsewhere. *Amakholwa* attended services twice and sometimes three times a day. They awoke at dawn to attend prayer, listened to long sermons in the afternoon, and responded to altar calls in the evening by getting down on their knees, confessing their sins, and experiencing the redemptive power of forgiveness and the rapture that came with being filled with the Holy Spirit. Two cases, however, puzzled Wilcox, individuals who he believed underwent consecration without the accompanying sanctification that should have followed. In the first, a man who was struck down during one of the services "as if with a sledgehammer" and then remained motionless for two hours before arising to confess "great sins." The man knelt in prayer and struggled for some time, but went home without being "brought around" into a new birth. As in America, it was unusual to undergo consecration without sanctification, but it must not have been unknown.

It is the second case, of a woman in Simungu's congregation, which provides a glimpse into the very different meanings that *amakholwa* and the American missionaries derived from the sanctification experience. More importantly, it illuminates why the dramatic events that shook the AZM in the years following the revivals can only be understood in the context of those revivals. *Amakholwa* wept over their wrongdoings, publicly confessed their sins, were shaken by the power of the Holy Spirit, and felt moved to share the "Good News" with all those who had not yet heard, because they believed that doing so made them fully Christian in a way they now believed they had failed to achieve before sanctification. But with this "surrender to Jesus," they expected, and indeed were all but promised by Weavers and his acolytes, that sanctification brought with it the authority in their sacred lives that had so far escaped them in their secular ones.

The woman in question, a leader in the opposition meetings, finally relented after Kuzwayo arrived and attended a service under the big canvas tent. She was, however, seemingly unmoved by the experience and went home following an afternoon service to work in her garden. It was there, among the ripened ears of maize that God first spoke to her, commanding her to go and pray. She stole away for quiet prayer and asked God to reveal her sins, "but she could see no wrong." Later, in bed for the evening, she lay uneasily, tossing and turning and, surprisingly for the chilly winter nights of Natal, sweating profusely. Concerned she prayed: "Lord, if I have no sin, why do I sweat so?" God did not answer and sleep did not come so she kept praying "that the Lord would show me my state."

Finally, toward morning: "God took me by the neck and threw me down on the floor and lifted me up and turned me around." She cried out: "Oh Lord, what is this for?" And he answered: "You have scoffed at the meetings where they are getting the Holy Spirit. You drove the missionary out of your house and you drove the Spirit out with him." She also, the Lord informed her, had been a leader of strife, fomenting division instead of building up the congregation. The Lord demanded she seek forgiveness for her actions and she hurried out of her house, tracking down Wilcox some time later just as he began a small kraal service off the mission reserve. She told him what had just occurred and implored the missionary: "Umfundisi can you forgive such as I?" Wilcox responded: "Yes, mother. It is alright." She ignored his outstretched hand and threw her arms around him, sobbing with happiness in the embrace of the astonished missionary.

But for Wilcox the story ended sadly. He believed she failed "to come fully around" and claim the sanctification she had earned through her difficult experience of consecration, for she remained a member of Simungu's breakaway congregation. To Wilcox, her failure to listen to God when he rebuked her for being a leader of strife and division provided sufficient evidence that she had not achieved the "higher life." But Wilcox failed to closely examine what God had spoken to her. The Lord's criticism was not that she had joined the independent congregation; he did not command her to return to the AZM or obey the American missionaries, but rather castigated her for her conflicts with other Christians. Elsewhere, revival led to the healing of difficult interpersonal quarrels within the churches and while the AZM hoped that this might translate into the return of the lost sheep to the fold, it seems to have meant the same at Table Mountain as elsewhere; long held grudges and grievances were given up, but this occurred on a narrow personal level, where hostilities did the most harm to individuals and the local *amakholwa* community. In other words, the woman needed to ask forgiveness from Wilcox for her actions towards *him*, not her stance towards the AZM. There was no reason to ask for forgiveness for joining Shibe's congregation because it was well understood by all involved that Simungu had been unjustly dealt with and standing up against injustice was no sin. Cleansed of the sin of anger she could seek her own sanctification.

More profoundly, if Wilcox had thought carefully about God's message to this woman, he might have anticipated the revolutionary changes that were soon to overtake the AZM churches, transforming them, during the course of the next three years, into a body of believers nearly completely in charge of their own affairs. For God's harshest rebuke was that she had driven the missionary out of her home and in doing so had driven the Holy Spirit out with him: "For he had the Spirit." The missionary, in God's own judgment as related by this Zulu woman at Table Mountain, derived his spiritual authority from the presence of the indwelling spirit. In this, however, sanctification served as the great leveler, for the central feature of the revival message was that all Christians shared in the powers that the Spirit's presence imbued. With the Spirit came not just personal salvation, but a commission to act and so *amakholwa* took up their own missions, policed their own moral borders, and claimed authority over their churches. Wilcox believed that consecration should have led to obedience because he still viewed the relationship of the AZM and its Zulu converts as father to child; what he didn't realize was that *amakholwa* believed that their sanctification marked their passage into Christian adulthood, and they fully intended to claim the autonomy that this implied.

That *amakholwa* of the AZM succeeded so remarkably in asserting their spiritual independence speaks both to their faith and to the opportunities that the revivals gave them to demonstrate the depth of their newfound devotion. Over the course of two revival seasons, first from 1896–1897 and then again from 1899–1900, participants committed themselves and their communities to a path that demanded they be first and foremost people of faith. This was far different from their earlier identity, that of a successful *amakholwa* community leading their traditionalist brethren into the civilized world through their own hardworking example, but it offered hope in the face of their failure to achieve this initial ambition.

Of course revival was not the only opportunity for re-imagining the *amakholwa* community. Some sought their fortunes in more radical visions of the civilized African Christian. But for almost a decade it was the revival message that held sway as the dominant response to the challenges of the twentieth century. And for a time it appeared that through sanctification Zulu Christians could actually lay claim to a level of independence unavailable elsewhere. The American missionaries could not deny the spiritual legitimacy *amakholwa* had acquired through revival, and in quick order they handed over control of the churches to the congregations. It was a remarkable development that belied nearly every other development involving Africans in Natal at that time, but it was to be fleeting. Terrified by anything smacking of "Ethiopianism," the Natal government ultimately found ways to restrict the autonomy Zulu Christians briefly made possible for themselves through their faith.

ALTERNATIVE VISIONS OF AN *AMAKHOLWA* FUTURE

Although it was the most enthusiastically embraced, the opportunity to transform their community through revival was only one of several *amakholwa* responses to the troubles they faced with the turning of the century. In the face of increasing marginalization, *amakholwa* were intrigued by, put their hopes and savings in, pursued, and acted on a bewildering array of schemes designed to rescue their rapidly waning fortunes in the wake of Natal being granted responsible government.[4] Some, such as a proposal to remove themselves to a part of the continent where they might be free of European control, proved entirely unworkable. But others, such as a project to buy land in Natal through thinly disguised cooperatives fronted by whites, or an industrial school operated and run by Zulu, were more successful. Minor though they may have been, they offered important alternatives to the *amakholwa* community who chose not to rely on the power of the Holy Spirit offered by revival.

The first of these was perhaps the most radical. Joseph Booth launched his campaign for an African Christian Union (ACU) from Durban on September 7, 1896, with the rousing watchwords "Africa for the African."[5] An English missionary who had spent time in Australia, the United States, Central Africa and elsewhere, Booth believed passionately that African Christians from across the continent needed to unite in creating their own African colony or face the slow loss of their lands and rights to a flood of white settlers. His proposal, as laid out in several Natal newspapers that day, initially centered on an effort to organize enough *amakholwa* capital to purchase a 150,000-acre coffee plantation in Nyasaland.[6] African Christians would operate this plantation, using their profits to buy surrounding land and convert it into tea, cotton, sugar, coffee, and cocoa plantations. A steamer would be bought and eventually Booth hoped to convince the United States to pay for the restoration of black Americans to their African homeland.

For the better part of a year, Booth traveled throughout southern Africa, raising support and encouraging prominent members of the African Christian community to serve on the ACU's board of governors.[7] His success in bringing these men together reflected the central frustration of the *amakholwa* community, the refusal of white settlers to extend to them the rites they believed they had earned through their conversion. Indeed, the published proposal cited a letter that had been carried in one of the local newspapers just two days earlier, in which a settler wrote that not only must Africans be "kept down with a strong hand" but that not a single penny should be given to missions as it was: "No good preaching to these creatures. I hardly think they can have souls."[8] In response, Booth exhorted: "Let the African be his own employer; develop his own country; establish his own manufactures; run his own ships; work his own mines, and conserve the wealth from his labour and his God-given land for the uplifting of the people and the Glory of God." Booth believed his plan would allow African Christians to participate in the benefits of "civilization" without submitting themselves to European rule.

The proposal generated considerable attention throughout Natal, with colonists roundly condemning it, missionaries of the AZM worrying that "His scheme flattered the pride and pandered to the prejudices of the natives," and *amakholwa* greeting it with cautious interest.[9] A meeting was set for the following month at which Booth planned to make a start towards his goal of raising the £75,000 (by selling £1 shares) needed to launch the project. Several hundred *amakholwa* from all parts of Natal gathered one evening to listen to Booth's proposal and while the meeting apparently started out well, someone eventually pointed out the troubling problem that Booth, a white man, proposed to be head of the "Africa for Africans" project.[10] They demanded that he apply his principles by excluding himself. He refused, arguing that without him there would be no plan. The argument raged until, about dawn, Booth lost his temper and apparently insulted the audience, who promptly rose in mass and left the room. Booth, bankrupted by the endeavor, quit Natal for greener pastures and the missionaries of the AZM praised the "good sense of the natives" while worrying about their readiness to "take up with an entire stranger even after being cautioned."[11] Years later, they pointed to Booth's arrival as one of the generators of the Ethiopian movement, blaming him for sowing the seeds of later discontent.[12] Convinced of the necessity for change, however, some looked elsewhere.

When John Dube withdrew his name from consideration for the Inanda pastoral position in 1895 he did so unhappily and when (just before Weavers arrived in Natal) he returned to America backed by funds from his royal family, the AZM worried that the son of their most celebrated pastor might return only to work against their efforts.[13] While in America, Dube finished an education at Oberlin cut short ten years earlier by illness, was ordained a pastor after attending the Union Missionary Training Institute in Brooklyn, and unveiled a plan for his Ohlange Industrial School, an institution inspired by a meeting with Booker T. Washington at Tuskegee.[14]

Before his return to South Africa in 1899, Dube raised some £1,000 for the school, and he soon put this sum to work by building a school house, buying tools, building a shop, and opening the doors for the first semester in August of 1901. And while the mission disapproved of his starting what amounted to a competitive institution to the AZM's Amanzimtoti

Seminary,[15] fears of the Americans over his intentions were largely dispelled soon after his return, when he accepted a call from the church at Inanda to be the pastor of their congregation.[16] Despite his prestige, Dube remained an anomaly, a Zulu pastor not commissioned within the mission and one who frequently proved more occupied with the political and material affairs of his people than their spiritual well-being. His commitment to Ohlange eventually caused a split with Inanda, a situation that also drove a wedge between him and the AZM.

The irony of both the mission's criticism of Dube and his own critique of the AZM, is that they represented a moment frozen in time before the revivals, an ideal long exalted by the mission of a self-sufficient, self-made, muscular Christianity in which faith was welded to status gained through material achievement. Dube believed in this vision and clearly felt that the AZM had failed in the task of producing such Christians. He intended to fill the gap between expectation and reality through his own efforts. An excerpt from his Ohlange School prospectus reads:

> When we have Native Missionaries who will not only preach on Sunday, but teach the people how to live a Christian life of toil six days a week, we shall then see the curtain of darkness lifting. Teach my people trades by which to supply their wants and gratify the desires which their enlightenment creates, and then we shall see a great and grateful people eagerly competing with their brethren in the manufactures and commerce of the world and glorifying the Lord our God.[17]

Although there is no record of it, Dube must have been disappointed when he returned from America to find his people transformed in an entirely different way. Indeed Dube's proselytizing vision, as laid out in Ohlange's prospectus, ran much closer to that of the AZM missionaries than that of Weavers and the *amavoluntiya*. Dube argued that education was *the* path to successfully spreading the Gospel, "because a religion whose teachings would enable him to build a two-room house, manage a plough, make a wagon, raise tea and coffee, grow sugarcane and do many other things, to do which now they know not how, is a potent argument to show the Zulus the superiority of Christianity." It should be noted here that I not believe that revival replaced the worldly ambitions of participants; it did not. But the secular world had been largely uncoupled from the spiritual and instead of conquering the former by lifting themselves up with the latter; *amakholwa* could now employ their faith to both console themselves over the intransigence of settlers, and as an outlet for stifled ambitions.

Yet Dube did not lose his faith in the value of industrial education. He traveled across the AZM throughout 1901–1902, holding meetings and exhorting *amakholwa* to send their children to his school. He bought a press the following year and began printing what would become the most important Zulu language newspaper of the early twentieth century, the weekly *Ilanga Lase Natal* (The Natal Sun). He built a dormitory, hired additional staff (there were three teachers the first year, himself, his wife and a cousin) and continued to trumpet the cause of Zulu Christian industry. Not surprisingly, his activities attracted the attention of the Natal government, which detained him briefly in 1902 as he barnstormed through Natal raising funds for Ohlange from chiefs and warned him against holding "political meetings."[18] But it was not until after the events of 1906, when Dube was arrested for sharply condemning atrocities committed by Natal's defense forces in putting down the Bambatha rebellion, that he became fully politicized. He remained within the Congregational church, but his attentions were almost fully drawn outside of it as he became, for a time, the single most important voice in the early struggle for African rights in Natal and beyond.[19]

Dube, the founder of the South African Native National Congress in 1912, and a man with a vision for black South Africans from across the religious and geographical spectrum, is understandably a more commented upon figure than Dube the man who sought to lead *amakholwa* of the AZM into a positivist future of industrial Christianity. But as late as November of 1905, the latter remained his primary ambition. At a speech given to a local Christian Endeavor Union, Dube opened his comments by noting with gratitude that if it were not for Daniel Lindley carrying the gospel to his father, he himself would probably still be a "half-clad, ignorant, superstitious native."[20] Instead, however, he was the pastor of a congregation of 400 members, "all clothed in European dress and living in good, square houses, with tables, chairs, etc." This vision was not a threat, as so many settlers believed, but rather he argued, a financial benefit to the colony, "for these things must be bought and were chiefly purchased in Durban." Indeed, Dube believed, an industrially trained Zulu workforce would help Natal as there would then, "be no need of either Chinamen or Indians." "Ours," he explained, "is an industrial mission, and our aim is to teach the Zulu that work is honourable and manly."

But while Dube's school educated scores of *amakholwa* children in the following decades, he never realized his vision. Amanzimtoti and Inanda remained the most prominent schools for blacks in Natal and a skilled Christian community did not spread out across the countryside bringing with them the joined Gospels of Jesus and the hammer. The Natal government insured the later would not happen, while the revival provided Zulu Christians with a much different vision of what their faith meant at the beginning of the twentieth century than that which had animated them in the previous century.

TABLE MOUNTAIN, JOHANNESBURG, AND INDEPENDENCE

While the revivals were underway elsewhere in the mission, a different sort of excitement brewed at Table Mountain Mission Reserve. Located near Pietermaritzburg, at a considerable distance from any other AZM station, *amakholwa* at Table Mountain had gone decades without a resident white missionary. At times this had been a source of anxiety, but in 1888 the mission assigned Simungu Shibe, one of their more promising young preachers, to the station and by all accounts he tended his small flock admirably.[21]

Poor and off the beaten path, however, the reserve did not grow wealthy in the decade following Shibe's arrival, and in an 1895 report critical of the use of mission reserve land, the government reserved its harshest criticism of the American missionaries for the state of Table Mountain.[22] Unable to meet the government's request for a missionary to be stationed there, the AZM entered into an agreement in July of 1896, to oversee the reserve with the Natal Congregation Union (NCU), the local organization of white Congregational churches. In what amounted to a ten-year lease, the NCU agreed to work closely with the AZM in running Table Mountain, report regularly, choose native preachers from the AZM's approved list, and hand over the church's annual collection to the *Isithupa*, the leadership committee for the churches composed of representatives from the congregations and the mission whose particular task it was to handle each institution's finances. For the NCU, Table Mountain gave local colonists an introduction to mission work without the trouble of launching their own mission.

The satisfaction that accompanied the agreement soon faded, however, as conflict quickly flared between the Table Mountain congregation and George Pugh, the NCU's first missionary to the station. The Table Mountain congregation, which looked skeptically on being led by a local settler, rejected Pugh and insisted on Shibe's continued leadership, even though he was away from the reserve for the year, taking classes at Lovedale Institute in the Cape Colony. Pugh reacted by insisting on Shibe's removal and his own right, as part of the NCU agreement with the AZM, to appoint another Zulu preacher in his place. Surprisingly, the *Isithupa* approved this request and reassigned Shibe to Noodsberg.[23] Distressed by the unfolding events, the Table Mountain congregation wrote the AZM to express their dismay at being "sold" to the NCU. They were little comforted when the Americans replied that they should now address such appeals to the NCU.[24] When Shibe finally returned from Lovedale at the end of 1896, the congregation urged him not to accept the reassignment, a request he agreed to after some contemplation. From that moment on, he became the public persona of the conflict.

For their part, the American missionaries clearly understood that the situation had been badly handled and they gave Shibe and the congregation at Table Mountain every opportunity to repent, offered up "earnest prayer" for "wisdom in deciding the questions relating to Table Mountain" and turned down several requests by the NCU to have Simungu removed.[25] The mission, concerned that *any* decision was likely to cause conflict with either the congregation or the NCU, resolved to settle the matter through negotiation. When he eventually met with a missionary representative, Shibe noted that his main complaint was similar to that of other AZM preachers, the mission shifted ministers from one place to another without consulting the affected congregations.[26] For a time an amicable resolution seemed possible, but Pugh ratcheted up the hostilities later in the year when, in a bout of frustration, he called in the Natal Mounted Police to have Simungu thrown off of the reserve (an action that was later overruled by the local magistrate), occupied the house Shibe had built, took over his gardens, and forbade the children of those who supported Shibe from attending the mission school.[27]

The congregation made one final appeal to the Americans, calling on them to ordain Shibe. Simungu, they argued, was a true and loving preacher, a man who had taught them much: "Yes, we knew nothing of the word of God; but since he came among us we learnt more. Yes he worked with heart, mind, soul and strength and now is getting on for ten years."[28] They detailed the despotism of Pugh, noted that the mission itself had encouraged them in the letter of self-support circulated the previous year to select their own pastor, and protested against Pugh and the NUC being forced upon them. Besides, they argued, they were members of the AZM and Pugh, as a member of the NUC, did not belong to their church. The appeal fell on deaf ears and for a time the matter appeared stalemated, with Pugh still on the reserve, Shibe still in possession of the loyalties of most of the people, and the mission refusing to choose between the two until events intervened elsewhere.

In early May of 1896, a disturbing letter arrived in the hands of the chairman of the AZM detailing a host of complaints against Reverend Goodenough, the American missionary who had arrived in the city the previous year to administer to the spiritual needs of the booming *amakholwa* population on the Witwatersrand.[29] Goodenough, it alleged, had spent more time looking after business interests in the city than administering to the needs of the congregation. Worse, the letter charged, one of these businesses was a boarding house abutting the church, "swarming with Dutch Bastards and half-cast people" whose rooms were frequent sites of "adultery and licenciousness [sic]." The letter concluded with the congregation calling on the AZM to appoint their Zulu preacher, Fokoti Makanya, as pastor in place of Goodenough. They assured the mission that if Goodenough hadn't misused the funds, recent church collections were sufficient to maintain Makanya as their pastor. They were unsure if they could keep Fokoti, however, as he did not want to send his girl to the school run by Goodenough as it was full of colored children who snubbed her and "put their fingers to their noses when going by her."

The mission, scandalized, hurriedly sent a deputation to investigate. After interviewing both Goodenough and church members, they found that their colleague had "not been careful enough to carry the church with him."[30] The church had expected that Fokoti would be appointed as their pastor, not a preacher, and they had wanted to hire another *amakholwa* preacher but Goodenough had insisted on hiring a teacher to work with the colored children (which the mission approved of even though it clearly vexed the Zulu congregation). They also concluded that Goodenough had reacted with unfortunate anger when the congregation had insisted on "receiving" Fokoti at an official ceremony. Further inflaming matters he had berated the congregation for trying to replace him with Fokoti and shouted out, "I am *umkhulu* [big man] here. I am not under you."

The deputation recommended greater transparency in matters of church funds, urged Goodenough to separate his businesses from his mission responsibility by transferring them to his wife, and wrote to the church expressing gratitude that they turned to the mission to discuss their troubles and looked to the AZM for guidance. But the deputation also cautioned the congregation that they should hold no meetings without Goodenough's knowledge, and that Goodenough's property was a matter for the AZM to deal with (and they were sorry that the congregation did not understand how difficult it was to live in Johannesburg on a small missionary salary), and insisted that only official church members could vote on church affairs.[31]

For a time the matter appeared resolved. Goodenough appointed Fokoti to lead Elandsfontein, one of the Johannesburg outstations, and in the middle of the year a band of revivalists came to Johannesburg. The experience moved Goodenough to breathlessly exclaim: "God has been doing wondrous things for us and the work. We have had and are having glorious meetings, with manifestations of the Spirit of God. Personally I have never had so much joy in the work as now."[32] He concluded, cautiously, that the recent difficulties had passed and the work could now move forward.

But even before Goodenough's note appeared in the Board's newsletter, the Johannesburg congregation shattered its hopeful optimism with a renewed call for the missionary to be replaced by their own man. Their concerns were twofold; they wanted Fokoti to be their pastor, and they believed Goodenough had unjustly put his and the American Board's name on the church's deed of property when it was their money that had been used to purchase the property.[33] As at Table Mountain, they looked to their preacher for leadership and as with Shibe, Fokoti responded by aligning himself with the disaffected congregation. Together they rented a building near the AZM church to hold separate services.[34]

The mission formed another deputation, and on April 24, 1897, they met with several members of the Johannesburg congregation in another attempt to resolve the dispute. The breakaway party explained that they wanted Fokoti as their pastor, that they believed he had been sent to Elandsfontein because of Goodenough's desire to protect his outside interests, that they would sleep on the church's benches in protest until the missionary had agreed to allow them to meet in the church, and that they desired their congregation to be similar to Impapala, aligned with, but largely independent from the AZM. The Johannesburg congregation, Ndeya Makanya explained, was like men on a hunting trip. They had located their game, tracked and cornered it, when suddenly a stranger stumbled along, killed it, and then claimed the beast.[35] Ndeya acknowledged that it may have been legal for the stranger to claim the prize, but it was unjust—as had been Goodenough's handling of matters at Johannesburg.

If the mission understood the moral of the parable, they failed to evidence it, and once again the central concerns of the Johannesburg congregation went unaddressed. The mission refused to remove Goodenough, ordain Fokoti, or sign over the lease of the Johannesburg church. The opposition group continued to meet in a separate location and the matter dragged on through the end of the year. Then in February, Shibe traveled to Johannesburg, met with Fokoti and his congregation, and the two had themselves ordained on the twentieth as the first pastors of the Zulu Congregational Church (ZCC), one of the earliest independent African churches legitimately larger than a single congregation.[36]

The two men approached the moment carefully. They consulted a lawyer who, for the steep sum of £5, mapped out how they should proceed. They had the disaffected congregations of Johannesburg and Table Mountain approve a resolution calling on the two men to be their pastors. The resolution was passed from hand to hand collecting signatures and when the time came, they held an installation ceremony mirroring the AZM's own. Afterward they announced their actions, sending out a circular to the churches of the AZM in which they took pains to explain that their deeds were in accordance with Congregational principles.[37] They wanted their independence, but didn't want to lose the legitimacy that came with membership in a mainline church. The emphasis Table Mountain and Johannesburg placed on cleaving to Congregational practices speaks to the fine line they walked.

Indeed, even as the mission acted to cut off the offending members, the leaders of the ZCC sought to reassure the missionaries of their continued, albeit drastically reduced, allegiance. Shibe wrote several times reminding the mission that his actions were necessitated by the unjust treatment he had received. When the mission responded by calling on him to renounce his "so called" ordination or risk being excommunicated, Shibe responded, "I didn't plan to separate myself from you, if I planned to break away from you I would have joined other congregations."[38] His ordination at Johannesburg was ethical, he argued, because it was the will of the Table Mountain congregation and he couldn't find a law, "that said I should leave a congregation that needs me."[39] Despite the AZM's threats, neither Fokoti nor Shibe backed down, and the mission responded by rejecting their ordinations, and informing the Natal government that they were not performed by any "recognized religious body in South Africa." More immediately harmful to the ZCC, the mission refused to recognize any baptisms, ordinations or marriages performed by the either man, stripping them of ceremonial authority.[40] By the end of 1898, the mission had fully ostracized the breakaway congregations.

REVIVED CHRISTIANS AND THE QUESTION OF ALLEGIANCE

Considering their mounting frustrations, it is remarkable that in the end so few *amakholwa* joined the ZCC. Second and sometimes third generation Christians were often better educated than white settlers, and yet they found fewer and fewer avenues open to their growing ambitions. As Booth and Dube demonstrated there was significant *amakholwa* interest in making their own way. And there was an early movement to do just that. Small ZCC branches sprung up on many of the mission stations soon after the ordinations of Fokoti and Shibe. At Amanzimtoti, Durban, and Umtwalume, the ZCC generated enough enthusiasm to cause the mission concern over the future of its work, and missionaries could not dismiss the movement, as it had Ngidi's, as merely representing those looking for an easy middle ground between Christianity and traditionalism. Shibe, Fokoti, and their followers were serious believers seemingly committed to orthodoxy.[41]

One missionary, at least, believed that were it not for the mission's control over the station lands, "there would be an opposition church on every reserve."[42] This bleak view of the relationship between the mission and its congregations suggests a model of interaction based on simple coercion; African Christians remained in the churches not out of faith but fear. Concerned to protect their already fragile existence, they were little inclined to actions that might get them removed from their valuable plots of mission reserve land. But this model does not survive scrutiny, for the mission never forcibly removed Simungu or Fokoti, or any other ZCC member. *Amakholwa* must have quickly grasped that missionary threats of such action were hollow. Indeed, the mission became so frustrated with their inability to maintain "order" that the following decade they eventually agreed to what had been the unthinkable, signing over their authority on the mission reserves to the Natal government.

If *amakholwa* were not held to the mission by a fear of losing their lands, then what kept them? It is significant, I believe, that those stations that had hosted Weavers responded the least enthusiastically to the ZCC's message of separation. It is not that they did not crave independence, or that revival somehow undermined their political will, rather, following their sanctification, they now felt confident enough in their own legitimacy that they could lay claim to that which they felt was already theirs. The men and women of the AZM had raised the churches, schools, and surrounding buildings with their own hands and now, after undergoing sanctification they stood on the verge of claiming them. Better yet, the American Board had provided what appeared to be the legal document through which they could act, the 1896 letter of self-support. Why throw that away?

Zulu Christians began flexing their newfound spiritual authority almost immediately after the revivals, calling for their own pastors at a rate faster than the mission's theological seminary could produce men the mission felt sufficiently prepared to answer the call.[43] Before the revivals, communities often viewed pastors as an unnecessary financial burden, but in the three years following the end of 1896 the number of Zulu pastors more than doubled, going from four to nine, an unprecedented increase reflecting the community's belief that the time had come to be administered by their own.[44] The mission, shaken by the ongoing struggle with the ZCC and concerned that the calls might be being made merely to satisfy a "love of independence," tried to slow the movement by issuing a series of provisions churches needed to fulfill before calling their own pastor.[45] But these proved surmountable hurdles and by the end of the decade Zulu pastors and preachers ran every AZM church in Natal.[46] Although they didn't realize it yet, the missionaries' days had passed, a reality *amakholwa* moved to formalize.

In 1896, the *Isithupa* had agreed to the mission's plan of handing over Table Mountain work to the NUC and reassigning Shibe to Noodsberg, but by the following year they were challenging the mission's handling of the matter. On March 17, *amakholwa* preachers and pastors gathered by themselves at Amanzimtoti and after much discussion voted to send letters to

Simungu and Fokoti urging them both to hold to their positions.[47] Later, armed with the language of revival and the legalese of the self-support letter, Zulu pastors met with their American counterparts and charged: "We see that you are contradicting your own words that we must take the lead in our church matters. Though we say Simungu must remain at Table Mountain it goes for nothing. We see that it is not the Spirit of God that sends Simungu to Noodsberg. It is Mr. Pugh's will."[48]

Although initially inclined to let this intransigence go, the formation of the ZCC convinced the Americans that they needed to end what they feared was becoming a full-fledged independence movement. At the 1898 NAM held that June in Umvoti, the mission reiterated an earlier warning against any effort by *amakholwa* to do away with them entirely. The American churches, they argued, had sent their delegates to preach the Gospel, raise up churches, and train, ordain and guide a native pastorate to a time when the control of the Americans was no longer needed. But, they continued: "It is evident to us that the time has not come when the American missionaries are no longer needed among you." Recent events, however, suggested to the missionaries, "that there is a feeling among you that the Americans are no longer needed here and may leave and go elsewhere." Should the churches ignore the input of the AZM when ordaining pastors, calling councils, and handling monies, the warning concluded, they risked losing the fellowship of the American churches.

The irony was, however, that by the time this warning was issued the churches had already decided to remain connected to the AZM. At a special meeting prior to the regular NAM, delegates had gathered to discuss the nature of the upcoming meeting. ZCC representatives had arrived and attempted to pass a resolution banning missionaries from participating in the event, but the regular delegates, after praying that: "God's guidance and control might be manifest" not only voted by a large majority to accept the Americans, but turned against the ZCC, demanding an explanation for the group's decision to form their own body.[49] The ZCC's position deteriorated rapidly during the rest of the NAM as delegates first determined that the Table Mountain representatives had arrived without a letter of invitation and therefore could not be recognized as regular members, and then did not allow them to lodge complaints. The limits of the revolution had been reached and while they were willing to push for self-control, most sought this benefit from within the political *and* spiritual legitimacy that the established church provided.[50]

Not surprisingly the continued effects of the previous year's revival infused the conference. Martin Luthuli (the father of Chief Albert Luthuli, the man who would become one of the first presidents of the African National Congress and a Noble Peace Prize winner before his death) began the services by opening his Bible and reading from Acts 19:2 and asked: "Have you accepted the Holy Spirit since you started believing?"[51] Wilcox followed by noting that the meeting should imbue in its participants an increased sense of community and love for each other, just as it should also broaden their minds so they could be led to wisdom and holiness. He cautioned, however, against those who had come simply to visit, or show off their beautiful clothes, and he warned against those there to "destroy everything" and raise a disturbance. "Satan" he warned ominously, "will use those people to destroy the work of the Holy Spirit."

But where Wilcox employed revival language to warn, Jeremiah Langeni who was ordained as pastor over Umvoti at the conference, used it to reach out to all Christians. Reading from Romans 16:16 he noted that Paul commanded: "Great each other in the Holy Spirit," an admonition he argued meant, "we should extend our love to all our Brethren." Mbiya Kuzwayo, the event's official evangelist, led the Sunday services and he, along with many others, filled the church well before dawn in what turned into an impromptu revival. By then revivalism had become so ingrained into *amakholwa* culture, that an altar call yielded quick results with many of those in attendance coming up to confess sins, ask for forgiveness, or seek sanctification. While many admitted to sins ranging from adultery, hatred, the use of tobacco and beer, and even a case of *ukuhlobonga*, perhaps the most noteworthy confession was that given by one of the Johannesburg delegates who confessed to "selfish and egoistic behavior."[52] Those only arriving at 7 A.M., for the first services' appointed hour, were surprised to find the church already full and the assembled in full swing.

THE SECOND COMING:
WEAVERS AND THE REVIVAL OF 1899–1900

In late January of 1899, Weavers addressed the Hephzibah church, bidding them farewell as he set off for a return visit to South Africa.[53] He called on them to join him in taking up missions and complained that that for every 100,000 Christian Americans, only twenty-one volunteered to bring the Gospel to other lands. This failure meant that very few of what he estimated to be the 200,000,000 strong population of Africa had heard the gospel. Anticipating an argument, he agreed that the heathen at home also needed looking after but admonished his audience that: "Their [African] souls are as precious to the Lord as yours are here in America." He warned that every ship carrying a missionary to Africa also carried "barrels and barrels of rum, to damn souls and pull down the Word of God" in its hold and saved his harshest rebuke for English and American officials who answered the pleas of Africans not to ship them any more alcohol with the answer, "We must keep up our governments by blood money!"

Weavers reminded the audience of his previous trip and noted that even as they gathered in Iowa, Christian Zulus were working for the salvation of their people; but they needed help. While in Natal he had urged *amakholwa* to give up wearing fancy clothes and instead devote themselves to spreading the Word. He was pleased that their answer had been, "by the grace of God we will give these things up and help our Zulu brothers." Even better, he could report that they having done so they had then come out with, "a plain pilgrim band [*amavoluntiya*] for God." The coming of the Lord was at hand, he concluded, and he was only happy that he had been chosen to serve as an ambassador for Christ in Africa. He also urged his audience not to delay their mission experience and suffer the same fate he had when a Zulu Christian had approached him and sadly asked: "Why did you not come sooner? Now you are old and your hair is gray." Weavers could only reply: "I do not know why!" Three months later he was back in South Africa, and on April 22, 1899 he arrived in Johannesburg by train from Cape Town.[54]

Once more Weavers arrived in South Africa at a time when most of its inhabitants felt the great dread of looming disaster. This time however, it was not natural causes such as rinderpest (that had succumbed the previous year to a combination of science and its own apocalyptic successes as it burned through available hosts) but from the rumblings of impending war.[55] After the failure of the Jameson Raid in 1896, a farcical attempt by pro-English businessman to instigate rebellion in Johannesburg, Paul Kruger's re-election in 1898 signaled the likelihood of imminent conflict between Britain and the Boer republics. Everyone knew it was coming, it was just a matter of when, where, and what side one would take when the shooting started.[56]

Arriving at the epicenter of this strife, Weavers found to his consternation that the people along the gold reef were too busy making as much money as they could in the face of impending war to concern themselves with the state of their souls. That is not to say he didn't have some success, he spent over a month in Johannesburg and working with Goodenough, Worcester, and several *amakholwa*, he pursued a frantic schedule throughout the city of two and sometimes three-a-day services at which many "found the true way." But after two weeks in the city he wrote: "The city is grand, some fine buildings. Men are making money here. But they do not want the Gospel we preach."[57] A week later he went up into the hills surrounding the city. Looking out across the hive of frantic activity that was each of the mine compounds, he observed mournfully, "Oh how busy they are for the things of this life. But no thought for the life to come."[58]

Of Weavers' visit, a noticeably disappointed Goodenough reported that while the Sunday services had been excellent, and many Christians had been "quickened" (a state in which the already sanctified felt a renewed urgency over their spiritual lives), attendance during the week was "not as good as it should have been."[59] Weavers, it seems, had learned a hard lesson; the urban areas of South Africa offered tremendous potential for revival, but only with great difficulty and a different set of skills than he possessed. Revivals in the countryside were not hampered by the constraints of the workday or municipal laws that forced Africans off of the streets early in the evening.[60] In America, revivalists such as Billy Sunday and D. L. Moody were perfecting techniques to skirt these urban problems, building up tension and offering salvation in convenient evening sessions.[61] But Weavers represented an older, rural revival tradition, and it is not surprising that after receiving several invitations, he returned to Natal and more familiar ground away from the speed of the city.

His first stop, responding to a request from Pugh, was at Table Mountain.[62] Remarkably, Weavers makes no mention of the discord that had recently rent the *amakholwa* congregation there, focusing instead on several faith healings that occurred during his two weeks, and a sustained effort to convince a local chief interested in Christianity to give up his wives. The healings were dramatic successes, the effort to bring the chief into the Christian flock, despite the man's stated earnest desire, was not and it seems likely that Weavers, who had himself felt justified in breaking away from a mainline church in America, found nothing worth commenting on or acting upon in Simungu's defection.

The congregation(s) at Table Mountain, fully prepared by their experience with Wilcox and Kuzwayo, responded eagerly to the event. The church was often full, many of the meetings were "grand" affairs, and a notable enthusiasm, missing in the Johannesburg meetings, filled the air. Believers danced, rolled on the floor and shouted out in exuberance when they were "filled with the Spirit." After one service the congregation marched out of church with their hands in the air, singing and praising God as they went. For weeks revival services, sometimes as many as three a day and lasting up to six hours each, took up much of their time. Before he left he urged them not to let the experience end with his departure and to go out and preach to the surrounding peoples; a charge many accepted, coming up to him later and saying they were "willing to go where the Spirit led them."[63]

From Table Mountain, Weavers accepted a return invitation to Inanda, where for he held a series of large meetings with the church and smaller ones with the girls in the seminar. Here, as at other churches he returned to, the maturation of the Christian community into the ways of Holiness was evident. While many came forward at Inanda to confess their sins, undergo consecration, and receive the Holy Spirit in sanctification, most of the congregation had already experienced these changes and were more likely to participate in the quieter act of witnessing to God's active role in their lives. These "testaments," as they were called, can and should be read as the confident assertion of the *amakholwa* community in their own righteousness. Sanctified two years earlier, they continued to claim this spiritual statues and in doing so felt not so much a need for confession, as an outlet to thank God for what he had wrought in their lives. Christians not only claimed their continued sanctification, but also its accompanying privileges. The missionaries at Inanda and elsewhere noticed this phenomenon and remarked that there were "less emotional manifestations" of this revival then previously and that the "already saved" were instead quickened and brought to a "more established faith."[64] When Weavers and Mbiya Kuzwayo visited Umzumbe in October of 1899, the missionary there reported that unlike the first revival, "there was not so much confession of gross sin, as the felt need of holiness in every detail of the life."[65] Here was the *amakholwa* community grappling with what their Christianity now meant to them.

Following Inanda, Weavers revisited Durban in early July, attending what must have been one of the first "Holiness conventions" in South Africa. Afterwards, he made his way with Wilcox to Esidumbini and Noodsberg, where that year's NAM was to be held. Continuing a tradition launched by Mbiya Kuzwayo the previous year, *amakholwa* pastors and preachers met for devotional services prior to the start of the NAM. This year's meeting, held at Esidumbini, began on July 16 and Weavers preached to a packed house of Zulu leaders for the next three days. Many at the meetings "got all broke up" by the experience and the last one concluded with a long service of joyful testaments by these preachers and pastors to the "power of God in their lives."[66] They could now travel to Noodsberg confident, like pilgrims of old, that they would arrive at their destination purified and powerful enough to overcome obstacles to their spiritual duties, whether these took the form of missionaries or the ZCC.

At Noodsberg, Weavers served as the 1899 NAM evangelist and conducted a series of meetings to full and enthusiastic congregations. In many ways, these annual affairs had long reflected an idealized *amakholwa* identity; how they wanted to see themselves and how they wanted the outside world to view them. In previous years this had meant elaborate and expensive preparations by the hosting community and regal attire donned by the delegates. While those at the 1899 NAM no doubt wore their best outfits to the event, these material signs of their success had taken backstage in recent years to demonstrations of their sacred lives. As one of the missionaries in attendance at Noodsberg noted, "the most important aspect of the Native Annual Meeting was the deep spiritual tone that prevailed throughout."[67] In this way participants announced to themselves and the AZM that they were prepared, and expected, to take on full responsibility for *their* churches. It was with this confidence that they again rejected an overture by the ZCC, admonished them for creating factionalism, and renewed their ties to the AZM while insisting that the missionaries find a way to reconcile with the breakaway congregations.[68] A new era had arrived in which the future direction of the churches would now be dictated not by Americans, but by their *amakholwa* congregations.

A week later Weavers returned to Mapumulo. Working once again with Mbiya Kuzwayo, Weavers held a series of meetings, including one just for Christian women, that grew in strength as the week passed. As Kuzwayo's base, the people of Mapumulo well understood the ingredients of a good revival and Weavers happily recorded that by the end of his stay services like those from his previous visit, with expressive and dramatic bouts of consecration and sanctification, were underway. But here also, the congregation took the opportunity, on Weavers' final day at Mapumulo, to voice their testaments and declared the fitness of their community before God and Man.[69]

For the next month, Kuzwayo traveled with Weavers, once again serving as his interpreter.[70] They crisscrossed their way through the northern stations and Durban before making their way to the AZM stations in southern Natal. It was the first time Weavers visited either Ifafa or Umtwalume and events here proceeded much as they had elsewhere during Weavers' first tour of Natal. At Ifafa, twice-daily services began early in the morning and frequently lasted well into the night. By the third day, the church was full and the congregation confessed a multitude of sins; disobedience to parents, lying, lust "in many forms," theft, adultery, a stabbing, and even a murder were all revealed. Charles Ransom, the missionary overseeing the southern stations, was particularly shocked by the actions of a few enterprising *amakholwa*, who confessed that they had been turning a profit by brewing and selling alcohol to *amabhinca*.[71] Worse, these women (there gender was not specified but as noted earlier brewing was almost entirely a women's affair among Zulu, Christian or otherwise) sinned twice in one stroke by both peddling their wares and doing so on the Sabbath. Some needed a great deal of time to make their confessions. The youth of the station, Ransom sadly reported, "frequently acknowledged they had broken all the commandments." One former Christian, who was "known to be a polygamist, thief, liar, and seller of love-charms" and who had been put into prison for fighting, stood up and confessed all, then accepted his sanctification with the promise to give up all his old ways.

Sanctification healed their souls and empowered them to strengthen their community. As elsewhere, old enmities were aired, forgiveness sought, and with much joy, the wrongs buried. Several leading members of the church, bitter enemies for years, confessed their sins, "one with tears and agonizing cries and confession of being a servant of the devil," and then forgave each other publicly. One after another plead guilty to backbiting and hatred, cried out to God for forgiveness, and having found it, rejoiced at being both individually cleansed and communally unified. "Love breathed over the community," Ransom reported, as the revivalists departed for Umtwalumi.

While geographically distant, this station stood at the crossroads of events shaping *amakholwa* identity. Always poorer than stations such as Inanda or Groutville, residents at Umtwalumi had taken earlier than others to migrant labor, working in the cities to acquire capital that they generally turned into cattle back home. Rinderpest swept much of this away in 1898 and the looming prospect of war threatened their ability to recover from the disaster. Of all the American stations outside of Table Mountain and Johannesburg, the ZCC made the greatest inroads here. Indeed, when Fokoti died unexpectedly in 1898 the Johannesburg congregation managed to lure away Umtwalume's pastor, Sunguza Nyuswa, to take Fokoti's place, much to the dismay of both the AZM and his congregation. That most of those in the church did not go over to the ZCC with Nyuswa probably speaks to the skills of Gardiner Mvuyana, who worked with Kuzwayo as Weavers' interpreter in 1896–1897 and served as an interim pastor at Umtwalume following Nyuswa's departure. He was also assisted by a particularly active band of *amavoluntiya* who had based themselves there after the first round of revivals.

After two years of *amavoluntiya* services, Umtwalume's congregation understood the dynamics of revival and lively services broke out the day after Weavers' arrival. Accompanied by a rash of minor miracles (illnesses healed, the removal of small infirmities, lameness cured, and, in one particularly dramatic case, an evil spirit cast out) the experience of consecration and sanctification proved even more intense here than at Ifafa.[72] For nearly two weeks the residents of Umtwalume and the surrounding outstations underwent revival. Those who initially chose not to attend, particularly ZCC members, soon yielded to pressure (*amavoluntiya* members showed "a great fervor in going from house to house" to stir interest for the event) and the church filled. Drawn to the spectacle, *amakholwa* from the surrounding outstations made their way over the hills to participate and by Weavers' last Sabbath at Umtwalumi, over 600 attended a service that filled the church to overflowing.[73] The congregation celebrated their new lives as sanctified Christians by taking over two hours for some 150 *amakholwa* to deliver "heartfelt testimonies—with such joy in their faces and such an earnest ring to their words as to fill the house with praise. One felt as if a great light was breaking on the multitudes."[74] The next day the community gathered one last time with the revivalists, built a bonfire and burned all those items they had lain upon the altar during Weavers' stay: snuffboxes, tobacco, pipes, Western medicines, charms, armbands, love medicines, and other traditional potions. Together they sang *Inkosi uJesu, Sitande, Sikenze Imihla, ngemihla*: "Let us give thanks to the Lord Jesus, Love Him, Serve him, day by day."[75]

While his trip to Ifafa and Umtwalume proved the most remarkable of his experiences from his second tour of South Africa, several further events are worth noting. In November, Weavers accepted an invitation from the mission to teach a short course on Holiness to the theology students at Amanzimtoti. Taking them to a waterfall one day, the woods another, and a nearby hilltop a third, Weavers spelled out his views on consecration and sanctification, divine healing, and the millennium using only the Bible as his reference.[76] As a generation that had already internalized Weavers' revival techniques, these future preachers and pastors quickly grasped the fundamentals of this theology and it became a central feature of *amakholwa* Christianity in the decades to follow—it was these men most fully involved in the naturalization of the faith that followed.[77]

Finally, while most of the missionaries welcomed Weavers when he first returned, many soon fell out with him over the issue of divine healing, belief in which the Holiness minister held as a final step for those who "were willing to take the Lord at his word."[78] Kilbon, whose son was studying to become a doctor, was one of those who rejected this practice and he and several other missionaries spent several days in the middle of December arguing unsuccessfully with Weavers for the necessity of Western medicines after the revivalist taught a course on the biblical basis of healing through prayer to the *amakholwa* seminarians.[79] The disagreement did not end the relationship, but it clearly dimmed the enthusiasm many of the Americans felt for the Holiness preacher.[80]

Weavers spent his last two months in Natal crisscrossing the countryside, revisiting stations for second and even third times. He received numerous requests from other missions for his services, but stuck with the familiar, working almost exclusively with either AZM or Holiness churches.[81] But these kept him busy enough. When the South African war finally began in October, he was forced to curtail several trips and news in late January that Boer forces had crossed the Thukela cost him his interpreter when a concerned Kuzwayo returned home to look in on his family, and then accepted a position as "acting pastor" of Mapumulo.[82] In his last weeks in South Africa, Weavers passed quickly through Umtwalume, Ifafa, Umvoti, Inanda,

Imfume, and Durban; as in his previous visit these took on the nature of a victory lap, with *amakholwa* offering up their testimonies as both thanks to God, and an audible statement of the purity and power they felt they had achieved through sanctification. Any doubt over their fitness to run their own churches lingering after the first revivals was burned away in the fires of the second. When Weavers boarded the steamer for home, on February 24, 1900, he left behind an *amakholwa* community confidently claiming the fruits of their spiritual labors. [83]

CLAIMING THEIR OWN

As during Weavers' previous tour, the revival that began with his visit did not end with his departure. *Amakholwa* once again proved not only willing, but often eager, to first perpetuate the experience at home and then spread it elsewhere. While in 1897 Mapumulo's *amavoluntiya* had been revival's most vigorous proponents, the force behind the work in the years after 1900 came from Umtwalume's *amavoluntiya*. Over thirty strong, they repeatedly ventured out, often no farther than nearby outstations, but as their reputation for rousing revivals grew, other churches began inviting them to conduct services and they trekked as far as Amanzimtoti.[84] Imfume, where they arrived in May of 1901, proved typical of the revivals they launched; consecration and sanctification that resulted in breathtaking confessions, periods of spiritual drama, and the final "conquest" of Christ. They left only after encouraging the revived church to follow their example. The Imfume congregation, like others, "were greatly stimulated, and became more earnest about preaching in the kraals. They no longer waited for Sunday, but sallied forth by two and threes on weekdays."[85] Evangelism had become a central concern for revived Christians.

The Umtwalume *amavoluntiya* made the most dramatic application of one of the group's central practices, renewing "backslidden" or flagging individual *amakholwa* and communities, *amavoluntiya* elsewhere steadfastly labored away with smaller, less publicized efforts. When Kuzwayo resigned his pastorate following the end of the war, Mapumulo went without a pastor for nearly four years. Instead of sinking into moral negligence as missionaries feared, their *amavoluntiya* kept the congregation's Holiness fires burning and the mission noted with pleasure that not only was the church "drawing from the heathen population outside a good number of converts" but also maintaining its own "strictness of discipline, not even snufftaking being allowed in the church members."[86] Indeed the mission directly linked Mapumulo's moral state with the earlier revivals, writing: "It has not yet lost the spiritual uplift gained in the great revival of 1896 under Elder

Weavers' faithful labors."[87] At Durban, in the years following the second revival, some thirty volunteer preachers gathered every Sunday morning before dawn, held an hour of preparation through prayer, counsel, and testimony, and then spread out into every corner of the city, holding services in barracks, backyards, and the "kaffir quarters" of small businesses.[88] They returned to the church before the 9:00 P.M. curfew to report on their activities, discuss the messages they delivered, and hand in any tithes received. A clearly impressed missionary noted that in the one exhausting Sunday he had traveled with them, one such band of *amavoluntiya* had preached to well over 2,000. "Remember," he urged his readers, "they do not receive a penny. These men have been at their daily tasks right through the week. It means something for them to be up just as early Sunday as on other days."[89]

For most, being an *amavoluntiya* member may not have involved the same level of sacrifice, but it still demanded considerable dedication. At Ifafa a "humble, consecrated band" of eight carried forward the revival work, buying a stock of Bibles and hymnals and dividing the surrounding area into districts to ensure each area had the opportunity to hear the word of God.[90] At Inanda, a small group of women ventured forth weekly into the surrounding hills. At their services each took turns giving their testimonies. "I wish you could have heard us women!" enthused a missionary wife who accompanied them on one of their trips, "Each in turn feeling that we had brought Jesus, to give Him to them for life and eternity."[91] At Amanzimtoti in the years after the South African War, "an earnest band" of young boys continued the tradition begun by their predecessors nearly a decade earlier, waking early on Sundays to range far from the school with the revival message, their principal proudly noting that they had "been the means of bringing many into the light."[92]

Throughout the mission *amavoluntiya* played a critical role in maintaining and occasionally extending the reach of the Holiness message; that sanctification, a state of absolute grace in which equality with all other Christians in sacred matters was assured, was had by simply confessing sins and giving over ones all to God. By 1901 the mission estimated that north of Durban alone, some 150 "volunteer lay preachers" were "spreading the knowledge of the truth in the by-ways of all the stations."[93] And every year they grew, for the revival perpetuated itself through a continuous cycle of conversion and renewal. Mbiya Kuzwayo held a revival at Emputyani, an outstation of Amanzimtoti, in 1902 and the congregation not only grew by a third, with twenty-two new members, but a group of "very energetic lay preachers" emerged from the revival frustrated that *amavoluntiya* from Amanzimtoti already claimed the nearby area as their province, leaving Emputyani without a field for their newfound zeal in witnessing to the power of Jesus. They appealed, unsuccessfully, to Amanzimtoti, asking their "mother" church to surrender some of the area.[94] In half a decade, evangelism had gone from a relative rarity among *amakholwa*, to a competitive hunt for new spheres of work.

THE ROLE OF MISSIONARIES IN A REVIVED CHURCH

The ambivalence many missionaries felt following the first revivals in 1896–97 deepened after Weavers' departure in 1902. They believed in its efficacy in deepening their congregation's moral lives, but many also grew increasingly wary of how it had shaped the churches and how it continued to do so through the work of the *amavoluntiya*. Many disapproved of the strong emotions revival generated, fearing that these were quickly forgotten, but they also worried that Congregational usages were being ignored just as the churches claimed their independence, pushing aside the missionaries. Frederick Bridgman's visit to Imfume, following the revivals of the Umtwalume band, offers a revealing glimpse at the expectations and worries generated on both sides of the pulpit by the religious awakening. Arriving in July he expressed his amazement at the depth of the continuing commitment of the congregation to their renewed faith, pleasure at their willingness to take the message off of the station, and surprise at the record levels of tithing.[95]

But during a Sunday service, just as Bridgman began reading his sermon, a "heathen" women dressed in an animal skin petticoat rose in the back of the church, walked slowly up the aisle until she reached the pulpit and , "shot a bare arm straight above her head, and pointing heavenward said, with a clear voice '*Ngiketa iNkosi*' (I choose the Lord.)"[96] A startled Bridgman, who never worked with Weavers and was clearly uncomfortable with the altar calls that made up the heart of a revival service, asked her a few questions probing the depth of her faith, encouraged her to seek further training in an inquirer's class, and sent her back to her seat. Starting again he worked his way through a few more sentences when another woman stood up. Wearing only a blanket covering her from shoulders to knees, her hair carefully strung with blue and amber beads, the young woman also marched up the aisle, stood before the altar and proclaimed, "*Ngiketa iNkosi.*" Annoyed by the interruption, Bridgman promised to give the matter further attention in the future and sent her back to her seat. Twice more, Zulu looking to "choose the Lord" interrupted his sermon and he handled them similarly; a response that after their recent excitement the congregation at Imfume must have found puzzling. Later, when writing of the matter, he justified his actions by noting that there were many cases in past revivals were converts had answered an altar call only to later backslide and after months of hearing only exhortation, he believed the people "now needed instruction."

Bridgman's reaction reflects the angst missionaries felt as they searched for a role in the revived churches. By and large they now accepted that their time of actively shaping the daily lives of individual *amakholwa*, or even the weekly affairs of the churches, had passed. In its place, however, they insisted on their right to serve as supervisors, school principals, and the keepers of heterodoxy. Arguing that the mission needed to concentrate its forces on the cities and the schools, the principal of Amanzimtoti urged his fellow missionaries to think beyond the mission's initial function for, "The second stage has come, when our chief work is to reach the people through trained leaders."[97] Another acknowledged that while the Americans believed *amakholwa* would be better off submitting to mission control, this was no longer likely, and while this worried the AZM, he now had confidence in the religious state of Zulu Christians and believed they would develop "a character of their own, rather than an imitation of American Christianity.[98]

As part of their narrowing responsibilities, missionaries looked to reign in what they saw as the undereducated excesses of the *amavoluntiya* who, without training, claimed both prophetic abilities and doctrinal leadership. The missionary in charge of the theological school was dismayed in 1900, to find that, "There seems to be a strange idea popular, that men with the Bible in their hands have no need to go to school to learn what it means."[99] His concern was echoed later that year when, at their annual meeting, missionaries agreed that in matters of church doctrine, "It is a time of much irregularity and of presumption on the part of novices."[100] The mission encouraged Zulu pastors to hold Bible studies with lay preachers, conducted their own trainings, and laid down restrictions on the duties of volunteers in the churches.[101] However, when missionaries met with Zulu pastors to discuss the issue of limiting *amavoluntiya* activities, they were forced to admit that no law in the Bible restricted certain duties to ordained men but that it was part of the policy of the Congregational church that services be led by those under ordination.[102] And while the mission agreed that it was the "duty of all Christians to spread the word of God and the spirit of revival" they also strongly urged the pastors to standardize *amavoluntiya* by meeting with them monthly, taking reports and discussing each group's successes and failures.[103] After a lengthy conversation, the pastors agreed to the Congregational usage of the benediction and promised to discuss the second matter at the upcoming NAM. But *amakholwa* delegates made no changes then or later, and *amavoluntiya* continued to act as an unregulated, albeit very enthusiastic, semi-official arm of Zulu Christianity.

MAKING AN INDEPENDENT ZULU CHURCH

In less than a half a decade of revival, the number of church members in the AZM had doubled, as had the number of lay preachers. In 1896 there were 1,947 full members of the AZM churches, 144 lay preachers and 148 different locations the mission recognized as preaching places. Four years later the census of 1900 counted 3,256 full members, 287 lay preachers and 205 preaching places.[104] This dramatic increase, combined with the sheer force of faith *amakholwa* demonstrated during the revivals, forced the mission to accept the call for a local leadership of Zulu pastors and preachers. Despite scattered missionary resistance, by the end of the second series of revivals *amakholwa* had largely secured a significant degree of freedom in managing their own churches and outstations. Emboldened by this success, Zulu Christians looked to consolidate their position by claiming some authority at the mission-wide level as well. They wanted not just a say in mission policy, as the AZM had recently permitted, but to direct it. The issue that tested this desire was the mission's relationship with the ZCC and at a meeting in June of 1899, Zulu pastors urged the mission to reconcile with the ZCC.[105] The Americans resisted; they wanted to let the movement "run its course and come to an end" and had had no contact with the breakaway body in eighteen months.[106] After a short dispute, the Zulu pastors won the day and while the mission believed such an effort would be "worthless" they agreed to send two of their own to accompany an *Isithupa* delegation appointed at the NAM the following month.

The first meeting between the AZM and ZCC proved difficult to arrange for the war made the Johannesburg branch of the ZCC temporarily homeless. For several months prior to the war's outbreak, a steady stream of refugees had poured into Natal. Arriving from the Witswatersrand, most were determined to both be clear of the city before the shooting started and to avoid conscription as porters in Afrikaner commandos. One of those fleeing the city was Pastor Nyuswa, who took shelter with friends at Imfume before the conflict started. It soon became clear that Nyuswa's presence at Ifmume was a fortunate circumstance, for, after several false starts, it took a threat to forbid him from attending communion to arrange a conference between the various parties.[107]

The two groups finally met in Durban on November 14, 1899. "With the help of the divine Spirit" and much to the missionaries' surprise, the meeting proved a success.[108] A subcommittee was formed to draw up a paper documenting what stood in the way of union or at least cooperation, and another meeting was called for January 30, 1900. The subcommittee's report was rejected in favor of a separate scheme put forward by Nyuswa,

who detailed the exact grievances of the ZCC and proposed a plan for unifi-
cation. Working from an idiom readily familiar to every Zulu, the displaced
pastor urged those present to think of the American Board as a kraal encir-
cling many cows, one of which, the AZM, had begat a calf, the ZCC, which,
while within the protection of the Board and a child of the Zulu mission,
was its own unique, and independent, being.[109] The days of an American
missionary "behaving like a bishop of the Anglican church" should end, he
declared, and each congregation should direct its own affairs independent
of missionary involvement.[110] Another meeting was scheduled for March to
give both sides time to review the document.

After considering Nyuswa's proposal, the mission worried that it "aimed
at entire independence" leaving missionaries as mere figureheads, props
against future threats from the settler government.[111] When Zulu pastors
gathered with the Americans for their semi-annual meeting, the matter was
discussed in great detail, and while the pastors "manifested a loyal spirit
toward the Mission and were hearty in their expressions of the same," they
also did not hesitate to express their "desire to have more responsibility
and reach a more complete independence as soon as possible."[112] Remarkably, considering the issues being discussed, the meeting proved to be
one of great warmth. Inspired by the recent revivals, the two groups held
a series of devotional meetings, gave their individual testaments, joined
together in prayer, and even socialized together. They parted with the
Americans reassured of the spiritual fitness of their Zulu counterparts, the
Zulu pastors confident in the coming changes, and both sides filled "with
hope for the future."[113]

Instead of rejecting Nyuswa's plan, the Americans made several small
adjustments: emphasizing the interconnectedness of churches along Congregational lines, restricting "absolute" independence by positioning
themselves as the spokesmen of the ABM, and maintaining their continued
rights over the mission reserve properties. But the fundamentals remained
untouched; Zulu congregations, working together, would be free to call,
dismiss, and reassign pastors as they chose, these pastors would be answer-
able to each other and their congregations first, and the Americans would
be largely restricted to the roles of mentors, councilors, and teachers. At
the March meeting, ZCC representatives disputed some of the changes to
Nyuswa's proposal, but *amakholwa* on the committee from the AZM clearly
understood the remarkable degree of autonomy they stood on the verge of
acquiring and carefully shepherded both sides through several difficult moments to a mutual agreement.[114]

One final delay remained, as the various parties presented the finalized
document to their constituents for ratification. The Americans passed it

with little trouble; *amakholwa* of the AZM did so with much fanfare by voting to "extend the right hand of fellowship" to the ZCC during that year's NAM, but the ZCC split over the issue.[115] The group had always been only loosely connected and unlike Nyuswa, who had only recently become pastor at Johannesburg, Shibe had fought a long and sometimes bitter battle with the AZM over his right to remain at Table Mountain.[116] His congregation also appears to have diminished following the revivals of Wilcox/Kuzwayo and Weavers, with all but the most hardcore returning to the AZM fold. Not surprisingly, Shibe's faction chose not to follow the lead of the Johannesburg congregation and remained unreconciled.[117]

The various parties met at the AZM chapel in Durban (which, like many other properties outside of the original mission stations, went into a joint mission/*amakholwa* trust as part of the agreement) on September 11, 1900, and for several days they hammered out the final details.[118] Nyuswa, it was decided, had never been released from his appointment at Umtwalume and was to return as their pastor, the ZCC's baptisms, marriages, and other sacred acts were endorsed, and the tricky business of deciding who was a member of the Johannesburg church and whose membership now reverted to the home congregation they had left to join the ZCC was tabled for another day. The dominant topic, however, was choosing a new name, for it was clear to *amakholwa* that "American Zulu Mission" was no longer an appropriate title. Nyuswa argued forcibly for retaining "Zulu Congregational Church," explaining: "This shows the background of who owns the church. It has been named by the Zulus for the Zulus."[119] But his reasoning was exactly why others at the Durban gathering found the name objectionable, arguing that it was a "tribal" title without wider appeal. Someone suggested African Congregational Church (ACC) instead, and after a short discussion the assembled voted in favor of its use.[120]

Mbiya Kuzwayo and several others were drafted to write up the future constitution. But for the time, a governing body of five members was chosen to run the ACC, two from the ZCC, two *amakholwa* from the old churches of the AZM, and one missionary.[121] As one of the final orders of business, the delegates drafted a note to the Natal government informing them of the new church body and asking that the general manager of the railways grant the reduced "minister" rate to the pastors and preachers of the ACC. These matters settled, reconciliation was formerly announced and those gathered celebrated by praying and singing hymns together. In only a half a decade, *amakholwa* of the ACC had successfully completed a remarkable revolution; they transformed the nature of their practiced Christianity, forced missionaries to recognize the new realities, and laid claim to the workings of their churches in nearly every form from top to bottom. By all appearances, a new era had begun.

In writing of these events, the mission recognized the extent to which Zulu Christians had claimed their autonomy, referring to the ACC constitution as an *amakholwa* "Magna Carta in matters ecclesiastical" and noting that "a change amounting to a revolution" had taken place in the Zulu churches.[122] "At first threatening disaster," they wrote, "it has with wise dealing resulted in a much larger degree of responsibility for the conduct of its own affairs being assumed by the native church, thus freeing the missionary for wider service."[123] This was, perhaps, the best spin missionaries could put on their losing power. For *amakholwa* it meant much more. Ten years earlier their community had threatened to break apart under the weight of scandal, disasters, and defections. Burdened by an identity based on an idyllic Christian agrarian community that eluded them as circumstances pushed it further and further out of reach, they had grasped onto revival as an answer to multiple crises. If they could not thrive in the secular world, at least Weavers' message promised absolute success in the sacred. In sanctification, they found a theology that allowed them to assume the mantle of sacred leadership. For decades, missionaries had told them that they were not quite fully Christian, not quite moral or pure enough to assume full authority of their religious affairs. Sanctification provided *amakholwa* with the authority to proclaim their equality through actions that missionaries could not deny. African congregations throughout South Africa made similar claims of independence at this time, but almost invariably these ended in Ethiopianism, the breaking away of congregations from their parent mission churches (a phenomenon discussed in greater detail below). This did not occur in the American churches because the revivals allowed *amakholwa* congregations to claim the empowerment of the Holy Spirit and in doing so demonstrate to all their fully realized Christianity.

RECOGNITION AND REFORM

In 1903 a delegation of the ABM's leadership arrived in South Africa. This was the first time such a committee had come to Natal and they departed, after touring the stations, deeply impressed by what they witnessed, holding up the ACC as a model for their missions elsewhere.[124] Certainly the ACC made its presence felt. A deputation from the newly titled body met the Board delegates soon after they docked, and at each of their stops the Americans met with local church leaders who identified themselves first with the ACC and then with the Board. They regarded the AZM as a sister organization and they urged the Board to impress on its missionaries this new relationship of shared authority.[125]

Where the ABM leadership was truly impressed, however, was with the fervor of *amakholwa* religious celebration. At Mapumulo they received a rousing welcome, the people packing the church for meetings with the deputation who left feeling that the congregation "furnishe[d] an excellent illustration of the fact that a native church can, in good degree, conduct its own affairs and prosecute its own activities, holding its people together and making some advances upon the surrounding heathenism."[126] At Umtwalume, hundreds gathered, overflowing the church and leaving the Board delegates awed by the "devoted, prayerful, and energetic" actions of a "large band of young people calling themselves 'volunteers.'"[127] On the last day of the 1903 NAM, some 2,000 Zulu delegates gathered to celebrate the Sabbath with the Board deputation. An experience that led them to write: "No one could fail to see that the gospel of Jesus Christ had secured a mighty hold among the Zulu people."[128] They departed South Africa believing that the Board's work in Natal was drawing to an end because, "today all the Zulu churches are presided over by Zulu pastors and all the station schools, with 4,000 pupils, are taught by native teachers under the occasional supervision of missionaries."[129] In just over half a decade Zulu Christians had translated the spiritual power of revival into almost complete autonomy.

Missionaries of the AZM were forced to face a similar conclusion, and acknowledge their own growing irrelevance. In a wistful, almost despondent report, one of the missionaries wrote:

No other department of missionary work offers so much practical instruction on the text, "He must increase, but I must decrease" as does Supervision work. The withdrawal of the missionaries from the work will began at the point of Supervision and already the door is opening before him for his departure. Even now he must report the work of others and wonder how much his personal effort has counted for establishing the kingdom.[130]

There is no doubt, of course, that missionaries were vital in introducing Christianity to the continent, but as it should now be equally clear, Africans needed to experiment with and adapt Christian theology to their own spiritual, cultural, and political realities. Missionaries of the AZM realized this truth as early as 1903 and were clearly preparing themselves for the end of their mission. But even as the mission envisioned its imminent withdrawal from Natal, the white government was pursuing policies that ultimately kept the American missionaries in the area much longer than they or their Zulu converts could have anticipated.

THE NATAL GOVERNMENT AND AFRICAN
CHRISTIANS AS "THE THREATENING EVIL"[131]

Through most of the two revivals, the activities of *amakholwa* evangelists
such as those of the *amavoluntiya*, had gone largely ignored and unregulated by Natal officials. But sometime before June of 1900, Solani,
a resident of neighboring Pondoland and a Christian, crossed into Natal
and began proselytizing. Like so many other African lay preachers and revivalists then spreading the Word, his presence would have gone uncommented upon by government officials except that he was heard preaching
that the Bible "said the black man ought to have nothing to do with the
white man and should therefore govern himself."[132] Any mention of independence set off alarm bells at Natal's Secretary for Native Affairs (SNA)
office and after a hurried investigation, a local magistrate reported that
Solani belonged to a church calling themselves *amakutshe*, or Ethiopians.
After several years of fermenting in the Cape Colony, "Ethiopianism" had
seemingly arrived in Natal.

The Ethiopian movement was not really a movement. That is to say
that while British colonial authorities feared a larger conspiracy of African
Christians breaking away from their home churches to establish independent congregations and then act together to pursue secular independence,
no such unified action ever occurred. Instead, throughout the history of
the Church in southern Africa, a number of Christians grew frustrated
with their inability to advance up denominational hierarchies and left,
carrying (as in the case of Shibe and Fokoti discussed in the previous
chapter) some, if not often all, of their congregations with them. Not
until 1892, however, did this phenomenon have a name, derived from
Mangena Mokone, a Methodist pastor in Pretoria, naming his breakaway
body the "Ethiopian Church" after a prophetic line in Psalms proclaiming, "Princes shall come out of Egypt; Ethiopia shall soon stretch out her
hands unto God" (Psalms 8:31).[133] Later in the decade, when Mokone's
congregation fractured over the issue of aligning with the American-based
African Methodist Episcopal Church, a number of the schismatic bodies
also took "Ethiopia" in the title and this seems to have convinced colonial
officials that this was a wider conspiracy. Whatever the name, government
officials soon became obsessed with stamping it out in the sundry forms
they feared it might take. So when Solani entered Natal they viewed him
not so much as an individual rabble-rouser, but part of something much
more ominous. After a year of spying on Solani (using native informers)
the government of Natal refused to renew his visa and he was thrown out
of the colony after being charged with doing nothing more than "preaching sedition under the cloak of religion," an accusation that became the

basis of government complaints against many African preachers, independent or otherwise.[134] From this moment on the government regarded African evangelization in any form as potentially dangerous to their larger interests.

On October 10, 1902, Frederick Moor, who as SNA also served as the acting head of the Natal Native Trust, sent a letter to the AZM detailing a new policy in response to the Ethiopian "threat." "The Natal Native Trust (NNT)" it was advised, "is unable to permit the establishment of missions on location land unless they are placed under the control of a permanent resident white missionary."[135] This was the opening salvo in an effort by the government to reign in both groups like the *amavoluntiya*, who wandered the countryside largely unregulated, but also the ACC which had only recently claimed responsibility for evangelistic outreach. Another letter, on October 17, and a further one on November 6, clarified the policy and affirmed, much to the mission's alarm, the intention of the government to enforce it. In the future, it was explained, no Zulu pastors, preachers, evangelists, or teachers would be allowed to work on location land unless they were under the direct supervision of white missionaries. For a government that had paid them no heed, it must have come as a shock to realize that Zulu preachers and revivalists had worked their way into nearly every corner of the colony—and perhaps more importantly that they were suddenly respected and their message powerfully effective. Certainly the government's sweeping reaction smells of the panic of an administration that believed they had overlooked something very important, and perhaps very dangerous.

Although the mission expressed their astonishment at this move, they could not have been surprised, for the government had groped its way towards this position for the better part of a year. Harry Bulose, a young revivalist, became the first ACC preacher to be cut off from his work when the SNA removed him from location land in January of 1902.[136] The mission protested, but the SNA coolly noted that they did not expect to allow Bulose to return unless a white missionary accompanied him. The problem was, the SNA maintained, that local natives had become upset by a series of "open air night services" Bulose had led. Many of the area's young men and women attended these services and while they spoke "loudly of Jesus Christ" at the events, families feared that their youth "played Satan on the way home."[137] This was just the type of issue that drove Natal's government to act, perpetually concerned, as they were, with maintaining patriarchal authority in the hopes of suppressing rebellious youth.[138] The mission, unaware that this was a developing policy, made several requests to send other Zulu evangelists in Bulose's place, each of which the SNA denied.[139] Finally, an exasperated Wilcox wrote a sharply worded reply to one such refusal: "I presume your letter is not to be interpreted that we are to be obstructed in our work of preaching the gospel to the natives in the locations . . . In other words, it cannot be expected that we are to stop sending out our native evangelists to those branches of our church as we have been doing all along."[140] But, as this new policy was hammered out over the course of the year, this became exactly what the Natal government expected and by the end of the year the SNA forced many ACC preachers and evangelists from their work and tore down or boarded up several roughly constructed outstation chapels and schools.[141]

Any hope that the government's policy might simply be ignored vanished the following year when the SNA began pulling down churches.[142] One of the first to go was a small church begun, as were so many in the years after revival, by an evangelist who felt the call to work among traditionalists after his sanctification and subsequently built a small chapel on location land not far from Inanda. By 1904 the first few converts there had grown to sixty members, too many for the initial structure. In response the congregation built a more substantial structure with seating for seventy from more durable materials.[143] But in late April of that year the local magistrate sent word that they must abandon the church and pull it down. They refused and three days later a group of Natal Mounted Police rode up, dismounted, and took axes to the building; slowly and in small methodical pieces, chopping it down. Most of the congregation was present to witness this outrage and the women and children began, "crying very much with sorrow," unable to believe, as the police rode away, what had just occurred.[144] In defiance, the congregation held services for several weeks under the spreading branches of a nearby tree, but the police returned and ordered them to stop. They responded by sending a delegation to the local magistrate, asking, at the very least, that they be allowed to carry on their services in the open air. But he refused and the fearful congregation had little option but to make the long trek to Inanda to worship.

Three other churches were destroyed in a similar fashion and one other was only saved when a local chief intervened, leading the AZM to darkly note, "We have the edifying scene of this heathen entreating a representative of King Edward VII to spare the house of God!"[145] While many other churches remained standing on location lands, the government had made its point and both the ACC and the AZM became loath to start or even pursue work off of the mission reserves until the matter could be settled. The mission, slow at first to respond, beat a steady path to the door of the SNA after the events near Inanda. They pointed out that the government's actions halted the development of trained native evangelists and in doing so threatened to "extinguish the great hope of expansion in mission work in Africa," and that while they understood the order "has its origins in the fear of Ethiopianism which the ruling class dread as threatening their ascendancy over the natives," they warned that its practical effect was to "cause the very spirit which it is aimed to suppress."[146] Fundamentally, they believed, as did the *amakholwa* congregations, that the government's actions were both wrongheaded and unjust:

> For the government, by way of impossible conditions, to decree the closing up of a church or a school dear to the people, and this, too, on land especially given to native occupation, where a native would seem to have a peculiar right to work for the Christianization of his race, to be prohibited to work here even under responsible missionary supervision, fills him with a sense of being wronged. This provokes criticism of the government which tend to aggravate that discontent and restlessness so much feared."[147]

Having committed to supporting the aspirations of the ACC, the American missionaries persisted in their efforts to change the government policy, writing directly to the SNA, encouraging local Congregationalists to do the same, and drumming up support from other missionary societies.

Although they did not have nearly the number of Zulu evangelists as did the Americans, other churches, particularly the Anglicans, Wesleyans, and Presbyterians, faced similar difficulties with this new policy. Like the Americans, they simply could not hope to place a white missionary at every byway their evangelists reached. United in their opposition to this new policy, they petitioned the government together on several occasions. In December 1904 they met with the new SNA George Leuchars who had replaced Moor (just one of many changes at the SNA accompanying the unstable condition of Natal settler politics at this time) and he explained to them that while he understood the improbability of stationing a white missionary with each black one, he saw no other option to contain the spread of Ethiopianism.[148] He assured the delegates that his predecessor had very good reasons for adopting the current policy and that it was his "firm conviction that the native preachers and evangelists are, as a rule, unfitted to be invested with the authority necessary for the maintenance of good order and progress on any mission station." He could not, he assured them, recommend that the government alter its policy.[149]

CRUSHING THE COMMUNITY

While the government tore down churches and pushed Zulu evangelists off of the locations, an amendment was quietly passed by Natal's legislature revising the law regulating the marriages of *amakholwa*. The bill redefined Christian marriages in several small ways, but also contained several clauses forbidding ministers from solemnizing weddings unless they had been licensed to do so by the government, a license they would need to reapply for annually.[150] The AZM initially supported the bill, indeed it was their repeated calls for the SNA to investigate Shibe's authorization to minister wedding ceremonies that prompted this piece of legislation, but by the end of the year they had every reason to regret having done so.[151]

In compliance with the law, *amakholwa* pastors submitted their license requests in April of 1904. Then they waited. As winter arrived and African ministers from other mission societies began receiving their "marriage officer certificates," *amakholwa* pastors of the ACC asked American missionaries to look into why they had not yet received their own. The Americans sent several letters to the SNA and then met with the USNA in July, but no explanation for the delay was forthcoming.[152] Answers were not yet possible because the government was taking a particularly hard look at the applications of the ACC pastors. The request of Pastor Jwili Gumede for a license serves as illustration for what was common with all of them. Gumede submitted his application on April 16, 1904, shortly after the law came into effect and listed himself as a minister of Umgeni Church, a congregation organized as of June 1, 1898.[153] He noted that he was working under the ACC and the local magistrate gave him high marks, commenting that he was a fit and proper person to be "entrusted with the power to solemnize native marriages according to Christian rites." What follows, in the SNA report, is a month's long discussion investigating Gumede; where he was located, how long he had served as a pastor, how long he had served as a teacher before that, his performance in both, etc. Nothing overtly unsatisfactory about Gumede could be found, but the questions persisted. Then, after several months' delay, the government sent out letters to all the ACC pastors on October 14, 1904, informing the ministers that their applications had "been submitted to his Excellency the Governor and have been refused."[154] No further explanation was attached.

The mission was quickly becoming adept at the art of the formal protest, and following the SNA's decision several Americans marched to Pietermaritzburg within the week, hoping to persuade the government to reverse this decision. To their amazement, it soon became clear that the licenses had been withheld for what had occurred four years earlier in Durban, on September 11, 1900, the formation of the ACC.[155] Leuchars, holding up an article written by Bridgman shortly after the event and published in an international missionary magazine, noted that it "would seem that reconciliation was not obtained by the missionaries without grave concessions." It was the opinion of the government, he informed them, that native churches needed to be kept under the strict control of European men, something that was clearly not the case with the ACC. He was right, of course, and the missionaries could only weakly reply that while yes, they had given up some power, they had made no concession not provided for by Congregational policy.[156]

The SNA, not dissuaded from his criticism, also noted that several of the applications from *amakholwa* pastors had listed other *amakholwa* as the primary moderator during their ordinations. "I look upon it as being very serious," he charged, "that your society should have to appoint a native as a chairman of any meeting. I take it you do it because it is policy to do so, because the native party is stronger than you in these councils. It is very unsatisfactory." One of the Americans responded: "I do not think it has been done because it was necessary. Of course we differ, very likely, but if a native is worthy and has the ability, I say frankly we have no objection to his being put in the chair." Here, of course, was the heart of the debate, in claiming autonomy, even in their sacred affairs, *amakholwa* threatened the ideology of racial supremacy that became a set of laws in Natal, and that ultimately served as a part of the foundation for the apartheid state. The Natal government, run by settlers, would not stand for such an affront, and the SNA leaped to the attack: "Yes, that is just where we differ. It is inadvisable to give them too much control. My opinion is they should be kept in a subordinate position as much as possible." Indeed, he argued, the Americans should thank him for the government's actions, for it put them in an excellent position to force the ACC to return the concessions granted in 1900. The missionaries, long aware of the deeply racist nature of many of Natal's settlers, but likely never having heard it articulated in such a naked way by a government representative, could only proclaim that they wanted no such change and repeated their requests; to allow their evangelists to preach off of the mission reserves, and to grant their pastors the marriage certificate. The SNA promised them nothing.

The AZM again marshaled its forces, writing letters of complaint and urging friends of the mission to do the same. But the government had found one of the few tools it could exploit in limiting the independence of the ACC and simply refused each request. In restricting *amakholwa* pastors from celebrating marriage, the government effectively undercut both their spiritual *and* worldly authority, for marriage was one of the few church ceremonies that intersected and intertwined the sacred and the secular. Zulu Christians could have their vows solemnized by a reverend not carrying a marriage license, but they risked not having their marriage recognized by the state, which meant, among other problems, their children would be considered illegitimate by the very same state. In just a few short years after they had laid claim to spiritual independence, Zulu pastors of the ACC found it necessary, once again, to have American missionaries at their side when conducting one of the basic services of their faith, a serious blow to their autonomy.

Perhaps unsurprisingly, as the government restrictions began to bite, members of the ACC reacted angrily toward the mission. They voiced their suspicion to ABM delegation that missionaries were collaborating with the government to keep *amakholwa* preachers off of the locations, they suspected the AZM had interfered with their marriage license applications, and they worried that the mission had simply forgotten to report to the proper authorities the name change of the churches to the ACC.[157] Members of the ABM delegation expressed a great deal of sympathy for these concerns as it became clear to them that the intransigence of the government meant crushing the dreams of an ACC that "aches to conduct independent work, which shall be under their own control and known as theirs, with no other hands upon it."[158] As they realized, however, that missionaries were not colluding with the government, the ACC insisted that they do more, and, barring their ability to find a solution, that they should let the Zulu pastors and preachers "try for ourselves."[159]

In February of 1905, the AZM successfully arranged an interview between the SNA, themselves, and a group of pastors from the ACC. The interview did not go well. The SNA argued that other pastors had received their licenses because applicants had clearly stated they were under the *immediate* control of their missionaries. The members of the ACC responded by arguing that, within the limits of the Congregational church, they too were under the ABM. This did not suffice and the SNA charged them with being "more or less independent."[160] With each protest of innocence, *amakholwa* pastors surrendered a little bit more of their independence until, at the end of the interview and with the SNA still refusing to change his position, William Makanya, one of the younger pastors, felt compelled to proclaim:

> The European missionaries are over us in every respect; we look to them for guidance, for advice, for direction in our affairs; we regard them as being over us in the same manner as the heads of other churches are over them. There is nothing we do if they have refused us permission to do it or signified their disapproval of it, and we do nothing outside of them. We take their views and we take their guidance and they teach us and show us the way we should go. There is nothing whatever either financially or administratively or otherwise which is done without their advice or without their knowledge.

Although this startling statement can be dismissed as Makanya simply saying what needed to be said to appease Leuchars, it should be more carefully read as the perceptive recognition by the young Zulu pastor of just how much of their independence the ACC would need to surrender in order to lessen government persecution. It was to be a crippling blow and one that gave truth to the mission's assessment that the government policy would ultimately lead toward a dramatic increase in Ethiopianism. Revival had provided the tools to transform the theological structures of their Christianity and in so doing claim significant freedom in both secular and sacred matters, but their nearly complete independence now ran into the hard realities of Natal's settler government.

After the interview, the governor of Natal, Sir Edward Harry Macallum, wrote the AZM that: "His Excellency's Ministers are of the opinion that there is nothing to justify, [the granting of marriage licenses to ACC pastors], seeing that the American Zulu Mission has so far failed to show that these men are under the ecclesiastical control of the representatives of the ABM. They appear to be members of the independent Native Church as fully as the ZCC."[161] Both the mission and the ACC made further protests, but time was running out. The following year all of KwaZulu-Natal was thrown in chaos when a number of Zulu clans refused to pay a new poll tax on top of the hut tax they had already paid. Led by Bhambatha kaMancinza, a minor Zulu chief located in Natal, this tax protest became a "rebellion" when the Natal government panicked over the killing of two European tax collectors in February of 1906, and badly mishandled subsequent events.

The deteriorating social and economic conditions that helped spark revival among *amakholwa* of the ACC were mirrored in traditional society at the turn of the century; drought, disease, migrancy, and land pressures all contributed to the disintegration of Zulu society.[162] Aggravating this growing crisis the Natal government looked to the African population as a politically expedient means to reduce the debt the colony had accrued during the South African war by forcing it to pay for the very systems of repression being established by the settler state. Residents of the mission reserves were one of Natal's first targets. After much wrangling, the AZM had finally handed over control of their reserves to the government in 1903, believing that they had negotiated fair conditions for themselves and their African charges.[163] But the government dismissed repeated requests by both *amakholwa* and missionaries to allow Christians to buy land outright and the following year the government imposed a £3 rent on the land, a staggering increase from the 10 shillings most had paid up to that point. Protests were in vain and the rent stood.[164] In 1905, the Natal government again reached into the pockets of its African populace, imposing a £1 poll tax on every unmarried man in the colony. Already carrying a disproportionate share of their families' financial burden, young men returning from the harsh conditions of the Witwatersrand goldmines became angry over this new tax, and when colonial officials attempted to collect it in February of 1906, resentment flared into open violence.

As rebellions go, the Bhambatha "rebellion" was a fitful affair. Throughout northern Natal, small groups of Africans refused to pay their taxes, the colonial state sought to punish *ambutho*, and young Zulu men mobilized in self-defense and resistance. The main engagement, at Mome Gorge on

June 10, ended in a massacre of some 600 Zulu, who stood little chance against a governmental force equipped with repeating rifles and Maxim guns.[165] But scattered acts of resistance continued, most notably in and around Mapumulo. As elsewhere, colonialists reacted brutally, killing indiscriminately, burning huts, pulling down fences, stealing cattle, and ransacking even the European-style homes of *amakholwa*, the vast majority of whom did not participate in the uprising.[166] At Esidumbini, where a handful of church members joined a rebel regiment, Pastor Sivetye flew a Union Jack from the roof of his house in the hopes that this might spare him from the excesses of colonial troops bent on forcing submission through terror. It did not. After tearing down the flag, colonial troops stole money he had hidden and then burned his house to the ground.[167] After destroying other *amakholwa* homes, the soldiers moved to the church, smashing pictures, pews and other items before stealing the silver communion set.

As Zulu Christians were swept up into the battle, worry about their standing in the colony tinged their initial correspondence, but it was afterward, when the government insisted on the connection between the rebellion and *amakholwa*, that any hope they had of overcoming institutionalized racism and increasing government obstacles while retaining their autonomy was shattered. Within a decade the ACC found itself forced by government policy to resubmit to a mission which, just a few years earlier, had envisioned withdrawing altogether from the area and leave the work in what it had come to believe was good hands. This was no longer possible as without active white oversight the government of Natal had demonstrated it was willing to crush any African churches, whatever their affiliation. While the changes *amakholwa* had made to their Christianity persisted to the present day and allowed for the rapid spread of the faith across southern Africa, the expectation many had that claiming this identity would allow them to fully control their own churches within the traditional mission-based institutions never fully came to pass during the colonial era. Still, at a time when the world *amakholwa* had so carefully constructed was collapsing, sanctification promised purity and legitimacy—a powerful combination. And while the ACC was forced to abandon its name and hand back much of its autonomy, the Natal government could not force them to surrender a faith that no longer felt foreign.

NOTES

1. The following account is taken from AZM A/3/41, Mapumulo and Groutville station report, 1896–97.

2. No mention is made of Simungu leading this resistance, which appears largely directed by his congregation. It is likely that he was in Johannesburg, organizing several independent churches into a wider communion.

3. A grateful Wilcox wrote of Kuzwayo's success: "He was instrumental in getting most of the opposition to come to our meeting and that the opposition meetings be given up."

4. Bill Guest, "Towards Responsible Government, 1879–93," in A. Duminy and B. Guest (eds.), *Natal and Zululand From Earliest Times*, 245.

5. Weavers, who had arrived in Durban on August 22, must have left the city for Mapumulo shortly before Booth's announcement.

6. *Natal Witness*, September 7, 1896.

7. Dr. Nembula was the most prominent member of the AZM to sign on as a director.

8. Ibid. While this opinion was extreme even for the openly racist Natal settler community, another idea raised in the same letter, that the "school kaffir invariably turns out a blackguard," was a common sentiment among most whites.

9. ABM 188/436, Amanzimtoti Station Report, 1896–97.

10. The following account is from ABM 189/643–44, Annual Letter of the AZM, 1896–97 and AZM A/1/8, 1903 committee report, "The Ethiopian Movement and other Independent Factions."

11. Booth eventually landed in Malawi where his radical vision of African political independence expectedly ran afoul of British colonial authorities and, as we have seen, his association with John Chilembwe eventually led to an uprising that colonial authorities viciously repressed. See Landeg White, *Magomero*; Karen Fields, *Revival and Rebellion in Colonial Central Africa*; Harry Langworthy, *"Africa for the African": The Life of Joseph Booth* (Blantrye: Christian Literature Association, 1996).

12. AZM A/1/8, 1903 Committee Report.

13. ABM 191/240, Goodenough to Smith, October 17, 1896. Speaking of Booth's recent efforts to separate the *amakholwa* community entirely from the European state, Goodenough fretted: "I fear that John Dube's motive in returning to America is very much the same."

14. For a fuller description of his experience see, Robert Vinson and Robert Edgar, "Zulus Abroad: Cultural Representations and Educational Experiences of Zulus in America, 1880–1945." *Journal of Southern African Studies*, 33 (2007), 56–58.

15. Although even they were forced to admit that while the "importance of Industrial work has passed beyond the point of theory and experiment and has become established fact," insufficient funds prevented them from offering anything but the most basic training at Amanzimtoti. ABM 189/750–60, Pixley to Mary and Margaret Leitch, March 18, 1899.

16. AZM A/3/42, AZM Annual 1900–01. This is, of course, the exact position over which the church had so bitterly divided prior to his departure. That Inanda called Dube to be their pastor speaks to both his own considerable skills, and the power of revival to heal the deep divisions that had wracked the church prior to 1897.

17. ABM 189/747–49, Ohlange Industrial School Proposal, enclosure.

18. SNA 1380/1902, SNA meeting with Goodenough and Bridgman, April 8, 1902. Dube spent much of his time shoring up the school's finances, a constant and often losing battle.

19. Shula Marks, *The Ambiguities of Dependence in South Africa: Class, Nationalism, and the State in Twentieth-Century Natal* (Baltimore: John Hopkins University Press, 1986), 60–61.

20. *Natal Mercury*, "Are Natives Spoiled," November 17, 1905.

21. ABM 188/565–71, AZM Annual Report, 1897–98.

22. ABM 191/249–50, Goodenough to Smith, April 12, 1897.

23. Ibid.

24. AZM A/1/2, minutes of semi-annual meeting, January 27–February 1, 1897.

25. Ibid and AZM A/1/2, minutes of annual meeting, June 16–29, July 6–9, 1897. In reply to these requests, they offered to form a joint committee to look into the matter. Later they noted that their native pastors were against the action and suggested that nothing could be done against Simungu unless definite charges were laid against him.

26. AZM A/2/29, intermission note dated August 23, 1897.

27. ABM 189/647, committee of Table Mountain to AZM, November 10, 1897.

28. Ibid.

29. ABM 192, Curzon to Chairman or Secretary of the AZM, May 1, 1896. Giving evidence to the early development of Johannesburg as a city with a remarkable social milieu, the letter was apparently written by a white man who had taken a particular interest in the quest of local black Christians to find a pastor and whose sympathies clearly laid with the *amakholwa* community.

30. AZM A/1/7, Committee Report on meeting with Johannesburg Church, June 9, 1896.

31. AZM A/1/7, Report of Johannesburg committee, June 9, 1896.

32. *Missionary Herald*, "The Religious Awakening," July 1897, 272–73.

33. AZM A/2/7, Ndeya Makanya and the American Zulu Church of Johannesburg to the AZM, March 8, 1897.

34. ABM 191/249–50, Goodenough to Smith, April 12, 1897. Goodenough noted that: "If they were only going into the work with a right spirit I should wish them Godspeed with all my heart and help them to become established. I am really glad to be rid of Fokoti and these malcontents." Speaking of the revivals going on elsewhere he sighed, "It is evident that this is to be a year of wonderful blessing in our mission and a year of sore trial."

35. AZM A/4/54, Special meeting concerning Johannesburg, April 24, 1897. Translated.

36. It is unfortunate that the correspondence between Fokoti and Shibe has not come to light and its absence leaves a critical hole in any history of these events.

37. AZM A/4/53, Appointment of Shibe as minister, February 20, 1897. Translated.

38. AZM A/2/10, Shibe to AZM, August 22, 1898. Translated.

39. Shibe also reassured the mission that he was not "hard-hearted" over the matter as he fully appreciated that is was they who had given him his first job. As

for their feelings toward his actions, Shibe explained that "there is no child that can be blamed by his father."

40. AZM A/1/2, minutes of special meeting, April 28, 1898; AZM A/1/2, minutes of annual meeting, June 18–July 5, 1898.

41. ABM 188/503–04, Report of Southern Stations, 1897–98.

42. ABM 190/450–51, Bunker to Smith, March 9, 1899.

43. On several occasions men left Amanzimtoti seminary early to accept a call from a church and in 1904 both Mbiya Kuzwayo and Gardiner Mvuyana entered the seminary only after accepting calls to the pastorate. AZM A/3/47, AZM annual letter, 1904–05.

44. AZM A/1/2, minutes of semi-annual meeting February 6–16, 1900. Nor did the five new pastors meet the desire of the *amakholwa* congregations, for at the 1897 NAM, delegates called on the mission to immediately ordain seven additional pastors. AZM A/1/2, minutes of semi-annual meeting February 2–10, 1898.

45. AZM A/1/8, Committee to draw up necessary conditions in calling a native pastor, June 1898. Churches were expected to have harmonious relations with the AZM and the NUC, be united and peaceable, be a body of believers whose Christian integrity the mission had confidence in, prove their ability to raise a pastoral salary, and be controlled and directed by Congregational principals. A stiff test to be sure, but one many churches passed.

46. The mission also laid out what it considered appropriate qualifications for its pastors. A pastor needed to be on the mission's list of approved preachers, have demonstrated success as a preacher, be faithful (presumably to the mission as well as in his personal life), be trained in biblical matter, demonstrate respect for the guidance offered by the mission, and be characterized by the "requirements of Paul in his epistles to Timothy and Titus."

47. ABM 191/249–50, Goodenough to Smith, April 12, 1897.

48. AZM A/4/54, Meeting with native pastors, June 22–25, 1897.

49. The following is from ABM 188/649–50, AZM Annual Letter, 1898–99; and AZM A/4/55, 1898 NAM Report. Translated.

50. The churches' refusal to join them probably didn't come as a surprise to the delegates of the ZCC, for earlier in the year pastors and preachers in the AZM had refused to grant letters of dismissal (a form necessary for *amakholwa* to leave one congregation and join another in the Congregational church) to those who wished to join the breakaway congregations. That prospective members of the ZCC sought these letters further indicates just how close to the tree the breakaway congregations believed they had fallen. ABM 191/266–67, Goodenough to Smith, May 9, 1898.

51. Acts 19:2 "He said unto them, 'Have ye received the Holy Ghost since ye believed?' And they said unto him, 'we have not so much as heard whether there be any Holy Ghost.'"

52. AZM A/4/55, 1898 NAM Report. Translated.

53. The following is taken from *Sent of God*, "Notes from Elder Weavers' Farewell Address," February 2, 1899.

54. Unless otherwise noted, the details of Weavers' second mission trip through South Africa are taken from his diaries for the years 1899 & 1900.

55. The fear of this looming disaster hung heavily on Natal for over a year as cattle in the various states surrounding the colony succumbed to the disease. Despite misgivings over the efficacy of quarantine, the Natal government invested in rinderpest prevention measures such as double fencing the border and employing several hundred guards, both black and white, to prevent cattle and other animals from making it into the colony. Regardless, in the middle of July 1897, the disease found its way in and began making its way through the colony. For white farmers, however, the delay proved efficacious as bile and serum vaccinations were finally produced that year, dramatically reducing cattle mortality. Unfortunately, most African farmers did not trust inoculation, or found the price prohibitive, and mortality rates among black owned herds remained high. Natal Blue Book, Annual report of the commissioner of agriculture for the year 1897. On a related note, Worcester wrote that he had canceled tabernacle meetings in Natal toward the end of the previous year because rinderpest had shut down all transportation in the colony and he could find no way to move the big canvas tent. *Sent of God*, May 19, 1898.

56. Fears over the future of South Africa also extended to the American missionaries, who in addition to discussing their approach to the ZCC and the revivals once again underway in their churches, placed at the top of their agenda for their June 1899 annual meeting: "The AZM and its churches in this time of war stress" and "Threatening aspects of South Africa." AZM A/1/2, minutes of annual meeting June 21–July 3, 1899.

57. Weavers' diary, May 2, 1899.

58. Weavers' diary, May 8, 1899.

59. AZM A/3/42, Johannesburg Station Report, 1898–99.

60. AZM A/3/41, Mapumulo and Groutville Station Report, 1896–97.

61. Robert Martin, *Hero of the Heartland: Billy Sunday and the Transformation of American Society, 1862–1935*, (Bloomington: Indiana University Press, 2003).

62. Weavers' diary, June 2, 1899.

63. Weavers' diary, June 16, 1899.

64. AZM A/3/42, Inanda Station Report, 1899–1900.

65. *Missionary Herald*, "Revival at Umzumbe," May 1900, 199.

66. Weavers' diary, July 18, 1899.

67. AZM A/1/2, minutes of semi-annual meeting, February 6–16, 1900.

68. Ibid.

69. Weavers' diary, August 12, 1899. It took several hours for everyone in the packed church to rise and thank God for the wonders He had wrought in their lives and express their joy for being fully in communion with Him.

70. Weavers' diary, September 9, 1899; AZM A/3/42, South Coast and Polela Report, 1899–1900.

71. AZM A/3/42, South Coast and Polela Report, 1899–1900.

72. Weavers' diary, September 11, 1899; AZM A/3/42, South Coast and Polela Report, 1899–1900.

73. Weavers' diary, September 24, 1899. Kuzwayo and several others went to a nearby Methodist station mid-way through their Umtwalumi stay and began holding services. This was probably an effort to relieve some of the burden of those who had been walking long distances to attend.

74. AZM A/3/42, South Coast and Polela Report, 1899–1900.

75. Ibid. They also gave Weavers £3 collected as an offering of thanks. This was an impressive sum for any of the AZM congregations, all the more so that it came from the rather impoverished Umtwalume community that somehow found a way to consistently give more than several far wealthier stations.

76. Weavers' diary, November 15–25, December 4–12, 1899.

77. Roy Briggs and Joseph Wing, *The Harvest and the Hope: The Story of Congregationalism in Southern Africa* (Johannesburg: United Congregation Church, 1970), 130, 295; Arthur Christofersen, *Adventuring With God: The Story of the American Board Mission in South Africa* (Durban: 1967), 93, 126.

78. Weavers' diary, December 17, 1899.

79. Weavers clearly understood the controversial aspect of this belief, as he rarely introduced it early in revival meetings and instead taught it as a sort of "advanced Holiness."

80. Michael Mahoney has suggested that the mission reacted indifferently to Weavers upon his return; this was clearly not the case. Even after their heated discussion over divine healing, the mission passed a resolution stating: "We desire first of all to thank our Heavenly Father for sending Elder Weavers to us in the spirit and service of an elder brother, to intercede for us and our families and for our natives and to undertake such a great labor of love as he has done in his evangelistic campaign from one end of our mission to the other. We desire to put on record our gratitude for the revivals at various stations under the preaching and prayer of our brother. We wish Elder Weavers a prosperous voyage home, blessing in his work, and command him to our Father's care and to the goodwill of any friends of the AZM in South Africa." AZM A/1/2, minutes of semi-annual meeting, February 6–16, 1900; Mahoney, "The Millennium Comes to Mapumulo: Popular Christianity in Rural Natal, 1866–1906," *Journal of Southern African Studies* 25:3 (1999), 387.

81. Weavers received a steady stream of invitations throughout this time. On October 5th, for example, letters from the Swedish Mission in Zululand, and the Salvation Army in Stanger, arrived asking him to come and lead services. Weavers' diary, October 5, 1899.

82. Weavers' diary, January 29, 1900; AZM A/3/42, Amanzimtoti, Umsumduze and Itafamasi Reports, 1899–1900. As it was, Kuzwayo already served intermittently as Weavers' interpreter. He returned home on several occasions, and he and Weavers stuck to the strategy worked out at Umtwalume; Kuzwayo often held revivals at nearby outstations while the old Iowan preached at the central churches. This not only helped them control crowds that had outgrown the carrying capacity of most churches, but also allowed Kuzwayo to flex his own considerable talents as a revivalist—talents that Weavers clearly recognized and appreciated.

83. Weavers' diary, February 24, 1900.

84. AZM A/3/42, Southern Stations Report, 1901–01

85. *Missionary Herald*, "A Memorable Sabbath at Imfume," December 1901, 536–37.

86. AZM A/3/47, AZM annual letter, 1902–03.

87. Ibid.

88. Paul La Hausse, "'The Cows of Nongoloza': Youth, Crime and Amalaita Gangs in Durban, 1900–1936," *Journal of Southern African Studies* 16:1 (1990); David Hemson, "Dockworkers in Durban," in Paul Maylam and Iain Edwards (eds.), *The People's City: African Life in 20th Century Durban* (Pietermaritzburg: University of Natal Press, 1996).

89. *Missionary Herald,* "Durban—its Fakirs and its Christians," August 1902, 348–352.

90. AZM A/3/42, South Coast and Polela Report, 1899–1900; AZM A/3/42, North Coast Report, 1900–01.

91. *Missionary Herald,* "The Work of Women," September 1902, 373–74.

92. AZM A/3/42, Amanzimtoti Seminary Report, 1903–04.

93. Unless they spoke of specific events, such as a revival at one church or another, missionaries rarely referred to *amavoluntiya* groups by name, often calling them "bands of itinerant preachers," "volunteers," "lay preachers," or simply "unpaid evangelists." While a few of those referred to in this way were probably not associated with the group, it seems likely that most were. The group's position as the keepers of the revival flame, its existence on nearly every station, and its persistence through time, all suggest that while no definitive membership figures exist, the number of "unpaid evangelists" counted by the mission rose dramatically in the years following the first revival, are a close reflection of overall *amavoluntiya* strength.

94. AZM A/3/42, Southern Stations Report, 1901–02. Kuzwayo arrived at Emputyani after holding a long, difficult series of meetings at Amanzimtoti, which had suffered from a protracted dispute over the calling of their pastor. Helped by a day of fasting, the two sides finally came to a compromise and the congregation, which its delegates had called "spiritually dead" at the previous year's NAM, suddenly became particularly vigorous.

95. Increased tithing frequently accompanied revival, a natural reaction to accepting the message of surrendering the physical self to the Lord and trusting in His work in one's life. A combination of prewar jitters, post-rinderpest blues, and a rising number of pastors to support meant that the ZHFM ran into budgetary shortfalls in 1899. *Amakholwa* leaders called a special meeting, spent the day in fasting and prayer, asked the churches to do the same, and were overjoyed by the "remarkable" response to the call which not only made up the deficit but left a small surplus in its wake. AZM A/1/8, Native Agency Committee Report, 1899.

96. *Missionary Herald,* "A Memorable Sabbath at Imfume."

97. AZM A/3/42, Amanzimtoti Seminary Report, June 1900.

98. ABM 190/450–51, Bunker to Smith, March 9, 1899. While Bunker worried about their desire for independence, he believed, at least, that their spiritual lives were in the right place: "I do not believe, at least I have not heard, that there is any desire on their part to lower the standard of religious life or practice which they have been taught by the missionaries. It is this: We know our people better than the missionaries. We want to choose our own pastors, build or own churches in our own name, handle our own monies, and control our own local affairs without interference from the missionaries."

99. *Missionary Herald,* "Theological School Report," May 1900, 199.

100. AZM A/1/3, minutes of annual meeting, June 20–July 6, 1900.

101. Missionaries found that the popularity of the Bible studies often depended on the subject being taught. After one of his studies fell flat, James Taylor was surprised when the following day students spent over two hours eagerly devouring biblical texts on "Messianic Prophecy." Another study on "Sacrifices and Atoning Sacrifices also proved popular. *Missionary Herald*, "Eager Bible Students," March 1903, 121.

102. AZM A/4/54, pastors meeting, June 20–23, 1901. Translated.

103. Ibid.

104. AZM A/3/48, statistical tables of AZM for June 1896 and June 1900. In comparison, none of the other missions of the American Board came close to duplicating this level of active involvement by local unpaid evangelists. The closest in the 1902 Board census was the Indian mission at Marathi (one of the Board's oldest) which could only count 165 lay preachers. *Mission Herald*, "Tabular View of the Missions of the ABM for the Year, 1901–02," January 1903, 9.

105. AZM A/1/2, minutes of annual pastoral meeting, June 21–23, 1899.

106. ABM 190/361–70, Bridgman to Smith, December 15, 1899.

107. Ibid. Nyuswa asked for permission to attend but was informed that the mission did not see how they could allow "one to the communion who, while professing to be a brother in Christ, refused to talk over a difference in a Christian spirit."

108. AZM A/1/8, report of committee on reconciliation of ZCC, June 1900.

109. AZM A/1/2, minutes of semi-annual meeting, February 6–16, 1900.

110. A/4/54, agenda for pastors' meeting, February 7–8, 1900. Translated.

111. AZM A/1/8, report of committee on reconciliation of ZCC, June 1900.

112. AZM A/1/2, minutes of semi-annual meeting, February 6–16, 1900. Pastor Mvakwendhlu undoubtedly spoke for many when he noted that while "it was a sin that people who came with such wonderful news should be chased away," it also annoyed him that "white reverends tended to block congregations from seeking to run themselves." A/4/54, agenda for pastors' meeting, February 7–8, 1900. Translated.

113. Ibid.

114. AZM A/1/8, report of committee on reconciliation of ZCC, June 1900. Martin Lutuli and James Dube in particular are mentioned as being both "remarkably self-possessed, considerate and tactful" and also "endeavoring to impartially show the excellencies and defects on either side and to right misunderstandings."

115. As in previous years, Mbiya Kuzwayo organized and led a three-day revival for pastors and preachers in the week before NAM. This "emphasis on revival of the Spirit" carried over into the actual NAM when Kuzwayo gathered together the *amakholwa* leadership on several occasions for prayer, a very conscious effort by *amakholwa* to foster the spirituality that had enabled them to arrive at this moment. AZM A/1/8, report of 1900 NAM, June 1901.

116. The mission refused, for example, to pay Shibe for the house that he accused Pugh of stealing. The Americans maintained it was mission property, while Shibe claimed he had built it with his own hands. Writing to protest their actions Shibe expressed his belief that "beautiful Christians" would never "suck the blood of others." AZM A/2/10, Shibe to AZM, September 3, 1898. Translated.

117. AZM A/4/55, council of reconciliation, September 11–13, 1900.

118. AZM A/1/3, minutes of semi-annual meeting, January 23–February 4, 1901.

119. AZM A/4/54, agenda for pastors' meeting, February 7–8, 1900. Translated.

120. AZM A1/8, report of 1900 NAM, June 1901; AZM A/4/55, council of reconciliation, September 11–13, 1900. The mission representatives were leery of this name and argued, at the very least, that it should be changed to "African Congregational *Churches*" to reflect the Congregational nature of the body [Emphasis added].

121. Delegates at the NAM voted on future representatives, electing them for three or five year terms.

122. AZM A/1/9, committee report on the Ethiopian movement and other independent factions, June 1903.

123. *Missionary Herald*, "The Zulu in South Africa," February 1902, 63.

124. *Missionary Herald*, "Rev. Sydney Strong's Address," October 1904.

125. *Missionary Herald*, "Closing Experiences of Deputation in Natal," October 1903, 443.

126. AZM A/1/51, report of the deputation sent by the American Board to the missions in southeastern Africa in 1903.

127. Ibid. This is, of course, an obvious reference to the *amavoluntiya*.

128. Ibid.

129. *Missionary Herald*, "Rev. Sydney Strong's Address," October 1904. The deputation concluded from its visit that the AZM now needed to concentrate on raising up leaders so that "our direct work is finished within a limited number of years." *Missionary Herald*, "Closing Experiences of Deputation in Natal," October 1903, 443.

130. AZM A/3/42, report of Esidumbini division of north-coast stations, 1902–03.

131. SNA C25/1902, letter to governor, May 13, 1903. The SNA wanted the Prime Minister's opinion as to how far the British Colonial Office was willing to support the fight against "the threatening evil" of Ethiopianism, knowing that many church bodies were already angry over the actions of the Natal government.

132. SNA 630/1901, Solani's entrance into Natal, August 3, 1900.

133. Psalms 68:31. For what remains the most definitive account of the Ethiopian movement see, Bengt Sundkler, *Bantu Prophets in South Africa*, (London: Oxford University Press, 1964.)

134. SNA 2271/1901, magistrate's report, December 1900. Much to the SNA's consternation, he was accidentally granted another year's visa in 1902. Three fellow evangelists from the *amakutshe* church applied for passes in early 1901, were denied, snuck into the colony and were arrested for failing to take an inward pass. The three were each fined the hefty sum of £5 and ordered out of the colony as "undesirables." Solani eventually made his way back into Natal in 1922 and was arrested for preaching sedition after he was heard saying that Americans were on their way to South Africa to kick all the whites out of the country.

135. *Natal Mercury*, September 2, 1905.

136. SNA 77/1902, removal of native preacher Harry Bulose, January 1902.

137. SNA 1380/1902, meeting with Goodenough and Bridgman, April 8, 1902. This peripheral glance at revival offers insight both into how fully the ceremony had been absorbed into *amakholwa* sacred practice and more astonishingly, how little impact it had had on official consciousness. As mentioned previously, I would argue that it was simply too unthreatening to report beyond the local level to the SNA. Take the case of the young man from Mapumulo described in Chapter 4. He did not preach sedition, he just appeared to be "drunk with the spirit," a harmless lunatic who while perhaps making the daily reports at the local level, no Magistrate would have bothered reporting to the SNA.

138. For a fuller discussion of the complicated relationship between colonial authorities and Zulu patriarchal authority (particularly chiefs) see, Carton, *Blood From Your Children*; Nicholas Cope, *To Bind the Nation: The Zulu Royal Family under the South African Government, 1910–1933*, (Pietermaritzburg: University of Natal Press, 1994); and Aran S. Mackinnon, "Chiefs, Cattle and 'Betterment': Contesting Zuluness and Segregation in the Reserves" in *Zulu Identities: Being Zulu, Past and Present*, ed. Benedict Carton, John Laband, and Jabulani Sithole (New York: Columbia University Press, 2008).

139. It should be noted here that while the mission offered the names, it was the ACC that selected the candidates, the mission serving, as they had feared they might, as something of a front for the ACC's actions.

140. SNA 1007/1902, request by Wilcox to place Nduzane at Umbumbulu.

141. The SNA later maintained that this was not a new policy, but merely the application of guidelines for the reserves first established in 1892 but left largely unemployed.

142. In discussions with the Natal Native Trust, the SNA resolved in November 1903 to began pursuing this policy, but did not actually begin carrying it out until midway through the following year. SNA 347/1903, chief Kamanga asked for permission to erect a church on Location Land, report of November 5, 1905 meeting between the SNA and NNT.

143. The following account is taken from, *Missionary Herald*, "Restrictions Upon Religious Liberty," May 1904, 180–81. AZM A/2/11, Cele to Taylor, July 28, 1905.

144. The wailing appears to have disturbed the police, who "tried to make the people stop the noise and also told the people that it had nothing to do with them." When confronted over their actions the police employed the age-old excuse that they were merely carrying out government orders.

145. AZM A/4/59, statement regarding the obstructionist policy of the Natal government toward Christian work among the natives, June 1905.

146. Ibid; *Missionary Herald*, "The Government Restriction of Missionary Work in Natal—a paper read by Frederick Bridgman before the General Missionary Conference of South Africa, Johannesburg, South Africa, July 16, 1904," October 1904, 408–11. In a particularly perceptive statement, one of the American missionaries anticipated Lamin Sanneh's central thesis by nearly a century, arguing that "the genius of Christianity is the propagation of the Gospel by its converts, and in recognition of this fact every great missionary society in the civilized world has placed its main dependence for the evangelization of the heathen upon trained native evangelists

acting under supervision. This principal is freely recognized by governments the world over, as also by all the other South African colonies. Does Natal propose to be an exception?" *Natal Mercury*, September 2, 1905.

147. *Missionary Herald*, "The government restriction of missionary work in Natal," October 1904, 408–11.

148. SNA 2569/1904, deputation from Natal Missionary Conference, December 1904.

149. Leuchars is one of several unquestionably racist Natal farmers that occupied the post of SNA during this time and who were supported in their actions by the Governor of Natal, Sir Henry McCallum, a, "dyed-in-the-wool white supremacist who believed that Africans had to be kept firmly in their place." Lambert, *Betrayed Trust*, 165–166.

150. SNA 1322/1903, bill to amend the Law relating to marriage of natives by Christian rites. The bill did not come into effect until April 1, 1904.

151. Ibid. The mission sent a letter to the SNA in August of 1898 alerting the government that Shibe's ordination "had not been conferred by any recognized body." A stream of further correspondence from the AZM and the NCC followed, both seeking clarification on Shibe's status and warning the SNA of his actions. SNA 1622/1898, Goodenough letter. As part of the government's "Ethiopian" paranoia that followed the arrival of Solani, undercover police began watching Shibe in 1901. He was suspected of "preaching sedition under the cloak of religion" but no evidence was forthcoming and the most the government could do was warn him against officiating at weddings. SNA 1622/1898 & SNA 6526/1903.

152. AZM A/1/9, report on the committee on government difficulties, June 1905.

153. SNA 994/04, application of Reverend Jwili Gumede for marriage license, April 1904.

154. AZM A/1/9, report on the committee on government difficulties, June 1905.

155. SNA 931/1904, deputation of Reverends Bridgman and Taylor, October 18, 1904.

156. They also noted that in giving *amakholwa* say in running their own churches, they had avoided just that full independence the government so feared and that the *amakholwa* community was in "far more sympathy than previously possible" with the mission.

157. AZM A/4/59, pastors' conference, June 1903; *Missionary Herald*, "Closing Experiences of Deputation in Natal," October 1903, 443; SNA 2468/1904, excerpt from *Ilanga Lase Natal*, December 7, 1904. Translated. The deputation reported: "They desire to be recognized by government as the African Congregational Church and expect and almost demand that the mission secure for them this recognition."

158. *Missionary Herald*, "Closing Experiences of Deputation in Natal," October 1903.

159. AZM A/4/59, pastors' conference, June 1903.

160. AZM A/2/24, notes from an interview between the SNA and a deputation from the AZM and the ACC, February 16, 1905.

161. AZM A/3/49, AZM reply to Gov. Sir Edward Henry Macallum's letter of July 11, 1905.

162. For a detailed, if flawed, contemporary examination of these problems see, *Report of the Natal Native Affairs Commission 1906–07*, (Pietermaritzburg: 1907). For an excellent current account of the events that led to the breakdown of the Zulu homestead economy around the turn of the century see, John Lambert, *Betrayed Trust: Africans and the State in Colonial Natal* (Pietermaritzburg: University of Natal Press, 1995).

163. By 1899, the question of the mission reserves had become an intractable problem for the AZM. They recognized and supported the desires of the *amakholwa* community to own the land outright, going so far as to survey several of the reserves in preparation for selling the land to the Christian community. But the government resisted any such efforts and conditions on the reserves made them increasingly difficult to manage. The mission tried to farm out responsibility, but such agents rarely stayed on, as one such man complained: "When I accepted this position I had no idea of the quantity of work it entailed. It will take a man his whole time and he will require to have a good knowledge of court procedure to do it successfully." Ultimately, fearing that the reserves threatened to swallow up all their time and efforts in Natal without achieving the corresponding "goodwill or confidence" of the people, the mission approved the transfer. AZM A/1/2, minutes of semi-annual meeting, February 2–10, 1898; AZM A/1/2, minutes of special meeting with *amakholwa* over the reserves, October 11, 1899; AZM A/2/10, Hulett to Goodenough, January 14, 1899; AZM A/2/29, Dorwood to Goodenough, March 27, 1899; SNA 1456/1900, petition from AZM for the granting of title to individual holding to native residents lawfully occupying mission reserves; AZM A/2/24, general plan for dividing up the American Mission Reserves, 1900; SNA 954/1902, SNA to Goodenough; AZM A/3/47, annual letter 1903–1904.

164. The mission considered the rent part of the government's overall attack on Christian work detailed in the previous chapter. They noted that *amakholwa* could not possibly be expected to pay their taxes and pay school fees for their children, stipends for their pastors, and tithes to the churches. While no government records support this view, both *amakholwa* and missionaries came to believe that it was part of a deliberate attempt by the SNA to undermine the ACC's recent achievement of autonomy, stripping away the ability of Christians to support themselves financially in all aspects of their works of faith. AZM A/3/49, AZM to SNA, July 19, 1904; AZM A/3/37, AZM to Sivetye, April 4, 1905—translated; AZM A/1/9, report of mission committee on government difficulties, June 1905; AZM A/4/59, statement regarding the obstructionist policy of the Natal government towards Christian, June 1905; *Natal Mercury*, "copy of ACC petition to SNA," August 23, 1905.

165. The fullest account of these events remains Shula Marks, *Reluctant Rebellion: the 1906–1908 Disturbances in Natal* (Oxford: Oxford University Press, 1970). For a particularly insightful analysis of the generational origins of this conflict see Carton, *Blood from Your Children*.

166. The question of *amakholwa* involvement in the rebellion has received a surprising amount of interest from historians, flowing, most probably, from the Natal government accusations detailed above. Shula Marks has dismissed the government charges, believing, as did the American Board, that the accusations

against *amakholwa* were made by settlers and colonial officials who had developed a deep distrust of the democratic tendencies of the AZM. Mike Mahoney, however, has argued that the confusion over the number of Christians who participated in the rebellion stems from a general blurring of the line between *amakholwa* and traditionalist in the preceding years. I agree with his assessment and have made a case earlier in this work for an understanding of what it meant to be Christian that embraces those who gathered in churches made of thatch around altars made of tree trunks and who went years without seeing either white or black reverends, participating in communion, or being baptized and thus were often not counted by either the missions or the state. There are limits, however, to how broadly one can stretch this tent and I would also argue that part of this debate has been shaped by a Natal government that sought to deflect criticism of its handling of the affair, a point elegantly made by Marks. Mike Mahoney, "The Millennium Comes to Mapumulo: Popular Christianity in Rural Natal, 1866–906," *Journal of Southern African Studies* 25:3, (1999), 388–91; Marks, *Reluctant Rebellion*, 80–81, 330–31; but also, *Natal Mercury*, "letter from Goodenough," October 1, 1906.

167. *Natal Mercury*, "The Natives: Grievances Enumerated," July 5, 1906.

Conclusion

CELEBRATION

In early July of 1905, the newly constructed Beatrice Street Church opened its doors for the first time. It is difficult, knowing what was about to occur, not to read accounts of the celebration that accompanied the church's dedication without trepidation, for despite the recent government moves against them *amakholwa* of the African Congregational Church celebrated the event as an important first step in their lives as autonomous Christians. And in a way it was. In the four years after the formation of the ACC, believers had raised numerous outstations and schools (some of which of course the government had subsequently pulled down) but this was their first truly substantial structure, an impressive building, largely paid for with *amakholwa* contributions, that they would own jointly with the AZM. That it was in Durban, the rapidly expanding heart of Natal, only served to emphasize the significance of the ceremony.

Missionaries from the AZM and other societies, local businessmen who had contributed to the new building, prominent white Congregationalists, and even mid-level government officials, all attended the two-day ceremony.[1] Yet despite the presence of these white dignitaries, *amakholwa* made the event their own. They electrified the assembly with their worship, awed them with their singing (hymnals, but almost certainly also *isicathamiya*, the a cappella music most often associated today with its most famous practitioners, Ladysmith Black Mambazo) and impressed even hardened settlers with the power and thoughtfulness of their sermons.[2] A reporter from the *Natal Mercury*, a paper that often spoke for the local European population, commented: "The ceremony and the service which followed were most impressive and those who have not attended anything of this character before could not but be struck with the heartiness and genuine pleasure with which the natives entered into the service."[3] With an average Sunday congregation of five hundred spread over several services at the old church, the new one, with six hundred seats, had been built to accommodate the growth the church had experienced since revival. When even all these seats were taken at the opening, *amakholwa* lined the walls and stood in back of the long building, and when no more could fit in, the rest gathered outside. Some three hundred of them stood under the midday sun and, unable to hear, they took turns leading each other in hymns until a Zulu preacher was dispatched outside to minister to their needs.[4]

Inside the new church, prominent *amakholwa* led the services. Martin Luthuli, serving as choirmaster, directed a group of children from Umvoti in a stirring round of hymns, their beautiful voices captivating the audience.[5] William Makanya, the pastor of the new church, recalled his sadness the day before when strong rains had fallen and threatened to spoil the opening, but when the new day had dawned and clear skies greeted him, he knew that the previous day's weather had been a prophecy that the remaining debt on the building would soon be cleared, the downpour, "a promise of the way in which the money was to be showered upon the contribution plate this afternoon."[6] When John Dube addressed the assembly he too called for contributions, but he also used the opportunity to promote his version of a Zulu future. It was time, he believed, for *amakholwa* to awaken like the city of Durban at dawn, rising from their slumber to become industrious leaders. For Dube the new church at Beatrice Street represented an important moment in the civilizing project.

Most *amakholwa* in attendance at the opening ceremonies had experienced one if not several revivals, so common had they become in the churches during the previous decade. For these men and women, Reverend Umvakwendhlu Sivetye's sermon resonated with their own ideas of what the new church symbolized. Sivetye, astonished by the magnificence of the new building, compared it favorably to Solomon's temple. It was an unlikely comparison, of course, but Sivetye should be forgiven this bit of hyperbole for the building was a marvel of the modern age. With sides and roof constructed from corrugated iron, "but with the appearance of a church," a spacious sanctuary, separate classrooms, a pastor's office, the entire building electrified, and even the mission's first stained glass windows, there was much to marvel at for parishioners.[7] But it wasn't these wonders, Sivetye stressed, that made the building more glorious than Solomon's temple, but rather the presence of the Holy Spirit among them. Echoing

the Holiness message *amakholwa* had successfully deployed in transforming their communities, Sivetye argued that, like this new building, each
person present needed to undergo sanctification, for only if "Christ entered
the temples of our bodies should we be truly blessed." In articulating their
empowerment through Christ and the Spirit of God, Sivetye repeated what
most *amakholwa* in attendance firmly believed, that through their sanctification they had achieved not just a salvation in the next life, but justification
in the present.

For the American missionaries, who had earlier transferred much of their
authority to their Zulu counterparts just as they now handed over control of
the Durban church, Sivetye's sermon offered reassuring words for the future
of Christianity on the continent. Perhaps the theology he espoused wasn't
fully orthodox, but the religion of their fathers was now clearly the religion
of his sons and in this moment the legitimacy of their actions appeared
settled. In the same way the legitimacy of Sivetye standing at the front of
the church delivering the sermon appeared unquestionable. As one of the
Americans noted: "His argument was convincing, powerful, spiritual, and it
helped us all." Revival had moved the missionaries from the pulpit to the
pews and while six months later the violence wrought by the settler state in
their frenzied efforts to suppress the Bambatha rebellion left the immediate
amakholwa dream of achieving some degree of secular equality in tatters,
Christianity was now as fully theirs as it was the missionaries who had first
arrived almost a century earlier.

FAITH, HOPE, AND POLITICS

The image of smoldering *amakholwa* homes and shattered churches serves
as a ready metaphor for the damage done to the community's aspirations.
During revival, the Zulu Christians had rallied from the malaise of the
previous decade and used the authority they gained from sanctification
to first heal their fractured body and then claim control of their churches
from the AZM. The ACC may not have been completely autonomous, but
it was as near a coupling of secular independence and spiritual legitimacy
as any group of African Christians attained in South Africa during the
colonial period. Government antagonism and open violence provided
revivalists with a harsh lesson in the realities of twentieth century Natal.
The earlier fight over marriage certificates and the rights of *amakholwa*
evangelists gave way to a desperate defense of community following the
"rebellion." The government accused Christians of not just joining the
uprising, but doing so in disproportionate numbers and providing both
prayers and leadership to the cause. It was made clear, through both official

channels and the newspapers, that the government would no longer tolerate the independency of the ACC, and in June of 1906, the Governor of Natal expressed his belief that the spread of Ethiopianism was one of the primary contributors to the violence.[8]

So it was a sullen NAM that met at Impapala in 1906 and voted to change their name to "The Congregational Churches of the American Board," surrendering the autonomy symbolized in African Congregational Church in the hopes that the Natal government might allow their work to go forward.[9] It is not that revival went away; rather it became institutionalized, and revivals, usually inspired by *amavoluntiya* visits, occurred intermittently throughout the Congregational churches during the decades to follow. But the violence of the state, and more importantly its active interference in the spreading of the word by Zulu evangelists, took much of the starch out of the movement, and it became a local phenomena designed to right individuals and churches going astray. The larger evangelistic and communal aspirations of those who had most passionately embraced the movement withered under government restrictions. Unlike many Ethiopians, legitimacy mattered a great deal to those who stayed in the Congregational churches, and they proved loath to challenge the Natal government over this issue.

Not everyone stayed. For several decades after revival the Congregational church led an unprecedented period of growth for all of the traditional churches across Natal. From well under 10 percent of the population, by 1911 just over a million Africans counted themselves as Christians, or approximately 26 percent of Africans in what would become South Africa.[10] By the end of the Second World War this had grown to some 4 million African Christians, or over half of the population. At this point, however, the numbers began to level off for the AZM and for the next several decades AZM church rolls barely held steady as some members looked to other Christian organizations to meet their aspirations. Many who left joined African Initiated Churches that allowed them to exercise the autonomy they had lost when the ACC had been eradicated. Others pursued the more radical promises of Holiness by joining Zionist churches, places where they could radically separate from the troubles of this world and lay claim to the power of the next by immersing themselves wholly in questions of the Spirit. Wherever they went, however, they brought with them the Christianity they had crafted at the turn of the century, and today the theological emphasis on the daily workings of the Holy Spirit, the power of prophecy, and personal power attainable through the church are almost universal, regardless of denominational affiliation, across the land.[11]

Most Congregational Christians, however, did remain within the church, but disconnected the more revolutionary promises of revival from their political aspirations. John Dube, Pixley Seme, and Martin Luthuli, among other prominent Congregationalists, helped found the South African Native National Congress (which would eventually become the African Native Congress) and even played a prominent role in the resuscitation of the Zulu royal house, promoting Zulu ethnicity over the universalizing aspirations embodied in revival and the former name of the their church, the *African* Congregational Church.

Given all this, one is tempted to dismiss the revival as yet another failed liberation movement, one of many floating in the backwash of Natal's colonial past. But this would be judging the movement by standards *amakholwa* viewed as at best parallel to revival's primary objective. Those who participated did so first and foremost to experience personal and communal spiritual transformation. In this, revival was an unqualified success, so much so that it remains imbedded in the conscious of church members today as the moment of the community's birth.[12] After a half decade of missionary efforts, this was the theology that moved *amakholwa* into a passionate embrace of their faith. That it was Holiness teachings chosen isn't a surprise; the message preached by Weavers offered a Spirit filled religious experience, empowering and uplifting those who participated. At a time when the world they had carefully constructed was collapsing around them sanctification promised both purity and legitimacy. Yet it would be a mistake to overemphasize Holiness, for when Weavers returned (for the last time) to Natal in 1903 with the intention of establishing an independent missionary body, he departed the following year deeply aggravated by his failure to attract any significant number of the very Zulu Congregationalists he had led in revival services. Indeed even Mbiya Kuzwayo, who sent his son to Tabor, Iowa, to be educated at Hephzibhah's school, remained within the church. Zulu Christians needed certain aspects of Holiness theology to transform their faith, but once that was accomplished they felt little compulsion to jump ships. That was the beauty of what they had accomplished; they no longer felt compelled to do so.

Political power and social legitimacy in white Natal may not have followed, but the evangelization that revival inspired propelled one of the most intense periods of *amakholwa* proselytizing the area had seen and within a generation Christians had gone from a small minority to a majority in the area. Revival also brought an unsurpassed creative moment when *amakholwa* solved central problems to the adoption of the faith in southern Africa by emphasizing the role of the Holy Spirit, making salvation a more spontaneous gesture, and giving congregations a powerful role in molding their own spirituality. It is for this reason that the revivals are recalled even today as a "golden age" of the faith, a time of power perhaps never again equaled.[13] As B. K. Dludla, the pastor of Beatrice Street Congregational Church (which looks today much as it did a century ago) recalled when I spoke with him in 2001 about the impact and nature of the revivals:

> So he [Weavers] started working and he was emphasizing the revival of the spiritual life of the church, so people could be totally committed to expanding the news of the Gospel beyond the present [?] reach of the local church. We required quite an extensive inspiration in those years and many people gave themselves to the Lord and worked for the Lord even though they themselves were not ordained, like me.[14]

While it is impossible to accurately quantify such a movement, the revivals of 1896–1901 certainly played a major role in transforming Christianity from a mission-led faith fitfully adopted, to a lived faith fully naturalized. As later revivals across Africa highlight, this was the model for the future of the faith on the continent.

NOTES

1. The manager of the Natal Government Railways, Sir David Hunt, had the honor of turning the key to open the church door for the first time. Although it was never explicitly stated, it does not take a great leap of logic to suppose that Hunt was chosen to do so with the hope that his participation in the ceremony might lead to a softening of the government's position. If this was the wish, it went unfulfilled.

2. Viet Erlmann, *Nightsong: Performance, Power, and Practice in South Africa* (Chicago: University of Chicago Press, 1996), 46–47.

3. *Natal Mercury*, July 10, 1905.

4. AZM A/4/59, Cowles to Friends, July 25, 1905.

5. Natal Mercury, July 10, 1905. Having sat in on Zulu church services, I can attest to the moving magnificence of Zulu choral singing.

6. AZM A/4/59, Cowles to Friends, July 25, 1905.

7. *Missionary Herald*, "New Church at Durban," November 1905, 582–83.

8. For a summation of the Governor's views see, *Natal Mercury*, "Causes of the Rebellion," January 7, 1907.

9. *Mission Herald*, "An Eventful Meeting," November 1907, 533–34. The move garnered the *amakholwa* pastors their marriage certificates, but it wasn't until the end of 1912 that the government relented and allowed Zulu preachers to work on the locations. ABM *1913 Annual Report*, (Boston: 1913), 41.

10. John De Gruchy has argued that these numbers may be inflated by as much as a third, but even if that is so the figures are impressive. See, *The Church Struggle in*

South Africa (Grand Rapids: Eerdmans, 1986), 245. Loraine Gordon et al., *A Survey of Race Relations in South Africa: 1977* (Johannesburg: Institute of Race Relations, 1977).

11. For a window into the remarkable similarities across denominations see, Richard Elphick and Rodney Davenport (eds.), *Christianity in South Africa: A Political, Social, and Cultural History* (Berkley, University of California Press, 1997).

12. Rev. B. K. Dludla, interview, Durban, May 20, 2001; Ms. Suka Benqaba, interview, Groutville, June 24, 2001; Mr. Brightman Mbambo, interview, Groutville, June 24, 2001.

13. Roy D. Briggs and Joseph Wing, *The Harvest and the Hope*, 199.

14. Rev. B. K. Dludla, interview , Durban, May 20, 2001.

Bibliography

1. ARCHIVAL HOLDINGS

Natal Archives, Pietermaritzburg

A. (AZM) American Board Mission Inventory
   a. Section A/1: Minutes of Meetings and Committee Reports
   b. Section A/2: Correspondence Received
   c. Section A/3: Correspondence Dispatched
   d. Section A/4: Internal
   e. Section A/5: Divers Matters
B. (SNA) Secretary for Native Affairs Papers
   a. I/1: Letters Received
   b. I/4: Confidential and Semi-Official Correspondence
   c. I/6: Miscellaneous Correspondence
   d. I/8: Letters Dispatched
   e. II/3: Magistrates Commission (1891)
   f. II/4: Native Affairs Commission (1903–1905)
   g. III/1: Resolutions and Minutes of Meetings (Natal Native Trust)
   h. III/2: Correspondence
C. Other Official Correspondence
   a. Report and Evidence of the Natal Native Affairs Commission, 1906–1907
   b. Blue Books: Natal, 1884–1903.

Houghton Library, Harvard

A. (HAZM) American Board Mission Collection
  a. (ABM) American Board of Commissioners for Foreign Missions microfilm
    i. South Africa, 18
  b. Miscellaneous Letters: Goodenough, Bridgman, Cowles, and Wilcox.

Nazarene Archives, Kansas City

A. Papers of Hephzibah Faith Missionary Association
  a. Diary of Elder Weavers
  b. Unsorted documents and artifacts

Killie Campbell Library

A. Proceedings of the Natal Missionary Conference
B. Papers relating to Rinderpest
C. Papers and Photos of American Zulu Missionaries
D. The American Mission Reserves—paper presented by Rev. Goodenough to the Natal Missionary Conference, July 1895
E. The Mission Reserves Bill— paper presented by Rev. Charles Kilbon to the Natal Missionary Conference, July 1895
F. Colenso Collection—letters to missionaries

Tabor Town Library

A. *History of Freemont County.* Iowa Historical Company, Des Moines, 1881
B. Collected Cuttings of Hephzibah Faith Missionary Association

2. NEWSPAPERS AND PERIODICALS

American Board of Commissioners Annual Reports, 1812–1910
ABM Herald, 1846–1910
Congregational Church Magazine, 1892–1897
Christian Science Monitor, 2008
Ilanga Lase Natal, 1904–1910
Inkanyiso Yase Natal, 1891–1895

Mills County Tribune, 1893–1924
Natal Mercury, 1879–1910
National Catholic Reporter, 2003
Shine On! Inanda Girl's School Annual, 1960–1978
Tabor Beacon, 1894–1924
The Sent of God (SOG), 1891–1912
Umvo Neliso Lomzi, 1896

3. INTERVIEWS

Ms. Suka Benqaba, Groutville, June 24, 2001.
Rev. Scott Couper, Groutville, June 22–24.
Mr. Vukile Kumalo, Adams (Amanzimtoti) Seminary Committee, November 14, 2000.
Rev. B. K. Dludla, Durban, May 20, 2001.
Captain Mgobhozi, Groutville, June 24, 2001.
Mr. Brightman Mbambo, Groutville, June 24, 2001.
Rev. Susan Valiquette, Inanda, June 16, 2001.

4. BOOKS, ARTICLES, AND THESES

ABCFM. *First Ten Annual Reports of the American Board of Commissioners for Foreign Missions*. Boston: Crocker and Brewster, 1834.

Abzug, Robert. *Passionate Liberator: Theodore Dwight Weld and the Dilemma of Reform*. New York: Oxford University Press, 1980.

Anderson, Benedict. *Imagined Communities: Reflections on the Origins and Spread of Nationalism*. London: Verso, 1991.

Atkins, Keletso. *The Moon is Dead! Give Us Our Money!: The Cultural Origins of an African Work Ethic, Natal, South Africa, 1843–1900*. Portsmouth: Heinemann, 1993.

Ballard, Charles. "'A Reproach to Civilisation': John Dunn and the Missionaries 1879–1884." *South African Historical Journal* 9 (1977): 36–55.

———. "Natal 1824–44: The Frontier Interregnum." *Journal of Natal and Zulu History* 5 (1982): 49–64.

———. "A Year of Scarcity: The 1896 Locust Plague in Natal and Zululand." *South African Historical Journal* 15 (1983): 34–52.

———. "The Repercussions of Rinderpest: Cattle Plague and Peasant Decline in Colonial Natal." *International Journal of African Historical Studies* 19 (1986): 421–50.

———. "Traders, Trekkers and Colonists." In Andrew Duminy and Bill Guest, (eds.), *Natal and Zululand from Earliest Times to 1910*. Pietermaritzburg: University of Natal Press, 1989.

Ballard, Charles and Giuseppe Lenta. "The Complex Nature of Agriculture in Colonial Natal: 1860–1909." In Bill Guest and John Sellers (eds.), *Enterprise and Exploitation in a Victorian Colony: Aspects of the Economic and Social History of Colonial Natal*. Pietermaritzburg: University of Natal Press, 1985, 121–50.

Barrett, David, George Kurian, and Todd Johnson, *World Christian Encyclopedia*, 2nd ed. New York: Oxford University Press 2001.

Behrend, Heike. *Alice Lakwena and the Holy Spirits: War in Northern Uganda, 1985–1997*. Ohio University Press: Athens, 1999.

Beidleman, T. O. *Colonial Evangelism: A Socio-Historical Study of an East African Mission at the Grassroots*. Bloomington: Indiana University Press, 1982.

Berglund, Axel-Ivar. *Zulu Thought-Patterns and Symbolism*. Bloomington: Indiana University Press, 1989.

Bird, John (ed.), *The Annals of Natal: 1495–1845, Volume I*. Pietermaritzburg: Natal Society Publishing, 1888.

Bonner, Paul. "Family, Crime and Political Consciousness on the East Rand." *Journal of Southern African Studies*, 14 (1988): 393–420.

Booth, Alan. *Journal of Rev. George Champion*, Cape Town: Struik, 1967.

Bozzoli, Belinda, *Women of Phokeng: Consciousness, Life Strategy, and Migrancy in South Africa, 1900–1983*. Portsmouth: Heinemann, 1991.

Breckenridge, Keith. "The Allure of Violence: Men, Race and Masculinity on the South African Goldmines, 1900–1950." *Journal of Southern African Studies* 24 (1998): 669–93.

Bredekamp, Henry and Robert Ross. "Introduction: The Naturalization of Christianity in South Africa." In Bredekamp and Ross (eds.), *Missions and Christianity in South African History*. Johannesburg: Wits University Press, 2001, 1–10.

Brierley, Jean and Thomas Spear. "Mutesa, the Missionaries, and Christian Conversion in Buganda." *The International Journal of African Historical Studies* 21 (1988): 601–18.

Briggs, Roy D. and Joseph Wing, *The Harvest and the Hope: The Story of Congregationalism in Southern Africa*. Johannesburg: United Congregational Church of South Africa, 1970.

Brooks, Edgar and Colin Webb. *A History of Natal*. Pietermaritzburg: University of Natal, 1965.

Brown, Karen. "Tropical Medicine and Animal Diseases: Onderstepoort and the Development of Veterinary Science in South Africa, 1908–1950." *Journal of Southern African Studies* 31 (2005): 513–29.

Brown, Kenneth. *Indian Springs Holiness Camp Meeting: A History of "The Greatest Camp Meeting in the South."* Hazelton, PA, Holiness Archives, 2000.

Bundy, Colin. *The Rise and Fall of the South African Peasantry.* London: James Currey, 1979.

Campbell, James. *Songs of Zion: The African Methodist Episcopal Church in the United States and South Africa.* New York: Oxford University Press, 1995.

Carton, Benedict. *Blood From Your Children: The Colonial Origins of Generational Conflict in South Africa.* Charlottesville: University of Virginia Press, 2000.

———. "'We Are Made Quiet by this Annihilation': Historicizing Concepts of Bodily Pollution and Dangerous Sexuality in South Africa," *The International Journal of African Historical Studies* 39 (2006): 84–106.

———. "Awaken *Nkulunkulu*, Zulu God of the Old Testament," in Benedict Carton, John Laband, and Jabulani Sithole (eds.), *Zulu Identities: Being Zulu, Past and Present.* New York: Columbia University Press, 2008.

———. "Faithful Anthropologists: Christianity, Ethnography and the Making of 'Zulu Religion' in Early Colonial Natal," in Benedict Carton, John Laband, and Jabulani Sithole (eds.), *Zulu Identities: Being Zulu, Past and Present.* New York: Columbia University Press, 2008.

Chidester, David. *Religions of South Africa.* London: Routledge, 1992.

Chirenje, J. Mutero. *Ethiopianism and Afro-Americans in Southern Africa, 1883–1916.* Baton Rouge: Louisiana State University Press, 1987.

Christofersen, Arthur. *Adventuring With God: The Story of the American Board Mission in South Africa.* Durban: Julia Rau Christofersen, 1967.

Clark, Francis. *Christian Endeavor in All Lands.* Philadelphia, P. W. Zeigler Co., 1906.

Cobbing, Julian. "The Mfecane as Alibi: Thoughts on Dithakong and Mbolompo." *Journal of African History* 29 (1988): 487–519.

Colebrander, Peter. "The Zulu Kingdom, 1828–79." In Duminy and Guest, *Natal and Zululand From Earliest Times to 1910.* Pietermaritzburg: University of Natal Press, 1989, 83–115.

Comaroff, Jean. *Body of Power, Spirit of Resistance: The Culture and History of a South African People.* Chicago: University of Chicago Press, 1985.

Comaroff, Jean and John. *Of Revelation and Revolution: Christianity, Colonialism, and Consciousness in South Africa*, Volumes I & II, Chicago: University of Chicago Press, 1991 & 1997.

Conkin, Paul. *Cane Ridge, America's Pentecost.* Madison: University of Wisconsin Press, 1990.

Cooper, James Jr. "Enthusiasts or Democrats? Separatism, Church Government, and the Great Awakening in Massachusetts." *The New England Quarterly* 65:2 (1992), 265–83.

Cope, Nicholas. *To Bind the Nation: Solomon kaDinuzulu and Zulu National-ism, 1913–1933*. Pietermartizburg: University of Natal Press, 1993.

———. "The Zulu Petit Bourgeoisie and Zulu Nationalism in the 1920s: Origins of Inkatha." *Journal of Southern African Studies* 16 (1990): 431–51.

Coplan, David. *In Township Tonight! South Africa's Black City Music and The-atre*. London: Longman, 1985.

Crais, Clifton. *White Supremacy and Black Resistance in Pre-Industrial South Africa: The Making of the Colonial Order in the Eastern Cape, 1770–1865*. Cambridge: Cambridge University Press, 1992.

Davenport, Rodney. *Christianity in South Africa: A Political, Social, and Cul-tural History*. Berkeley: University of California Press, 1997.

Deichmann Edwards, Wendy. "Forging an Ideology for American Missions: Josiah Strong and Manifest Destiny." In Wilbert Shenk (ed.), *North American Foreign Missions, 1810–1914*. Grand Rapids: Eerdmans, 2004, 163–191.

De Gruchy, John, *The Church Struggle in South Africa*. Grand Rapids: Eerd-mans, 1986.

Dieter, Melvin. *The Holiness Revival of the Nineteenth Century*. Metuchen, NJ: Scarecrow Press, 1980.

Dinnerstein, Myra. *The American Board Mission to the Zulu*. Ph.D., Columbia University, 1971.

Draper, Jonathan. "The Bishop and the Bricoleur: Bishop John William Co-lenso's *Commentary on Romans* and Magema Kamagwaza Fuze's *The Black People and Whence they Came*." In Gerald West and Musa Dube (eds.), *The Bible in Africa: Transactions, Trajections, and Trends*. Boston: Brill Press, 2000.

Du Plessis, J. *A History of Christian Missions in South Africa*. Cape Town: Struik, 1965.

Elbourne, Elizabeth. "Early Khoisan uses of Mission Christianity." In Henry Bredekamp and Robert Ross (eds.), *Missions and Christianity in South Af-rican History*. Johannesburg: Wits University Press, 2001.

———. *Blood Ground: Colonialism, Missions, and the Contest for Christianity in the Cape Colony and Britain, 1799–1853*. Montreal: McGill-Queens Uni-versity Press, 2002.

———. "Word Made Flesh: Christianity, Modernity and Cultural Colonial-ism in the Work of John and Jean Comaroff." *American Historical Review* 108 (2003): 435–459.

Eldredge, Elizabeth. "Sources of Conflict in Southern Africa, c.1800–30: The 'Mfecane' Reconsidered," *Journal of African History* 33 (1992): 1–35.

Elphick, Richard. "South African Christianity and the Historian's Vision." *South African Historical Journal*, 26 (1992): 182–190.

———. "Introduction: Christianity in South African History." In Richard Elphick and Rodney Davenport (eds.), *Christianity in South Africa: A Political Social and Cultural History*. Berkeley: University of California Press, 1997: 1–15.

———. "Writing Religion into History: The Case of South African Christianity." In Henry Bredekamp and Robert Ross (eds.), *Missions and Christianity in South African History*. Johannesburg: Wits University Press 2001: 11–26

———. "Evangelical Missions and Racial 'Equalization' in South Africa, 1890–1914." In Dana L. Robert (ed.), *Converting Colonialism: Visions and Realities in Mission History, 1706–1914*. Grand Rapids: Eerdmans, 2008: 112–133.

Erlmann, Veit. *Nightsong: Performance, Power, and Practice in South Africa*. Chicago: University of Chicago Press, 1996.

Eslinger, Ellen. *Citizens of Zion: The Social Origins of Camp Meeting Revivalism*. Knoxville: University of Tennessee Press, 1999.

Etherington, Norman. "Mission Station Melting Pots as a Factor in the Rise of South African Black Nationalism." *The International Journal of African Historical Studies* 9 (1976): 592–605.

———. *Preachers, Peasants and Politics in Southeast Africa, 1835–80: African Christian Communities in Natal, Pondoland and Zululand*. London: Royal Historical Society, 1978.

———. "The Historical Sociology of Independent Churches in Southeast Africa." *Journal of Religion in Africa* 10 (1979): 108–26.

———. "The 'Shepstone System' in the Colony of Natal and Beyond the Borders." In Duminy and Guest, *Natal and Zululand From Earliest Times to 1910* Pietermaritzburg: University of Natal Press, 1989: 275–301.

———. "Recent Trends in the Historiography of Christianity in Southern Africa." *Journal of Southern African Studies* 22 (1996): 201–19.

———. *The Great Treks: The Transformation of Southern Africa, 1815–1854*. New York: Longman, 2001.

Fast, Hildegarde. "'In At One Ear and Out At the Other': African Response to the Wesleyan Message in Xhosaland, 1825–35." *Journal of Religion in Africa* 23 (1993): 147–73.

Fields, Karen. *Revival and Rebellion in Colonial Central Africa*. Portsmouth: Heinemann, 1997.

Finney, Charles Grandison. *Lectures on Revivals of Religion*. Cambridge: Harvard University Press, 1960.

Flint, Karen. *Healing Traditions: African Medicine, Cultural Exchange, & Competition in South Africa, 1820–1948*. Athens: Ohio University Press, 2008.

——. and Julie Parle, "Healing and Harming: Medicine, Madness, Witchcraft and Tradition" in Benedict Carton, John Laband, and Jabulani Sithole (eds.), *Zulu Identities: Being Zulu, Past and Present*. New York: Columbia University Press, 2008, 312–321.

Ford, John. *The Role of Trypanosomiases in African Ecology*. London: Oxford University Press, 1971.

Foster, Stephen. "A Connecticut Separate Church: Strict Congregationalism in Cornwall, 1780–1809." *The New England Quarterly* 39 1966: 309–33.

Foucault, Michel. *The History of Sexuality, Volume I*. New York: Vintage, 1980.

Freund, Bill. "Indian Women and the Changing Character of the Working Class Indian Household in Natal, 1860–1900." *Journal of Southern African Studies* 17 (1991): 414–29.

Fynn, H. F., J. Stuart and D. McMalcom (eds.), *The Diary of Henry Francis Fynn*. Pietermaritzburg: University of Natal Press, 1950.

Gaitskell, Deborah. "'Wailing for Purity': Prayer Unions, African Mothers and Adolescent Daughters, 1912–40.'" In Shula Marks and Richard Rathbone (eds.), *Industrialisation and Social Change in South Africa: African Class, Culture, and Consciousness, 1870–1930*. New York: Longman, 1983, 338–357.

——. "Devout Domesticity? A Century of African Women's Christianity in South Africa." In Cheryl Walker (ed.), *Women and Gender in Southern Africa to 1945*. Cape Town: David Philip, 1990.

——. "'Praying and Preaching': The Distinctive Spirituality of African Women's Church Organizations." In Henry Bredekamp and Robert Ross (eds.), *Missions and Christianity in South African History*. Johannesburg: Wits University Press, 2001.

Gardiner, Allen. *Narrative of a Journey to the Zoolu Country in South Africa*. Cape Town: Struik, 1966.

Gewald, Jan-Bart. *Herero Heroes: A Socio-Political History of the Herero of Namibia, 1890–1923*. Athens: Ohio University Press, 1999.

Githieya, Francis. *The Freedom of the Spirit: African Indigenous Churches in Kenya*, Atlanta: Scholars Press, 1997.

Goodhew, David. "Working-Class Respectability: The example of the Western Areas of Johannesburg, 1930–55." *Journal of African History*, 41 (2000): 241–66.

Gordon, Loraine et al., *A Survey of Race Relations in South Africa: 1977*. Johannesburg: Institute of Race Relations, 1977.

Gourevitch, Philip. *We Wish to Inform You That Tomorrow We Will Be Killed with Our Families: Stories from Rwanda*. New York: Picador, 1998.

Gray, Richard. *Black Christians and White Missionaries*. New Haven: Yale University Press, 1990.

Groom, Winston. *Vicksburg, 1863.* New York: Vintage Press, 2010.

Grout, Lewis. *Zululand: Or Life Among the Kaffirs of Natal and Zululand.* Philadelphia: Presbyterian Publishing Society, 1864.

Guest, Bill. "The New Economy." In Duminy and Guest, (eds.) *Natal and Zululand From Earliest Times to 1910: A New History.* Pietermartizburg: University of Natal Press, 1989, 302–23.

———. "Towards Responsible Government, 1879–93." In Duminy and Guest, (eds.) *Natal and Zululand From Earliest Times to 1910: A New History.* Pietermartizburg: University of Natal Press, 1989, 233–48.

Gunner, Elizabeth. "Power House, Prison House: An Oral Genre and its Use in Isaiah Shembe's Nazareth Baptist Church." *Journal of Southern African Studies* 14 (1988): 204–227.

Guy, Jeff. "The Destruction and Reconstruction of Zulu Society." In Shula Marks and Richard Rathbone (eds.), *Industrialisation and Social Change in South Africa: African Class Formation, Culture and Consciousness, 1870–1930.* London: Longman, 1982, 167–94.

———. *The Heretic: A Study of the Life of John William Colenso 1814–1883.* Johannesburg, Witwatersrand University Press, 1982.

———. "Analysing Pre-Capitalist Societies in Southern Africa." *Journal of Southern African Studies* 14 (1987): 18–37.

———. "Gender Oppression in Southern Africa's Precapitalist Societies." In Cherryl Walker (ed.), *Women and Gender in Southern Africa to 1945.* Cape Town: David Phillips, 1990

———. *The Destruction of the Zulu Kingdom: The Civil War in Zululand, 1879–884.* Pietermaritzburg, University of Natal Press, 1994.

Hamilton, Carolyn, and John Wright. "The Making of the AmaLala: Ethnicity, Ideology and Relations of Subordination in a Precolonial Context." *South African Historical Journal* 22 (1990): 3–23.

———. (ed.). *The Mfecane Aftermath: Reconstructive Debates in Southern African History.* Bloomington: Indiana University Press, 1996.

Hanretta, Sean. "Women, Marginality and the Zulu State: Women's Institutions and Power in the Early Nineteenth Century." *Journal of African History* 39 (1998): 389–415.

Harries, Patrick. "Kinship Ideology and the Nature of Pre-Colonial Labour Migration." In Shula Marks and Richard Rathbone (eds.), *Industrialisation and Social Change in South Africa: African Class, Culture, and Consciousness, 1870–1930,* London: Longman, 1982.

———. "Plantations, Passes and Proletarians: Labour and the Colonial State in Nineteenth Century Natal." *Journal of Southern African Studies* 13 (1987): 372–99.

———. *Work, Culture, and Identity: Migrant Laborers in Mozambique and South Africa, c. 1860–1910.* Portsmouth: Heinemann, 1994.

Hastings, Adrian. *The Church in Africa, 1450–1950*. New York: Oxford University Press, 1996.

Hattersley, A. F. *The British Settlement of Natal: A Study in Imperial Migration*. Cambridge: Cambridge University Press, 1950.

Healy, Meghan. "'Like a Family': Global Models, Familial Bonds, and the Making of an American School for Zulu Girls." *Journal of South African and American Studies* 12 (2010)

Hemson, David. "Dockworkers in Durban." In Paul Maylam and Iain Edwards (eds.), *The People's City: African Life in 20th Century Durban*. Pietermaritzburg: University of Natal Press, 1996, 145–173.

Holden, William. *A Brief History of Methodism and of the Methodist Missions in South Africa*. London: Wesleyan Conference, 1877.

Houle, Robert "Constructing an AmaKholwa Community: Cattle and the Creation of a Zulu Christianity." MA, University of Wisconsin–Madison, 1998.

———. "'Today I am delivered': Revival, Holiness, and the naturalization of Christianity in Turn of the Century Colonial Natal." Ph.D, University of Wisconsin–Madison, 2003.

———. "Mbiya Kuzwayo's Christianity: Revival, Reformation and the Surprising Viability of Mainline Churches in South Africa." *Journal of Religion in Africa* 38 (2008): 141–70.

———. "The American Mission Revivals and the Birth of Modern Zulu Evangelism." In Benedict Carton, John Laband and Jabulani Sithole (eds.) *Zulu Identities: Being Zulu, Past and Present* New York: Columbia University Press, 2008, 222–239.

Hughes, Heather. "A Lighthouse for African Womanhood: Inanda Seminary, 1869–1945." In Cheryl Walker (ed.) *Women and Gender in Southern Africa to 1945*. Cape Town: David Philips, 1990.

———. "Doubly Elite: Exploring the Life of John Langalibalele Dube." *Journal of South African Studies* 27 (2001): 445–458.

Isaacs, Nathanial. *Travels and Adventures in Eastern Africa: Description of the Zoolus, Their Manners, Customs, etc.* L. Herman and P. R. Kinkby (eds.), Cape Town: Struik, 1979.

Jenkins, Philip. *The Next Christendom: The Coming of Global Christianity*. New York: Oxford University Press, 2007.

Johnson, Charles. "The Frontier Camp Meetings: Contemporary Appraisals, 1805–1840." *The Mississippi Valley Review* 37 (1950): 91–110.

Johnson, Curtis. *Islands of Holiness: Rural Religion in Upstate New York, 1790–1860*. Ithaca: Cornell University Press, 1989.

Johnson, Paul. *A Shopkeepers Millennium: Society and Revivals in Rochester, New York, 1815–1837*. New York: Farrar, Straus, & Giroux, 1978.

Keto, C. Tsheloane, "Race Relations, Land and the Changing Missionary Role in South Africa: A Case Study of the American Zulu Mission, 1850–

1910." *The International Journal of African Historical Studies* 10 (1977): 600–27.

Kingsolver, Barbara. *The Poisonwood Bible*. New York: Harper Torch, 1998.

Kling, David. "The New Divinity and the Origins of the American Board of Commissioners for Foreign Missions" In Wilbert Shenk (ed.), *North American Foreign Missions, 1810–1914*. Grand Rapids: Eerdmans, 2004, 11–38.

de Kock, Leon. *Civilizing Barbarians: Missionary Narrative and African Textual Response in Nineteenth-Century South Africa*. Johannesburg: Witwatersrand University Press, 1996.

la Hausse, Paul. *Brewers, Beerhalls and Boycotts: A History of Liquor in South Africa*. Johannesburg: Ravan Press, 1988.

———. "'The Cows of Nongoloza': Youth Crime and *Amalaita* Gangs in Durban, 1900–1936." *Journal of Southern African Studies* 16 (1990): 79–111.

———. *Restless Identities: Signatures of Nationalism, Zulu Ethnicity and History in the Lives of Petros Lamula and Lymon Maling*. Pietermaritzburg: University of Natal Press, 2000.

Lambert, John. *Betrayed Trust: Africans and the State in Colonial Natal*. Pietermaritzburg: University of Natal Press, 1995.

———. "Chiefship in Early Colonial Natal, 1843–1879." *Journal of Southern African Studies* 21 (1995): 269–85.

Landau, Paul. *The Realm of the Word: Language, Gender, and Christianity in a Southern African Kingdom*. Portsmouth: Heinemann, 1995.

———. "Hegemony and History in Jean and John L. Comaroff's *Of Revelation and Revolution*," *Africa* 70 (2000): 501–519.

Langworthy, Harry. *"Africa for the African": The Life of Joseph Booth*. Blantyre: Christian Literature Association, 1996.

Leverton, B.J.T. (ed.). *Records of Natal, Volume One, 1823–August 1828*. Pretoria: Government Printer, 1894.

Liardon, Roberts. *God's Generals: The Revivalists*. New Kensington, PA: Whitaker Press, 2008.

Mafeje, Archie. "Religion, Class and Ideology in South Africa." In M. G. Whisson and M. E. West (eds.), *Religion and Social Change in Southern Africa*. Cape Town: Rex Collins, 1975.

Mahoney, Michael. "The Millennium Comes to Mapumulo: Popular Christianity in Rural Natal, 1866–1906." *Journal of Southern African Studies* 25 (1999): 375–91.

Majeke, Nosipho. *The Role of the Missionaries in Conquest*. Alexandra, Cumberwood Press, 1952.

Marks, Shula. "The Ambiguities of Dependence: John L. Dube of Natal." *Journal of Southern African Studies* 1 (1975): 162–80.

——. *The Ambiguities of Dependence in South Africa: Class, Nationalism, and the State in Twentieth-Century Natal*. Baltimore: John Hopkins University Press, 1986.

Martens, Jeremy. "Enlightenment Theories of Civilization and Savagery in British Natal," in Benedict Carton, John Laband, and Jabulani Sithole (eds.), *Zulu Identities: Being Zulu, Past and Present*. New York: Columbia University Press, 2008: 122–132.

Martin, Robert. *Hero of the Heartland: Billy Sunday and the Transformation of American Society, 1862–1935*. Bloomington: Indiana University Press, 2003.

Maxwell, David. "Historicizing Christian Independency: The Southern African Pentecostal Movement, c. 1908–60." *Journal of African History* 40 (1999): 243–64.

——. *African Gifts of the Spirit: Pentecostalism and the Rise of Zimbabwean Transnational Religious Movement*. Athens: Ohio University Press, 2007.

McCord, James. *My Patients Were Zulus*. New York: Rinehart, 1946.

McLoughlin, William. *Modern Revivalism: Charles Grandison Finney to Billy Graham*. New York: Ronald Press, 1959.

——. *Revivals, Awakenings, and Reform: An Essay on Religion and Social Change in America, 1607–1977*. Chicago: University of Chicago Press, 1978.

Meintjes, Shiela. "Edendale, 1850–1906: a Case Study of Rural Transformation and Class Formation in an African Mission in Natal." PhD, University of London, 1988.

Meyer, Brigit. "From African Independent to Pentecostal Charismatic Churches." *Annual Review of Anthropology* 33 (2004): 447–474.

Mills, Kenneth. "The Naturalization of Andean Christianities" in R. Po-Chia Hsia, ed., *Cambridge History of Christianity: Volume 6, Reform and Expansion 1500–1660*, Cambridge: Cambridge University Press, 2007.

Mills, Wallace. "The Fork in the Road: Religious Separatism Versus African Nationalism in the Cape Colony, 1800–1910." *Journal of Religion in Africa* 9 (1978): 51–61.

——. "The Roots of African Nationalism in the Cape Colony: Temperance, 1866–1898." *The International Journal of African Historical Studies* 13 (1980): 197–213.

Mofokeng, Takatso. "Black Christians, the Bible and Liberation." *Journal of Black Theology* 2 (1988), 34–42.

Moodie, T. Dunbar, Vivienne Ndatshe and British Sibuyi. "Migrancy and Male Sexuality on the South African Gold Mines." *Journal of Southern African Studies* 14 (1988): 22–56.

Moore, Edward Caldwell. "The Naturalization of the Christianity in the Far East." *Harvard Theological Review* 3 (1908): 249–303

Moorhead, James. "Between Progress and Apocalypse: A Reassessment of Millennialism in American Religious Thought, 1800–1880." *The Journal of American History* 71 (1984): 524–42.

Morrell, Robert. "Of Boys and Men: Masculinity and Gender in Southern African Studies." *Journal of Southern African Studies* 24 (1998): 605–30.

Ndlovu, Sifiso. "A Reassessment of Women's Power in the Zulu Kingdom" in Benedict Carton, John Laband, and Jabulani Sithole (eds.), *Zulu Identities: Being Zulu, Past and Present*. New York: Columbia University Press, 2008.

Neill, Stephen, *A History of Christian Missions*. New York: Penguin, 1986.

Newton, Sidney. *Thanks, Tabor, for the Memories*. Council Bluffs: Midwest Publishing, 1990.

Ngubane, Harriet. *Body and Mind in Zulu Medicine: An Ethnology of Health and Disease in Nyuswa-Zulu Thought and Practice*. London: Academic Press, 1977.

Owen, Francis and Sir George E. Cory (ed.), *The Diary of the Reverend Francis Owen*. Cape Town: Van Riebeeck Society, 1926.

Padayachea, Vishna and Robert Morrel, "Indian Merchants and Dukawal-lahs in the Natal Economy, c. 1875–1914." *Journal of Southern African Studies* 17 (1990): 71–102.

Page, Jesse. *Captain Allen Gardiner of Patagonia*. London: Pickering and Inglis, 1830.

Parle, Julie. "Witchcraft or Madness? The *Amandiki* of Zululand, 1894–1914." *Journal of Southern African Studies* 29 (2003): 105–132.

———. *States of Mind: Searching for Mental Health in Natal and Zululand, 1868–1918*. Pietermartizburg: University of KwaZulu-Natal Press, 2007.

Paton, Alan. *Cry, the Beloved Country*. New York: Scribner, 2003.

Peel, J. D. Y. "The Colonization of Consciousness." *Journal of African History* 33 (1992): 328–29.

———. *Religious Encounter and the Making of the Yoruba*. Bloomington: Indiana University Press, 2000.

Peires, J. B. *The Dead Will Arise: Nongqawuse and the Great Xhosa Cattle Killing Movement of 1856–57*. Bloomington: Indiana University Press, 1989.

Penn, Nigel. *Rogues, Rebels and Runaways: Eighteenth-Century Cape Characters*. Cape Town: D. Philip, 1999.

Phillips, Clifton. *Protestant America and the Pagan World: The First Half-Century of the American Board of Commissioners for Foreign Missions, 1810–1860*. Cambridge: East Asian Research Harvard, 1969.

Phoofolo, Pule. "Epidemics and Revolutions: The Rinderpest Epidemic in Late Nineteenth-Century Southern Africa." *Past and Present* 138 (1993): 112–143.

Ranger, Terence. *Revolt in Southern Rhodesia, 1896–97: A Study in African Resistance.* Chicago: Northwestern University Press, 1967.

——. "Religious Movements and Politics in Sub-Saharan African." *African Studies Review* 29 (1986): 1–69.

Reynolds, David. *John Brown, Abolitionist: The Man Who Killed Slavery, Sparked the Civil War, and Seeded Civil Rights.* New York: Vintage, 2006.

Rich, Paul. "Race, Science, and the Legitimization of White Supremacy in South Africa, 1902–1940." *The International Journal of African Historical Studies* 23 (1990): 665–686.

Robeck, Cecil. *The Azusa Street Mission and Revival: The Birth of the Global Pentecostal Movement.* Nashville: Thomas Nelson, 2006.

Rosenbaum, Elise. "Patient Teenagers? A Comparison of the Sexual Behavior of Virginity Pledgers and Matched Nonpledgers." *Pediatrics*, 123 (2009): 110–120.

Ross, Robert. "Missions, Respectability and Civil Rights: the Cape Colony, 1828–1854." *Journal of Southern African Studies* 25 (1999): 333–45.

Sandgren, David. *Christianity and the Kikuyu: Religious Divisions and Social Conflict.* New York: Peter Lang, 1989.

Sanneh, Lamin. *Translating the Message: The Missionary Impact on Culture.* Maryknoll, NY: Orbis, 2008.

Schneider, Gregory. "A Conflict of Associations: The National Camp-Meeting Association for the Promotion of Holiness versus the Methodist Episcopal Church." *Church History* 66 (1997): 268–283.

Schoffeleers, Matthew. "Black and African Theology in Southern Africa: A Controversy Re-Examined." *Journal of Religion in Africa* 18 (1988): 99–123.

Scorgie, Fiona. "Virginity Testing and the Politics of Sexual Responsibility: Implications for AIDS Intervention." *African Studies* 61 (2002): 55–75

Scott, Shuanna. "'They Don't Have to Live by the Old Traditions': Saintly Men, Sinner Women, and an Appalachian Pentecostal Revival." *American Ethnologist*, 21 (1994): 227–244.

Simensen, Jarle. "Christian Missions and SocioCultural Change in Zululand, 1850–1906, Norwegian Strategy and Response." In Jarle Simensen (ed.). *Norwegian Missions in African History Volume I: South Africa 1845–1906.* New York: Scandinavian University Press, 1986.

Slater, Henry. "Land, Labour and Capital in Natal: The Natal Land and Colonisation Company 1860–1948." *Journal of African History* 16 (1975): 257–283.

Smith, Edwin. *The Life and Times of Daniel Lindley.* New York: Library Publishers, 1952.

Smith, Timothy L. *Revivalism and Social Reform: American Protestantism on the Eve of the Civil War.* New York: Wipf and Stock, 2004.

——. "Righteousness and Hope: Christian Holiness and the Millennial Vision in America, 1800–1900." *American Quarterly* 31 (1979): 21–45.

Southey, Nicholas. "History, Church History and Historical Theology in South Africa." *Journal of Theology for Southern Africa* 68 (1989): 5–14.

Spear, Thomas. "Toward the History of African Christianity." In Thomas Spear and Isaria Kimambo (eds.), *East African Expressions of Christianity.* Athens, Ohio University Press, 1999, 3–24.

Sundkler, Bengt. *Bantu Prophets in South Africa.* Oxford: Oxford University Press, 1964.

——. *Zulu Zion and Some Swazi Zionists.* London: Oxford University Press, 1976.

Switzer, Les. "The Problems of an African Mission in a White-Dominated, Multi-Racial Society, the American Zulu Mission in South Africa, 1885–1910," PhD Dissertation, University of Natal, 1971.

——. "American Missionaries and the Making of an African Church in Colonial Natal." In, *The London Missionary Society in Southern Africa.* John de Gruchy (ed.) Athens: Ohio University Press, 1999, 166–188.

Synan, Vinson. *The Holiness-Pentecostal Movement in the United States.* Grand Rapids: Wm. B. Eerdmans, 1971.

Thornton, John. *The Kongolese Saint Anthony: Dona Beatriz Kimpa Vita and the Antonian Movement, 1684–1706.* Cambridge, Harvard University Press, 1998.

Tyler, Josiah. *Forty Years Among the Zulus.* Boston, Congregational Publishing Society, 1891.

Van Onselen, Charles. "Reactions to Rinderpest in Southern Africa, 1896–97." *The Journal of African History* 13 (1972): 473–88.

——. *Studies in the Social and Economic History of the Witwatersrand, Vol. 1–2.* London: Ravan Press, 1982.

Vilakazi, Absolom. *Zulu Transformations: A Study of the Dynamics of Social Change.* Pietermaritzburg: University of Natal Press, 1962.

Vinson, Robert and Robert Edgar. "Zulus Abroad: Cultural Representations and Educational Experiences of Zulus in America, 1880–1945." *Journal of Southern African Studies* 33 (2007): 43–62.

Volz, Stephen. "Written on our Hearts: Tswana Christians and the 'Word of God' in the Mid-Nineteenth Century." *Journal of Religion in Africa* 38 (2008): 112–140.

Waldrep, Christopher. "The Making of a Border Society: James McGready, the Great Revival, and the Prosecution of Profanity in Kentucky." *The American Historical Review* 99 (1994): 767–784.

Walker, Cherryl. "Gender and the Development of the Migrant Labour System c. 1850–1930: An Overview." In Cherryl Walker (ed.), *Women and Gender in Southern Africa to 1945*. London: David Philips, 1990, p.168–196.

Ward, Kevin "*Tukutendereza Yesu*: The Balokole Revival Movement in Uganda," in Z. Nthamburi (ed.), *From Mission to Church*. Nairobi, 1991.

Webb, C. de B. and J. B. Wright, (eds.), *The James Stuart Archive of Recorded Oral Evidence Relating to the History of the Zulu and Neighbouring Peoples Volumes I–V*. Pietermaritzburg: University of Natal Press, 1976, 1979, 1982, 1986, 2001).

Welsh, David. *The Roots of Segregation: Native Policy in Colonial Natal, 1845–1910*. London: Oxford University Press, 1971.

West, Gerald. "Mapping African Biblical Interpretation: A Tentative Sketch," in Gerald West and Musa Dube (eds.), *The Bible in Africa: Transactions, Trajectories, and Trends* Boston: Brill Publishing, 2000, 29–53.

White, Charles Edward. *The Beauty of Holiness: Phoebe Palmer as Theologian, Revivalist, Feminist, and Humanitarian*, Grand Rapids: Zondervan, 1986.

Wilson, Monica and Leonard Thompson (eds.), *The Oxford History of South Africa*. London: Oxford University Press, 1971.

Worcester, Paul. *The Master Key*. Kansas City: Nazarene Publishing House, 1966.

Wright, John. "Control of Women's Labour in the Zulu Kingdom." In *Before and After Shaka: Papers in Nguni History*, J. B. Peires (ed.), Grahamstown: Institute of Social and Economic Research, Rhodes University, 1981.

———. "Reflections on the Politics of Being 'Zulu,'" in Benedict Carton, John Laband, and Jabulani Sithole (eds.), *Zulu Identities: Being Zulu, Past and Present*. New York: Columbia University Press, 2008: 35–43

Index

Abraham, Andrew, 13, 37n60,
41n95, 99
abstinence, 63, 95, 99–102, 113,
165, 223n72
Adams, Dr. Newton, 10–13, 23, 63
Adams Mission Station. *See*
Amanzimtoti Mission Station
Adams Theological School. *See*
Amanzimtoti Seminary
African Christianity, xvii, xxv–xxvii.
See also amakholwa
African Congregational Church
(ACC), 255–56, 259–66,
295n140, 297n165, 279, 281–
82
amadhlozi (ancestral spirits), 21–22,
73, 95–97, 202–03
Amahlongwa Mission Station, 51,
79n19, 120, 141n161
Amazimtoti Mission Station, 48,
79n19, 82n52, 99, 107–10,
132n51, 216–17, 222n60
Amanzimtoti Seminary, 31, 56–57,
83n79, 113, 162, 178n2, 216–
17; revival at, 192–95, 197–98

amavoluntiya, xvi, xxxiii, 209–13,
218, 222n58, 223n64, 227,
243, 247, 249–50, 252, 258–59,
277n93
American Board of Commissioners
for Foreign Missions (ABM),
xxix, 8–10, 36n42, 64, 76, 98,
115; and letter of self-support,
98, 120–22; 1903 delegation to
South Africa, 256–57, 264–65
American Zulu Mission (AZM), xv,
xxiii, xxiv, xxxv, 11–15, 24–25,
37n47, 55, 67, 76, 83n71,
192, 210, 216–17, 253; and
Natal Government, 6, 115–17,
139n137, 259–65, 277n164;
changing nature of, 20, 41n104,
93, 97–99, 120–23, 163,
228–232, 246, 252, 274n129,
279–80; lands, 12, 48, 58, 90–
91, 114, 115–17; Missionaries,
xxviii–xxix, 9, 11–15, 22, 62,
81n41, 90, 130n25, 140n151,
156–57, 161, 187n89, 198, 203,
211, 222n41. 257–58. *See also*

amakholwa independence from AZM

Anderson, Rufus (Nguzana), 28–32, 45, 111, 140n155

Anglo–Zulu war, 32n2, 46, 48, 54–55, 75, 91–93, 107

apartheid, xxxvi, xxxviin, 5, 263

Beatrice Street Chapel, 111, 279–84

Beer and Liquor. *See utshwala*
    isibhalo (pressgang), 5, 26, 34n22, 42n108, 74, 118

Bhambatha Rebellion, 265–66, 278n167; *amabhinca* (traditionalist), 47, 49, 52, 55, 76, 92

Bible, xxii, xxxvi, 26, 39n81, 44–45, 59, 106, 193, 217–18, 248, 258; study of, 15, 23, 31, 61, 66, 102, 210, 210, 252, 273n101

Blind Johannes, 125, 142n173, 162

Books, 26–27, 39n81 50, 58–59, 168

Booth, Joseph, 231–32, 267n11

Boshi, 95–96

Bridgman, Frederick, 251–52, 262, 275n147

Bridgman, Henry, 95–96, 100

Carton, Benedict, 19, 79n15, 84n86, 86n115, 88n142

Cattle: *amakholwa* uses of, 19–20, 45, 52–53, 64, 81n42, 92, 97–99; disease. *See* rinderpest; *isibaya* (cattle enclosure) 47–48; in traditional society, xxiv, 2–4, 19, 25–26, 29, 33n9, 51, 80n35, 119

Cele, Maduba, 95–96, 100–101, 105

Cetshwayo kaMpande, Zulu king, 91, 128n2

Chief. *See inkosi*

Christianity: African, xvii, xxi, xxvii, xxxvi, 207–08, 255–56; global, xvi, xxii, 76–77, 147, 211; local, xvii, xxi, xxii, xxv, xxviii–xxx, 112,177,200–15, 253–56, 261, 272n98, 279–284; Christians. *See amakholwa*

Church membership, xxvi, xxx, 76, 94, 99, 102, 109, 152, 155, 212–13, 216–17, 238

clothing: as marker of Christianity, 26–28, 43, 45–47, 78n7, 90, 94, 102, 104, 109, 201, 234; as extravagance, 46, 78n13, 79n16, 80n29, 163, 168, 242–43; production of by *amakholwa* women, 46, 57, 62–63, 70, 78n12; shoes, 46–47; worn by *amabhinca*, 78n6, 133n59

Comarroff, Jean and John, xxii, 78n4, 221n24

Congregational Church, 112, 135n82, 209, 235, 262–64; practice, xvi, 95, 108, 119, 123, 202, 211, 252, 269n50

consecration: nature of, xxxiv, 148–54, 157, 179n19, 181n45, 211–12, 245; *amakholwa*, 145, 165–70, 189–92, 194–96, 204–05, 214, 228–30, 240, 246–47, 256, 281

conversion, 9–10, 14–20, 24–27, 45–46, 65, 67–68, 71–72, 102, 109, 133n159, 165, 201, 231, 250

Dingane, kaSenzangakhona, Zulu king, 3–5, 6–7, 10–11,78n14

divine healing, 154–55, 170, 176–77, 189, 191, 203–204, 218–19; opposition to by missionaries, 248, 271n80

Dube, John, xxviii, 60, 232

Durban, 3–4, 7, 29–31, 43, 58, 62–
    63, 90, 135n85, 136n92, 160,
    224n78; mission to, 110–12,
    135n82, 177, 216–17, 225n78,
    245, 255, 279–82

educated elite, xxviii, 60, 96–97,
    119–20, 140n145, 172, 232–34,
    267n13, 273, 280, 283
education: *amkholwa* teachers, 56,
    60, 82n55, 83n57, 132n43;
    schools, 6, 7, 38n68, 47, 55–61,
    68, 84n81, 106, 110, 113, 231–
    32, 237, 252; family schools,
    xxiv, 10, 15–16, 18, 21, 25–26,
    28, 38n66, 57–58, 92; and Natal
    government, 12, 58–60, 83n71,
    260–61; *See also* Amanzimtoti
    Seminary and, Inanda Seminary;
    Zulu desire for, xxiii, 57–60,
    82n55, 83n60, 87n131, 106–08,
    216, 231–33
Edwards, Mary, 62, 71, 84n86,
    85n98, 136n92
English language, 58–59, 60, 61,
    112, 118, 146, 165, 178n2, 193
Esidumbini Mission Station,
    37n56, 68, 73–74, 113, 121–24,
    141n161, 187n133, 190, 207,
    216, 266; revival at, 173–76,
    210–11, 245
Etherington, Norman, xxii–xxiv, 14,
    82n48
ethiopianism, xxvi, 104–105, 169,
    232, 258–59, 276n152
European settlers, 4–5, 12, 34n18,
    73, 74–75, 84n86, 87n139, 90,
    108, 115, 211, 231, 239, 263
evangelism. *See amakholwa*
Exempted Status, 105, 116–19,
    136n93, 139n131, 164, 184n94,
    215

female taboos, 95–96, 129n18
Finney, Charles Grandison, 148–
    49, 178n12, 180n31
Fokoti, 124, 142n165, 236–39,
    241, 247, 268n34
furniture, 50, 68, 70, 91, 234

Gardiner, Allen, 6–7, 35n24
generational conflict, 17, 26–27,
    72, 113, 137n105, 163, 169–70
Goba, Cetwayo, 119–20, 140n146
Goodenough, Herbert, 123–24,
    141n165, 236–38, 244, 268n34
Groutville Mission Station, xv–xviii,
    2, 20, 23, 27, 29–31, 43, 48–49,
    52–54, 56–59, 66–69, 75–76,
    79n19, 81n43, 91–95, 109, 115,
    129n16, 164, 168–69, 205, 216,
    223n66, 241–42, revival at,
    167–69, 201, 207, 210

Hawes, Benjamin, 112, 123,
    141n155
Hawes, Joel, 42n119, 94
Hawes, Thomas, 31, 38n69,
    42n119, 118, 139n139, 214–15
headring (*isicoco*), 24, 102, 167,
    212
hemp, 99, 138n116, 170
Hephzibah Faith Home Mission
    (HFHM), 152, 155, 157–60,
    180n32, 185n107, 242
Hlonono, John, 56, 87n131, 105
Holiness, xxxiv–xxxv, 149–54,
    158–60, 166, 175, 177,
    185n100, 200, 202–04, 208–09,
    211–12, 248
Holy Spirit, 64, 125, 145–46,
    149, 154–56, 165, 167–74,
    189–90, 200–01, 242; as key to
    naturalization, xvii, xxxii–xxxvi,
    202–08, 220n9, 228–30, 282–84

homes: Western, 43, 47–49, 50, 79n17, 91, 114, 234; Zulu (*indlu*), 43, 47, 201

Ifafa Mission Station, 109, 115, 246–48, 250

Impapala Church, 87, 108, 169–70, 185n113, 189, 210, 212–13, 216, 282

Inanda Mission Station, 27, 31, 57, 64, 79n19, 94, 96, 102, 119–20, 136n91, 161, 208, 232–33; revival at, 172–73, 176–77, 199–200, 210, 244–45, 250

Inanda Seminary, 61–62, 63, 71, 84n86, 85n98; revival at, 170–72, 190n91, 217

inkosi (chief), 2–3, 5–6, 13, 17, 22, 34n22, 48, 51, 73, 96–97, 105, 118–20, 137n115, 164, 169, 260

Isaac, Dalita, 84n87, 171–73, 199–200, 205

isililo (women's prayer groups), xvi, xviiin1, 222n58

isithupa (Committee of Six), 235, 240, 253

izifuni (seekers), 108–09

Johannesburg, 53–55, 60, 82n54, 90, 108, 110–12, 136n95, 208, 211; split from AZM, 123–24, 141n165, 236–39, 243–44, 255, 265

Jwili, Grace, 64–65

Kilbon, Charles, 83n63, 121–22, 248, *amakholwa* (believers): changing meaning of, xvii–xviii, xxv, xxviii, xxxv, 51, 91–94, 97–99, 103–14, 125, 132n51, 147, 153–58, 160–163, 185n100, 200–02, 206, 245, 280–83;

evangelism, 69–70, 134n66, 108, 161–64, 167–68, 189–90, 193, 205, 207–09, 222n60, 230, 243, 249–51, 264n80; independence from AZM, 124, 235–42, 247, 255–56, 269n50; *induna* (mission station chiefs), 48, 64, 94, 96, 102, 119–20, 124, 127, 139n140, 140n142, 145, 163–64; maintaining identity, xxiii, xxxii, 2, 20, 27, 43–54, 59–60, 65–70, 71, 75–77, 89–91, 94–99, 161, 234, 245–46; pastors and preachers, xxvi, 28–30, 42n119, 59–61, 96, 100, 107, 109, 119–23, 134n67, 135n87, 140n153, 161–62, 164–65, 170–74, 205, 213–15, 231–32, 234–38, 240–42, 247–49, 252–53, 269n44, 284; professions, xxiii, 29–31, 44, 49, 51–57, 62, 82n52, 83n57, 108, 111, 126, 135n83, 136n95; relationship with *amabhinca*, xxxi, 24–25, 28, 45, 42n110, 45, 68, 71–74, 87n131, 92–94, 98, 128n5, 246; relationship with AZM, xxx, 92–93, 95–96, 98–99, 112, 114–16, 120–24, 129n9, 137n104, 196–99, 211–15, 232–33, 235–42, 246, 251–56; relationship with Natal government, 6, 81n43, 116–19, 139n131, 184n94, 258–66, 277n64; women, 16–17, 26–27, 38n69, 42n112, 46, 50, 57, 61–65, 70–72, 84n86, 85n98, 96, 100–01, 130n25, 132n45, 136n92, 166, 170–72, 190–91, 195–96, 200–01, 218–19, 225n86, 228–30; youth, xxiii, 9–11, 17, 21–23, 26, 60, 113, 137n104–05, 147,

163, 166, 169–72, 189–96, 208–09, 214, 217, 246, 259–60. *See also* clothing, consecration, education, land ownership, and revival

Kuzwayo, Mbiya, xvi, 145–46, 165–68, 171, 176, 178n2, 189, 198–99, 255, 269n43; as mission revivalist, 205, 209, 217–19, 227–28, 242, 245–47, 249–50, 270n43, 283

Kuzwayo, Mfanefile, 114–16, 124–25, 127, 137n109, 163–65, 184n94

land ownership, 35n31, 49, 74, 115, 126n3, 129n16, 165

Lindley, Daniel, 11–12, 20, 31, 234

literacy, xxiii, 39n81, 110, 118, 206

lobola (bridewealth), 25, 28, 41n107, 93, 97–99, 105, 113, 129n9, 130n21, 137n104

locust plague, 91, 124, 162

London Mission Society (LMS), 7, 10

Luthuli, Martin, 241, 280, 283

Luthuli, Ntaba, xxvii, 29, 41n100, 43–44, 50, 52, 77n1

Mahoney, Michael, 105, 128n1, 183n78, 271n80, 278n167,

Makanya, William, 264, 280

Mali, Jeremiah, 60, 100

Mapumulo Mission Station, 61, 66, 72, 79n19, 82n54, 101–02, 105, 112, 114–15, 124, 125, 160, 162–67, 184n94, 204–05, 216, 257, 266; revival at, 145–47, 167–170, 185n105, 189–90, 209–10, 216, 222n58, 246–48

market gardens, 80n39, 91, 128n3, 172

marriage certificates, 141n165, 261–62, 281, 284n9,

Mdiwa, John, 110–11, 135n84

medicine: Western , 13, 21, 73, 155, 203, 209, 218–19, 248; Zulu, 9, 13, 17, 27, 42n112, 96–97, 105–06, 173, 192, 195, 202–05, 220n9

Mellen, Andrew, 27, 41n104,

Methodism, 7, 150, 222n55, 258

migrant labor, 106, 110, 34n68, 143n185, 172, 247

millennialism, 156–57, 196, 248

Mpande, kaSenzangakhona, Zulu king, 4–5, 20

Mseleku, Qanda (Banda), 206, 222n58

Mvuyana, Gardiner, 247, 269n43

imvuzelelo. See revival

Natal: British colony of, xxiii, 1–2, 3–6, 11–13, 17, 26, 32n2, 42n110, 48, 57, 59, 73, 90, 247, 269n43; native policy 59, 78n6, 115–16, 139n140, 163–64, 240, 257, 265–66; Responsible Government, 34n18, 90, 74, 114, 231

Natal Native Trust, 116–17, 139n130, 259–60, 275n143

Native Annual Meeting (NAM), 69–70, 90, 94–95, 97, 100, 113, 121–22, 125, 162, 241–42, 245, 255–57

Native Home Missionary Society (NHMS), 69–70, 94, 142n171

naturalization, xxv, xxvii–xxviii, xxxvi, xxxviiin, 192–93, 248, 266

Nembula, Dr. John, 40, 62, 85n89, 136, 267n7

Ngidi, Mbiyana, 66, 70, 94, 104–05, 175

Noodsberg Mission Station, 102–
03, 105, 139n139, 235; revival
at, 175–76, 201, 245–46
Nyuswa, Sunguza, 213–14, 247,
253–55

Oberlin, 148, 161, 178n12,
180n31, 232
Ohlange Industrial School, 232–34
outstations, xxxi, 50, 56–57, 107–
09, 115, 121, 134n67, 138n117,
174, 189, 193–94, 206–07, 212,
237, 250, 260

Parle, Julie, 17, 39n72, 191
Pixley, Stephen, 40, 141n162, 173,
197–98, 208, 220n222
plows, 45, 51–52, 54, 63, 72,
81n43, 104
polygamy, 6, 24, 39n80, 53, 71,
92–93, 98, 105, 109, 115,
129n16
possession, 18, 21, 38n72, 166,
185n100, 187n139, 190–91
poverty, xxi, 30, 38n67, 51, 54–55,
66, 79n19, 142n171, 235, 247
prayer meetings, 31, 44, 55, 66–67,
86n107, 112, 168, 173
purity, xxxi, 69, 89, 95, 98–99,
141n162, 147, 154, 165, 206,
212–13, 266

respectability, 64–65, 73–75, 90,
95, 103, 107, 136n93, 200, 215,
259
Revival: *amakholwa*, xxxiii, xxxvii,
146, 165–77, 189–97, 227–
30, 243–49, 253–55, 280;
American, 8, 147–52, 178n7;
mission discomfort with, 187n9,
197–99; nature of, xvi–xvii, xxxi,
xxxiii–xxxv, 147, 152–58; pre-

1896 southern Africa, 160–61,
183n89; tabernacle (tent), 151,
180n30, 190, 205, 211, 227–28,
270n55
rinderpest, 91, 125–27, 129n18,
142n176, 143n185, 162–63,
184n90, 215–16, 247, 270n55
runaway girls, 16–18, 61–62

Sabbath, 13, 19–20, 22–23, 29, 66,
75, 110, 112, 208, 246, 257
sanctification. *See* consecration
sexuality, xviiin1, 113, 131n35,
195, 220n16
Shaka kaSenzangakhona, Zulu
king, 2, 3, 20, 33n12
Shembe, Isaiah, xxln26, 188n144
Shibe, Simon, 227–29, 235–40,
255, 258, 262, 268n39,
273n116, 276n152
sin, xxxiv, 23, 69, 82, 92–94, 98,
102, 133n53, 147–49, 154, 159,
165, 171, 179n13, 181n45, 196,
202–04, 208, 212, 229,
Smith, Judson, 121–22
snuff. *See* tobacco
Soldiers for Christ, xvi, 158,
222n58, 223n64
South African Native Congress
(SANC), xxviii, 234, 241, 283
South African war, 222n58, 243,
247–250, 253, 265,
sugar, xxiii, 1–2, 34n18, 49, 54, 75,
81n43, 91, 99, 115, 141n157,
231
syncretism, xvii, 108, 202

Table Mountain Mission, 40n83,
115, 244; split from AZM, 227–
30, 235–41, 255
Tabor, Iowa, 152, 157, 177,
180n31, 221n25, 283

taxes, 5–6, 34n22, 42, 52, 116, 139n138, 164, 265, 277n165
Teachers' Institute, 57–58
tithes, 216, 277n165
tobacco, 25, 53, 109, 133n64, 138n116, 153, 168, 170, 179n26, 192, 212–14, 220n13, 248–49
traditionalist. *See amabhinca*
translation, xv, xxii, 3, 39n81, 59, 193, 198, 200, 275n147
transport riding, 45,52–57, 71, 80n36, 91, 125–26, 128n5, 143n182, 162–64, 184n90, 270n55

ubuthakathi (witchcraft), 17, 51, 166–67, 186n130, 205
Uhlanga Church, 104–05
ukuhlobonga. See sexuality
Umbalasi, 13–14, 62
Umsumduze Rules, 97, 99–102, 103–06, 113, 134n67
Umsumduzi Mission Station, 20, 26–28, 50–51, 56, 68, 74, 99, 129n9, 131n36, 134n67, 160–61; revival at, 173, 201, 214
Umtwalumi Mission Station, 49, 51, 54–55, 70, 80n29, 81n43, 84n80, 102, 118–19, 121, 141n161, 255, 257, 271n75; revival at, 213–14, 222n58, 246–50
Umvoti Mission Station. *See* Groutville
Umzumbe Mission Station, 68, 73, 75, 95–97, 100–02, 106, 113–14, 131n43, 162; revival at, 171, 195–98, 201–02, 206–08, 245
urban living, 58–59, 65, 78n6, 107, 110–13, 135n85, 136n90, 149, 169, 244, 279–80

village plan, 12, 48–49
violence, 42n110, 85n98, 166, 168–69, 202, 246, 265–66, 271, 281–82

wagons. *See* transport riding
walking and fighting sticks, (*udondolo/isikhwili*), xvi–xvii, 46–47, 72–73, 78n14, 79n15, 173n62, 177, 192
wealth, xxiii, 24, 35n31, 38n67, 48, 51–52, 55–56, 63, 71–72 75, 79n19, 81n42, 91–92, 94, 124, 202, 206
Weavers, George: in America, 150–52, 153–57, 159–60, 179n25, 180n27, 183n76, 208, 221n25, 242–43; in southern Africa, xvii, 145, 165–70, 171–77, 187n137, 198–99, 222n41, 243–47, 248–49
Week of Prayer, 77, 100, 207
Wilcox, William, 64, 124, 142n170, 160–61, 166–70, 183n89, 197, 227–30, 242, 259–60
witchcraft. *See ubuthakathi*
Witwatersrand Gold Mines. *See* Johannesburg
women's church, 62–65, 225n86, 185n107
Worcester, L.B, 152, 154–55, 158
Worcester, William, 158–60, 190, 219n3, 227, 243, 270n55

Zulu Congregational Church (ZCC), 238–41, 246–47, 253–55, 265, 269n50, 270n55
Zululand, 29–30, 32n24, 53, 91, 108, 118, 169–70, 189, 212

About the Author

Robert J. Houle is associate professor of history at Farleigh Dickinson University, New Jersey, USA.